FERENC II RÁKÓCZI
AND THE GREAT POWERS

BY
WILLIAM B. SLOTTMAN

EAST EUROPEAN MONOGRAPHS, BOULDER
DISTRIBUTED BY COLUMBIA UNIVERSITY PRESS, NEW YORK

1997

EAST EUROPEAN MONOGRAPHS, NO. CDLVI

Contents

Foreword

The author of this book did not live to see the publication of his manuscript. During his lifetime the results of his long and intensive work in numerous sources remained unknown to the scholarly community. Professor William B. Slottman was an extraordinary man. His remarkable achievements in the field of historical research, however, are known only to a few of his close friends. He was also a brilliant teacher, and many generations of students gratefully attest to that.

In order to pay homage to the life work of this distinguished colleague, two of his friends decided to introduce the present study with an extensive preface. Walter Leitsch is paying tribute to Bill Slottman's scholarly work, Gunther Barth to his accomplishments as a teacher. Introducing Bill Slottman's extensive achievements in this way may also provide an opportunity to indicate that the preface will deal not only with the published text but also with a related manuscript on which Bill Slottman worked for many years. Unfortunately, this second manuscript was not among the papers he left behind.

The friends of Bill Slottman are much indebted to Professor Stephen Fischer-Galati who made the long delayed publication possible.

Career and Work of William B. Slottman

The book before you was written long ago. Although its author, William B. Slottman, invested much time and energy in the manuscript, unfortunately, fate and circumstances deprived him of the satisfaction of seeing it in print. He became a much admired and very inspiring teacher in the University of California at Berkeley. His death, shortly after his retirement, came much too early and was a tremendous shock to his colleagues.

Since Bill Slottman never published a book, it is the purpose of my Preface to testify to his high research ethos and his mastery of prose. Conscientious to a fault, he devoted his talents to his tasks as researcher and writer. With the help of excerpts from letters he wrote to me between 1945 and 1969, I shall attempt to sketch his career. That approach to a discussion of his work will show his distinguished attainments as an author whose striving for perfection kept him from publishing his book-length manuscripts.

Bill Slottman's human and intellectual qualities speak not only from the book before you but also from a seven hundred-page manuscript which has disappeared. Its research and writing, however, is well documented in our correspondence about the Lord Paget study, as we called the manuscript. Bill Slottman's letters and my recollections of the problems he mastered will show the triumph of a scholar's mind over the trials and tribulations of research, writing, and publishing. A discussion of the Lord Paget study will also throw some light on the vicissitudes of scholarship and the tolls of excellence as they affected Bill Slottman. In the light of these considerations I shall append the history of the Lord Paget study, as far as I can reconstruct it, to the Preface as a personal tribute to my American friend Bill Slottman.

In 1952 I met a historian in Vienna, roughly my age, who came from Brooklyn and was searching in the Haus-, Hof- und Staatsarchiv for material to write a dissertation as formal completion of his historical studies at Harvard University. We were both working diligently and enthusiastically on seventeenth century topics and came to appreciate each other. Our liking grew to a friendship.

Since Bill Slottman was studying in Cambridge, Massachusetts, and I live in Vienna we kept in touch by mail. We wrote each other letters about a thousand things and about our families, but above all about our scholarly work and our academic aspirations. We both were at the beginning of our careers and we both wanted to become university professors. In due time our correspondence became quite a treasure trove of biographical material dealing with Bill Slottman's work and life which he ordinarily guarded from unsolicited intrusions. An account of the energy and time he devoted to his research and writing provides an intellectual portrait of his personality and a suitable introduction to the book.

From the onset of our friendship I was struck by Bill Slottman's amazing talents. Austrian history fascinated him, and I always considered it particularly fortunate for Austria that a man with his abilities cared for our history. Quite naturally it came to be expected that he would make important contributions to an understanding of Austria's past. That he did, indeed, but because his writings were never published a casual reader of these lines might puzzle about the odd circumstances: a young scholar passionately studied historical sources with the express intent to detect something new and to produce fresh insights. Furthermore, although he was able to create a breathtaking account of his discoveries he would consign the results of his splendid efforts to the privacy of his home.

In order to understand the complex situation, I have often asked myself what special talents brought Bill Slottman to the task. Above all he had an outstanding memory which enabled him to learn foreign language quickly. We have many historians in Austria who at one time in their lives began to study Hungarian. Hardly anyone got so far that he could read and could understand documents. I myself am one of these failures.

Bill took lessons in Hungarian with a Countess Zichy and soon he was able to understand Hungarian documents. He also could read texts in Slavic languages, handled French splendidly and presumably Italian, too, but I cannot speak about that from my own experience. He also worked in the archives in The Hague and could read Dutch.

Bill Slottman had the enviable ability to grasp anything new immediately. Initially, when I sat next to him in the archive and observed his work habits I wondered how he would be able to cope with his task. He worked for half an hour and then would take off to spend the next half hour somewhere else. Soon he would return, stay for another half hour, and then disappear again from sight. His routine startled me and I worried how much he actually could get done in a day. When I came to know him better and was able to assess the rate of his progress, however, I discovered to my great surprise that I had been sitting for four hours in the same place while he had achieved more in two hours than I did in four despite his coming and going.

I was reminded again of Bill Slottman's astonishing perceptivity during the past decade when I traveled extensively by car with various people from various walks of life. None of them was as gifted in reading a road map as Bill Slottman. He and I have traveled together many a mile in many different European countries but only once did he tell me to make a right turn instead of a left turn. I instantly began to worry that he was not well because I firmly believed that he could not be mistaken. Ordinarily he just glanced at a map and knew immediately which direction we had to take.

These amazing talents, however, at times led him to take on a work load which could hardly be managed even with his astonishing capacity for achievements. His striving for completeness and for excellence was remarkable. At times several people were working in various European archives to furnish him with material to speed up the progress of his scholarly research. It will make hardly much sense to describe the procedure in detail, but I shall try to account for his endeavors in general and to show how his ambitious plans affected his career.

1. The Beginning of His Career

In 1953 when Bill Slottman worked in the archive in Vienna he intended to write a detailed study of the cultural context of the negotiations leading to the Peace of Carlowitz (1699). It terminated the Austro-Turkish War which had begun with the Turkish attempt to conquer Vienna in 1683. Bill Slottman had to get on with the writing of his doctoral dissertation but he did not quite have his material together. In the Haus-, Hof- und Staatsarchiv he had seen the pertinent documents but had not yet found time to analyze them. The secondary literature had alerted him to the existence of other collections, such as the Harrach Archiv, but as yet he did not have an opportunity to look at the holdings. He described the dilemma on October 5, 1954.

"After a very brief stay in New York, I came on to Cambridge and the time since has been spent involved in negotiation for a number of positions. It is, of course, a question of supply and demand, and they can never be sure how many people will sign for the different courses. The great interest in history -- one can't explain it rationally -- created a demand for people like myself, and so I am now a tutor in History, committed to a year or two of gentle supervision of a large number of our nation's youth." (October 5, 1954)

He did not lack opportunities to work up his research, however, the problem hinged on the fact that his materials were thousands of miles away.

"My existence is oddly enough calculated to be the very best for a working scholar. I have a very definite routine (there is something almost monastic about it) and as I don't have to go far for my meals and snacks and my entertainment, a movie now and then, everything is wonderfully convenient." (March 20, 1955)

There was, however, a time limit to these favorable conditions.

"I have one more year until the zero hour, and then I must have the Ph.D. I have made a few enquiries already, and so I am hopeful that I will have a fairly decent job when I leave this place. I do hope to stay

on the East Coast, as I don't want to get too far away from Mother."
(May 29, 1956)

His filial obligations, which he observed meticulously, required
his attention. When he was two his father died, and Bill Slottman made
certain throughout her life to care for his mother. He often took her
with him on his European trips. I can vouch that she was always a
cheerful and a pleasant travel companion because occasionally, as on a
journey through France, I traveled with them.

In the face of these obligations his dissertation did not get
finished on time, and he had to look for a job.

"My own situation is extremely ambiguous at the moment, I don't
think that I will finish the thesis on time, and that will mean that I have
to move. (Actually I don't want to move away from here, even though
it will mean taking a sizeable cut in prestige and the extent of my future
possibilities. Fordham has been mentioned as a likely possibility, and
I am currently negotiating with them)." (February 19, 1957)

The task was somewhat easier because Bill Slottman was
regarded as a gifted and promising young scholar. Although he had not
yet completed his formal academic work, he was mentioned as a
successor of Oscar Halecki, an internationally well-known and
important historian who was teaching at Fordham University and
Columbia University. However, things worked out differently.

"I finally received an offer from Wesleyan University in
Middletown, Conn., halfway between here and New York. A two year
contract at a fine round sum, and a slight possibility of staying on there.
But it is a fine place to make a transition, and I am looking forward to
it." (May 4, 1957)

Harvard University did not want to let the promising young man
go; a clear indication of the degree to which his work was appreciated.

"A few days before I left Eliot House, I was asked to become
Senior Tutor. This is an administrative and a teaching post; actually half
of one and half of the other. It has a certain prestige about it and a
lovely set of rooms overlooking the Charles River. I accepted on the
proviso that Wesleyan would release me; the academic niceties should

be observed I think. This Wesleyan failed to do, and for a day or two I was a *cause célèbre* at Cambridge. The decision was finally made to have me come here for a year, and then to allow me to return to Cambridge." (October 9, 1957)

"Professor [Robert Lee] Wolff was none too pleased about my desire to become s Senior Tutor, but he did finally come around to the idea, and he got the History Department to offer me a job for the next three years as an instructor with a virtual blank check on a full year course in the history of the Habsburg monarchy." (November 12, 1957)

These changes provided Bill Slottman with good working conditions for the writing of his dissertation.

2. The Doctoral Dissertation

In the beginning the dissertation produced unexpected difficulties.

"My own situation in the matter of the thesis is not quite so happy. Professor Wolff leans strongly to Rákóczi, and when Professor Wolff leans strongly one has no other course than to agree with his position. My first chapter will be a boiled down version of what the more extensive treatment of the Carlowitz business would have been. This does call for a change in plans, and I shall write you in the very near future with more details on the new plan of attack. I know that it is a criminal practice to write a thesis bit by bit, but I really have no other alternative. The Harrach collection assumes even greater significance, and I should be very glad to hear, if you could crack the magic circle and take a look at the documents bearing on my problem." (October 5, 1954)

Working on Ferenc II Rákóczi, the leader of a Hungarian freedom movement against the Habsburg rule at the opening of the eighteenth century, had initially not been Bill Slottman's intention. He wanted to do a larger research project leading to a study of the broad cultural context of the negotiations leading to the Peace of Carlowitz. At the end of 1954 he had to change his original design. That created additional difficulties.

"The present state of the thesis is something of a problem. Feelers have been made just this week about the possibility of having most of it finished by next September -- an undertaking that staggered my imagination but which may be the golden opportunity of staying here for a few more years. The thing must be ready then within a year, and this will necessitate cutting some corners." (December 11, 1954)

An essential part of the source material had first to be obtained from Vienna, and he reported about it in the spring of the following year.

"I continue to realize that I am way behind schedule ... Even if I were to do a phenomenal job of writing and studying I don't think that I can complete the first four or five chapters before the beginning of the next school year in September. I shall have absolutely no excuses for not getting down to work, but I am too much a realist at this point not to see that I will not be able to perform miracles. The material is just too difficult for that." (April 24, 1955)

He was an extremely conscientious and thorough worker who intended to write a dissertation based on solid archival research. Now he faced the need to consult additional sources as well as the pertinent literature for the new topic.

"I have not quite settled down to writing though the actual production is only a day or two away. I found that I had to do a bit more of the background reading before I started on it." (July 4, 1955)

In the fall he was finally able to start.

"I am sitting down, believe it or not, and writing my thesis. It is going ever so slowly and it sounds like tripe, but I am forcing myself to stay at it. I absolutely have to get this summer to Europe for a change, and the trip to Hungary will be a pleasure trip if it ever comes off. Most of the thesis should be done before I go. If I ever can develop sufficient momentum, I should have much of it done by the beginning of the year." (October 1, 1955)

He soon faced a syndrome familiar to most scholars. New obstacles need to be cleared away first, if one just does not want to do a perfunctory job but aims at presenting respectable work. Even somebody who could think so effectively and write so well as Bill Slottman, needed time to complete a book-length manuscript.

"It is a matter of life and death now, and I can only hope that the motivation will not prove too stimulating. I shall save my bit on Hungarian social and economic conditions until the last." (September 24, 1956)

In the fall of 1956 the completion of the work was near.

"I am storming ahead with my thesis, and I am rather depressed with it generally and with my chance of having it completed this year. I do think that I will finish it by June, but they need it by April 1st if it is to be counted for the June Commencement. I shall do my best, but it is fearfully difficult going, and I now realize why I have temporized with it so long; it is just an immensely difficult piece of work, and it far exceeds my powers now and forever more." (November 15, 1956)

A particularly stressful time in his career accounted for his despair. Anyone familiar with scholarly writing knows rather well that in the midst of writing, doubt and despair can get the better of anyone. In Bill Slottman's case, however, the pressure to complete his studies swiftly and successfully was so great that he rallied and quickly mastered the difficulties. However, the delay with the completion of the dissertation had its consequences.

"What is going to happen is that I will be quickly and finally removed from this isle of learned leisure to a place where I have more than enough time to do the work which I now more than ever feel called upon to do ... You must not think that I am whining, or that I am going in for self-deprecation for the fun of it. I know that I have something on the ball, but I know with the same certainty that the present project is something which a man should do as he nears the time of his Festschrift and not at the beginning, however delayed it may have been, of his career." (November 30, 1956)

In the letters which followed I did not hear more about the difficulties. In the end the director of his dissertations was well satisfied with the work.

"The greatest problem collected with all of this was the thesis --

still unfinished. My director, Professor Wolff, finally put in an appearance, and he has now read a large portion of it. All that remains are brief chapters on Rákóczi and the Turks, the Swedes, and the Mediation. He seemed to like it, though he was rather depressed by the style. I continue to think that my letters are not that bad, but I may be wrong. I shall have to do more polishing, and I shall have to complete the remainder by the end of Christmas vacation. It will be a great relief to have it off my mind, and then, I tell myself, I can get down to 'what I really want to do'." (October 9, 1957)

Obviously, Bill Slottman faced complications that befall historians who write their manuscript in another language than in the language of their sources and their literature. Under such circumstances one loses touch with one's own language and uses all kinds of outlandish expressions.

In June, 1958, when he received his Ph.D., Bill Slottman had one major hurdle behind him. The future of his career, however, depended on the publication of a book. Undoubtedly, at one time or the other he must have told me why he did not want to publish his doctoral dissertation, but unfortunately I have forgotten the details. In any case, the reason never came up in his latter letters.

Perhaps, Rákóczi may not have been a topic that really enthralled him; perhaps, other projects on his mind may have struck him as more promising to leave a mark on the profession; perhaps as an overachiever he was inclined to shy away from committing himself to any action that might entail the slightest degree of failure. Although these speculations might have been valid reasons for Bill Slottman not to publish his dissertation, I am thrilled that it has found its way into print after his death because his dissertation is a distinguished piece of scholarship.

From the extensive archival work which Bill Slottman did for his dissertation two additional research projects emerged. One of them was devoted to the Lord Paget study, the other to the internal political constitution of the Habsburg monarchy. This work relied on the minutes of a commission, the so-called Deputatio, which played an important role in the Habsburg monarchy at the end of the seventeenth century. Nothing more needs to be said here about that study before it will appear as book.

It is surprising that Bill Slottman decided to research simultaneously the Deputatio and the negotiations which led to the Peace of Carlowitz. While pursuing these projects he also returned to a topic which he originally had wanted to include in his dissertation: the significant role of William 6th Baron Paget (1637-1713) as English Ambassador at Vienna and later at Constantinople, in bringing about the Peace of Carlowitz.

3. The Study of Lord Paget

Lord Paget's personality fascinated Bill Slottman. That I know from many remarks. He loved to talk about him and he even had something in common with him: both wrote wonderful letters. Lord Paget as an extremely talented letter writer captured the loyalty of Bill Slottman. He now concentrated his energy primarily on that project. Its origins reached further back.

Early on Bill Slottman encountered problems with Lord Paget.

"I know from the Kinsky-Schlick correspondence that Paget was to arrange for a payment, but I have no idea as to the recipients (Maurocordato and the Turk or just one of them), the amount, and the quid pro quo." (March 3, 1955)

Soon another difficulty appeared.

"One small problem has come up. In Hammer's account of the negotiations he declares on p. 648, 'Paget, welcher seinen Hofe die Ehre der Vermittlung um fuenfzigtausend Taler erkauft hatte ...', as far as I can see and as far as a few other savants [*sic*] have been able to see, he gives no source for this transaction ... This is not crucial, but it has puzzled a number of people and it might be nice to track it down to the source. I would not want 'Milford' to be accused of anything he can no longer answer for. I have come upon new leads as far as Paget's papers are concerned: they are in Wales, and the indefatigable Tappe at

London has just been looking at them. I plan to write him shortly to see if there is much that is relevant to Carlowitz in this collection (that of the Marquess of Anglesey)." (July 4, 1955)

Bill Slottman had just discovered a collection of documents which later on would greatly effect his completion of the Lord Paget study. He provided details about the collection.

"I wrote recently to the Marquess of Anglesey to inquire about some Paget papers. He sent me a very nice letter, urging me to come and have a look. I am too old a hand to think that it will turn up anything new, but a nice little prize may be waiting for me." (May 21, 1956)

Obviously he tried to play down his expectations so that he would not be too disappointed if the discovery of the correspondence should be irrelevant for his work. In the summer of 1956 he visited the county seat of the owner of the collection and reported his first impression.

"There was no long-expected revelation at Anglesey, but there is a fine collection of documents, which would make for a very tidy study of Paget -- brief and pungent perhaps -- that might well be the first publishable part of the thesis." (July 1, 1956)

Evidently, on his initial encounter with the material, Bill Slottman did not fully grasp its significance. He seems to have thought of publishing a short report if we consider the final size of the study that was based in part on the Paget material.

Even before the completion of his dissertation Bill Slottman planned the additional research project leading to the writing of two manuscripts he hoped to publish. He presented the plan to his dissertation director, Professor Wolff, who reacted positively.

"He is most enthusiastic about my working on Paget and my following up the business of the Deputation." (October 9, 1957)

Immediately after the completion of his dissertation Bill Slottman continued working on the great project. It had now taken the shape of two parts in his mind: the study of the Deputatio and the one on Lord Paget. He obtained copies of archival material from Vienna and Paris. He also intended to visit Simancas, Venice, and Rome in order to evaluate the significance of these archives for the Lord Paget study. Although he intended to work simultaneously on Paget and the Deputatio, he decided to move ahead with Lord Paget.

"I do hope to have Paget ready by the middle of the next year. I won't have to teach in the first term, and then there will be time to think about the Deputation." (March 26, 1960)

In his letters from 1960 and 1961 he continued to report about the work on the Lord Paget study and at the end of 1961 he indicated that he would start writing in June 1962. He not only found ways to obtain copies of European archival material but also traveled himself constantly to Europe to continue his archival work.

"Professor Wolff tells me that he hopes that I will get some money next year from a foundation, so that I will be able to devote all my time 'to the preparation of the two monographs -- one on Paget and the other on the Deputatio'. That means that I have to think about getting things from Brno again, and I surely will have to spend time at all the usual archives. I do hope that he is right -- I surely am convinced that it is now or never, for I have no wish to apply for any more assistance without having a publication or two to my credit." (October 12, 1961)

Now he was occupied in getting materials from Spain. Again the idea surfaced to write both studies simultaneously.

"The summer remains somewhat less obscure than before. As of May 1, I will get down for the first time to serious work on the two projects: Paget and the Deputatio. I hope that three months or so will have me well enough away so that I can really do most of the writing before I come to Europe next spring." (February 12, 1962)

Obviously the plan for an extensive archival trip had to be postponed for a year. It is perhaps a reflection on all of our experiences when Bill Slottman kept mentioning deadlines for one or the other project which he could never meet. Taking on a large project at times we succumb to the illusion that we could finish it relatively quickly. Additional difficulties, however, always appear during the writing. Furthermore, Bill Slottman had a lot of other things to do, and he could not devote his time exclusively to the production of the two books. Finally, he received financial support for a longer research trip to Europe.

"I finally have had good news about next year. Last week quite unexpectedly a letter arrived from the American Council of Learned Societies saying that they had voted to grant me an award next year. The sum is generous enough to make certain that I will be able to come this summer and next spring, too. In addition, there may be a chance of some additional help from the Fulbright people; I feel rather awed by all the support, emotional and financial, and even more determined now to do my very best with my poor old neglected Paget." (February 21, 1962)

Bill Slottman did not intend to use the new opportunity only for archival work. In 1962 the political situation in Eastern Europe was not as tense as in the previous years, and he now hoped to have an opportunity to visit the place where the most important phase of the events took place which occupied him.

"I will need some feeling for the country if I am to write about the Congress of Carlowitz," he wrote in the same letter. In fact, in September he traveled to Carlowitz. At that time it was a town of about six thousand inhabitants with the same Sremski Karlovci on the Danube in Yugoslavia, roughly forty miles northeast of Belgrade. Characteristic for his way of working he needed to see in what setting the events had taken place. With his quick and grasping intelligence, however, he did not need to linger long to absorb the ambience of Carlowitz.

During all these projects, the additional trips to find new archival evidence, the need to become acquainted with the location of the events, and the task of writing, Bill Slottman had to keep in mind continuously that any projected book would decisively influence his career. The talents of the young historian had not gone unnoticed.

"At the end of March I was approached for the first time by the University of California at Berkeley; I signified that I was interested and sent my thesis on to them. At the end of April they called me to tell me that they were thinking seriously to make me an offer ... I flew out there two weeks ago, talked with members of the Department and was required to deliver a talk on of all things the 'Austrian Enlightenment'. The impression seemed to have been a most favorable one ... Now the question is whether or not they will make me a formal offer (this would mean that I would be an Associate Professor and have tenure by the end of my first academic year at Berkeley in the event that poor Paget sees the light of day or is about to have that pleasure in the meantime). My reaction to California was so positive that I have been ready for the past two weeks to make the difficult step of leaving Harvard and setting out for the golden West. The climate, the beauty of the situation, the youthful character of the Department, the presence of so many friends." (May, 1962)

At the same time he was still in the midst of the work on the Lord Paget study.

"I am working fairly hard on Paget and expect to have written about two hundred pages of rough draft before leaving for Europe. If I can have the manuscript in some manageable form by the end of the summer I will be pleased. You would be startled, I think, to see me really working hard for once in my life -- perhaps when I get the hang of it I will continue to do so. The major problems are more technical than methodological (forgive me for the last word); it consists quite simply on going through all the microfilm from Anglesey (I have had some of it xeroxed for easier reading -- a wonderful method that) and constructing a simple orderly narrative on that basis. It doesn't sound like much of a job, but it will keep me busy until it is time to start operations in California." (End of 1962)

Although he had begun writing the manuscript he came to Europe. Shortly before his move to Berkeley, in July, 1963, he was in London.

"I have been working fairly intensively at the Public Records Office discovering that I should have worked on George Stepney [1663-1707, represented William III at various Central European courts, including Vienna] and not Lord Paget ('Ten years with the wrong diplomat'), still I have found a lot of nice things and may even produce an article on the strength of what I have found." (June 20, 1963)

Unfortunately, I cannot explain the comment which somehow seemed to disassociate him from his work on Lord Paget because I never held the manuscript in my hand. I know about it only from Bill Slottman's account.

It is a familiar dilemma of a historian who finds in archives important documents which have the potential suddenly to direct public attention at the discoverer that the expected renown will never come along if the new evidence is not published immediately. Any delay will naturally increase the fear that somebody else will also come across the documents, publish the insights faster, and reap the benefits. Such a threat caused Bill Slottman temporarily great concern.

"The first piece of news is that I am doubtful now that I will be going to Vienna this summer. In the past weeks it has become more and more apparent that I will have to spend the summer toiling on Paget (though now as you will see with a rather different point of view, alas!); the trip to Europe would be pure joy after a year of great isolation and remoteness from my friends and familiar places, but it would be something of a suicide expedition, for if I make no more progress than I am making there will be difficulties in the way of my promotion. The recipe, or better, prescription, then, is to spend almost all of the summer working on the manuscript, so that I shall have something to show the local talent and a publisher just before Christmas ... The sources seem ever more important than before -- a week or two in Vienna would make so much difference, but I must discipline myself." (April 3, 1963)

He explained in the same letter the reason for the rush when he reported about a meeting with the Ottoman scholar Sir Bernard Lewis.

"Sir Bernard mentioned the fact that there were good materials on Carlowitz, etc. After the lecture was over I went up with an eye of making polite conversation and asked him about this point. He told me straight off that a student of his has been working on a thesis on Carlowitz based on Turkish archival materials. That sounded ominous enough, and he turned away for a few minutes to talk with one of the other people; he returned to the case with the word that not only was he doing the Turkish things but that he had been working on the Paget papers. I am afraid that all of my small store of *sang froid* deserted me at that moment. It had been difficult enough to believe that there was anyone crazy enough to work on that whole business in this day and age; but difficult so it was one could appreciate the fact that the Turkish sources might have yielded a good deal. But the almost exact duplication of the work struck me as more than a difficult thing to believe -- it was a blow right at the very shaky structure of the Slottman system." (April 3, 1964)

Ultimately he relaxed and recognized the importance of the matter.

"Before I quit Paget and all of that I must say that I take a more thoughtful view largely because I believe as a matter of theory that one book is not like another and that I am bound to find things, to see things, to say things that Mr. X will not do, and vice versa. I just wish that he had touched all the bases with the exception of the Paget Papers. My book will not really focus on Carlowitz; it will be a fairly minute study of an English diplomat (read European diplomat) at work. With an eye to extracting as much as I can in what is generally relevant from a mass of minute and often trivial detail." (April 17, 1963)

At this moment Bill Slottman also mentioned a characteristic of Lord Paget's letters which he regularly stressed in his conversations. The correspondence contained letters to his wife at home, and in them Lord Paget mentioned many things which normally do not find their ways into diplomatic pouches but which are of great interest for the historian and anyone interested in history. Now, Bill Slottman reflected more calmly that the other scholar who had gone through the Paget Papers might indeed have other interests and would not necessarily rely on the same information he had culled from the correspondence. Ultimately, his concern about a race for the Lord Paget papers proved to be unfounded. From Berkeley he reported about it.

"I had a very curious meeting yesterday with the man who is working on Lord Paget. A young and rather breathless Englishman who wants to become an expert on the Ottoman empire in the seventeenth century. He went to Anglesey some years after I had been there and was told he was the first to use the collection! He managed to take the papers to London, catalogue them with great care, and prepare them for eventual return to Pla Newydd. At the moment he is working very carefully and successfully I think on some of the ground that I am covering at the moment. His orientation is more to the Turkish side and more in the way of straight diplomatic history; I have resigned myself to the biographical approach with a lot of social history and to a few outrageous pages on Austria in this period. He has a tremendous motive force behind him -- his life is blocked out for the next ten years at least. In his presence I felt a bit like an astrologer talking with one of the first astronomers. Still, one or two interesting things emerge: we are agreed on much of the situation and agreed on the figure of Paget. I also felt how curious it was that I immediately felt that the collection of papers is not as interesting as it looks straight off (the dilettante's guess); he catalogued them and took a year at it and only then did he come to the conclusion that things were not quite as hopeful as they seemed. Some of the more interesting things actually don't figure in his study at all. There will be two books then, and I have little doubt that he will go to work on mine when it appears -- but a fine fellow for all that, terribly decent and very much pleased to have found someone who shares some problems in common." (June 5, 1965)

The threat that somehow the beautiful subject could be taken from him kept Bill Slottman at his task. He continued to work diligently, his inspiration fueled by the danger that somebody could best him utilizing the precious material.

"Paget is proceeding somehow, and I am confident this time that if my resolve can be renewed each and every day that he will be off (in fairly disorganized form) but off to a Press before too many months are out. I have finally come to the point when it is necessary for my survival, and when it is necessary, too, for my peace of mind to have this behind me. I suspect that once that has been done (even though it won't be the way I want it to be) that it will be much easier for me to publish in the future. I feel more interested in my work, in my own language, and my life here is so monastic that even the good monks at Melk would find it dull. It has taken so many years for this to come about, but I can see now that it would have been impossible any other way. My only fear is that this signal change in my *regimen vitae* may have come a bit too late to spare me some difficulties this year." (August 28, 1964)

One of Bill Slottman's character traits saw him through the dilemma. Occasionally in conversations he had intimated that as a young man he had toyed with the idea to join a monastic order. In his way to react to a crisis or to organize his life in general there was much that a European observer might associate with the life of a Benedictine monk. Perhaps, it was more that Bill Slottman, irrespective of where he lived and what he did, always carried a bit of monastic life with him. Already in his description of his daily routine at Harvard he had used the comparison.

For some time he did not mention the projected book in his letters but it turned out that he was working at it tensely.

"Lord Paget is further advanced than he has been in years, and I am actually following a drastic schedule of forced marches. I hope that I survive him, but then I have very little confidence about my sources of energy." (August 15, 1965)

"One of the difficulties of working on a thing like Paget at this particular time is that American society really doesn't help very much; it only makes what one does seem doubly without meaning. We are certainly having our troubles, and it would be easy for me to adopt my usual pose of Cassandra." (July 21, 1966)

Finally, at the end of 1966, the manuscript was completed. Already at the beginning of 1960, when his employment at Harvard had been clarified, he pointed out that his position would also have the advantage that without great difficulty he would be able to publish. At the end of 1964 the manuscript had advanced so far that he speculated how he could best publish it.

"The final weeks were a bit hectic, but around the beginning of November I managed to present the Department and California Press with an almost complete version of the book. It runs to nearly seven hundred pages, and if I do make a few additions it will be over eight hundred. First reactions have been almost nonexistent. The kindly editor of the press read the first half and thought that I had been too ponderous in my introduction; one member of the Department is reported to have read it and to have been pleased with it. It looks as though it may be sufficient to carry me across the goal line (the football metaphor appears to be a favorite with editors, since he said that I deserved a five yard penalty of being too long in the huddle) and it also looks as though I will have to spend one additional summer really bringing it up to snuff." (December 18, 1966)

The completion of the manuscript had the anticipated effect on Bill Slottman's career.

"Did I tell you the Department recommended me for tenure? Even though reports have been so adverse the group apparently liked the book and me sufficiently to recommend an associate professorship. I am crossing my fingers that there will be no trouble." (March 25, 1967)

Now it looked as if there would be no more difficulties.

"Meanwhile I continue to boil down Paget with the hope of turning that in very soon. My future here seems very solid for once; all they want is a nod from a publisher or two that I can 'publish' with the best of them." (October 20, 1968)

I cannot say what caused him specifically to refer to his continuing "to boil down Paget." In any case the situation did not look too bad in the following March.

"I seem closer to having Paget between covers, and on or about the same time I hope to hear positively from the local people. Two books in the works after all these years should ensure my advancement here -- it can't come fast enough in view of the long wait I have had." (March, 1969)

Bill Slottman had to wait a while but then came the hoped-for success.

"I don't know whether I have told you that I have been finally promoted to full professor. They jumped me over the secondary step --

associate professor. I owe them something now, where before they owed me. It does make me feel more relaxed and will, I know, encourage me to publish as I have not managed to publish before." (October 16, 1969)

I cannot find anything more in our correspondence but I recall that Bill Slottman told me that the editor insisted that the manuscript needed to be cut considerably. Regarding the cuts as an unreasonable demand he was not prepared to listen to a person whom he could not recognize as expert to determine how long the book should be. A historian knows best how good his material is and how pertinent his commentaries are. Consequently he knows better than anyone else how long his manuscript should be. The reaction of the editor discouraged and frustrated Bill Slottman. He withdrew the manuscript and did not publish it.

I regret deeply that after Bill Slottman's death the Lord Paget study was not found among his papers. For that reason I consider it essential to add my recollections of the history of its research and its writing to the Preface of his published dissertation. They will enhance an awareness of Bill Slottman's distinguished contributions to scholarship and will reaffirm his position as scholar and author.

Walter Leitsch

William B. Slottman as Teacher

William B. Slottman was a brilliant teacher who enriched the lives of others during his thirty years in the University of California at Berkeley. He believed passionately that education is the education of individuals. His character and his schooling explain the sources of his conviction.

The roots of Slottman's belief fed on a deeply felt religious commitment. They were constantly nurtured by reading, thinking, praying, writing, and deeds. People from all walks of life benefitted from his gracious advice and generous actions. Friends and strangers, students and colleagues, anyone in need, poor or rich, became the beneficiaries of his care. For a teacher it was quite natural that his humanity would focus foremost on his students.

Slottman was born on February 7, 1925, in Williamsburg, Brooklyn, and for his secondary school work he attended Brooklyn Preparatory School. That classical high school conducted by Jesuits taught him to think of education as teaching in ways which spoke to each student personally. After he had seen combat during the last phase of World War II in Europe, Slottman concluded his undergraduate studies at Fordham University where he was graduated with *summa cum laude* in history in June, 1949.

His graduate work and his teaching at Harvard University enabled him to observe and to practice aspects of his educational belief. While working on his thesis, "Austro-Turkish Relations: The Peace of Carlowitz and the Rákóczi Rebellion," Slottman was a teaching fellow in General Education and History at Harvard College and a resident tutor in history at Eliot House. During the academic years 1957-58 he taught as an instructor in history at Wesleyan University. After he had earned his Ph.D. in 1958, he served as Allston Burr Senior Tutor at Eliot House and as an assistant professor at Harvard from 1958 to 1963 when he came to Berkeley.

Slottman's years in Eliot House provided his educational beliefs with an institutional model in the form of the individual tutorial system. Eliot House, named for Harvard's great president, Charles William Eliot, was an auspicious setting for thinking about educational innovations. Slottman linked the tutorial system to the development of the so-called elective system, the most radical curriculum change introduced during Eliot's administration.

Eliot believed in giving the individual college student a wide range of choice so that he might, in the words of Ralph Barton Perry, "acquire self-reliance, discover his own bent, rise to higher stages of attainment in his chosen field, and be governed in his work by interest rather than by compulsion." Eliot sought to ensure that the so-called liberal education was liberal indeed, and Slottman embraced that concern.

Slottman's major reservation to the Harvard tutorial system, as it was practiced during the 1950's and early 1960's, focused on an aspect of the college's admissions policy and the measure of exclusivity it spawned. In a letter to an Austrian friend Slottman's irony pricked a hole into the bag of pretension. While relating that he was asked to become Senior Tutor in Eliot House Slottman added, "You will certainly be amused to hear that deep in the wilds of New England, young Bill will be initiating our American first families into the Lore of the Habsburgs."

In 1963, when Slottman came to Berkeley, he felt that he had left behind him that modest enclave of social aloofness at the Charles River. Berkeley, stirring slightly as if anticipating the Free Speech Movement of the following year, seemed to be a place to implement his educational belief. The context bode well for innovation. The size of the student body at Berkeley and its bureaucratic structure challenged Slottman to find ways to reach the individual undergraduate. His kind and helpful nature constantly involved him in programs to develop institutional foci for students in search of directions.

With his commitment to education as the education of the individual, Slottman soon became involved in the residential program of Professor Woodbridge Bingham, one of his colleagues in the

Department of History. The program brought faculty and under-graduates together frequently in their residence halls, and Slottman centered his attention on the residents of Bowles Hall. He met regularly with as many of them as possible, listening to each of them while sharing with them his vast reservoir of historical lore. Subsequently he served for several years as Director of the Residential Program in History. In the late 1970's he directed the Summer Threshold Program, until limited funds made its continuation impossible.

The Summer Threshold Program was conducted under the auspices of the Division of Special Programs of the College of Letters and Science. During the summer Slottman sought to introduce incoming freshman to the campus in ways best suited to giving them a solid basis for subsequent college work. From his staff Slottman expected teaching directed purposefully at the individual student, in the class room, in the section, on field trips, and at the lunch table.

From 1983 to 1986 Slottman was Dean of the Division of Special Programs. He provided an alternative of individual majors for upper-division students not drawn to the established fields. A lack of funds and support kept Slottman from realizing his cherished notion of introducing Berkeley to a large-scale tutorial system as the core of an accessible undergraduate program.

After his deanship Slottman continued his Berkeley career as a brilliant teacher. He patiently upheld standards of scholarship and decency while maintaining a humane and humorous perspective on the tangled affairs of central and eastern Europe. The humanity and erudition which he instilled into his core course, "The History of the Habsburg Monarchy," made "Slotty" a legend for his students.

Without a tutorial program for undergraduates in "Letters," Berkeley's bashful substitute for "Liberal Arts," Slottman resorted to his own resources. Every week of the academic year he invited the students in his course to come to an open house at his home. There he talked with them about their concerns and about history, gently lacing his accounts with references to the complex Habsburg experience.

During these conversations a grasp of many cultures and their idioms enriched his splendid sense of humor. It often relied on the timeless tutorial wisdom: If you can make the student laugh she or he is apt to get careless and to go on listening. When his mind tossed off complex witticisms and epigrams, each of his students came away with the feeling that Slottman had addressed and helped her or him directly.

Despite Berkeley's limitations, before his death on May 4, 1995, Slottman had enjoyed the satisfaction of caring for individuals as well as teaching them.

Gunther Barth

Preface

In the course of a preliminary survey of the materials relating to the history of Hungary in the reigns of the Emperors Leopold I and Joseph I, which are preserved in Vienna's great *Haus-, Hof- und Staatsarhiv*, I came upon a large number of interesting 'tracks' of the Rákóczi Rebellion. Many of these had already been studied in detail by historians of greater learning and wisdom than I could ever hope to possess, and I had no wish to duplicate their efforts which were in many cases definite. But I did have the definite impression that a study of which would introduce this little known and yet important historical event to a Western audience would be useful. The Freiherr von Hengelmüller in his *Franz Rákóczi und sein Kampf für Ungarns Freiheit: 1703-1711* (Stuttgart-1913), had ,made a beginning in this direction, but he had not been able to carry his study of the rebellion beyond 1706. I thought for a time of beginning where he had left off (his book had been translated into English), but the continuation of a study written over fifty years ago when the Austro-Hungarian Monarchy was still very much of a living force would require of a modern student a superhuman effort to recapture the mood and the objectives of Hengelmüller's work. In addition, I felt an obligation to restudy the whole affair with an eye to introducing new material wherever possible and to presenting it in a manner that would obey the wise dictum that every generation should write with its own history.

In the manner of new materials, Professor Gyula Miskolczy of the University of Vienna called my attention to the collection of *Vorträge*, the minutes and the more formal reports based on them of the meetings of the Privy Conference (*Conferenz*), the equivalent of a cabinet in this period, in so far as they were concerned with Hungarian affairs, and, by extension of this principle, to other collections of the central organs of Austrian administration, which had not previously been used by students of the Rákóczi Rebellion.

The number of *Vorträge* in this category was disappointingly small, however precious they were for their indication of the views expressed by leading Austrian statesmen. But in the years before 1703, there were a large number which were concerned with the prehistory of the Rebellion, and this convinced me that it would be wise to concentrate my main attention on the diplomatic, political, and social origins of the revolt, rather than -- as most previous students have done beginning *in medias res* with its actual outbreak in 1703. This shift in emphasis to the origins led me quite naturally to the Peace of Carlowitz and to the internal conditions in a Hungary so recently recaptured from the Turks. In this way new light could be thrown on those external and internal forces which, operating as they did virtually automatically, brought Hungary to the brink of insurrection at the very moment when the attention of its Habsburg king was engaged elsewhere in the business of preserving the Spanish succession in his branch of the family. The failure of Leopold's absolutistic regime to solve the manifold problems posed for it by Hungary with ever greater urgency in the crucial years 1696 to 1703, was to fade imperceptibly into a diplomatic struggle between the Austrians and the Hungarians on a European-wide front. Insurrection now had its foreign allies, and its agents were to be found at trouble spots all over Europe ready to take advantage of the Emperor's embarrassed position. Success or failure in meeting this threat was to be quite as important a chapter in the formative days of the Habsburg monarchy as its showing in the same years on the battlefields of the Lowlands, Germany, and Spain.

The Hungarian diplomatic offensive, as I soon realised, ran directly counter to the almost customary work of mediation which England and Holland had carried on in Eastern Europe in an effort to free Austrian armies of the crushing burden of war on two fronts. The busy diplomatic maneuvering of the years 1704 and 1705, when George Stepney and J.J. Hamel Bruynincx, the English and Dutch envoys in Vienna, attempted to bring about a compromise between the Emperor and his rebellious Hungarian subjects, was a continuation of the efforts of Lord William Paget and Jacob Coyler, the English and Dutch envoys to the Sublime Porte, to bring about the final settlement at Carlowitz in 1699. The third appearance of this mediation was at the negotiations leading to the Treaty of Passarowitz in 1718, a topic to which I hope someday to return.

However congenial a task I found this introduction of an important and little known chapter in the history of Hungary -- indeed, in a broader sense, in the history of supranational government in the Danubian region -- I felt that it would be a good idea to situate this process against a background showing the dynamics of the European power politics of the day. In doing this, I would be approaching the relatively unknown from point of departure of the more familiar world of French, English, and even Russian statesmen and policies, which would have the additional advantage of allowing me to assess the rebellion's role on the European scene. And no more natural a way can be found for approaching these problems than through the eyes of Western diplomats whose observations might be expected to find a natural response from their 'descendants'.

These many strands of historical explanation and relevance have been joined in this study, not simply by *fiat*, but by the very nature of the process which it seeks to describe. In the first part there is a discussion of the Anglo-Dutch Mediation of Carlowitz, and here in an effort to introduce new material I have made use of the unpublished despatches of Lord Paget in London's Public Record Office and the published Dutch sources which have not received the attention they deserve. Conceived as a unified presentation of a diplomatic assignment, this part may at first seem extraneous to the history of the Rákóczi Rebellion, but I know of no better way to approach that subject, particularly in view of the continuity in the work of mediation by the two Maritime Powers and their increasingly close involvement in Eastern European affairs which I hope to establish.

The Peace of Carlowitz legally ratified the Habsburg claims to Hungary and Transylvania, and Leopold and his ministers were presented with a magnificent opportunity to create a new order of political and social life in those lands. In the second part of this thesis, "Hungary *Conquista et Neo-acquistica*: 1696-1703," the reactions of the Austrian government to this challenge are studied in some detail. Austria's fatal reluctance to provide a viable solution to Hungary's difficulties is not to be ascribed, as is so often the case, to violently anti-Habsburg feeling on its part but to the failure of men and material to weather a crisis of such proportions. This conclusion is based on the protocols of the *Deputation* (unpublished and previously unused), the *ad hoc* committee developed to meet just such an emergency. The picture of Hungarian society reflected in the musings of Viennese administrators is balanced by an impressionistic description of the milieu which produced Ferenz Rákóczi, the future leader of the Hungarian Malcontents.

In tracing the diplomatic history of the rebellion in the third part, I have made extensive use of the *diplomatica* of the *Reichshofkanzlei,* that perfect labyrinth of reports and instructions exchanged by Vienna and its diplomats in a wide variety of European capitals. One can perceive on the basis of such indications the degree of importance assigned -- it was in direct proportion to the harm it could do -- to the rebellion. The extended treatment of the Anglo-Dutch Mediation relies almost exclusively on the wealth of published sources.

This, then, is a work of introduction; it makes no pretensions to being a complete study of the Rebellion or in a more restricted sense of the whole sweep of its diplomatic successes and failures. An old and familiar story, as far as Hungarian historiography is concerned, is presented with a change of pace and emphasis, with the added fillip of a conscious effort to provide as many indications as possible of the living presence of a time and a place which have too long been shadowy and obscure. The almost bewildering complexity of this rebellion has evoked differing reactions from some of Europe's most distinguished historians of the past hundred years: Klopp, Noorden, Oswald Redlich, Srbik, Szekfü, to mention only the most outstanding. Their generations were radically different from our own, and the writing of history in their manner is no longer possible, however intrinsically desirable it might be. For where they concentrated on the diplomatic history of the nation-states, we incline to a graphic presentation of the whole range of contacts between peoples, a cultural history of international relations in which the diplomatic contacts are only the most evident and best documented. Where they had experience of the Habsburg monarchy as a political reality, we can know it only through the more recondite process of intuitive recreating. Where they were able to work securely within a well-defined historiographical tradition or school, we have no such support and little of their certainty in assigning meaning and value to the events we are studying.

But one pitfall we can avoid, and that is the temptation to substitute quite badly the events of our own day for those of the early eighteenth century in our work of evaluation. This search for historical analogies is doubly dangerous at a time when Hungary once more experiences all the frightening implications of its traditional role of *antemurale Christianitatis*. This would involve, for purposes of judgment, the substitution of the German regiments of Leopold I for the Soviet armor of Khrushchev, or the confusion of the strange contrarieties of Anglo-Dutch support of Leopold and the moral indignation they felt over his treatment of the Hungarians with our own hesitancies in policy. Such an ill-advised process can work both ways, and for some modern observers the present magnificence of the Hungarian Freedom Fighters may seem to be impugned, if Prince Rákóczi emerges, as he does in these pages, as all too human. But it is surely the melancholy task of the historian to present human beings in their weakness as in their strength, and if Rákóczi is certainly not canonized, he is placed once more on that more tenable eminence which Szefkü's great pioneer effort in his *A szamuzött Rákóczi* reserved for him.

It must be possible surely to honor the spirit of freedom and, at the same time, to bestow due recognition on the conscious efforts towards order which derive from other traditions and inspirations. The men who fought Rákóczi did so in the interests of the continued existence in Central Europe of a state which they hoped would not be inferior in its way to the best that was in the Holy Roman Empire and the Spain of Charles V and Philip II. The apparent similarities between the events of 1703 and 1956 must not lead us to the conclusion that what we have to do here with roughly similar processes, and that same relative positions are to be assumed by the powers of light and darkness. The only healthy point of departure (it has been adopted here) is that the Rákóczi Rebellion was unique in its time and place, and that a close study of its evolution will find relevance only in the degree to which the differences, essential and in a final sense not wholly explicable, between it and the uprising of 1956 are underlined.

Part One

The Anglo-Dutch Mediation at Carlowitz

Chapter 1

The Grand Alliance

"Je crois que la Maison d'Autriche est lasse de regner...."
William III

"....wee are lookt upon and entertained as People they need; yet not used like such as they desire or care to oblige, but as they are forced by pure necessity...."
Lord Paget

The 'Dutch Wind' that brought William of Orange's fleet safely to England helped to initiate a change in the whole political climate of Europe, for it made possible a project that had long been William's most cherished dream: the formation of an alliance of the two Maritime Powers and the second most powerful land power in Europe, Austria, to act as a counter-weight to the expansionist France of Louis XIV. Though his feelings toward his new subjects would always appear to be ambivalent, there was no doubt that William was anxious to commit their growing power and prestige as a nation to maintenance of the balance of power on the Continent.

In the first week of September, 1689, he saw to the practical arrangements. William, sixth Baron Paget, was named as his envoy to the Emperor, and in the letter which announced this appointment William spoke of his great desire to add further strength to the forces already combined against France in the Austro-Dutch alliance of May 12, 1689.[1]   A few days later he took a more drastic step, and this time without the countersignature of a minister or the acquiescence of Parliament, he caused the Great Seal of the Realm to be placed upon the official act of his adhesion, as King of England, to that alliance.[2]

This almost perfunctory conclusion of the Grand Alliance might seem to be an admission by the High Contracting Parties that such a solution was too obvious, too much a product of the logic of events to require prolonged discussion. But this alliance was in reality the end term of a long process, and as such, to use the expression of Cournot, was one part logic and one part chance. Since the signing of the Treaties of the Pyrenees and of Oliva, it had been manifestly clear to perceptive observers that France was the revolutionary force with which Europe must measure her welter of popularistic loyalties and liberties, but the transformation of this insight into a political reality had been difficult and time-consuming. The statesmen who felt the need for such a new alignment were few in number, and the forces of which they disposed were far too ponderous to be quickly brought into line. The actual paternity of the alliance, moreover, was something of a problem: a number of sires have been suggested, but none with a title clear enough to settle all doubts. Baron Franz Lisola, the sagacious imperial diplomat whose experiences had made him tiresomely aware of the French menace had in his books and pamphlets, above all in his *Bouclier d'Etat et de Justice*, become the first publicist for such a venture. Sir William Temple was the leading English candidate for the honor (he, too, combined the roles of diplomat and journalist), while Jan de Witt and William of Orange divided between them the Dutch claims to this great political invention.[3] The problem of the parent in this case is possibly insoluble; a number of gifted individuals, faced with the same overriding emergency, could easily have come to the same conclusions. One can suspect that we have here an independent discovery of a political calculus that would see good use for the next few decades. But the pressing need for such a new departure could not obscure the strangeness felt by the partners to such a novel undertaking. Defense could certainly bring them together into am *Interessengemeinschaft*, but the prolonged association required almost uninterrupted was would reveal the weaknesses of an arrangement of that kind. There would appear strains and points of the course of their association that were the natural consequences of a real divergency of views in the political sphere; but even more decisive was the growing cultural time lag between the Enlightenment world of London and Amsterdam and that of baroque Vienna.

Austro-English relations were very much in the experimental stage. In the history of both states there had been diplomatic exchange, but there was nothing that even the most optimistic could call a 'traditional friendship.'[4] In the thirteenth and fourteenth centuries they had been only dimly aware of one another's existence, and it was fear of France that has brought them together then, as it would in 1689, into occasional alliance. The meteoric rise of the Habsburgs under Maximilian I had required a new interest on England's part in the fortunes of this heir of the Burgundian inheritance on the Lowlands, but the division of the enormous possessions of the House of Austria between the Spanish and German branches resulted in a concentration of English attention on Charles the Fifth to the exclusion of Ferdinand I and his successors. In the subsequent century and a half there had been occasional English interest in the Emperor's wars in Eastern Europe and a fairly repetitive pattern of marriage negotiations which had uniformly collapsed after long periods of bartering. English policy towards Austria was "kept a blank to be filled by the writing of chance."[5] The contrast between the two states to the minds of Englishmen was too far-reaching to allow of anything even remotely approaching friendship and alliance. When tentative offers were made, they originated in Vienna which was naturally the first to realise the need for allies in its wars with the Bourbons. The timid advances of Leopold I and Charles II made it difficult for hardpressed Austrian statesmen to place much confidence in English dependability. Franz Lisola, who had spent many trying years on London, expressed their skepticism when he said that "as far as we are concerned we have nothing to fear nor anything to hope for from England."[6]

Unusual as the new found community of interests between England and Austria may have been, the alliance between the United

Provinces of the Netherlands and the Holy Roman Emperor was even more surprising.[7] Where in the English case the difficulty was clearly one of a long standing indifference, the trouble in the case of the Dutch was the very reverse of that, for there had been a very complicated history of relations connected with the fact that the United Provinces had originally been part of the Empire and that they had been for a time a possession of the House of Austria as well. The tie with the family had been the first victim of the Dutch struggle for independence; the connection with the *monstrum* that was the Empire had remained as a legal fiction. Rudolf II, for example, had caused frequent stalemates in negotiations by his insistence on regarding the seven provinces as parts of the Empire and addressing them in appropriate manner. But at Münster even the Emperor had been forced to concede that this alleged tie no longer existed. For the Dutch the new ties with Austria in the form of an alliance could not fail to stir old and unpleasant memories, while Austrian ministers and the prelates who so often influenced official policy were certain that any *foedera cum calvinistis et inimicis* were bound to be of very questionable value indeed.

It was characteristic of Austrian policy that the official friendship with Holland was produced under duress, and that, while the Emperor maintained a representative in The Hague from 1659 on, he only consented to receive a Dutch envoy to his Court ten years later. The first treaty of alliance was only concluded in 1673. Apparently the prospect of what seemed to be the mortal agony of the Dutch Republic moved the hesitant Emperor to such a decisive step. The opening of the dikes had not failed to have its repercussions at the *Hofburg*. Dutch subsidies and Imperial troops became one of the staples of European warfare; the fact that they so often failed to coincide became one of the constant sources of irritation. But such a symbiotic relationship made constant diplomatic intercourse a necessity. The *calvinisti* and their Catholic *inimici* settled down to accustom themselves to a process of continued alliance.

It was in this atmosphere so redolent of new departures in European politics that William Paget set out from Beaudesert Hall, his ancestral state in Staffordshire, to take up his post in Vienna.[8] Paget was very much of an English "Milord," and, if one can place much trust in Caroline portraiture, a handsome man, but he had little preparation for his long and difficult assignment in Eastern Europe. He was, as he said of himself, a "bad traveller," and his age (he was over fifty) made him an elderly novice in one of the most trying trades of the time.[9] His appointment was more of a testimony to the new King's sense of gratitude than to his usual perspicacity in choosing the right person for an important assignment. Paget had emerged from the obscurity of the life of a country gentleman to play a small and yet sufficiently impressive a role in the "Glorious Revolution" to attract the grateful notice of William III.

The new English government was faced with the difficult task of creating a new working corps of diplomats, for most of the veterans in the service of the Stuarts were ardent Jacobites and were currently intriguing with French diplomats in the interest of their deposed sovereign. William's criteria for his appointments were standard for the time: a sure loyalty to the monarch, a capacity for hard work (the amount of correspondence usually involved was immense), and an adventuresome spirit that could make light of the enormous inconveniences and dangers of travel and residence in foreign lands.[10] In selecting his envoy to the Emperor, William remembered that he was well represented at Vienna by a brace of Dutch envoys and that what was really required was a personable English peer by way of reciprocity for the Emperor's custom of sending nobles on his diplomatic missions to London. The very soundness of a man like Paget would give the lie to a good deal of the Viennese gossip and soul-searching about the new state of affairs in England. Vienna was, after The Hague, the most important diplomatic center in Europe, and, as His Britannic Majesty's envoy, Paget might well find himself in the position of being a focal point of all English diplomatic activity in Eastern Europe.[11] William's insouciance was all the more regrettable and but another indication of his cynical attitude towards Englishmen. He was not afraid to appoint mediocrities, and only time would show that this particular appointment was not such an unfortunate one after all.

Paget seemed in no hurry to reach his post in Vienna; his trip through Germany was a leisurely affair. In January, he was at Regensburg at the time of the election of the Archduke Joseph as King of the Romans. In obedience to the ancient customs which refused permission to foreigners to remain in the city during the election, Paget and the Papal Nuncio were required to leave the city for a brief period.[12]

At the very time that the new English envoy was travelling towards Vienna, the States-General decided to replace the aging General Hamel Bruynincx, who had served as their customary representative in Vienna since the establishment of the Dutch permanent mission there. Bruynincx was not one of the most distinguished diplomats in the Dutch service; and the value of his limited talents had been further reduced by his openly intransigent Calvinism in an atmosphere that was hardly less militant in its Catholicism. Continuing to live as he did in the mental and emotional world of the Wars of Religion, he could never comprehend the life that went on around him. His support of his coreligionists in Hungary and Transylvania did him much credit, but it could not fail to render him *persona non grata* to the imperial ministers who were pursuing an actively anti-Protestant policy. His activities at the Hungarian Diet at Ödenburg (Sopron) in 1681 had only confirmed the impression that he was actively interfering in the internal Affairs of the Habsburg monarchy.[13]

The States-General showed a similar lack of confidence in him, and on a number of occasions during his stay in Vienna diplomats of higher rank and greater ability had been despatched to represent Dutch interests at particularly critical junctures. Jakob Hop, the pensionary of Amsterdam and a man of wide experience in German affairs, had served on two such missions, and Coenraad van

Heemskerck had been sent in 1673 to direct the negotiations which had produced the treaty of alliance in that year.[14]   Despite his unmistakable desire to return to Holland, Van Heemskerck was forced to remain at Vienna to oversee the even more burdensome business of making certain that the Emperor would carry out his part of the bargain.   The Jakob Hop had returned in 1688 to conduct the first series of negotiations that would eventually lead to the Anglo-Dutch Mediation between the Emperor and the Sublime Porte. Purely a Dutch concern at first, it developed into a joint undertaking in which now the Dutch, now the English would take the lead.

It was Van Heemskerck's turn again when the States-General sent him to Vienna as their resident envoy in the spring of 1690. He and Paget arrived in Vienna at virtually the same time, and almost immediately they were to be closely associated in one of the most difficult and nerve-racking diplomatic good works of modern history. That the two men could not abide one another was soon apparent. This friction was natural; their personalities were vastly different -- Van Heemskerck had a more agile mind and specialized in quick and conclusive negotiation, while Paget was slower and perhaps better geared to the *lenteurs* of the Court of Vienna -- and beneath the facade of amity which they strove to maintain (they both served the same master) the lack of sympathy between English and Dutch was evident.[15]

For these recently arrived diplomats of the Maritime Powers the difficult business of acclimating themselves to one of the most complicated courts in Europe naturally consumed most of their time. Before one negotiated, one had to trace out however impressionistically the network of power relationships, the delicate links and interlacings which formed the nervous system of this other *monstrum* -- the Hereditary Lands of the House of Austria. And though Dutch and English diplomats did not ordinarily receive the training in penetrating observation of foreign politics and statesmen and the deft reporting of the daily activities of the courts to which they were accredited which still remained a trademark of Venetian diplomacy, their reports to London and The Hague, despite their more improvised nature, reveal natural talents of a fairly high order. Less conscious of what they were attempting to do, they nevertheless shed light on some of the more enigmatic aspects of the life of the Viennese court and to agree in a large measure with the reports and final relations of their Venetian colleagues.[16]

To the jejune minds of these Western observers, the Court of Vienna could only seem old fashioned and full of pretensions that had little contact with reality. The Austrians lacked the sheer will to power and its expression in art which was so characteristic of Versailles; there was a more ancient arrogance in Vienna that exerted itself by refusing to honor the pressing claims of princes whom it could only regard as parvenus. It was no mere dispute over trifles when Austrian statesmen refused to accord to younger members of the European family the honorifics to which they felt themselves entitled. The primacy of honor reserved for the Emperor was often more jealously guarded than any fortress of great strategic importance in Hungary or the Rhineland, and negotiations were often allowed to extend beyond their natural terms because of a dispute over the titles to be used in the official documents or the ceremonial to be used at the meetings. The baroque mentality retained an aggressively sensual and theatrical sense of the symbol, but it evoked deep-seated responses none the less, and the Austrians showed great virtuosity in treasuring up their reminders of past greatness against the day when reality and symbol would coincide once more.

And baroque it certainly was, this conglomerate of *Länder* and peoples; even in the confined area of a capital that was in large part still a medieval city one could feel the baroque in the mixture of external simplicity and interior elegance which characterized its retorations of ancient churches and the newly-built town houses of the nobles. The influence of French classicism was slight, because of a conscious effort to preserve a kind of cultural independence as well. The by now well-established time lag between Western and Central Europe was one of the most unfortunate by-products of the Thirty

Years' War, and the well-nigh constant state of alert in Eastern Europe. And when a breathing spell was granted them, it was understandable that they would give their cultural allegiance to neighboring Italy or to Habsburg Spain. For the few spirits who might wish to free themselves from this cultural inferiority, French culture was not as yet a social possibility. The Emperor had set himself against this threat from the West, and the Court took its cue from him in this, as in all other things.

For he was the very center of their 'solar system,' and the ideology which had developed about the figure of the absolute monarch flourished in Vienna, if in a much more modest and less self-conscious way then it did it in France.[17] Here the accent was more patriarchal, and the great prelates and magnates had not been reduced to the passive role of their French equivalents. They were accustomed to do his Imperial Majesty's bidding in their slow and selective way, and it was only in the presence of that highly perfected form of regal idolatry, the Spanish court ceremonial, that they might occasionally mistake mere earthly Majesty for the Divinity itself. And so they resolved with a truly Ptolemaic complication about their 'sun,' and if Leopold could not impose his will or his personality upon the age with the same undeniable success as his cousin Louis, the rapidly growing monarchy with which he alternatively struggled and temporized for nearly fifty years would owe much more to him of its future strength and weakness. The particular form which its growing pains took were made inevitable by its unique and baffling constitutional situation, but in a monarchy which was customarily regarded as the private preserve of a family, the personality of the reigning head of that family could often prove decisive. It is a paradox of history that this period of formation of Austria as a Great Power should take place under the aegis of a man who was certainly not one of the most gifted members of the Habsburg dynasty. His character strikes the modern observer as being similar in many ways to that of Franz Joseph. Here, indeed, a Great Power's last years of life were prefigured in its beginnings.[18]

Leopold had inherited from his father the Habsburg face (in him it was developed almost to the point of caricature), an "irresolute wavering temper," and a set of crowns for whose exacting responsibilities he had not been prepared.[19] Destined originally as a second son for an ecclesiastical career, he had retained a deep personal faith which made him almost morbidly aware of his duties to his God and to his subjects. Yet there was nothing of Escorial gloom about him; his tastes covered a wide range of interests. Strongest perhaps in languages and possessing a high degree of intelligence, he was musically gifted beyond the average. Hunting was for him, as for so many of his family, a positive fetish. His private life was full of festivities and innocent amusements; it was an exceptionally moral one, in marked contrast to those of his royal contemporaries. He proved himself a devoted husband to three wives and a loving father to a whole bevy of archdukes and archduchesses. His were the virtues that would have flourished in the more congenial setting of the palace of a spiritual elector or a luxurious abbatial lodge. He would have mastered that leisurely and benevolent kind of life with ease.

But the death of his older brother thrust him into a situation of continuing crisis where goodness and indecision would not often redound to his credit, and his 'inertia' would be forever contrasted unfavorably with the energetic habits of the King of France. The persistent threat of French hegemony would demand of him a constant effort to save his own possessions and those of the Princes of the Empire from French military execution and occupation. Bitter experience of his own weakness and that of his *Ländercomplex* taught him to believe without question in the direct intervention of the Almighty on his behalf. Politics was for Leopold the realm of the miraculous. Leibniz might express surprise at this state of affairs without being able to understand what was involved here.[20] The Emperor was grateful and modest in victory, and in defeat he never entirely despaired. This was not the stoicism that a long history of thwarted ambitions develops as a protective coloration, but a firm reliance on the will of God which serenely expected a favorable outcome no matter how desperate the situation might seem at any particular time. The intimate relation of this spirit of passivity to his own personality has never been entirely explained. One may suspect that the two were complimentary, that the unquestioning faith in Divine Providence provided an excuse for his reluctance to make decisions. And yet it was not entirely a rationalization of his weakness, for the very pressure of events seemed perennially greater than anything he could invoke against them, and the better part of valour was to temporize with the inevitable, until such a time as God was ready to come to his rescue.

His was a personality that felt secure only in the presence of the accustomed, and he habitually clung to policies and to advisors long after they had outlived their usefulness. A man of only middling political talent who is also Holy Roman Emperor finds it easier to give his confidence to men of roughly the same calibre, for inborn pride and a slight consciousness of inferiority would allow no mere subject to be greater than his Emperor. In time the men about him began to take on the characteristics of their master; they learned to discuss with almost inhuman care a multitude of projects which never became realities, and when Austrian affairs were at their lowest ebb, they came to expect that the outcome of the next battle or the next campaign would put all aright. There was gratitude on his part for all of this, and for once it was impossible to believe in the fabled ingratitude of the *Dank vom Haus Habsburg*. Boyhood companions never lost his initial confidence; no failure no matter how blatant and irremediable could destroy that trust. His unpleasant experiences with one small category of men -- his chief ministers -- in the early years of his reign, coupled with his innate reluctance to share his solitary responsibility, led to the resolution to be for the rest of his life his own "*Primo Ministro*."[21] He preferred to have two or three fairly distinguished ministers, who might represent his whole gamut of Baroque statesmanship. One might be suave, corruptible, a superb diplomat; another cold, unbending, a slave of the endless meetings and reports. The "last impressions" (one English observer felt) was the key to the hesitancies of Leopold's policies, for he appeared to be governed by his advisers in turn, "as if each commanded *de jour*."[22] But these men who were reputed to govern him in turn were acutely aware of the exact amount of pressure which could be applied and the possibility as well that at the end of series of dexterous manipulations the imperial will might be as unfathomable as before. He often resorted to the device of keeping some of his closest advisers in the dark about important state business; it was his way of keeping them in their place.

Though his Court was undoubtedly one of the few really interesting centers of European political and social life at the end of the seventeenth century, it did not have the good fortune to possess memorialists of the distinction of a Saint-Simon or a Dangeau, or letter writers like those who provide an unforgettable chronicle of the Cockpit and Kensington. Its leading figures with the possible exception of Eugene of Savoy -- and who would have the temerity to claim that he has ever been adequately understood? -- remain shades for the most part. Perhaps the eminence of the names they bore tended to obscure the actual contributions of any particular member of the family, and not a few careful scholars have confused brothers or cousins or have visited in a most un-Biblical manner the sins of the son upon the father. Greatness in a very striking way was rare in those nobles who formed the group of *Auliker* at the *Hofburg*, but if value is to be measured by lasting achievement, their contributions as individuals to the rise of Austria as a Great Power suggest that many of them have not received adequate recognition for their talents.

In contemporary accounts, such as the reports of our ambassadors, we are furnished with fairly complete lists and descriptions of the relative degree of importance and the particular spheres of influence of Leopold's advisers. References are continually made to the exceedingly involved clusters of family relationships; these ties of nature played a role in the recruitment of officials and in determining their subsequent adhesion to the parties at the Austrian Court. Of these, there was a disturbingly luxuriant growth. Van Heemskerck was able to distinguish seven separate "factien" in a prolonged report on internal politics, which he sent to the States-General in 1691.[23]

There was first and foremost the Neuburg party which had collected about the Emperor's third wife, Eleonora of Pfalz-Neuburg, who wielded in company with her brother the Elector Johann Wilhelm a surprising degree of influence. The fact that their sister Maria Anna was the wife of the sickly Charles II of Spain and thereby an important pawn in Austrian endeavors to secure the Spanish succession only strengthened the Neuburgers' position. A party with a much older tradition and hold on Court sentiment was the Spanish party, which was under the astute leadership of Carlos d'Este, Marques de Borgomanero, Spain's Ambassador in Vienna. The three smaller parties of Lorraine, Baden, and Bavaria were made up of the supporters of the three most successful military leaders of the Imperial armies in the recent campaigns against the Turks. In the years that had passed since the raising of the Siege of Vienna, Charles of Lorraine, Louis of Baden, and Max Emmanuel, the Elector of Bavaria, had with varying degrees of success driven the retreating Turks deeper and deeper into the Balkans. In these parties dynastic ties mingled with the prestige conferred by their victories, since each group could rely on ties by marriage with the Nost August House.

The sixth faction -- it was only in its formative stages -- was purely Austrian in orientation. Developed out of the conscious desire to replace the predominance of these foreign interests in the formation of Habsburg policy, this group sought to concentrate Habsburg interest on the destiny of the family's holdings in Central Europe. This was a view that would gain momentum in the next few decades, as the center of gravity of the Emperor's power shifted gradually towards the east. But that party's preeminence was not yet a fact, and its first feelers in this direction were tentative enough, as if it were uncertain of the role it was destined to play.

The seventh faction consisted of the chief prelates of the Austrian lands and members of religious orders like the influential Jesuits who served as confessors and spiritual advisers at the Court.

> I am now in a place where ecclesiastical power is extremely great; that no person (that is not of Civility or obtain any advancement, assistance or countenance, that is not a Transubstantiationist, and therefore you may suppose negotiations go on slowly, and heavily, while their Priests are continually buzzing in their ears Passive Obedience to Mother Church which forbids all concourse and sincerity of dealing with Hereticks;[24]

No foreign observer could doubt that its influence was enormous, even decisive at times, but Paget, and others like him, surely inclined to exaggerate scope and the effectiveness in any particular instance of ecclesiastical interference. A monolithic force it certainly was not, and its more outstanding leaders often supported persons and policies whose value to Holy Mother Church could never be conclusively demonstrated. The very influence of the Holy See on Imperial policy varied enormously from pontiff to pontiff, and the main trend was clearly in the direction of a greater measure of control by the Emperor of local church affairs.

The specific policies which were supported by these parties are more of a mystery; we suffer from a paucity of detailed information. But the foreign diplomats, having provided us with a bare outline of political forces operative at this Court, go on to describe in disappointing brevity, the party 'programs.' The Neuburg party, under the leadership of Count Stratmann, was the most powerful force at the moment. Its natural interest in a strong anti-French policy and in the defense of the Rhineland against further French encroachments made it particularly favorable to the Grand Alliance. It was this primary involvement in Rhenish affairs which enabled it to transcend the customary "bigotry" of the Austrian Court. Stratmann had the good sense "to mix a little politics with his religion," a compliment which that minister. marked for life as a parvenu, might not have entirely relished. The alliance found further support in the Spanish party, whose orientation was naturally westward and violently Francophobe.[25]

The Austrian party was in opposition to this bloc. Since its primary interest was the defense of Austrian interests against threats from the east, it was less anxious to support what it felt to be extravagant Habsburg commitments in Western Europe. On the crucial question of whether the Emperor should fight France or Turkey (it was assumed that war on one front was the only possibility), it inclined definitely to a continuation of the war with the Turks. The residue of a general spirit of Reconquista could be felt here; and if all of Europe could feel a sense of elation at the great victories over the Turks, this party understood that success as a sign of Divine intervention and a promise of even greater aggrandizement for Austria in Eastern Europe. A powerful ally in a good deal of its struggle for power was the party of the churchmen who quite naturally preferred a crusade against the Turks, so ardently desired and so devotedly supported by Innocent XI, to a war with Catholic France. Both groups were gravely troubled by the policy of close alliance with the Maritime Powers. But it would be a distortion of the facts to speak of any real combined operation of the two parties. In the matter of the crusade the glowing dreams of the clerics could not fail to outstrip the more limited objectives of the working statesmen in whose view Habsburg manifest destiny found its Archimedean point more and more in the Austrian lands, Bohemia, and Hungary.

The generals' parties vacillated between these poles of East and West, torn by an appetite for more glory, as a consequence of the inspired generalship of each particular hero, and the need for military security and an access of power for the German state he ruled. Their oscillations, when they could not be reduced to a mere struggle of personalities, could be explained in terms of the characteristically *Kirchtumpolitik* of German states of secondary importance. Thus, the Baden party found itself traditionally at loggerheads with the Neuburgers, though it was able to add further complication to this political mosaic by allying itself occasionally with the Spanish party. The position of the Bavarian party, so ostentatiously devoted to the alliance with Vienna, could not fail to become even more ambiguous as the struggle for the Spanish heritage involved Wittelsbach interests as well![26]

The Emperor's character and the existence of a variety of political factions did not reduce the ministers to the level of ciphers. Gifted men were needed to carry on the work of Austrian administration, and when they were discovered their effectiveness depended not so much on their presumed political attachments or their rank in the official hierarchy as on the confidence of the Emperor. Count Stratmann was a case in point. His position as Austrian Court Chancellor was certainly not the most prestigious, but it covered such a multitude of affairs, particularly those of a diplomatic nature, that he was brought into constant contact with the Emperor. And in such a favorable situation, this diplomat of long experience could not fail to win for himself the limited kind of pre-eminence possible in these circumstances.

"His beginning was ordinary," but industry and intellectual ability had brought him in successive jumps from Cleves, where he had served the Elector of Brandenburg, to Neuburg, and then to Vienna, where in the process of arranging a marriage between Eleonora of Pfalz-Neuburg and Leopold he had attracted the latter's attention and had been encouraged to enter the imperial service.[27] His great success had not been without great cost to his integrity; the carelessness it had produced now combined with the exhibitionism of a social climber who could never overlook the fact that he was not the scion of an old *Auliker* family. But his diplomatic gifts had survived, and his almost encyclopedic knowledge of the ways and means of petty German courts and, in a larger sphere, of Western European politics made him an indispensable figure at the deliberations of the Privy Conference. His political loyalties had not changed remarkably, as with the ease that was so natural to men of his time he had moved from one master to another; somehow he managed to continue in their favor long after he had gone on to greater things. He was a great favorite with the English and Dutch diplomats, because his contribution to the conclusion of the Grand Alliance had been, as far as they were concerned, a major one, and his expressed determination to bring the war to a successful conclusion gave him an air of "policy," which was not conspicuously present in his colleagues.

Count Leopold von Konigsegg, who had been for over twenty years the Imperial Vice-Chancellor, might well have been second to Stratmann in importance. It was conceded that he possessed a "good head and heart," but his days of real influence on the formation of policy were over. The pathological extravagance, which he shared with so many members of his class, had reduced him to financial need, a pitiful condition which made him prone to accept those gifts, which a less nuanced age would call bribes. His greatest political liability was the gout (this malady was the universal scourge of Austrian statesmen of his generation), and his experiences at Court were, for that reason, less and less frequent. He was respected for his years and eloquence, but neither the Emperor nor the ministers were likely to regret his gradual disappearance from the scene.

The opposite pole to Stratmann in character and in political convictions was Count Franz Ulrich Kinsky, the Supreme Bohemian Chancellor. Kinsky might impress his contemporaries with his great industry and zeal in the Emperor's service, but they were generally repelled by his *froideur* and his inflexibility of opinion. More of an intellectual than the other ministers, he possessed a weakness common to the intellectual politicians -- the overdeveloped sense of the extraordinary range of the possible in political activity. His close connection with a monarchy whose very existence seemed in perpetual doubt had taught him the virtue of limited objectives and of postponement of the inevitable. As devout or as bigoted as the Emperor -- depending on your point of view -- their accustomed manner of conducting affairs was very much the same, though their deeper reasons for their conduct were by no means identical. Where Leopold inclined to a political agnosticism, Kinsky had the pessimism of a man for whom the future holds little in the way of improvement. His was a mechanistic world of political equilibria, and a gain on one side necessarily entailed, according to this view, a corresponding loss on the other. Every situation was fraught with danger, and the wise man pondered the pro's and con's with the infuriating reasonableness of a pedant.[28]   Though Leopold finally came to depend almost exclusively on Kinsky, it was no secret that, while he esteemed Kinsky, he had loved Stratmann.[29]   And as long as that more attractive personality lived, Kinsky was doomed to remain a secondary figure.

The remainder of the offices, including even the crucial positions of President of the War Council and president of the Court Treasury, were held in succession by men whose prominence was often more genealogical than personal, men who were fixtures at this Court as their fathers and uncles had been. The Starhembergs, the Windischgrätz's, the Dietrichsteins, the Wratislaws, all were content and ready to serve and were able occasionally to produce an individual of real talent. A small and excessively inbred group, their contributions as individuals were not half as crucial as their unchanging pattern of life which yielded so little to the increasing need for a creative response to the monarchy's endemic problems. These men were willing now and again to carry their unusual sense of dignity to foreign courts as Imperial envoys, and once there, their *hauteur* was not calculated to win them or their master many friends. But they were in essence pleasant and uncomplicated gentlemen, *Wienerisch* before that complex of traits had become the possession of the lower classes. And the process of selection by which one of these gentlemen was preferred to another in appointments to high offices was itself based on family custom: the first-born divided his time between his estates and his official responsibilities, the second son might be a canon in an aristocratic cathedral chapter with hopes of further spiritual preferment, the younger sons followed a military career, travelled abroad, and searched in the age old way for heiresses to great estates in Bohemia and Hungary.

All of this rich mixture of political loyalties and statesmen by reason of talent or inheritance were usually concentrated in the frequent meetings of the Privy Conference. Some of the members were present because they presided over the various collegial administrative offices, while others, whose roles were restricted to Court functions, were in attendance largely on personal grounds. And this made for a variegated collection of advisers whose discussions and conclusions submitted for the Emperor's approval were of very uneven value.

This, then, was how their new field of operations appeared to such observers as Paget, Van Heemskerck, and Stepney. The Grand Alliance had been so recently concluded that the Austrians had not yet been able to grasp all of its startling implications. The sacrifice of the devoutly Catholic James II to the iron law of *ragione di stato* had been the occasion for some perfunctory soul-searching by Leopold and his spiritual advisers, and their conclusions in favor of the alliance with the Maritime Powers, while beautifully buttressed with learned theological argumentation, left them vaguely conscience-stricken.[30] And the alliance itself was subject to the apparently eternal laws which govern such combinations. When French pressure was most real, the allies could, indeed had to, overlook what separated them in political objectives, general culture, and religious belief. To speak of the liberty of all of Europe seemed for a time compelling enough of an explanation for their great experiment, but any noticeable relaxation of that pressure provided all too much scope for dangerous afterthoughts. And it was precisely this avenue of escape from the broader obligations imposed by the Grand Alliance which made problematical the measure of success that the two diplomats would have in their combined efforts to bring about a peace treaty between the Emperor and the Sultan.

Even their personalities were likely to evoke very different responses in Viennese circles. The English Milord could expect a fairly sympathetic reception from his Viennese peers. His Anglican faith would be a stumbling block, but his education and his life as a gentleman permitted of a certain sharing of interests with the Austrian nobles. The absence of any diplomatic experience would not be regarded as a handicap by men who, for all their years of service, were perennially amateurs.

The Dutch diplomats were on the surface at least far better equipped to acclimate themselves to the Viennese atmosphere. They were customarily at their ease in German, and they came equipped with a ready sense of the forms of Austrian political life. Though Holland's ties with the Holy Roman Empire had been cut, memory of the ancient connection served to provide the Dutch with an inborn sense of the political facts of life, as far as the Empire was concerned, and when memory failed, the very actuality of Holland's involvement in German affairs made good any deficiencies. Then, too, the Dutch diplomats were professionals in a way that was still fairly uncommon in the English diplomatic circles. Their period of apprenticeship was usually a long one, and when they did rise to the rank of an ambassador or a minister they were likely to spend long periods of time in the country to which they had been sent as the official representative of Their High Mightiness.

But the tensions that existed between Austrians and the Dutch were far deeper than those that obtained in Anglo-Austrian relations. The fate of their Calvinist co-religionists in Hungary and Transylvania had a far more imperious claim on Dutch attention that it did on that of the English, however much these last were attached to the Protestant cause. The militant Catholicism of the Court of Vienna was certainly a great obstacle to harmonious relations, but the Dutch were liable to grasp this difficulty not in narrowly ecclesiastical terms but in the serious difficulties they experienced with the consequences of the Counter-Reformation theology in Austrian political and social life.

The stoutly independent and no nonsense tradition of the Dutch patrician class was particularly apt to take offense at the tone of Austria's aristocratic society. Their frequent complaints as diplomats about Austrian *lenteurs*, Austrian pretensions, and Austrian touchiness must be traced to this deeper disquiet. Holland's society was, to be sure, built on privilege, and its leadership was sustained by ties of blood, but there remained the clear imperative of proving one's merit as an individual that was not evident in Austrian practice. One trait above all the Dutch mentality had learned in the course of its evolution to question and that was what it described as *deftigheid*. This meant a stateliness that bordered on pomposity, a distinction of manner that did not correspond with distinction in mental and moral equipment. In a word, a description of the atmosphere prevailing at the Court of the Emperor Leopold as seen by an alert Dutch observer.[31]

The consequences in the realm of politics of this profound tension will be noted in the activities at Vienna of men like Hop, Van Heemskerck, and Bruynincx, father and son, and it may have something to do with the tendency of the English representatives, however repugnant they might be as individuals to the Austrians, to assume a predominant role in any Anglo-Dutch combination in negotiations with the Austrians. The effect of this tragic lack of understanding was certainly to diminish the value of any collaboration of the Habsburg monarchy and the United Provinces. The merchant and the magnate would never really appreciate one another, and this was particularly true in the years in which the Austrians and the Dutch were required by the pressure of power politics to act in concert against the pretensions to European hegemony of Louis XIV.

Notes to Chapter 1

[1]Onno Klopp, *Der Fall des Hauses Stuart und die Succession des Hauses Hannover in Gross-Britannien und Irland im Zusammenhange der europäischen Angelegenheiten von 1660-1714* (Wien-1876), IV, 491), and the *Anlage*, 526.

[2]A.F. Pribram, *Österreichische Staatsverträge; England* (Veroffentlichungen der Kommission fur neure Geschichte Osterreichs, 3) (Innsbruck-1907), I, 185-190.

[3]The case for Lisola has been presented by A.F. Pribram, *Franz Paul Freiherr von Lisola* (1613-1674) *und die Politik seiner Zeit* (Liepzig-1894), see particularly 415-423; "Damais (1665) nun tauchte zuerst der Gedanke jener "grossen Allianz" auf, die ein Viertel jahrhendert später Frankreichs Ubergewicht und Terrorismus sich gegenüberstellte. Das Eigentumsrecht an der idee bleibt den Nierderlandern, *die Priorität aber gebuhrt nicht William III. und auch nicht Lisola, sondern de Witt*." (italics my own), Heinrich Ritter von Srbik, *Österreichische Statts-verträge: Niederlande* (Veroffentlichungen der Kommission fur neuere Geschichte Osterreichs, 10) (Wien-1912), I, 52.

[4]This is the theme of Sir Charles Firth's article, "England and Austria", *Transactions of the Royal Historical Society*, Third Series (XI), 1917, 1-34. The brief review of Austro-English relations that follows is based on the now classic treatment to be found in Pribram, *op. cit., passim*; this treatment is summarised in the introductory chapter of his *Austria-Hungary and Great Britain 1908-1914* (London-1951).

[5]C. Brinkman, "The relations between England and Germany, 1660-88," *English Historical Review* (XXIV), 1909, 249.

[6]A.F. Pribram, *Lisola*, 49

[7]The background of Austro-Dutch relations is based on the work of Srbik, *Osterreichische Staatsverträge: Niederlande*, 3-185; he approaches the material from the Austrian side, though he made extensive use of archival materials in Holland. For a Dutch view of the history of the establishment of permanent diplomatic relations between the two states, see G. von Antal, J.C.H. de Pater, *Weensche Gezantschapsberichten van 1670 tot 1720* (Rijks Geschiedkundige Publicatien, 67) ('S-Gravenhage-1929), I, vii-xxii. (Henceforth, *W.G.*)

[8]A brief account of the life of William Paget, sixth Baron Beaudesert, is to be found in the *Dictionary of National Biography*. A good portion of his papers,

public and private, survive in the great collection of the *Paget Papers* preserved at Plas Newydd, Anglesey, the residence of the present Marquess of Anglesey.

[9]Letter of Paget to Sir William Trumball, Oct. 11/21, 1689, *Historical Manuscripts Commission: Report on the Manuscripts of the Marquess of Downshire* (Hist. MSS. Comm. -1924), I, 384.

[10]The condition of England's diplomatic service under William III has been treated by Margery Lane, "Diplomatic service under William III", *Transactions of the Royal Historical Society*, 4 series (X), 1927, 87-109.

[11]*Ibid,.* 93.

[12]Klopp, *Der Fall des Hauses Stuart*, V, 40.

[13]*W.G.*, xxv-xxvii.

[14]A description of Jakob Hop is to be found in H.J. van der Helm, *Het archief van den raadpensionaris Anthonie Heinsius* ('S-Gravenhage-1867), I, 93ff.; for Heemskerck's background, *W.G.*, xxvi.

[15]In a letter of October 22. 1695, Stepney roundly denounces the Dutch envoy, Schonenberg, at Madrid as 'not less troublesome to him (Alexander Stanhope, English representative there) than Mr. Heemskerck was to my Lord Paget, Mr. Amerongen to Mr. Molesworth, and Mr. Ham to Mr. Johnson at Berlin and to me at Dresden.", Margery Lane, *loc. cit.*, 103; the speed of Dutch diplomatic operations was strikingly exemplified in both the cases of Hop and Van Heemskerck. Much of their speed was due to their often expressed desire to return to Holland, since they obviously did not relish thier assignments in foreign parts. Never had a state been served by more reluctant, and yet capable, diplomatic agents than the United Provinces in this period. For Hop's homesickness, see the description of his role in the Austro-Turkish discussions of 1689; as for Van Heemskerck, "Zijn taak was het bovenal tot snel en krachtig handelen, san een hof (i.e. Vienna), waar de tragheid en omslag ook toenmals spreekwoordelijck waren.", H.J. van der Helm, *Het archief,* I, 102.

[16]We are fortunate to possess two published accounts, one by the English diplomat George Stepney and the other by Coenraad van Heemskerck, of the state of the Court of Vienna *circa* 1690. The two accounts have not received the attention they deserve, and I have made liberal use of them here. An effort

has been made to present a picture of the reactions of diplomats of the Maritime Powers when faced with the culture of the Austrian *Barock*.

The first is a "short account" sent by Stepney, then representing England in Vienna as Secretary, to His Majesty's Secretary for the Northern Department, possibly Sir John Trenchard; it is published in the collection of *Prior Papers*, in the *Bath MSS.*, III, 8-14. The letter was sent just after the death of Count Theodor von Stratmann on October 20, 1693 N.S., but it surveys the political situation and personalities in Vienna in Stepney's accustomed pungent style. The account of Conraad van Heemskerck is shorter, but it is particularly valuable for the light it sheds on the cliques and factions at the Court. Their High Mightinesses had expressed an interest in receiving a report on the "constitutie" of the Austrian Court, and Van Heemskerck had compiled on November 13, 1681, *W.G.*, 494-499.

In an effort to produce as balanced a picture as possible on the basis of contemporary reports, I have also made use of the collection of the final relations of the Venetian ambassadors at Vienna in this period. They are to be found in Die Relationen der Botschafter Venedigs uber Deutschland und Osterreich, Hrsg. Joseph Fiedler (FRA, 27) (Wien-1867). The reports of the Federigo Corner (1690) and Hieronymus Venier (1692) in that volume were particularly helpful. The general impression has long existed that the Venetian diplomats inclined to be more sympathetic to things Austrian than the representatives of the Maritime Powers, but in this particular case, barring the striking difference in discussing religious and ecclesiastical questions, the accounts substantiate one another in a striking way.

[17]A contemporary allusion to this ideology of the Emperor is made by no less a worthy than Alexander Mavrokordatos, the Grand Dragoman of the Sublime Porte. If one makes allowances for a fulsome style that he had developed in his occupation of translating official Turkish documents into Latin or Italian his remarks are most revealing: "L'Augustissima Maesta Caesarea essendo sola sole risplendente con i raggi di tutte le regie, et adorabili virtu, si come non e dubio, che li suoi primi Ministri, a guisa di tante stelle quanto piu s'accostano, tanto piu partecipano della sua luce, cosi non e meraviglia, che alcuni delli piu rimote, restino meno riscaldati, e piu privi di quella soprafine tempre che si puo chiamere la vita interiore del ben essere.", Letter to Count Kinsky, Pottendorf, March 23, 1689, *Documente privitore la Istoria Romanilor,* culese de Eudoxiu de Hurmuzaki (Bucuresci-1885), V/I (1650-1699), 242. (Hereafter, Hurmuzaki, *Documente,* V/I) This is the sign certainly of the existence of a political

theology in the Austrian atmosphere. No study of the relation of theology, particularly theological cosmology, and politics in the era of Leopold I exists, however; the blank space may well attract students in the near future.

[18]The similarity in many ways of the two men has been already noticed by Heinrich Ritter von Srbik.

[19]"But as His Imperial Mjesty is observed to be of an irresolute wavering temper, on which the last impressions ever make the deepest marks, this occasions that he is frequently torn several ways by the different inclinations of his ministers, who in a manner governed him by turns as if each had commanded *de jour* (to which may be attributed those delays which have ever been too visible in all the designs and enterprises at the Imperial Court)"; Stepney to Sir Trenchard (?), Vienna, October 20, 1693 N.S., *Bath MSS.*, III, 9.

[20]"Man nennt es Mirakelgeld denn es herrschte die Meinung, dass in der Zeit grosser Noth der Kaiser Leopold immer ein Mirakel zur Rettung bei der Hand Habte.", Liebniz to the Princess Sophie, Vienna, I/II May, 1690, quoted in Klopp, *Der Fall des Hauses Stuart*, V, 194.

[21]"...bleibe Ich Herr und kann ein ander nicht vantiren, dass alles von ihm dependire; so kann ich es besser verantworten, dann alles ich mir selbst attribuiren muss.". Leopold to Potting, Feb. 18, 1665, quoted in A.F. Pribram, *Lisola*, 268.

[22]Cf. page 25, note 2.

[23]"...ende offwel Syne Keyserl. Maj'. tegen hetgunt voor deesen by desselfs voorsaeten meest in gebruyck te sijn, geen eerste minister heeft, soo nochtans heeft voorsz. slapheyt occasie gegeven tot verscheyde factien ende jealosies, die d'eene over 't credit ende aensien van d'ander heeft geformeert ende opgevat.", C. van Heemskerck to the Raadpensionaris, Vienna, November 13, 1691, *W.G.*, 494. THe discussion of the factions at the Austrian Court is based largely on this report.

[24]Lord Paget to Sir (?), Vienna, May 3, 1690, *Add. MSS.* (British Museum) 8880, 14.

[25]Stratmann had, according to George Stepney, supported the Alliance with the Maritime Powers "and supported his arguments with the credit of the Spanish

Ambassador, who (true to the principle of the King he serves), has ever been irreconcilable in his hatred To France and in his opposition to an universal Monarchy; which last consideration I look upon to have been the true one, why the Emperor so readily entered into a league with those they call heretics, and has continued firm in it, notwithstanding the offers France has made and the frequent solicitations of the Pope to that purpose.", Stepney, *Bath MSS.*, III, 9.

[26]"...oock kan Baden de Nieuwburgse partye niet betrouwen...Baden begint eerst weder te leven, heult aen de Spaense, soekende door een animositeyt tegen Vranckrijck sigh daer en elders recommendabel te maeken, om by een goeden uytal van de oorlogh sijn reckenigh aen de kant van den Elsas te vinden."; Bayeren is bekent, dat de presumtive erfgenaeme van Spagne in houwelijck heeft, vooraf niettemin gerenuncieert hebbende aen de successie van de Croon in 't generael tegens een cessie van de Nederlanden, by den Keyzer in sulcken geval gedaen; hoe verre dit ter wederzyden op sijn tijd plaets sal vinden, staet te besien;", Van Heemskerck's *report*, *W.G.*, 498.

[27]This characterization of Count Stratmann is based on the reports of the diplomats and on the published dissertation of Brigitte Kuczynski, *Theodor Heinrich Altet Stratmann* (Berlin-1934).

[28]"Wie baer alle Menschliche Sachen, zumahlen die Politische, Einen Unumbganglichen nexum in sich haben, also an welchen theill Euer Kayserl. Mayestät leiden wurden, wuerde derselbe (i.e. the continuation of the war with the Turks) den andern unfehlbar in Consensum ziehen, und Euer Kayserl. Mayestät interesse in grosse Gefahr seczen; dan solte Esz mit Frankreich unglücklich ablaufen, so stunten grosse Gefahr E.K.M., in augenscheinlicher Gefahr die Cron Böheimb und incorporierte Länder zu verliehren, deren feindtliche Eroberung das übrige such in die Gefahr desz Ebenmässigen Verlussts ziehen wuerde;" Relation of the Deputation *in Turcisis* to the Emperor, October 30, 1688, in Hurmuzaki, *Documente*, V/I, 166.

[29]Kuczynski, *Stratmann*, 178. But the correspondence of Leopold with Kinsky, a magnificent source for the Emperor's day to day reactions to official business and for his relations with Kinsky which is preserved in the collection of *Grosse Korrespondenz* (*Haus-, Hof- und Staatsrachiv*, Wien) suggests that the Emperor's feelings did go beyond esteeming Kinsky; aunfortuantley, a fair portion of the correspondence is illegible (Leopold had perhaps the worst hand in recorded history) and the number of lacunae render it difficult at times to

make a judgment on the relations of the two men. For Leopold's reaction to Kinsky's death, *vide infra*.

[30]Klopp, *Der Fall des Hauses Stuart*, IV, 424-436, and see also the *Anlagen* VI and VII, presents the detailed opinions of the theologians who were consulted by Leopold on the morality of recognizing William of Orange as King of England. The theologians generally concluded that the Emperor could do this without endangering his soul.

[31]My discussion of 'deftigheid' owes its impetus to the remarks of Jan Romein in his Die Biographie: *Einführung in ihrer Geschichte und ihre Problematik* (Bern, 1948), 48-49.

Chapter 2

The Congress of Vienna That Failed

"La plupart des gens croyent que l'on veut continuer les deux guerres, quoique tous les gens de bon sens et bien intennionez pour le bien public en enragent et connaissent bien que ce sentiment là peut setre soutenu que par les moins."

The treaties of Carlowitz, which were signed on January 26, 1699, have generally been regarded as proof that the Sublime Porte regarded Eugene of Savoy's victory at Zenta as a sign that the military and political situation in Eastern Europe had been radically modified to its disfavor.[1] Historians have been very well aware of the existence of a long series of negotiations, stretching over ten years, which preceded the actual Peace of Carlowitz, but the final achievement has often thrown the earlier tentatives into obscurity by depriving them of any organic connection with itself. A closer investigation of the whole course of the negotiation between the Emperor and the Turks during some fifteen years of war suggests that there was much more in the way of continuity of objectives, of individuals involved, and of accompanying political and psychological situations throughout this whole series of contacts than has been previously recognized. Any wider perspective, particularly one which has for its unifying theme the role of the Anglo-Dutch Mediation, may well amplify the usual version of Carlowitz, whose error is one of presuppositions rather than any faulty description of particulars. It would be foolhardy at this point to speak of any major revision of the traditional view of the Carlowitz negotiations. What is involved here is an effort to produce a version that is much closer to the historical original as experienced by the nations and individuals concerned. Any close involvement in these negotiations as they actually developed which does not fall into the error of judging the preliminaries simply in terms of their relation to the final outcome provides greater freedom for the interplay of historical chance and necessity and thus avoids the tautologous conclusion that Carlowitz happened, because it had to happen that way. That there were alternative solutions and possibilities as almost every turn of the long road to Carlowitz becomes immediately apparent once a close study of the relevant sources has been undertaken. Such a *point de départ* has the additional merit, as far as this study is concerned, of highlighting the real threat existent in an obscure rebellion in Hungary to the maintenance of the recently reestablished peace between the Emperor and the Turks -- one of the most ticklish problems raised by the Rákóczi Rebellion in the context of the *Grosse Politik* of the War of the Spanish Succession and the Great Northern War.

An observer with a mathematical disposition of mind might come to the conclusion, after considering the whole course of negotiation, that a number of conditions that were absolutely necessary before peace could be achieved can be isolated without great difficulty. The 'formula' for Carlowitz would be derived from the variables: Austrian victories and incipient Turkish decline, the presence in Eastern Europe of the Holy League, which was eager to take advantage of this state of affairs, the ever more unmistakable signs of the approaching demise of Charles II of Spain, which had the effect of making his Austrian relatives and would-be heirs more accommodating in the East, and the decision, finally, of Louis XIV to patch up a compromise with the Grand Alliance without any diversion in the West. It would have to take into account the growing exhaustion on both sides which sixteen campaigns had produced and the consequent internal weaknesses that became more evident in both Constantinople and Vienna. A really adequate mathematical expression would have to include the contrasting psychological rhythms of Austrian and Turkish political life. Peace could be achieved at the very moment in which the tortoise of Viennese *lenteurs* overtook the hare of swift and capricious Turkish decisions.

But the small group of English and Dutch diplomats who were to carry on the work of mediation did not possess any extraordinary ability to take in -- in one sweeping view -- the situation in which they found themselves. They did make rough calculations as to the possibility of peace, but these were the speculations of tyros in great part and revealed no special clairvoyance. When one of these men had managed to survive (the possession of good health was a necessary prerequisite for success) long enough to acquire a sufficient amount of painful experience, he learned to expect everything or nothing; and the variations in their attitudes as a group varied far more wildly and dramatically than the circumstances allowed.

The first years of this process were purely a Dutch affair. In the years immediately preceding the Grand Alliance, the States had appreciated the wisdom of keeping the Emperor's forces free for action in Western Europe, and when the activities of the Grand Vizir Kara Mustapha began to point in the right direction of a major war with the Austrians, Their High Mightinesses decided to throw the weight of their influence and prestige in the Levant on the side of last minute Austrian efforts to reach a compromise. The Imperial mission headed by Count Albert Caprara, which arrived in Adrianople in the spring of 1682, was an attempt on the part of the Emperor and his advisers to maintain the *status quo* which had been created by the Treaty of Vasvar in 1664, and was undoubtedly inspired by the feeling in Vienna that the real enemy was France. The rudimentary Dutch 'mediation' which followed had the unusual distinction of preceding the actual outbreak of hostilities. The Dutch Ambassador in Constantinople, the veteran Justinus Coyler, had already been instructed to work for the settlement of the growing tension between the two empires. He had had long acquaintance with the endless vagaries of Turkish policy and was able to advise Caprara on the manner of negotiating best suited to his purposes, but the situation soon became so tense that it was decided that continued Dutch assistance would only act as a stimulus for further Turkish "extravagances."[2] It was an axiom of Imperial diplomacy that any display of great solicitude in such a negotiation only encouraged the Turks in their wholly erroneous belief that the Emperor was desirous of peace because of his weak position. Coyler tactfully withdrew, and Dutch 'mediation' in this very primitive and informal form had suffered its first defeat.

The ensuing outbreak of hostilities neatly coincided with Justinus Coyler's death in December, 1682, and the succession of his son Jakob, only twenty-six at the time, to his father's post. It had seemed to the officials in Holland a wise and economical plan to allow the son, who had the added advantage of being well-versed in Turkish affairs and being on the scene as well, to inherit his father's position. This hereditary arrangement was to be repeated in Vienna: the Coylers and the Bruynincx's represented Dutch interests in these two important capitals for over half a century. These posts were not particularly attractive to ambitious young Dutch diplomats, and they became family affairs almost by default. But the second generation developed into particularly valuable and trusted representatives of their country. Their lifetime of service gave them a great advantage over their English colleagues which served to create another source of constant friction.

At the moment, there was little for the young Dutch Ambassador to do but watch the extensive preparations for the expedition against Vienna. The mood of the Turkish army was one of "playful excursion"; never in recent history had the Turks seemed so menacing and so confident of their power.[3] The Siege of Vienna was for Europeans of that generation a great *crise de conscience*, for a crusading spirit returned to a Europe which had only imperfectly retained its vision of a united Christendom in arms against the infidel. Gentlemen of uncertain prospects and admitted zeal in the common cause enrolled themselves in the Imperial army, and the pleas of Pope Innocent XI and his sizable contributions of funds added strength to wavering imperial spirits. When the siege was actually raised on September 12, 1683, Europe was able to breathe freely again, and the

Imperial Court, which had anxiously awaited the outcome first at Regensburg and then at Linz, could once again indulge its belief in divine intervention on its behalf. But this would not be an isolated miracle, for it was followed by a series of stunning blows to Turkish military and political pretensions that brought the Imperial armies within the space of a few years into the Balkans, and made the Emperor the effective ruler of Transylvania and the wasted Hungarian plain, a dramatic reversal of fortune which entailed a parallel modification in the traditional Austrian policies in this area.

Success on such a great and unexpected scale could not completely corrupt men of the stamp of the Emperor and his closest advisers; they were not to be shaken so easily out of their habitual pessimism and policy of short-term objectives. But they found it increasingly easy to dream of expansion and to resurrect claims to the conquered territories which only fitfully survived in the memories of antiquarians. In these years, Austrian statesmen learned to appreciate the great sweep and grandeur of the medieval Kingdom of St. Stephen. The young and promising Archduke Joseph was crowned the first hereditary King of Hungary at the conclusion of the Diet at Pressburg (Pozsony) in 1687, as if to underline the quickening of interest in Vienna in Hungarian affairs, and to make absolutely certain that territorial gains made in the name of Hungary would be secured for the Habsburgs as well. The vision of a revival of pre-Mohacs Hungary under Habsburg auspices was something with which European diplomacy would have to reckon in its future. For it was as successors of the Arpads and the Angevin kings that Leopold and his successors would present themselves as rightful claimants to Transylvania, Slavonia, Bosnia and Herzegovina, and even Moldavia and Wallachia.

In Western Europe, particularly in Holland, this unusual elan in Vienna evoked mixed emotions. It was rumoured that the Emperor was already considering the partitioning of the Balkans -- it might be possible to find compensation in Thessaly for what had been lost in Lorraine. Dutch sea captains, whose spirit of adventure did them more credit than their faulty sense of Holland's commercial interests in the Levant, proposed that a naval assault be made on the Dardanelles by a combined force of Dutch and Imperial ships. Johann Cramprich, the Imperial Minister at The Hague, displayed interest in such an expedition. But the natural coolness of Dutch official demand commercial interests and the fact that the Emperor could not possibly provide naval support condemned this proposal to an early demise.[4]

The Turks were not slow to take the measure -- and it was an accurate one -- of Imperial strength, but their perilous political situation made it difficult for them to adjust quickly to such undeniable indications of Austrian preponderance and renewed Turkish decline. Ibrahim Pasha, Kara Mustapha's successor, found it practically impossible to give even the slightest indication that he was negotiating for peace; it was important for his political future and, in addition, for his personal survival that he be regarded as a leader willing to prosecute the war at all costs. But even he managed to make the first peace feelers through the intermediary agency of a Greek dragoman. The two Greek dragomans of the last Imperial embassy had remained in Turkey at the outbreak of the war, and with the approval of the States-General had been taken under the protection of Jakob Coyler. One remained with him at Pera; the other, Joannichio Porfiriti, was detained at Adrianople. It was to the latter that Ibrahim Pasha turned with the suggestion that he sound out the Imperial Court to see whether or not the Emperor was disposed to enter into negotiations for a treaty of peace. When Porfiriti agreed in the autumn of 1685 to do this on condition that he be allowed to make use of the Grand Vizir's seal in communicating with Vienna, the Grand Vizir decided that this was too dangerously overt an action, and the matter was allowed to drop.[5]

Ibrahim Pasha was deposed soon after this, and Suleiman Pasha, who had shown a good deal of political acquiring the post of Grand Vizir, was given an opportunity to display his talents in making peace overtures to the Emperor in the event that victory in the field continued to elude the Turkish generals. After the fall of Buda, which the Grand Vizir had been powerless to prevent, he began to sound out responsible Imperial commanders in Hungary; letters were accordingly dispatched to Charles of Lorraine and to the Margrave Hermann of Baden, the president of the Hofkriegsrat. The choice of correspondents was a perfectly natural one, but there is the definite suspicion that the Turks may have wished to exploit the well-known rivalries between Imperial generals.[6]

Difficult negotiations of this kind, which demanded a knowledge of such details of Imperial politics, required successive Grand Vizirs to rely more and more on the diplomatic experience and the broad knowledge of European affairs of Alexander Mavrokordatos, the Grand Dragoman of the Sublime Porte.[7] He was one of the few people who managed to survive the treacherous changes of policies and personnel for long periods of time, and he was able, as a result, to provide a kind of continuity to the Turkish side of the extended peace negotiations. Involved in the fall of Kara Mustapha, he had narrowly escaped death; imprisonment and the loss of all his considerable property had been judged sufficient punishment for his close connection with the debacle at Vienna. Suleiman Pasha found it wise to restore Mavrokordatos to his former position of trust at a time when his talents were most needed.

As a Greek from the island of Chios, Mavrokordatos possessed to a striking degree that unfailed sense of the realities of a situation so characteristic of the Chiotes. His father had been a prosperous merchant who had managed to marry the widow of Alexander Mihnea, a Voevode of Wallachia, and it was due to her enlightened foresight that Alexander was sent as a boy of twelve to Italy to acquire a European education. He showed a precocious ability to adapt to his milieu by evincing interest in the union of the Greek Church with Rome. He studied for a time at the College of the Propaganda. But this phase of his activities was brief, and he pursued philosophical and medical studies soon after at Bologna and Padua. He learned by instinct to make the maximum use of the opportunity for travel and study his family had given him, and he retained throughout his life the distinguishing features of a graduate of the Italian universities he had frequented as a young man. It was as a physician with the best possible medical education for the time that he returned to Turkey, and he soon had established a very lucrative practice in Constantinople. Nicholas Panagiotes, a fellow Chiote, was at the time (1671) winding up a long career as the first Greek to be Grand Dragoman, the chief assistant to the Reis Effendi, the Turkish official who was charged with the conduct of foreign affairs, and he turned to the up and coming Mavrokordatos for assistance. When Panagiotes retired two years later, his assistant naturally succeeded him; he as to retain this post except for a brief period after the fall of Kara Mustapha for an impressive total of thirty-six years.

The office of Grand Dragoman was largely that of intermediary between the Turkish officials and the foreign diplomats; he met frequently with the European envoys or their dragomans and drafted the official and unofficial communications which passed between the Sublime Porte and foreign courts. It was something of an art to transmute the awesome periods of the Turkish statesmen into a Latin or Italian prose that Westerners could understand and even occasionally appreciate, and he soon proved himself a master of this difficult art form. In addition, he was one of the rare individuals in the Turkish government with whom European envoys could converse on roughly the same footing even if they learned not to expect complete candour from him. They respected him for his evident mastery of his calling, and they none too subtly flattered his enduring interest in European scientific and scholarly developments by presenting him with whole cases of the latest books from Europe. The professional physician in need of the most recent medical literature was understandable enough (the Dutch Ambassador was particularly helpful here), but his interest in books dealing with contemporary politics would at a later date be taken as a most suspicious sign by Austrian officials.[8] They felt that it was dangerous to provide Mavrokordatos with even the most banal accounts of Imperial campaigns against the Turks. But he would have plentiful opportunity to learn about Turkey's ancient adversary in Vienna at first hand.

The spectacle of his success in the service of the Sultan occasions certain questions as to his loyalty to his Turkish master. No hint of outright dereliction of duty has come to light, but there is plentiful evidence that he was willing to make adjustments favorable to the parties with whom he was negotiating, if he was promised compensation.[9] This practice was by no means unusual in Turkey, and it was a failing which he shared with a number of his European contemporaries, since at the time there was little of the moral opprobrium that we so instinctively feel attached to the acceptance of "presents." An exchange of gifts was usually made on formal occasions at the Porte, and this made the business of bribery appear normal and acceptable. A Greek in his position had to make the maximum use of the brains with which he was endowed and position of influence which he had achieved, and he might dream of an even more glorious future for his descendants as voevodes in the Danubian principalities. Five years after his death in 1709, his oldest son fulfilled the father's dream by becoming Voevode of Wallachia.

The natural talent for diplomacy which Mavrokordatos possessed was to undergo its supreme test in the years which followed the dispatch of the Vizir's letters to the Imperial generals, for the Turkish situation was becoming increasingly serious. The Turkish attack on Vienna had brought John Sobieski, the Emperor's Polish ally, to the city's rescue and, in due course, to participation in the great work of freeing Hungary from its Turkish masters, but there was always the good chance that French intrigue and the normal processes of deterioration of a successful alliance, once the enthusiasm inspired by the initial successes had worn off, would cause the Poles to make a separate peace with the Turks. Sobieski's French queen was encouraged to intrigue for the establishment of one of her sons as King of Hungary. It required all the enormous prestige of Innocent XI and the zealous day-to-day negotiating of his nuncios in Vienna and Warsaw, Buonvisi and Pallavicini, to settle such causes of tension.[10] The Pope was anxious to broaden the scope of the war by bringing Venice in on the side of the allies, and after much persuasion the Austrians and Poles accepted Venice as an ally on terms of equality. The Pope was to act as the guiding spirit of this Holy League (*sacrum foedus*), and the members made no secret of the fact that they required material help as well, for without his annual contributions to the allied cause they could not hope to be as effective as he expected them to be in ridding Europe of the Turks.

The Holy League, which was concluded on May 24, 1684, made a concession to its membership by according them a large measure of freedom in carrying out their part of the initial agreement to exert the maximum pressure possible all along the Turkish frontier in Europe. It did provide for constant consultation and mutual assistance, but in practice the three powers (Russia would join in 1687) were left pretty much to their own devices in their particular spheres of influence. The *Reconquista* might continue to exist as a current of public opinion, but as a political force it had been transformed into Austrian, Polish, and Venetian expansionism in Eastern and Southeastern Europe. As if this was not a sufficient break of restless enthusiasm, the hesitancy of Vienna, the perennial anarchy in Poland, and the financial straits of Venice would further blunt the crusading spirit to which the Holy League was in its protestations of high purpose at least a touching tribute.

It was customary for there to be a continual exchange of messages between Imperial and Turkish generals about terms of surrender for particular fortresses and the usual exchange of prisoners, and it was relatively easy then, when an opening had to be made, merely to attach a postscript in which the desire of the Turks for a just and honorable peace was brought to the attention of the Austrians. Mavrokordatos, who had accompanied Suleiman Pasha to the Hungarian front, sent three separate letters of August 26, October 8 and 18, 1686, to the Margrave Hermann of Baden. His excuse for writing was a request for the release of Selim Kiatub, who had been captured by Imperial troops at Buda, but after this preliminary gesture he went on to suggest the summoning of a peace congress. The Margrave's answer was not very helpful. It had obviously been written only after consultations with Vienna. The Margrave spoke in glowing terms of Leopold's love of peace and his disappointment at the failure of Count Caprara's embassy to Adrianople before the war. The blame for the war was laid squarely at the door of the Turks, and it was clear that definite reparation would have to be made for this act of Turkish aggression. Some wan hope was offered in the assurance given to Mavrokordatos that the Emperor had decided to communicate the contents of the Grand Dragoman's letters to his allies. It was not much in the way of favorable response, but at least the question of peace negotiations had been officially raised for the first time.[11]

Suleiman Pasha took advantage of this none too encouraging opening to address the Margrave with a letter of his own. It was a curious mixture of diplomatic platitudes and Islamic theology, but the state of the negotiation required a certain amount of camouflage. The loss of so much territory and prestige was explained not in terms of Austrian victories but of the dictates of the Almighty, and with a fervent sigh of "*Fiat voluntas Altissimi*" the chief minister of the Sultan announced that he was ready to discuss a peace settlement. He would be happy to despatch a trusted subordinate to treat with the Austrians; beyond that he could not bring himself to be more specific.[12]

The Austrian reply repeated the tiresome refrain of the Emperor's pacific intentions and went so far as to clear Suleiman Pasha of any personal responsibility for the war. The Austrians did expect that the Turks would make concessions; it was easy to speculate on their magnitude at a time when the allies were preparing for another victorious campaign. And though the Imperial government was ready to negotiate, it required sufficient proof that the Turks had reasonable conditions in mind before it would consent to the holding of a peace congress. Continued Turkish support of Count Imre Thököly, the leader of the Hungarian *kurucok* (insurgents), who had been fighting on the Turkish side since the beginning of the war, was regarded in Vienna as fairly conclusive proof of the superficiality of Turkish peace overtures.[13]

Suleiman Pasha received this letter while he was in winter quarters at Belgrade. In his next letter he announced that he was despatching the Kapidji Bashi Mehmed Aga to the camp of General Count Caraffa.[14] Mehmed Aga had little of real interest to offer the Austrians -- he brought neither concrete proposals nor presents with him. In addition, the Grand Vizir had complained about the recent loss by the Turks of the fortress of Verad; their old arrogance had not completely deserted them by any means. When the Turkish emissary requested permission to continue his discussions in Vienna, Caprara made ironic reference to the fact that Mehmed Aga had arrived empty-handed. The Turks always expected gifts from European envoys arriving for the first time in Turkey, and if Mehmed Aga thought of approaching the Emperor at closer range the very best present he could bring along was the person of Thököly. The Kaidji Bashi returned then to Belgrade to confer with the Grand Vizir, but the Turks, for their part, were unwilling to make that kind of gift.[15] In a letter to Mavrokordatos, Caraffa expressed his disappointment at the failure of the Turkish emissary to make any concrete proposals ("*non ha fato veruna proposizione di questa sorte*"); the Grand Vizir was surely using these exchanges as a device to sow discord among the members of the Holy League at the very beginning of the campaign of 1687.[16] The Emperor had been regularly transmitting reports on Turkish peacefeelers to the member powers (it was proof that his intentions in regard to the League and its objectives were completely honorable), but this naturally gave some substance to the undercurrent of fear in Warsaw and Venice that the Emperor might make peace with the Turks without troubling about his allies. These suspicions were mistaken, and in any event these negotiations had reached such an impasse that the only further Imperial advances and pressure from the Dutch on the two main belligerents could remove.

In the course of this exchange of letters the Dutch had not shown much interest in offering their mediatory offices to the Emperor and the Sultan. Hamel Bruynincx spent most of the years 1685 and 1686 in Holland, where he was content to receive reports from his "Amanuensis" in Vienna that there had been a series of contacts with the Turks.[17] Coyler showed a similar indifference. It was not until it became clear that the war was seriously harming Dutch trading interests in the Levant that the Dutch began to pursue a more active policy. The Dutch factors in Turkey had great influence with Their High Mightinesses, and their reports for a number of years had been uniformly depressing.[18] This financial distress, combined with the fear felt by the *Stadhouder* William III that France would not long remain a passive observer of continued Imperial expansion in Eastern Europe, prepared official circles in Holland for a proposal of Daniel de Hochepied, Jakob Coyler's brother-in-law and, in the cozy manner of the Coyler family's monopoly in Pera, the secretary of the Dutch Embassy. Hochepied was on embassy business in Holland in the last months of 1687, when he suggested to Nicholas Witsen, one of the most influential members of the States-General, that the United Provinces should offer its mediation to the Emperor and the Turks. This proposal -- it was made presumably at the behest of his brother-in-law -- received an extremely favorable response, for on January 2, 1688, it was decided that the opportunity "provided by the accession of Sultan Suleiman should be used to urge upon the Turks the benefits to be derived from a treaty of peace."

The States-General can be excused for its serious misreading of a very unsettled Turkish internal situation; the 'opportunity' afforded them by the accession of the new Sultan was for a time more apparent than real. A revolution of the military had deposed Sultan Mohammed IV and the clique about him which had vainly tried to maintain its control in the face of constant defeat in Hungary, but the revolution had not been able to establish much in the way of stable government. Coyler should not have been surprised, as he said he was, to receive "an indifferent answer" to his offer.[19] The Grand Vizirs in such a different period followed one another in quick succession, and they were forced to concentrate all their energies on the uninspiring business of preserving a modicum of order and thereby maintaining their precarious position in Adrianople.[20] Only with the accession of Mustapha Pasha of Rodosto in May, 1688, did matters improve so far as Coyler was concerned. The new Grand Vizir admitted that he had grave fears about the outcome of the current campaign (it required no great insight to see that internal instability made defeat in Hungary inevitable), and for once there was real evidence of a desire to use influence in Vienna to bring about a peace settlement. By the beginning of July, Coyler was able to report that the Sultan and the Diwan had decided to send an embassy to the Emperor to discuss a peace treaty. The Turks seemed ready to call upon Dutch assistance, though no formal declaration had been made, and the Turkish envoys who had been selected for this difficult undertaking, Sulfikar Effendi and Alexander Mavrokordatos, were provided by Mustapha Pasha with an important letter to the Dutch envoy in Vienna.[21]

Sulfikar Effendi and Mavrokordatos arrived at Belgrade with their large entourage, six camels included, just two days after the capture on September 6, of that stronghold of great strategic importance by Max Emmanuel of Bavaria and his truly international army. The conquerors received the Turkish party with great courtesy and made arrangements for it to proceed with all the necessary supplies and with an escort whose size was discreetly measured to the embassy's dignity. After a month of travelling through Hungary, where travelling conditions were especially difficult, the Turks arrived at Schloss Pottendorf, a short distance from Vienna, on October 13. There they were held virtually incommunicado until the time when they were allowed to have an audience with the Emperor and present the letters of the Sultan and the Grand Vizir to him. If they expected that this would occur soon after the arrival at

Pottendorf, they were doomed to disappointment.   The whole
European situation had changed so radically during their long trip that
the Imperial government had to resort to its well-worn device of
procrastination, while it assessed the rapidly evolving threat of a
general war in Western Europe.[22]

    The fall of Belgrade was a defeat for Turkish arms comparable
to the loss of Buda and the disaster at Mohacs, but its internal
repercussions were in its case slight compared with the lightening
swift reaction in Western Europe. The report of this latest and most
irritating victory of the Emperor convinced Louis XIV that he should
abandon his policy of sitting idly by, and French armies were soon
pouring into the Palatinate. The French Ambassador at The Hague,
alarmed at the many signs of Dutch preparations for an expedition to
England, warned the Dutch that the King of France would give his
full support to King James, if the Dutch intervened. This had the
unwanted effect of forcing William III's hand, for the speedy
deposition of James was absolutely necessary, if England were to be
detached in time from her tie with France and brought into the
concert of powers which would have to be formed to meet the latest
act of French aggression.

    The swift change in Western European affairs created a
quandary of the first order for Leopold and his ministers. War on
two fronts had always been a Habsburg nightmare, and it was
virtually an axiom with them that they could not seriously entertain
the possibility of such an extreme effort, for the very existence of
Austria as a power in Central Europe might be called into question.
Ardent as their faith in God's special protection was, they had no
wish to *va banque* and thus tempt Divine Providence. It was their
humiliating duty to interest themselves in the problem of mere
survival, when the statesmen of other countries had advanced beyond
that primitive stage, but their crossroads position did not allow them
the luxury of some degree of isolation from Europe's general
conflagrations.   There had been an extraordinary improvement in
Austrian prospects since 1683, but the statesmen retained habits of

mind which ill accorded with the recent gains. Even these might suddenly be swept away at any time by the slightest shift in the alignment of the European powers, and as they watched and waited through the autumn of 1688, they pondered not simply the attitude to be taken to any proposals the Turks might make but the future of Austria as a Great Power.

Leopold looked about him for advise, and he turned, as was his custom, to men like Father Marco d'Aviano, who had been so influential in firing up an authentic crusading zeal in Austrian hearts. But even this loyal Capuchin had little to offer in the way of advise; he could merely echo the Emperor's sense of puzzlement in the face of a truly historical decision of this kind. The factions at the Court were not able to be any more helpful. They polarized far too quickly, and their ready reactions did not bring much illumination to the Emperor, who was familiar with the limited number of options they espoused.[23] The ecclesiastical party and the 'Austrians' tended to support the continuation of the Turkish war through the medium of a compromise with France. The smaller parties were torn between their involvement in Rhenish politics, where the threat of French expansionism was brutally actual, and the dreams of exotic compensation for their heroes in the Balkans. Only the Spanish party worked with determination for peace with the Turks; it was willing to make real concessions to the peace mission at Pottendorf. The main duty of the Habsburgs -- Spanish or Austrian -- in Borgomanero's opinion was to hold the Bourbons in check in Western Europe, and there were many people in Vienna who were sympathetic with this somewhat outmoded view. But fresh support for such a policy appeared in the form of Jakob Hop, who arrived in Vienna in November to negotiate a new Austro-Dutch treaty of alliance and to offer Dutch assistance in the settlement of Austro-Turkish difficulties.[24]

The early reactions of Leopold's ministers were not much of an improvement on the views expressed by the political groups, even though his close advisers were more sensitive to the practical implications of the two courses which could be adopted. They were being particularly circumspect, as they were well aware that any violent espousal of a position might involve a tremendous loss of prestige, if their recommendations should lead to disaster. The arrival of the Turks gave them an excellent opportunity to present their tentative conclusions for the Emperor's consideration. He had established a special *ad hoc* committee, the Deputation in *Turcisis*, of selected members of the Privy Conference who could best advise him on the course he should take in the forthcoming negotiations. The Deputation's manageable size, the proven distinction of its members, and the certainty that the two major poles of opinion would be represented there made this body in theory at least an immensely valuable agency for the accomplishment of the difficult work assigned to it. Count Kinsky, who was regarded as something of an expert on Turkish affairs, assumed the chairmanship. The three other members of this quarter were Count Caraffa, a protege of Kinsky's who acted as the official go-between with the Turks at Pottendorf, Count Starhemberg with an aura of military glory clinging to him and charged now with the direction of the *Hofkriegsrat*, and Count Stratmann.

Its first full-fledged meeting took place on October 30, 1688, at Kinsky's residence, and Caraffa was asked to begin with a report on the conversations he had had with the Turks.[25] He reported that the embassy was armed at long last with specific proposals, but they refused to make these known without the preliminary concession of an audience with the Emperor. This was a troublesome condition for them to impose, for it was not established protocol in Vienna to permit representatives of an enemy power to enter the august presence of His Imperial Majesty. But the Turks were adamant on this point, and refusal would be interpreted as a sign to return to Adrianople without making any further effort to discuss terms.

Caraffa's report was followed by the *vota* of the members on the general policy to be followed in treating with the Turks. The whole European situation was so fluid at the time, that the opinions expressed were more than usually imprecise. And if they appreciated the need for a determined policy, they were not inclined to allow any opportunity to pass in which they could demonstrate their prowess in worrying even the simplest problem with a flood of Baroque rhetoric. On one point they were all agreed; the crisis in Imperial finances, the desperate state of unpreparedness for the next campaign, and the French entry into the war made it absolutely necessary for the Emperor to avail himself of the opportunity provided by the presence of the Turkish envoys to reduce, if possible, the war on two fronts to war on one. Once this principle had been enunciated, the members of the deputation differed widely in their reasons for such a conclusion and in the stress which they placed on the necessity of such a settlement.

Caraffa was a typical representative of the Italian generals (his relative Montecuccoli was an archetype) who had played such an important role in the seventeenth century wars in which the House of Austria had been involved. Unmoved by any national feeling or local attachments, these were professionals who fought a textbook war in conditions radically unsuited for such exercises. Hungary only annoyed them with its abundance of surprises, especially in the regrettable custom the Hungarians had of resorting to guerrilla warfare in aid and support of the Turks. Caraffa's name would always be associated with the bloody revenge he had taken for such activities, when he had executed completely innocent men at Eperjes, and he had earned the reputation of being one of the leading opponents of Hungary and Hungarians.[26] In this particular instance, he voted for a peace treaty, because he feared the consequences of a more powerful Turkish campaign than usual in the spring of 1689. The Turks, he felt, would find new courage at the sight of the French diversion in the West, and, in addition, he was of the opinion that it was pointless for Austria to advance any deeper into the Balkans. The southern part of Hungary, which had been recently added to the Emperor's possessions, was of little use to him (a few fortresses were exceptions to this rule); in fact the prohibitive cost of defending and administering such a wilderness made expansion in that area a real liability. He voted for peace with the Turks, but he did not think that their demand for an audience with the Emperor was a *sign qua non* for the accomplishment of this. He was inclined to call the Turkish bluff once more.

Stratmann admitted that a treaty with the Turks was necessary, but his general reaction was far different from what might have been expected from the leader of the Neuburg party. There was little enthusiasm for such a treaty in his excessively dry and formalistic opinion; he appeared to be keeping an open mind at the beginning -- perhaps he was waiting to hear what his rival Kinsky would say before committing himself more definitely. He was incredibly finicky about questions of ceremonial, for he wanted no settlement that would lower the dignity of the Emperor in the eyes of Europe. All the legalistic refinements, the loving and often inaccurate knowledge of precedent, the whole stock in trade of the Baroque diplomat was trotted out for inspection. Interest in the preservation of Imperial prestige was not simply a maneuver to gain time; it often had a tranquilizing effect on hard-pressed Austrian ministers who were able to forget for a moment in the warm security of such eternal values the real perplexities of the moment. Stratmann agreed with Caraffa on his point that the Turks would negotiate without an audience; Turkish difficulties at home, which he enlarged upon at some length, would render them more cooperative than such a demand seemed to suggest.

The chairman's conclusions were even more unexpected; he made a strong appeal for peace with the Turks. Kinsky believed that it was impossible to fight two wars, and, since one had to be chose, the war with France would be less burdensome, because it would be fought for the most part in the territories of the Electors and Princes of the Empire. There was no fine feeling for the traditional solidarity of the Emperor and the Empire, and this was one of the many indications in his remarks that his primary concern was the safety and well-being of the Austrian Lands. He showed little patience with the technical difficulties, which had been pointed out by Stratmann; details of this sort could be overlooked in the present "labyrinth" in which Imperial policy found itself. Spring might see a repetition of the life-and-death struggle of 1683, and there would be even less chance that the Emperor would triumph over two enemies than there had been when he faced only one. The dramatic effects of the last two weeks had clearly profoundly disturbed Kinsky; they had succeeded in robbing him momentarily of his usual *sang-froid*. But his phlegmatic nature would soon restore the balance, though for a time he would support the notion that Austrian interests were better served by concentrating all the available military power in the West. He sounded very much the Supreme Bohemian Chancellor, when he reminded the Deputation of the great danger to Bohemia that would exist, if it were not adequately protected against French incursions. The flickering remains of a Bohemian particularism converted him to the initial position which his colleagues had taken.

Leopold, when he received the customary report on these deliberations, added his own resolutions. These were scrawled in his own illegible hand, whose mysteries have defied the learning and devotion of generations of historians and archivists, and the sections of his comment which are legible, reveal that the Emperor was for once more farsighted than his ministers.

> There is little doubt in my mind .... that it would be very difficult, *though not impossible* (italics my own) to fight two such wars. In the meantime, since we are not certain that the negotiations will be brought to a successful conclusion, we have to put ourselves in a state of readiness to fight two wars, if need be.[27]

On the minor problem of the audience, he added that he was willing to receive the Turks, since there seemed to be no way of avoiding it.

This was a brave little straw in the wind for a man of Leopold's character, for it meant that he definitely entertained the adventuresome notion of fighting both the French and the Turks. There was nothing final about his observations, but they made it possible for his ministers to return in their own discussions to such a revolutionary policy, and in this they were supported by the thought of the assistance which the Maritime Powers (the success of William's undertaking was still not clear by any means) might be able to furnish Austria in a struggle of such magnitude. It was a fateful change of emphasis, this substitution of "possible" for "impossible," since it set a tone for the negotiations with the Turks which was highly prejudicial to their hope of success. The Austrians no longer felt that they had to accept Turkish proposals, if they were reasonable enough.

Only in January did the question of admitting the Turkish envoys to the Imperial presence become actual, and the Deputation, reinforced on this occasion by the presence of Count Starhemberg, met to make the necessary arrangements for the audience and the meetings of the peace conference which would follow.[28]   They requested that the Emperor name, as soon as possible, his own representatives to the conference, and he speedily confirmed the four of them as his delegates with the occasional addition, if they saw fir, of other officials who might be especially suited to assist them on any particular question that might arise.

The Deputation was uncertain as to the extent to which the Venetian and Dutch Ambassadors should participate in the discussions. Stratmann believed with some good reason that the acquisitive instincts of the members of the Holy League were incompatible and that it would be dangerous to let the Turks, at this very difficult point, become acutely conscious of tensions in the League. He did not deny that a member of the League could not make a separate peace, but it would be necessary now to interpret that clause as loosely as possible. The Austrians had very good reasons for making peace, and they could not allow themselves to be greatly hampered by the often conflicting wishes of their allies. The diplomatic niceties must be maintained by inviting the Venetian Ambassador to attend the first few general discussions, but it was expected that he would conduct his own negotiations with the Turks privately. If the conclusion of peace treaties *seorsim* was forbidden by the terms of the Holy League, negotiation *seorsim* was not. The attitude to be taken towards the Dutch offers of mediation was more of a problem. The ministers were apprehensive that, if Hop was allowed to become the "Padrone" of the congress, the House of Austria would receive no profit from the peace settlement, since they suspected that the Dutch might exploit their role as mediator in Venice's behalf purely out of consideration for commercial advantages. Hop, they decided, was to be allowed to treat privately with the Turks and to interpose his good offices, when the need might arise; he might secure a certain *relachement*, if the Turks began to pitch their demands too high. The Austrians were not willing to go beyond this -- there was no intention of formally accepting Dutch mediation. It was just that the practical advantages of Dutch assistance and the danger of seriously offending a power with whom they were presently negotiating an even closer alliance could not be lightly dismissed.[29]

Somewhat in the character of an afterthought, the suggestion was also made that a series of conferences be held on the subject of the proposals which they would wish to see embodied in the peace treaty -- the *Idea Pacis*. It seemed high time indeed for the Deputation to concentrate its wavering gaze on such a consideration. Nearly three months had passed since the arrival of the Turkish embassy, and there was as yet no clearly-defined Imperial policy with which to measure the degree of acceptability of the Turkish proposals. It was not a shabby device by any means for fobbing off the Venetian Ambassador, when he became too pressing in his demand for information on Austrian objectives, to say that the Emperor had, as yet, no specific demands, since he was compelled to wait for the revelation of the contents of the Turkish offer. There was some excuse for the delay in framing a program; they could expect that the Turks would propose, as they had on all other such occasions, the fundamental principle of "*Possideatis uti possidetis*," and the first show of activity was to display an extraordinary degree of interest in the exact extent of the Emperor's holdings in Hungary and in the Balkans and in suggestions as to how these might be augmented by negotiation. Caraffa was able to be of some assistance; Count Herberstein and Count Piccolomini were asked to submit their opinions, and ecclesiastics who had seen some service in diplomatic missions in these areas were asked for their advice. The Bishop of Nicopolis and Father Dunod, who had served on missions to Serban Cantacuzene, the Voevode of Wallachia, were among those whose opinions were considered. The Emperor was moved to let his wishes in the matter of the *Idea Pacis* be known: the Austrian proposals must be so framed that they did not, by any extreme harshness, appear to exclude the possibility of peace, but, on the other hand, they must not be so mild as to suggest that Austria was willing to be content with very little -- an allusion certainly to the Treaty of Vasvar.[30]

While the members of the Deputation were attempting to fill this Imperial prescription, the long-awaited audience took place. On the afternoon of February 6, 1689, the Turkish envoys and a great entourage of one hundred and sixty people arrived in Vienna, and an entire *Wirthaus* on the *Landstrasse* was placed at their disposal. They had expressed great interest in the ceremonies to be observed at their audience and at the first sessions of the peace conference, and, on the very next day, a subordinate of the Imperial Court Chamberlain Prince Dietrichstein and the usual interpreter Lachowitz went over the ceremonial with them in great detail.

Their official reception on the next day did not differ markedly from those accorded to the other envoys; it was very much like the one Paget experienced a year later. Once in the audience chamber, Sulkikar Effendi and Mavrokordatos added an oriental touch by making deep reverences in the Turkish manner at the door, the middle of the room, and at the steps of the throne. The aged Turkish diplomat and his Greek companion then made as if to kiss the Emperor's coat; this part of the ritual was so abhorrent to both men, for very different reasons, that it was not actually performed. Their letters were then placed on a table near the throne. Sulfikar Effendi was the first to speak; he addressed the Emperor in Turkish, and his speech, which varied little from the standard for such occasions, was then translated. A deputy of Count Konigsegg, who was as usual indisposed, replied in the name of the Emperor, who stood quite motionless throughout the interview. Their return to their lodgings followed the pattern of their arrival -- in reverse -- with equal care. Now that they had been satisfied on their demand for an audience, the actual conferences could begin.[31]

Two days later, the members of the Deputation, supported by representatives of Venice and Poland, met with the Turks in the palace on the *Herrengasse* of the *Stände* of Lower Austria.[32] The same care had been lavished on the arrangements here, and care was taken to see that only those of ambassadorial rank (this did not include the Turks) were provided with armchairs. The meeting was taken up largely with formalities and in none too subtle attempts by each side to sound out the other. The Turks coyly waited for the Austrians to present a series of proposals first, though it had been generally understood (and the Turks had not objected when the point had been raised before) that the Turks would take the lead. But before they took such a drastic step, they wished to be absolutely certain that a most ironic spirit of moderation would be the leitmotiv of the conferences. They hinted rather broadly at the need on the part of the Holy League for a willingness to compromise and to make concessions to the Turks which would salvage something of lost Turkish prestige. The Turks, they said, had not shown arrogance when the Almighty had favored their designs, and they expected a certain amount of reciprocity now that conditions were reversed. In the manner of proceeding in the discussions themselves, they mentioned two possibilities: the first method was to produce a treaty piecemeal by discussing each provision separately; the other was to exchange a complete list of proposals which could then be accepted or rejected *in toto*. The last method was fully in accord with the summary manner of dealing of Turkish diplomats at the height of Turkish power, but the Imperial commissioners agreed to follow this method even though it was a significant departure from their usual practice. It was finally agreed that the Turks would submit their proposals at the next conference.

An illuminating contretemps occurred between the Effendi and Count Kinsky, as the meeting was breaking up. The Turkish official made the informal comment to the Imperial ministers that if they really wanted peace it would be an easy manner to arrange it; his long white beard testified to his experience in business of this kind. Kinsky quickly riposted that there would be no difficulty, provided the Turks presented acceptable proposals, for the Emperor, too, had men who had grown old and wise in his service, and if it were their custom to let their beards grow, they would have quite as impressive a display as the Effendi. The Turk received this piece of childishness with great good humour, and both sides parted with the pleasurable conviction that their masters' prestige had not suffered any harm.

At the next conference, the Turkish proposals finally were revealed.[33] The first provision made a distinction between a lasting peace (*firma Pax*) without limit of time and a treaty (*foedus*) with a definite expiration date. If the Emperor desired the former, he would have to return to the Sultan a portion of the territories which had been won from the Turks in the recent campaigns (here was his chance to demonstrate his moderation in the very flush of victory); if he settled for the treaty with a limited duration of time, the principle of *Uti possidetis* would be applied. The second and third points were to cause the Austrians the most difficulty: Transylvania, which had been occupied by Imperial troops since 1687, was to be restored to its previous status as an independent principality under the joint protection of both rulers and with the obligation of paying annual tribute, as it had done before, to the Sultan, the four great fortresses in the border regions -- Gyula, Temesvar, Grosswardein (Nagyvárad) and Kanizsa, still in Turkish hands, though completely surrounded by Imperial forces, were to be freely provisioned and supplied by Turkish convoys. The fourth point provided for an armistice which would be in force during the peace congress.

This wa₃ *Uti Possidetis* with a difference, a perceptible shift had been made to a stronger set of talking points, which was certainly related to the news which had penetrated even to the Turks in their enforced seclusion at Pottendorf that the French had come to their rescue at last. Their first point meant that Leopold would have to pay rather dearly for the assurance that the Turks would not attack from the rear when the greatest part of his forces was committed in the West. The loss of Transylvania would work a real hardship, for that principality was regarded by the Viennese officials as the most valuable of the recently acquired territories; the *Hofkammer* would sorely miss its tax money at a time when Imperial finances were in very sore straits indeed. Then, too, if Transylvania recovered her semi-independent status it would be able to provide a clandestine base of operations and a place of refuge for the Hungarian rebels still fighting Habsburg dominion, whose position would be psychologically and materially weakened, if Transylvania continued for any length of time under Austrian rule. The demand for an armistice placed a definite limit, even in the far from likely case that the congress would be brief about its business, to the further advances that the Imperial generals could legitimately hope to make in a few months' time. To be sure, an armistice would stabilize the frontiers, and it would be an easier task to determine what was in Austrian possession and what belonged to the Turks. But this did not remove all sources of tension; the amount of ignorance by both parties of the actual limits of their territories was as much a testimony to the primitive state of the cartography of this area as to the absence of any detailed and reliable reports on conditions. The Austrian government had good reason to be disappointed with the Turkish proposals, but it was no more capable of preparing provisions which would serve as a working foundation for any reasonable agreement. The preparation of the *Idea Pacis* required still more time, and in the month that followed attention was centered on the case of Count Thököly and on the first discussions between the Poles and the Turks.

The Turks, in presenting specific proposals had complied with on of the prerequisites for a peace congress which had been stipulated by the imperial ministry. One other stipulation remained to be discussed and acted upon, and this was the demand for Count Thököly. The Turks admitted in the course of one of their meetings with the Austrians that the leader of the *kurucok* was not in favor in Adrianople, for he was held partially responsible for the disastrous war which had resulted from Kara Mustapha's energetic support of his rebellion. Thököly was in their quaint phrasing the "dog of the Padishah," and they had no intention of surrendering him to the Austrians. They agreed under pressure to discuss this question again, but they continued to expect an overall agreement before discussing individual cases of this kind.[34]

This was a chance for Hop to make use of his position, and, at the instance of Count Stratmann, he approached the Turks with the intention of sounding them out further on Thököly. He had only recently established contact with the Turks. At his appearance on the scene in November, they had refused to treat him until the Emperor should announce his formal acceptance of Dutch mediation.[35] Matters had remained at that impasse until the Turks, moved by the general atmosphere of good feeling immediately after their audience, relented to the extent of contenting themselves, as the Emperor appeared to be doing, with Hop's good offices. It was something of a humiliation for both the States-General and Hop, but he was a man of sturdier stuff than most, and he had no intention of being frustrated by mere technicalities. His main interest was to return as soon as possible to Holland, and thus he was ready to accept whatever came his way in the hope that this would speed up the negotiations. In discussing the question of Thököly with the Turks, he reminded them of their reference to the Hungarian rebel leader as a "dog"; certainly this meant that they would find it relatively easy to part with him. But the Turks were not to be trapped by such use of their own expressions; he certainly was a dog, as far as they were concerned, but at the command of the Padishah, his master, "he could become a roaring lion."[36]

The diplomats from the Allied states were not having much better luck at this Congress. The complaints from Venice and Warsaw about the injustice of the Emperor's negotiations with the common enemy had given place to Venetian and Polish participation in the Congress. But the Austrians evinced little desire to allow the Allied diplomats much freedom in treating with the prisoners of Pottendorf. If the Austrian ministers were suspicious of Holland's pro-Venetian bias they were by that token doubly suspicious of the activities of the Venetian representative. Moreover, Poland's recent inactivity in the war had been unambiguous enough to suggest the predominance of the French party in Warsaw, and even the once guarded enthusiasm for Sobieski was a thing of the past.

When the Venetian and Polish proposals finally did make an appearance and were submitted in writing to the Turks, they were so immoderate as to make absolutely certain the Turkish rejection which they received.[37] The sweeping character of their demands may have been partially a reflection of the Allied diplomats' conclusion that peace was impossible in any case, and that the best they could do was to furnish an impressive postscript to the Congress' failure. The decision on war and peace rested solely with the Austrians, and the Allies were well aware of this. The very essence of the deliberations of this Congress was in the musings of the Emperor which led him to the opinion that his territories would be able to continue the war on both fronts.

The Deputation had spent the balance of February discussing the *Idea Pacis*, and their obvious reluctance to come to any conclusions, however typical it was of Viennese procedure, only irritated the Turks. They continued *Uti possidetis* for a time, but then decided to replace it by a set of legal claims to territories still held by the Turks. They were accustomed to make their first demands extreme, so that in the inevitable process of bargaining which ensued they would be able to make concessions and still emerge with

impressive gains.   That this practice did not accord with the
diplomatic procedure of the Turks, who did not have the patience for
prolonged negotiation, did not apparently strike the ministers as an
obvious weakness of their plan.   Starhemberg, for example, suggested
that they demand the surrender of Wallachia with Moldavia thrown in
for good measure as a protective cover against Tartar raids.   This
flight of imagination could not fail to cause immediate friction with
Poland, whose lively interest in Moldavia was well-known, and it
would certainly encounter the maximum degree of resistance on the
part of the Turks.[38]   On March 1, in a similarly expansive mood, the
Deputation advised the Emperor to the permanent cession of
"Hungary and all its appertinences, Bulgaria, Herzegovinia, et
cetera."   Kinsky was commissioned to combine these points into an
organized whole, and his final draft was handed to the Turks on
March 12, after it had been approved by the Emperor.[39]

The very first clause incorporated the suggestions which had
been made at the meetings of the Deputation: the Emperor required
the cession of the Kingdom of Hungary and all the territories which
had been annexed to it in the past (Wallachia, Bosnia and
Herzegovinia, and Bulgaria were presumably referred to here), and
the renunciation by the Sultan of any further claim to the Principality
of Transylvania, which would remain an Austrian possession. After
this momentous demand, the other articles were in contrast less
controversial and far more specific. They were commonly phrased in
reference to both parties, but it was abundantly clear that the
Austrians were anxious to place subsequent Austro-Turkish relations
on a footing more favorable to their own interests. Both Empires
would be permitted to fortify their frontiers; and depredations (the
Tartars were specifically mentioned) carried out by either side against
the other were to cause, and if they did occur proper punishment was
to be meted out to the guilty parties and sufficient satisfaction was to
be given to the innocent victims. Both states were to refuse their aid
and asylum to rebels -- an obvious allusion to a constant source of
annoyance with Turkey.   The subjects of each state were to be

allowed to trade freely in the territories of the other, and Imperial consular officials, possessing the usual privileges, were to be established at important trading centres in Turkey. The next two clauses spoke of restoration: the return of captives and prisoners and the restoration of the Holy Places in Palestine to the Franciscans. Provision was to be made for the conduct of Austro-Turkish relations on the basis of international law and established European diplomatic practice. Satisfaction was to be made by Turkey to the Emperor's allies, Poland and Venice, and Moldavia was to be cleared of Tartar bands. The four attenda to the draft treaty concealed a well-worn theme in a mass of technicalities. The first three points covered the mechanics of the ratification of the treaty and of the work of the commission to adjudge disputed boundary claims (the confusion experienced by the diplomats on these points always necessitated the establishment of a boundaries commission), while the fourth provided for the surrender of Thököly.

The Turkish rejection was prompt and negative; in a discussion of the Imperial proposals with Hop, they gave vent to their great disappointment and urged him to prevail upon the Imperial ministers to modify their tone. The Turks declared that they were limited in any case to negotiating on the basis of their own proposals, which were the "*ultimatum*" (no pun was intended) which they had been authorized to accept. Hop was asked to press Kinsky and his confreres for a "categorical answer" to their offer with the stipulation that, in the event neither a permanent peace nor a treaty for a limited period of time was acceptable on the Turkish conditions was acceptable to the Austrians, the envoys were prepared to break off the talks and entrust the justice of their cause to the decrees of Divine Providence.[40]

Hop was in an understandably depressed mood when he sounded out the ministers about the possibility of even "the appearance of concessions." If they did not at first give any indication of their readiness to concede anything to the Turks they moved rather quickly to limit their demands to the *acquistica,*

Wallachia, and the fortresses still held by the Turks in Hungary. But this concession did not help matters at all, because the Turks refused to allow any of their territory which had not been occupied by Imperial armies to pass into Imperial possession. The Austrians tempted them with a permission to send a courier to the Grand Vizir for fresh instructions on the second set of Austrian demands, but they refused this offer on the ground that they were certain that the Sultan would never agree to the surrender of the fortresses and Wallachia. Their refusal of the offer of a courier was especially striking, since they had not been allowed to correspond with Adrianople during their stay in Pottendorf and Vienna.[41] When the Imperial ministers made reference once again to the historical claims of the Crown of St. Stephen, Mavrokordatos made the acidulous observation that it would be ridiculously easy to carry that sort of argument back to Adam and Eve and to pretend on that score to claim many other countries as well.[42] The Turks had been in actual possession of Wallachia and the other territories, which had once been a part of the medieval empire of the Magyars, for so many centuries, that it was outside the limits of possibility to expect the Turks to cede them out of respect for claims of greater antiquity. As for the fortresses, "*Porta neque lapidem arcis unquam voluntarie cedit.*" The war might continue for as long as ten years (a remarkably accurate prediction) with even greater disadvantage to the Turks, but the could not think of surrendering the four fortresses without a fight.[43]

Both sides were now in a deadlock; they had gone as far as they were prepared to go in the way of compromise, and if there was any flicker of hope of any further benefit to be derived from negotiation in their minds, it was not publicly expressed. The Austrians were congenitally unwilling to give the "categorical answer" that would automatically terminate the peace congress; there was also the slight chance that sufficiently impressive Austrian victories might make the Turks more tractable, and they were required out of respect for the wishes of their allies to wait for the arrival of the Polish and Venetian peace proposals. These eventually appeared in April and were communicated in due course to the Turks. The Poles demanded the key fortress of Kameniec on the Dniester, a prize for which Poland and Turkey had been vying for generations. Venice had more extensive demands: the Negroponte and Athens with the adjacent countrysides and the Bosnian littoral as well. These tardy proposals were, if anything, more unacceptable to the Turks than the Austrian draft treaty had been.[44]

The opportunity for serious peacemaking had passed, and it was high time to begin the next campaign. The prospect of war of such magnitude continued to depress the Austrian ministers, though they could derive some comfort from the offer made by the States-General through Hop of an offensive and defensive alliance to be in effect in the subsequent period of peace. The Dutch government was disturbed at the thought that much of the force of this alliance would be dissipated, since a large part of the Emperor's armies was needed in the Balkans. Hop was once more urged to do what he could to bring about an Austro-Turkish settlement, so that the Emperor might be able to concentrate his effective forces against France. But in event that war with the Turks continued despite all their appeals to both parties (the Dutch had read enough of Hop's despatches to regard this eventually as highly probable), they were anxious to know how many Imperial troops would be available for the Western front.[45] Hop was informed by Count Stratmann that thirty thousand troops could be expected as the Emperor's contribution, which would necessitate a change from an offensive to a defensive posture in the Balkans, but he would require Dutch subsidies to make this possible. Hop gave the necessary assurance that the requisite financial assistance would be forthcoming, and once the two states were convinced that a satisfactory, if excessively optimistic, balance between soldiers and subsidies had been struck, the alliance was formally concluded on May 12, 1689.[46]

Hop had had notable success in carrying out the first part of his instructions. His signal failure in the department of the Austro-Turkish peace negotiations was due, he felt, to the stubbornness of both sides and to the distrust with which the Austrians had received his offers of assistance. The ministers had gone so far as to let him know through a third party that "the less the States of Holland troubled .... the sooner would the Turks be disposed to make concessions."[47] Once again, the Austrians felt, and not without some justification -- there was the well-founded suspicion that Coyler had painted an excessively gloomy picture of the Emperor's position in an effort to move the Turks to initiate negotiations -- that the display of any excessive interest in peace by a third party was enough to convince the Turks that Austria was weak. The presence of Jakob Hop seemed further proof of Turkish suspicions; he was one of the most distinguished men in Dutch political life, and he had the reputation of being a diplomatic trouble-shooter -- witness his extraordinary status as a Dutch representative to the Court of Vienna.

But an even more basic reason for this failure of his efforts was the truly paradoxical situation in which every increment in Viennese circles of a feeling of dependence on Holland and on England, now securely in the hands of William III, substantially reduced the need for the "good offices" of the Dutch in the Austro-Turkish talks and, indeed, for the treaty itself. It did not occur to Hop to establish a causal connection between the two apparently unrelated processes, though in a meditative moment at the end of the crucial month of March, he was perilously close to such an insight. "The wished for newes of the Prince and Princess of Orange's elevation to the throne of Brittaine arriveing about the same time that the Turkish treaty of peace broke up and ended, occasioneth many and weighty reflections to be made upon both."[48] If his own reflections did not reveal to him the operation of the simple political mechanism involved here it did not escape the Emperor and his closest advisers, though they did not openly allude to the fact.

The initial divergence of the view of Leopold and the Deputation on peace with Turkey was not very marked, and the suggestion has been made that Leopold, whose abundance of peaceful settlements was so typical of him, sincerely desired peace with the Turks. As evidence for this view, an Imperial rescript to his ministers at The Hague in the middle of November is cited. Cramprich, who did not have any special claim to the confidence of the Emperor, was told that, while little could be done on the Western front that fall, a full force of Imperial troops would take to the field in the spring, if a peace had been arranged in the meantime with the Turks -- "of which there can now be little doubt."[49] This optimism was calculated to reassure the Dutch on that score (Austrian diplomats were quick to see rays of hope when questioned about the peace negotiations in London and The Hague), but it does not prove that Leopold had entirely abandoned the notion of fighting both the French and the Turks.

Hop began to see that Leopold was waiting in expectation of a major diplomatic revolution in Western Europe; a change in alignments important enough to embolden him to make a break with the family axiom of fighting one enemy (of the importance of France and Turkey) at a time.

> The Spanish Ambassador the Marques Borgomanero confirmed what is above mentioned, to wit, that Ronquillo (the Spanish Ambassador in London) and Crampvich (sic/) hade used their devoirs to make the house of Austria interest itself in the English affaires. That he himself hade orders from Spain to concert with this Court thereupon; but that it was unanimously judged unadviseable to trouble themselves with them, by reason that this expedition to England was looked upon not only as sufficient, but likewise as the only meane of quickly extricating Europe. Count Stratman assured Mr. Hop that the Emperor inwardly, but now also spareth not to avow the same openly, would not be dissatisfied to see the affaires of England upon another footing.[50]

The Venetian Ambassador had a similar impression: the long postponement of the actual meetings with the Turks was due to the desire to wait until Vienna had an accurate measure of the size of the French offensive and until affairs in England had had time to clarify themselves.

In January, the Emperor revealed his own innermost thoughts to his intimate and spiritual adviser, Padre d'Aviano. The wish to continue the successful crusade in the East, which had been their

great common task for a number of years, was still of primary
importance to him.

> And so I shall bring all the power at my disposal to bear on these two
> redoubtable enemies. It will be extremely difficult, but it is not outside the realm of
> possibility, especially if the Princes of the Empire carry their part of the burden vis-a-vis
> France. It certainly would be a thousand times better not to make peace with the Turks,
> as that would halt any further advance of our holy faith in that part of the world. In any
> event, I shall not allow myself to enter into any agreement from which Christianity would
> not derive great benefit.[51]

He did not completely exclude the possibility of a treaty, but he
would only agree to one, if the terms were very favorable to Austria
and to Christendom. The four points on which the Turks insisted as
their "*ultimatum*" neatly disposed of that possibility, and the *fermezza*
of his delegates to the peace congress had his full support. The
members of the Deputation may have been displaying a jealous care
for the interests of the Emperor, but they may have taken their cue
from him in their policy of increased toughness. Early in March,
when they were discussing the Turkish armistice clause, Starhemberg
urged its acceptance in order that the Imperial troops in Hungary
could be transferred to Germany, but Kinsky and Caraffa disagreed
with him -- this would denude Hungary of troops, and Hungary was
more important to the Emperor than the Empire.[52] This marked a
clear evolution of their positions over their reactions in October; they
had recovered from the shock of the French invasion of the Palatinate
and they were assuming an attitude closer to that of Leopold. Their
remarks must not be understood to mean that the primacy of interest
in Western European affairs was to be abandoned by the House of
Austria in favor of its grandiose dreams of a crusading mission in
Eastern Europe. The center of its political gravity had not yet shifted
so dramatically, but this was fresh evidence that the Emperor, when a
choice had to be made between his responsibility to the Empire and
his proprietary interest in the Kingdom of Hungary, would be advised
to choose the latter.

The modern scholar may experience feelings of impatience that Austrian policy at this important juncture was not more conscious of the alternatives it faced and more certain of the goals which it should pursue. The very multiplicity of interests struggling to hold the Emperor's attention was partially responsible for this state of affairs. The secular trend was away from a life and death involvement in the affairs of the Empire itself -- the Habsburgs had made their great effort to establish their kind of order in the Empire at the beginning of the century, and something of the disillusionment of Ferdinand III had passed to his son, but powerful forces in the Emperor's entourage sought continually to counteract this growing indifference. More narrowly dynastic concerns were many and complex. Spain was in the position of primacy here, and there is no question but that the pursuit of the Spanish prize was the largest single continuous undertaking of Leopold's long reign. First by marriage, then by diplomacy, and finally by war, he did his best to make certain that the possessions of the Spanish branch of the *Casa d'Austria* would fall to his own descendants.

But there was the growing involvement in Eastern Europe as well, and a whole range of religious, economic, and political motivation (would it be too foolhardy to suggest that the motives fell into precisely that order?) would struggle for mastery with the more traditional ties to the West. In Western Europe, Austria was faced with a rising pressure from France and from small states within the Empire which were on their way to becoming Powers in their own right, and the consequence of this evolution was a tendency to confine Austria to her Central European base and to turn her own expansionism towards the East. While the West pressed ever harder, a power vacuum was beginning to develop in Eastern Europe, and occasional talk was heard in Austrian circles of a drive towards Constantinople. This was grandiose rhetoric and had little practical significance, beyond the fact that it presaged an interest that would flower in a later period. The tremendous strain of Habsburg resources incurred by the wars with Louis XIV and the war with the

Turks insured that, for the moment, Austrian penetration into the Balkans would be kept within reasonable bounds. There was no chance that the statesmen of this generation would have the foresight to see beyond such limiting factors and to make a radical break with acquired mental habits by consciously turning their attention from Western Europe to the East. There was simply too much mental inertia, for one thing, and it would be difficult to expect them to abandon their pretensions in Western Europe until they had been literally forced to do so. In the world of politics at that time, and perhaps at any time, states and individuals have seldom had the good taste to yield gracefully.

One must not judge these men too harshly. Admittedly, they were bereft of great and liberating breadth of vision; they were notoriously pedantic and fussy about their work. Recent history and their own experience was to blame for this; a virtually continuous pattern of disaster had made it difficult for them to rise above the level of political immediacy and day to day decisions. Neither time nor leisure for more sublime speculation on political problems had been vouchsafed them, and in the years immediately following upon the collapse of the peace negotiations at Vienna in 1689 there would be even less opportunity for such recreations. The situation was still far too fluid to be reduced to the brittle if brilliant categories of a Wenzel Kaunitz, and it would remain precisely the task of that later generation to comprehend what had been accomplished by these lesser men and to digest the acquisitions they had made. Leopold and his ministers had not been wholly without distinction, but they had lived in a world where it was possible to carry on high political discourse at the level of preferring 'castles in Spain' to 'fortresses in Hungary.'

Notes to Chapter 2

[1]The preliminary peace negotiations leading to the Peace of Carlowitz and, indeed, the Congress at Carlowitz itself. have not received the attention from modern scholars that they perhaps deserve. The difficulties of such studies are, of course, immense. The number of nations which figured in this complicated pattern of diplomatic starts and stops was extremely large; virtually all the major powers of Europe were involved in one way or another. Publication of source has not been in any way complete; the Turkish sources for the problem may well remain a mystery, but the documents in French, English, Dutch, and Austrian archives have in large measure gone unnoticed. The present chapter and the two following it should be regarded as a preliminary effort to overcome the all too formidable obstacles posed by archives and linguistic barriers. Its virtue may only consist in the fact that it is a beginning, but the attempt to view the negotiations from a generally European point of view may constitute an improvement.

Four previous studies having to do with the Peace and, occasionally, its preliminaries are worthy of note. Joseph von Hammer-Purgstall in his *Geschichte des Osmanischen Reiches* devotes a large section of the sixtieth book of his classic (it is to be found at the very end of the *6. Band*) to the work of the Congress, and in the course of the fifty-ninth book frequent reference is made to the preliminary talks. His study of the documents now preserved in the collection of the *Turcica* (*Haus-*, *Hof- und Staatsarchiv*, Wien) was by no means complete, but much of the picture of Carlowitz that survives in mode modern studies is based on his work. His discussions of the importance of the Peace in European and Turkish history has certainly set the tone. The next study in point of time is the work of R. van Zuijlen de Nijevelt, *De vrede van Carlowitz* (Utrecht, 1883). In essence a doctoral thesis, it may be regarded as the first attempt at a more detailed treatment. It, too, had been prepared on the basis of a rather cursory examination of the *Turcica*, but its importance is largely in its discussion of the form of mediation as a diplomatic practice. Anyone who is particularly interested in this related problem will find some aid and comfort in this rather antiquated Dutch thesis. I have strenuously avoided the larger question of mediation as a diplomatic practice in my own investigations. Where the problem is raised, it is confined simply to Carlowitz, and my view of mediation is almost coincident with that of the participants at the Congress of Carlowitz. The next entry is the work of one of Hungary's most distinguished historians in the late nineteenth and early twentieth centuries Ignac Acsady. On the occasion of the bicentenary of the Peace he prepared a brief monograph which quite naturally approached the problem from the Hungarian point of view. While he did not study the materials in Vienna, he was aware of the secret correspondence of Count Kinsky and Count Schlick; he quotes from it at times. The work is full of sound historical sense, and it does not fail to convey his disappointment that the Kingdom of Hungary was not officially represented at a peace conference which had so much to do with its historical evolution. He was understandably weak on the Mediation; he refers to Paget as being one of the best diplomats that England had (this certainly is hyperbole) and Sir William Hussey is transformed into "a hollandi Houssay". The full title of the work, etc., is Acsady Ignac, "A Karloviczi beke" (*Ertekézesek a történeti tudományok körébol*, XVIII. kötet, #4) (Budapest-1899). The most interesting study is clearly that of J.H. Hora Siccama, "De vrede van Carlowitz en wat daaraan voorafging", *Bijdragen van vaderlandsche geschiedenis*, IV (1910), 8, 43-185. This study follows the whole chain of events from the prehistory of the Dutch mediation efforts to the triumphant conclusion at Carlowitz. Its main merit, for my purposes, was its liberal quotations from the letters of Jacob Coyler, the Dutch Ambassador, and the orders from the States-General to their representative in Turkey. In this way, I have used this work as virtually a primary source. When combined with published reports of the Dutch envoys in Vienna, a fairly accurate picture of the role of the Dutch in the Mediation can be attained. (In referring to this work henceforth, I shall use the form *Hora Siccama*.)

[2]*Hora Siccama*, 44-46.

[3]"een speelreijs", Letter of Coyler to the Griffier, Sept. 26, 1683, quoted in *Hora Siccama*, 47.

[4]*Ibid.*, 50; "Das gewaltige Vordringen des Kaiserlichen Waffen gegen die Türkei, das mit der Befreiung Wiens ... einsetzte, löste in Holland keineswegs grosse Befriedigung aus. Politische und Kommerzielle Rücksichten legten den Wunsch nach Frieden im Osten nahe; daher das beständige Drängen der Republik nach einer Aussöhnung Leopolds mit der Pforte durch die der Kaiser freie Hand gegen Ludwig XIV. gewinnen und dem Orienthandel eine ungestörte Entwicklung gesichert werden sollte. Der scharfe Blick für die gedeutung der jeweiligen politischen Lage, die ausserordentliche Anpassungsfähigkeit und der Kühne Unternehmungsgeist, der dem höllandischen Kaufmanne zu eigen war, bewogen ihn aber bald zu dem Versuche, aus den geänderten Verhäitnissen Nutzen zu ziehen.", Srbik, *Österreichische Staatsverträge: Niederlande*, 278.

[5]The Dutch envoy in Para was also expected to maintain constant contact with the Dutch envoy in Vienna so that any peace feelers from the Turkish side might

be passed on as quickly as possible to the Austrian ministers, cf. *Hora Siccama*, 48-49.

[6]This correspondence is published in the main part in Hurmuzaki, *Documante*, V/I, 120-151 *passim*. I have discovered that great care must be taken in using this collection, and only actual comparison with the documents themselves can settle some difficulties. On a number of occasions, *vide infra* for an example, the dating of a document may be wrong in the heading.

[7]The best brief account of Mavrokordatos in a language accessible to me is to be found in Otto Brunner, "Eine osmanische Quelle zur Geschichte der Belagerung Wiens im jahre 1683", *Mitteilungen des Vereins für Geschichte der Stadt Wien*, V, 1925, 37-41. I am grateful for the suggestions of Mr. George Christos Soulis in regard to Mavrokordatos, particularly in bibliographical matters.

[8]A brief discussion of the contributions of the Dutch to the Grand Dragoman's education is to be found in K. Heeringa, *Bronnen tot de Geschiedenis van der Levantschen Handel* (Rijs Geschiedkundige Publicatien, 34) ('S-Gravenhage-1923), II, 140n.

[9]An extensive discussion of the bribing of the Reis-Effendi and Mavrokordatos will be found in a section entitled, "The Affair of the Boursillo" which follows Chapter Four.

[10]It is characteristic for the study of this area of Europe at this crucial period that there is no detailed study of the Holy League. The best treatment, based on the materials in the Vatican Archives and biased naturally in regard to the influence of the Holy See, is that of Ludwig, Freiherr von Pastor, *The History of the Popes*, trans. Dom Ernest Graf, O.S.B. (London-1940), XXIV, 192-201. The text of the *Sacrum foedus* is in Hurmuzaki, *Documente*, V/I, 102-107.

[11]*Ibid.*, 118-119; Letter of the Margrave of Baden, the *Hofkttegsratpräsident*, Vienna, Nov.10, 1686, *ibid.*, 121-122.

[12]Suleiman Pasha to the Margrave of Baden, Varadin, November, 1686, *ibid.*, 123-124.

[13]An extract from this letter serves to reveal the temper and the taste for rhetoric which was prevalent in Austrian official quarters. "Divino et omniun gentium jure palam est, non tolli a Porta culpam illati injuste belli litato paucorum

consulentium sanguine, multo minus illo satisfactum esse laesae Maiestati Sacratissimi imperatoris mei, sed oportere resarciri illata injuste Damna, de non inferendis posthac idonee caveri, praesatrique impensam in bellum factam, et simul satisfieri vocatis in necessariam defensionem belli sociis; haec regula et justitae Divinae et gentium ... Novit Sacratissimus imperator, vos in persona Vestra a pacifragio fuisse alienos ...", Margrave of Baden to the Grand Vizir, Vienna, January 17, 1687, *ibid.*, 128-129.

[14]Suleiman Pasha to the Margrave of Baden, February 15/25, 1687, *ibid.*, 129-130.

[15]Cf. the account of this mission in David Angyal.

[16]The letter of Count Caraffa to Alexander Mavrokordatos is dated April 18, 1688, in Hurmuzaki, *Documente*, V/I, 151; according to its contents it should be dated 1687.

[17]*Hora Siccama*, 49n.

[18]The directors of the Dutch Levant Company had been complaining to the States-General of a "vermindering van de negotie", *ibid.*, 50n.

[19]*Ibid.*, 51-53.

[20]I have based the necessarily brief allusions to Turkish internal affairs on Hammer-Purgstall, *Geschichte des Osmanischen Reiches*, VI, 499-678 *passim*.

[21]Coyler reported the views of the Grand Vizir to the Griffier, Pera, July 3, 1688, and mentioned the desire of the Turks that the Dutch should play a role in the forthcoming negotiations: "Ende ten laatsen nademael haere Ho. Mo. de goetheyt hadden believen te hebben de hooge Keyserl. Porta te doen aenraden tot het maken van deselve Vreede met hoogstged[en] Keyser, Coning van Poolen, de republycq van Venetiën ende andere waermede deselve tegenwoordig in oorlog is, men deselve soude sien te bewegen de mediatie van dit groote werck te willen aennemen ...", *Hora Siccama*, 54-55.

[22]An account of their trip is contained in the "Relation des Dollmetschen Lachowiz über die Turkisch en Ablegation den 8ten 7[bris] in dem Lager vor Belgrad beschehene ankhonfft, ferner Raisz nachher Pottendorff, und hernachmals in der zu Wienn den 8ten Februar 1689 gehabten Kayserl. Audienz

mit ihnen observierten Ceremonialen.", Hurmuzaki, *Documente*, V/I, 153-154.

[23]Jakob Hop in his letter to the Griffier, Vienna, February 27, 1689, reported that four groups at the Court preferred peace with France to peace with Turkey. On the basis of his description it is possible to surmise that the 'Austrian' party and the ecclesiastical party were at the forefront of this agitation; *W.G.* 418-420. In this letter he describes his efforts and those of the Marques de Borgomanero to counteract the work of the Francophiles.

[24]"... in conformite met t'hoogwijs advijs van Syne Hoogheyt der Heer Prince van Orange, dat een bezendinghe aan Syne Keizerlycke Majesteyt sal worden gedecerneert, om on der andere alle goede officiën aan te wenden, ten eynde een goede ende vaste vrede tusschen Syne Keyserlycke Mayesteyt ende de Ottomanische Porte mag worden getroffen.", Secr. Resolution of the States-General, The Hague, Sept. 20, 1688, *W.G.*, 390.

[25]We are fortunate to possess the complete relation of this session of the Deputation *in Turcicis* in Hurmuzaki, *Documente*, V/I, 162-169.

[26]A nuanced view of this general that does not manage to exculpate him finally of his brutality in dealing with the Hungarians is but one of the many minor masterpieces of Gyula Szekfü, the greatest modern Hungarian historian; see his *Magyar Történet* (Budapest-1932), V, 387-188.

[27]"Es ist pro 1mo kein Zweiffel dasz dise 2 Krig, wo nitt unmöglich, doch sehr schwer auszuführen sein werden. Indeme man aber noch sehr ungewis ob man mitt dem Friden zu Einem Endt wird gelangen können. So musz man sich stellen, als wann man beede Krig füren müste. Was 2do anlangt, soll man den Turcken Audienz geben zwar: kan sich iedoch so aigentlich nicht reculiren."; the resolution of the Emperor Leopold, Hurmuzaki, *Documente*, V/I, 170.

[28]The Relation of the Session of January 3, 1689, *ibid.*, 174-179.

[29]"... findet man bedencklich, dasz den Hollandischen Abgesanten Hop des Fridenswerck, und die angesuechte general Erlaubnisz (i.e. to visit and confer with the Turkish delegation) dergestalt illimite Einzuraumben, dass Er sich gleichsamb Padrone des negotij machen khönte, in deme wohl zu erachten, dasz Sy Hollander Eur Kayserl. Mayestat und dero Löbl. Erzhausz bey diszen Fridens-Tractaten so wenig avantaggia alsz Immer möglich, verlangen-und gonnen werden, auch wohl sein khonte, dasz Sy Eines und das andere, weiches

Euer Kaiserl. Majestät Convenienz gemäsz wäre, lieber in der Venedigs als
Euer Kaiserl. Majestät sechen derfften, sonderlich wan Sy des geringeste
vermerckhen solten, wordurch Ir Commercium schwarer gemacht werden
khönte, nichts desto weniger weilier Er seine officia beederseiths zu
interponieron von seinem Principale befelcht, selbige auch von Euer Kayserl.
Mayestät allergenädigst angenomben worden ... gestalt er seine intention nur
dahinzuzihen vor-gibt, damit dir Türcken Ire Propositiones nicht so absone
Einrichten, als Sy in Sünn haben ...", ibid., 178-179.

[30]Cf. the marginal notation of Emperor Leopold: "Ist höchst nöthig, und wirdt
Man wohl ohne Vorschub der vogeschlagenen subiectorum ire Mainungen
vernemben miesszen, damit sodan die Deputierten Mir eine fundierte ideam
vorlegen khönen, so wohl wirdt miesszen dahin gesehen werden, dasz Sie nicht
nahte seyn, das Man gar Es pro impossibili halten khönne; Esz musz aber auch
nicht so Eingerichtet sein, damit die Türckhen nicht glauben Wir wolten unsz
mit Einem wenigen contentiren, indem Einmahl gott unsz solchen Vorthl an die
Hand geben hat, dessen man sich Nuczlich bedienen muesz.", *ibid.*, 190n.

[31]The *Relation des Dollmetschen Lachowiz* contains a description of this solemn
audience; ibid., 155-156.; the *Tarichi Sulfikar Effendi*, a history in Turkish of
this affair by Sulfikar Effendi, recounts the pleasure he and Mavrokordatos
experienced in violating the ceremonial; they did not actually kiss the Emperor's
garment.- Hammer-Purgstall, *op. cit.*, VI, 531n.

[32]A floor plan of the meeting place in the *Landthaus* is included in Hurmuzaki's
publication of the interpreter's report, *vide supra*; the relation of the first session
of the Congress is to be found in Hurmuzaki as well, *Documente*, V/I, 224-228,
under the misleading heading of February 19, 1689. The first session actually
took place, as the date at the conclusion of his printed relation reveals (this is
also substantiated by Lachowitz' report), on February *10*, 1689.

[33]The four Turkish propositions (in a Latin translation by Mavrokordatos), *ibid.*,
229. The first proposition is of special interest for the light it throws on the
distinction between a *pax* and a *foedus* (an agreement for a limited length of
time): "Ne futuris quoque temporibus inter utrumque imperatorem aliquod
intercedat dissidium, sed firma Pax coalescat, Caesarea Maiestas aliquam
partem restituens, reliqua vero retinens moderationem et aequanimitatem
ostendat, *si autem abnuerit, retentis occupatis foederi terminus temporis
praefigatur.*"

[34]Sulfikar's *History*, 29, quoted by Hammer-Purgstall, *op. cit.*, 536-537.

[35]Confusion was introduced into an already complicated situation by the Turkish tendency to confuse mediation and good offices as they were then understood in European diplomatic practice. Western diplomats were on occasion none too certain of their use of these terms, as when Van Heemskerck, *vide infra*, declared power on the part of two belligerents was tantamount to the acceptance of its Mediation. According to Jakob Hop, the Emperor had only agreed to accept the good offices of the Dutch, while the Turks insisted particularly on Dutch Mediation, cf. his letter to the Griffier, March 10, 1689, *W.G.*, 427-428.

[36]Hammer-Purgstall, *op. cit.*, 536-537.

[37]*Ibid.*, 538 ff.

[38]Hurmuzaki, *Documente*, V/I, 234-235.

[39]This period of the negotiations has been studied carefully by Otto Brunner on the basis of the *Konferenzprotokolle* and the *Turcica*. His findings were incorporated in his "Osterreich und die Walachei währed des Türkenkrieges von 1683-1699", *MIÖG* (XLIV), 1930, 302-303. The text of the Austrian proposals is in Hurmuzaki, *Documente*, V/I, 238-140.

[40]Hop discusses the Turkish reaction at some length and comes to the mournful conclusion: "Uyt alle hetwelcke Haer Ho. Mo. dan sullen gelieven te sien, in wat desperaten staat dese negotiatie is gevallen en hoeseer het is te duchen, dat beyde hoogststrydende parthyen, by hun gepraetendeerde ten wedersyden blyvende persisterenm deselve in weynig daagen afgebroken soude kunnen werden.", Hop to the Griffier, March 17, 1689, *W.G.*, 429-431. Cf. also, Hammer-Purgstall, *op. cit.*, 536-538.

[41]Hop to the Griffier, April 24, 1689, *W.G.*, 434-437; Hammer-Purgstall, *op. cit.*, 541.

[42]"Auf diesse weiss könnte man sagen, dass alle von Adam und Eva herkomben und könnten sy ex hoc ratione viel andere Länder praetendieren, in deme sy aber Wallachei und selbige Länder so lange zeit possidierten, als wissen sich nicht, wie man ihnen der Abtrettung zumuthen könne." - Mavrokordatos on April 13, 1689, *Turcica*, quoted by Otto Brunner, *loc. cit.*, 304n.

[43]Brunner, *ibid.*, 303-304.

[44]The text of the Polish note of April 4, 1689, is in the Hurmuzaki, *Documente*, V/I, 245-246; the Venetian demands are discussed by Hammer-Purgstall, *op. cit.*, 538-539.

[45]Hop to Count Stratmann, April 23, 1689, *W.G.*, 434.

[46]Hop to Heinsius, May 5, 1689, *ibid.*, 438-440; Hop reported on the conclusion of the alliance in a letter to the Griffier, May 13, 1689, *ibid.*, 440-444.

[47]Mr. Hop's journal in English translation in *The Lexington papers; or, some account of the courts of London and Vienna at the conclusion of the seventeenth century*, ed. H. Manners Sutton (London-1851), 387.

[48]The actual Dutch text is as follows: "Tzedert dien tijd is alhier aengebracht de tydinge van de voorgevallene verandering van saken in Engelant door de seer gewenste verheffing van haero jegenwoordige Konincklycke Majesteyten tot de Kroon, en is wyders de Turckse vredehandel desperaat en ten eynde gelopen. Op beyde dese soo notable veranderingen sijn verscheyde seer gewichtigs reflexien by dit Hoff gemaeckt ...", J. Hop to the Griffier, April 3, 1689, *W.G.*, 431-432.

[49]Leopold said on November 13, 1688, in a rescript to his envoy at The Hague: "Im Frühling, sofern bis dahin der Friede zwischen uns mit unseren Bundesgenossen und den Türken zu Stande kommt -- *woran fast nicht mehr zu zweifeln* -- soll die im Felde gestandene vollige Armada folgen (italics my own)."; quoted by Klopp, *Der Fall des Hauses Stuart*, V, 196, in support of his view that the Emperor was personally very anxious for Peace with the Turks. The context of the statement makes it very doubtful that this can be taken as an adequate representation of the Emperor's views.

[50]"Mr. Hop's Journal", *Lexington Papers*, 330.

[51]Onno Klopp, *Das jahr 1683 und der folgende grosse Türkenkrieg bis zum Frieden von Carlowitz* (Graz, 1882), 188.

[52]O. Brunner, "Österreich und die Walachei", *loc. cit.*, 302n.

Chapter 3

The Accidents and Perils of Mediation

"I hope whoever succeeds Mr. Harbord, will arrive quickly at Adr^{ple}, before the Port settles things, and gives Order for next Campagne, which perhaps it will be too late to treat, and if this Ambassador must accompany the Vizir to Belgrad, and bee not one of robust complexion, in the bad aires, and watters, he runs the danger of his life, or a sever sicknesse, which will stop, or much retard any negotiation. A peace here would much contribute to the common good, but unlucky accidents still crosse it..."

Thomas Coke

"D'accidenten die gedurende de onderhandelinge door een bysondere bestieringe van den Hemel sijn voorgevallen bennen remarcabel en fattael, ende verden bij veele Turcken selfs voor quade teeckenen aengenomen."

Jakob Coyler

While the depressing failure of peace negotiations in Vienna in April 1689, did not put an end to Anglo-Dutch efforts in that direction, attention was now focused on developments in Turkey. The foreign embassies in Constantinople and Adrianople became the backgrounds for protracted and extraordinarily complicated diplomatic maneuvers. Jakob Coyler and Sir William Trumbull, the English Ambassador, were soon involved in a combined effort to curb French influence and to encourage the Turks in their thoughts of peace. Even before the collapse of the negotiations in Vienna, Coyler had been particularly worried by the report that Girardin, the French Ambassador, had offered the Turks an offensive and defensive alliance with the most Christian King. Louis XIV would promise, according to the terms of this purported agreement, not to make peace with either the Emperor or the Empire until the Porte had received full satisfaction -- a reference perhaps to the *status quo ante bellum*. Two circumstances had thwarted this French intrigue. It had been still too early, in January, for the Turks to be pessimistic about the outcome of the talks in Vienna, and the French Ambassador's sudden death had momentarily removed the source of the alleged offer.[1]

But late that spring, Coyler noted a renewed interest on the part of the Turks in such a tie with France, and his reports moved the States-General to dispatch a learned treatise on the state of affairs in Western Europe for presentation to the Grand Vizir -- all this in the easy confidence that the Ottoman Empire cared about the political situation in the West. The document tried to convince the Turks that France's position was not as favorable as Girardin had reported it, but the Turks did not take to this lesson with any enthusiasm. And when the new French Ambassador, the Marquis Castagneres de Châteauneuf, arrived the following autumn, the Grand Vizir was so unconvinced by Dutch political science, that he gave orders that the French Ambassador visit him at his camp at Sophia. Coyler became desperate at this menacing turn of affairs, and he appealed for permission to go to Sophia as well.

The Kaimacam of Constantinople, receiving his request, assured him that there was sufficient awareness in Turkish official circles of French duplicity, and he did not encourage Coyler to make the trip. This was tantamount to refusal of his request, and Coyler was left to fret in Pera, doubtless imagining a whole series of *coups* on the part of the wily Marquis. A small degree of comfort was contained in the constant assurances that "the Porte would take no account of the propositions which would be offered by the French." The Grand Vizir was, officially at least, cool to French overtures, and he reminded Châteauneuf of the failure of France to honor similar promises in the past.[2] There was the good likelihood that the Dutch and the French would be encouraged to engage in a diplomatic duel with the Turks as interested and amused spectators, but the sudden removal of the Grand Vizir in the wake of a general Imperial offensive, which had advanced deep into Bosnia and Albania and captured the important fortresses of Nis, Semendria, and Vidin, introduced a radically different atmosphere at Adrianople.[3]

The new Grand Vizir was Mohammed Köprülü, the son and nephew of previous vizirs of that name, who soon revealed that he was the rare person who could halt the runaway process of military defeat and internal chaos. He did not immediately reveal his plans for a more vigorous prosecution of the war, and Coyler was encouraged to confer with him at Adrianople. In his audience with the Grand Vizir on December 14, 1689, he reported his warnings about the dangers to Turkey in a French alliance. The undercurrent of disorder then prevalent in Constantinople was sufficient proof for him that the Turks desperately needed peace with the Emperor. He offered the assistance of the States, if the Turks were interested. Köprülü seemed to favor these suggestions, and Coyler had the rare pleasure of reporting to The Hague that the Turks were fully inclined to conclude an honorable peace with the Emperor and his allies.

Hamel Bruynincx was able on the strength of Coyler's optimism to approach the Imperial ministers. Would it not be possible for them to provide Coyler with some talking points, so that the process of peacemaking could be resumed? Coyler, it was felt, would have to have a respectable set of proposals to make any headway with a Turkish statesman of the stamp of Köprülü. The Austrians agreed, and word was dispatched to Coyler that a peace treaty now depended on *Uti possidetis* and the surrender by the Turks of the fortresses which they held in southern Hungary. This was cold comfort indeed for Coyler, coming as it did at the very beginning of the campaign of 1690. The Grand Vizir became almost violent when he was informed of the Emperor's latest proposal; the Imperial "terms" were rejected as "scandalous and wholly unacceptable," and Coyler was informed by way of superfluous afterthought that the Grand Vizir intended to bring the enemies of Turkey to reason by military means.[4]

For once, the Turkish threat carried weight, and the long and uninterrupted series of Imperial and Allied victories was broken at last. The reason for this new development was that the combination of renewed elan in the Turkish armies and constant French pressure on the Western front forced the Emperor to spread his forces very thin. Indeed, it was the depressing task of the Imperial strategists to abandon their offensive posture in the East. The recapture of Belgrade by the Turks was a sure sign that the war in Eastern Europe had entered upon a new phase. Coyler could no longer have any illusions as to the peaceful intentions of the Grand Vizir, and he returned to Pera to hold himself in readiness for the next favorable opportunity for the offer of his good offices.[5] Such an opportunity seemed very remote in 1690, but Coyler was not the kind of man to give up easily. The frequent reports of a treaty of alliance between the Turks and the French may have depressed his spirits, but he did not jump to any conclusions. He might entertain a number of suspicions as to the exact nature of Turco-French complicity, but he did not mention this alliance in his reports to The Hague. The rumour was current for many years in Constantinople, and only a few people -- the Grand Vizirs and the Marquis de Châteauneuf -- were in a position to know that no such treaty of alliance existed.

While Coyler had been occupied in 1689 and 1690 in efforts at mediation, help had arrived from a wholly unexpected quarter. Sir William Trumbull entered the field, and thereby earned for himself the honor of being the first English diplomat to offer the mediation of the King of England to either of the belligerents.[6] Trumbull had had the misfortune to be chosen to represent the King of England and the Levant Company at the Porte at a most difficult time. There were the usual annoyances connected with the post -- troublesome dragomans and disputes over finances with the Levant Company -- and in addition the "Glorious Revolution" had forced him to make the transition, as best he could, from the service of James II to that of William III. When James was still England's undoubted King, Sir William had reported on the departure of the Turkish embassy for Vienna and had proposed (the idea may have emanated from a French source) that the King order him to be "assistant in bringing a peace to a conclusion." The Levant Company decided that this matter was quite outside their competence and, therefore, beyond Sir William's normal call of duty as well.[7] But this line of attack was to prove useful to him in making his peace with the new King, whose interest in arranging a peace between the Emperor and the Sultan was well-known, and, a year after the failure of his first offer, the Levant Company had itself discovered the desirability of such a peace and had suggested to Whitehall officials that a man of Trumbull's unquestioned talents be permitted to undertake a mediating role.

It was only at the end of January 1690, that William III finally empowered this survivor of James's diplomatic corps to "interpose a peace between the Grand Signor and Germany .... that we might have some good effects of it upon our trade."[8] The exact nature of Trumbull's subsequent offer and of Turkish reactions to it are not known; the Turks, who had not yet accustomed themselves to the new realignment of diplomatic forces in Pera by which the English had abandoned the French for the Dutch, did not bother to reply to the offer. But his role in these negotiations was still uppermost in Trumbull's mind when he wrote to Paget in May and thus quite incidentally introduced him to the work which was to provide him with his lasting claim to fame.

> The Dutch Ambassador after 5 months stay at Adrianople returned hither a week since; But without any Effect of his Negotiation; indeed it was not probable that he should succeed, having onely Orders from the States Generall to do what he could to dispose the Turkes to a Peace; but None from the Emperor of any Foundation for a Treatie; And after all their Misfortunes, these people retaine their Pride; They will not stoop to aske what they would be glad were preferred them, and they would receive Proposals, but would not begin themselves, looking upon it as an Advantage, as well as Honour, to have an Overture made to them and not to make any themselves. Neither (in my poor opinion) will anything be done unless His Imperial Majesty would condescend to an Overture by a Third Hand, or of one or more Mediators, who might begin and (with His Approbation) end this Affaire.[9]

It was clear that Trumbull had an inaccurate picture of Coyler's negotiations, but his recipe for a peace treaty was sound enough. He was still picturing himself as one of the Mediators when he was informed that Sir William Hussey had been appointed to succeed him as English Ambassador at the Porte.[10]

William III had been planning for some time to replace Trumbull; new blood was needed in Pera to make a more effective presentation of the case for peace. The new appointee was instructed to "use his best endeavours to attempt the conditioning of tearmes for a Peace," and in order that he might be armed with up to date proposals from the Emperor, Paget proposed that Hussey travel overland to Constantinople, so that he might confer at Vienna with the Imperial ministers about an offer which he could then present to the Grand Vizir.[11]   Hussey was dilatory enough in starting his journey, but the "brief stay" he had planned on making in Vienna delayed him even more, for it extended to five months of waiting for the Imperial ministers to make up their minds. There was little more that he and the resident envoys of the Maritime Powers could do but wait until the Austrians were ready to provide him with instructions and the passport that would conduct Hussey safely through the Imperial lines to the Turkish outposts. "Importunity indeed gets fair answers and promises," -- Paget was already a truly philosophical veteran of Viennese procrastination," -- "but these answers and promises have no effect."[12]

But even promises were an indication of the growing influence of William III in Vienna, and Hussey was quick to realize, for all his inexperience of such affairs, that the Austrians now intended to derive very practical advantages in their policy in Eastern Europe from their tie with the King-Stadhouder. "As their hopes now depend upon his Majesty for protection in the West, they now also translate his genius to the East, for their guardian angell hic et ubique."[13] There was as yet no formal Austrian acceptance of William's mediation, but the Emperor's capitulation on this point (it meant that he would have to tolerate a certain measure of Anglo-Dutch interference in his own affairs) could not be long delayed.   Van Heemskerck to sweeten the bitter pill for the Austrians by suggesting to Count Kinsky that the mere acceptance of the good offices of the Maritime Powers by both belligerents was in itself an acceptance of their mediation. Kinsky was not moved by this disingenuous suggestion, and even the more ominous reminder that William III did not expect that such little regard would be shown by the Emperor for the well-intentioned advice of England and Holland did not cause him to yield. But the subsidies, which Van Heemskerck tactfully failed to mention, provided the English and Dutch with an ever more pressing claim to attentive consideration of their advice at the Court of Vienna.[14]

Lord Paget's hopes were high when he reported that Sir William Hussey had finally departed for Turkey, but he was quite correct in his reservations about the proposals which Hussey carried with him -- "they were not so full as I would have had them." Further cause for alarm was to be found in the failure of the Austrians to provide Hussey with a full power to enter into a treaty on the basis of these proposals with the Turks. *Uti Possidetis* was the fundamental principle about which the various conditions had been arranged, but the real interest lay in the variations which were to be played on this familiar theme. In the case of Hussey's proposals, the variation made certain that Transylvania, which was once more in Imperial hands, would be the real bone of contention.

In the conference with his ministers in which they had discussed these proposals, Leopold had declared that a boundary line which ran from the Iron Gate westward along the Danube to its confluence with the Sava at Belgrade and then along the Sava to the Unna River, the boundary of Bosnia and Croatia, would be the one most satisfactory to him. This would involve the surrender to him of the remaining fortresses in Hungary in Turkish hands, and the admission on his part that all territory south of this proposed line was Turkish. But in March, 1691, such a settlement of the boundary question erred by being far too generous to Austria, and Leopold found it necessary to invoke the *Uti possidetis* and to demand the recognition of his claim to Transylvania as well, since that principality could not yet be considered an undisputed Imperial possession.

If the Sultan refused to agree to these proposals, Leopold was willing to go part of the way in meeting Turkish demands of two years before by agreeing to the restoration of the *status quo* in Transylvania. This meant that the Transylvanians would once more be permitted to enjoy their traditional state of autonomy vis-à-vis the Emperor and the Sultan and a wide range of political and religious liberty. The Transylvanian Diet had formally elected Michael II Apafy, as the successor to his father Michael I, and Leopold now declared that he was prepared to recognize Apafy's election as Prince of Transylvania -- a step which he had up to this time been reluctant to take. The Turks would be expected to match his generosity with a concession of their own -- the cession of Várad, Gyula, Lippa, and Temesvár. The Privy Conference agreed that the remainder of the proposals should follow the form of the draft treaty of 1689, and that a time limit of June 1, 1691, should be established, because the campaign might entirely alter the situation.[15] These terms revealed an increasing Austrian desire for a peace in Eastern Europe, though they were not likely to find a favorable reception from Köprülü, who continued to hope that Turkish power in Hungary and Transylvania would be fully restored. The latest Imperial peace terms had the added advantage of giving some assurance to the envoys of William III that the Emperor was willing to cooperate.

Thanks to the care and solicitude of the Imperial government Sir William Hussey had been provided with a most talented young assistant. Now travelling with him as his secretary Count Ludovico Marsigli, a protégé of Count Kinsky. This young Bolognese nobleman, like so many of his nation and status, had come to make his fortunes in the crusades against the Turks. A war of this size offered manifold opportunities to a gentleman of his talent. He had duly served as an officer, had been captured and enslaved, and had finally managed to escape, and in the process he had added a detailed knowledge of the state of the ottoman Empire and a fluent command of the Turkish language to his endless collection of interests and achievements. A walking academy of sciences, he managed to collect a bewildering number of disciplines into a well-ordered unity that any baroque polymath could envy, and his renown as a cartographer, as an expert on Turkish affairs, and as a student of Danubian flora and fauna, made him on first sight an ideal companion for the inexperienced Hussey.[16] But his assignment was not merely to be a technical assistant, he had been added to the English Ambassador to the Sultan's entourage to observe Hussey's activities and, if the occasion should present itself, to negotiate secretly with Turkish officials.

There was much that was attractive in this young Italian, but his connection with Count Kinsky did not fail to arouse suspicions in the minds of English and Dutch diplomats. His role in Hussey's embassy is one of the preciously few indications of the general tenor and direction of Kinsky's Turkish policy in these years. Since the collapse of the talks in the spring of 1689, Kinsky had been encouraged to devote much of his time to Turkish affairs, and he was generally acknowledged as the responsible minister in this area of political decisions. At the moment, he was retiring as gracefully as he could under strong pressure from the Maritime Powers, but he had no intention of ending an extraordinarily successful war in the Balkans until the ministers were absolutely certain that the maximum advantage had been secured. The campaign of 1690 underlined the wisdom of feeling out the Turkish position once more, but a delicate operation of this kind required something better than a rank amateur and outsider like Hussey, and Marsigli was an obvious choice.

In the course of the long journey from Vienna to Adrianople, Sir William doubtless received a good deal of advice from his secretary, and when he finally reached the presence of the Grand Vizir, he was uncertain what tack to take in opening his negotiations. Whether Marsigli was to blame for this hesitancy is not clear, but the fact is that Hussey was curiously uncommunicative when questioned by Köprülü.[17] He asked if he had any proposals to make, and he avoided a direct answer to that question. Instead he seemed anxious to learn if the Turks sincerely desired peace. In the event that they did, he demanded to know if they would allow him to act as mediator. No mention was made of Jakob Coyler and his previous offers of mediation, and the Dutch veteran of this 'campaign' was much chagrined when he learned of this omission, though he did not, however, blame Hussey for his lapse. At the conclusion of what was clearly the strangest interview in the course of these peace negotiations, Hussey, finally satisfied to his own satisfaction that the Turks really wanted peace, informed the Vizir that he would send Count Marsigli to Vienna for the necessary *pleinpouvoir* and detailed instructions, so that the work of preparing the peace treaty might be carried through as expeditiously as possible.

Marsigli hurried off to Vienna with an extremely unfavorable report on Hussey's conduct; the all too innocent English diplomat had fallen into the trap prepared for him by the Austrians. The Imperial ministers found themselves no longer able to entrust Sir William with the responsibility of negotiating in their name in Adrianople, but instead they sent the necessary full power to Louis of Baden, so that he could treat directly with the Turks on the battlefront. But since it would be unwise to overlook the presence of Coyler and Hussey in Constantinople, their assistance in the forthcoming talks with the Turks. The two diplomats or their representatives were to join the Grand Vizir at his camp at Belgrade.[18]

Hussey and Coyler were now burdened with the extensive preparations for a trip of very doubtful value to the cause of peace. To an observer with long years of experience of Turkish customs like Thomas Coke, the outspoken secretary of the English Embassy, the proposed journey was a "solemn absurdity" that was doomed to failure. The Grand Vizir had doubtless already crossed the Sava on his way to the front, and he would be well out of reach of the mediators when they arrived in Belgrade after a long and arduous trip.[19] Marsigli, who had returned to Adrianople with the Austrian request for the assistance of Hussey and Coyler, was sent to Louis of Baden's camp near NagyVárad to obtain passports for the Turkish envoys who were to treat with him. The Italian go-between was on the return trip to Adrianople in October, when a party of marauding Serbs who were quite unaware of his identity attacked his party, killed the Turkish Chiaus commanding the Turkish escort party, and left Marsigli himself badly wounded.[20] The devious maneuver by which he had been planted in Hussey's retinue was doomed from them on to failure, for in the aftermath of the Serbian raid the whole range of his activities -- they included secret talks with the Turks and tampering with the letters of English diplomats -- was disclosed. His guilty secret was one no more, and the Emperor was given a full report by Paget of this nefarious plot. Paget believed that Leopold had been purposely kept in the dark about Marsigli's activities by Count Kinsky , but though Paget brought the whole story to the Emperor's attention he made no move to reprimand Kinsky for what had been done.[21] It was difficult to blame the Supreme Bohemian Chancellor for pursuing am policy of spirited independence of Anglo-Dutch interference in Eastern European affairs; it bore a very striking likeness to the line he had adopted in the peace negotiations in 1689. But Paget left no doubt in the minds of the Austrians that they would have to be more circumspect in dealing with representatives of William III. The royal honor of the King of England had suffered an affront in that hid diplomatic representatives had been callously exploited as a cover for "a private and separate negotiation" between the Austrians and the Turks.[22]

Hussey and Coyler continued their preparations for the trip to Belgrade in blissful ignorance of Austrian duplicity, and they had reached Adrianople when the report arrived of a great Imperial victory at Szlankmen on August 16, 1691. Köprülü, a courageous but not particularly gifted military commander, had fallen on the field of battle, and these two great blows to recently revived Turkish optimism gave renewed impetus to the envoys' plans for their trip to Belgrade. Ali Pasha, Köprülü's successor, was reported to be more favorable than his predecessor to peace with the Holy League, and he had given them added encouragement by asking them to join him in

Belgrade as soon as possible. But the two men were no longer in any position to act upon this request. They had established their camp just outside Adrianople, precisely at the spot where an epidemic of malignant fever appeared, and both were taken seriously ill. Hussey died on September 24, and though Coyler, too, was expected to die, he surprised everyone by making a slow recovery. In the long period of his sickness and convalescence, the French Ambassador had been extremely active in distributing large sums of French money to influential Turkish officials, and when Coyler was sufficiently recovered to carry on with the work of mediation alone, it was apparent to him that the Turks were no longer interested in peace negotiations. The sudden death of Hussey and the accident which had temporarily incapacitated Count Marsigli (Paget was of the opinion that this had more to do with the Turkish loss of interest than the death of Hussey) created a temporary hiatus in the peace negotiations.[23] Another favorable opportunity had passed, and this time it was no the content of the suggested peace terms which was responsible for the debacle, but the chain of historical accidents which had suddenly removed by death, sickness, or injury, the men responsible for these delicate preliminaries of a full-blown peace conference.

   To Coyler, as he made the usual return trip to Pera, it was all a very personal disappointment -- he had not come quite so close before to the ardently desired climax of all his sacrifices and ceaseless endeavours in the cause of peace. Great expectations had been raised by the conjuncture of a great Turkish defeat and the apparent willingness of the Austrians to negotiate with the Turks through the medium of the Dutch and English Ambassadors to Turkey. Marsigli's mishap, Coyler's prolonged indisposition, and Hussey's death had suddenly intervened, and the Turks, encouraged by French bribes and a wanton hope of victory in the next campaign, had regained their equipoise. It was time in any event for the Turks to go into winter quarters. The survivors of the Anglo-Dutch mediation (it was not as yet formally recognized as such by either the Turks or the

Austrians), Paget and Coyler, had gained in experience of Turkish and Austrian political procedures; it was a thorough grounding which would serve them well in the future.

The lessons provided by the Viennese ministry had been particularly informative. A makeshift plot to exclude the would-be mediators from the peace parleys had failed, and Kinsky had been revealed to them as the evil genius of the whole plot and of the unfortunate policy which the Austrians tended more and more to pursue in regard to the Turks. Paget was certain that only with the removal of Kinsky could there be a real advance in the Austrian attitude; only then could something be salvaged from the wreckage of the recent talks, whose sudden collapse was partially Kinsky's responsibility.

> I am, humbly, of opinion, that, so long as Count Kinski is president of the council for Turkish affairs, no good will be done in them, since one can not honorably (considering what has already past) undertake to manage any thing of which he is to have the Direction; if the Emperor would put another in his place, some good, I think, might yet be don; but the Emperor (far from disturbing him) will not so much as reprehend him for what he has don;[24]

In arriving at such a conclusion, Paget had revised the spectre of the Schuldfrage in the failure of the talks. The moral indignation of a Paget and a Hop was understandable and perhaps forgivable, but the failure to grasp the wider implications of Austrian diplomatic transgressions was not. They failed so often to see that the Habsburgs had vital interests in Eastern and Southeastern Europe, which their rigorously Western minds could not fail to regard as of secondary importance. And while it must be conceded that the Imperial ministers primarily responsible for the defence of these interests were embarrassingly uninformed as to their exact limits, a little healthy experimentation to clear up some of the doubts deserved a better reception from England and Holland. But this presupposed the presence in London and The Hague of an intuitive and automatic sympathy for Austria's perennially perplexing position, and it was in precisely that area of emotional involvement that the Grand Alliance was so weak. The Austrian reaction to this Western indifference to what was felt to be essential for Austrian survival was natural enough; it involved going one's own way as much as possible, and permitting the interference of outsiders only when such a concession was absolutely unavoidable. Kinsky, when considered from that point of view, was a devoted champion of the real, as opposed to the imaginary, interests of his Emperor and neither better nor worse than the median of political morality of the time.

If the deeper roots of their differences with the Austrian ministers were not perceived by Paget and Coyler, one very practical conclusion had been drawn by them from the failure of the latest attempt at mediation. Timing was of the greatest importance; the sense of the right moment had to be cultivated, and diplomats empowered to act decisively at a favorable juncture had to be continually on the scene.

> Count Marsigli is of the same opinion with as that with these people scarce a Peace or Truce can be made, except the Emperor, with his Allyes, sends over a Full Power to the Ministers of Your Majestie, and Their High Mightinesses, or even one from his Court authorized thereunto, in order to assist us therein, that so, in case of a change in the Government, or a consternation by another Victory, or Incursion of the Imperiall Forces, a Peace or Truce may *ipso facto* be concluded, for as soone as all feare is past, these People take courage agine and easily change their Resolution, as is now done ....[25]

That this judgment found support for Marsigli is an ironic commentary on the failure of the recent negotiations, whether public or private. The Imperial government suddenly appeared to have learned its lesson, and at the end of December 1691, Van Heemskerck informed the States-General that the Emperor had finally accepted *in forma* the mediation of the States and the King of England.[26] This long-delayed recognition of Anglo-Dutch efforts was made with all the appearances of an afterthought, but it could not fail to give much needed encouragement to men who had been sorely tried by the thankless task of bringing the abnormally touchy Austrians and Turks to their senses.

Meanwhile, a successor to Hussey had to be found, and there was wan hope that the new man's appearance almost immediately with the necessary full powers might breathe new life into the affair. The prospect of the trip to Constantinople and of prolonged residence in Turkey was not an attractive one (Hussey's fate had done nothing to improve matters), and it was difficult to find men willing to undertake such a responsibility. Mr. William Harbord, an early partisan of William's cause who had obtained the post of paymaster of the army in Ireland, seemed overly anxious, however, to follow in Hussey's footsteps. His motives for seeking the appointment were not clear, though there was the suspicion that the aura of financial peculation which he had acquired in Ireland had something to do with it; the prestige of a diplomatic *coup* in Turkey might erase other less favorable impressions. His qualifications for the post were undeniable: he had travelled in that part of the world as a younger man (he had taken part in the capture of Buda), and he had announced that he was ready to leave at a moment's notice. William did not tarry to weigh other alternatives. Mr. William Harbord's name was duly presented to the Levant Company for formal election to the post, and in a relatively brief time another English Ambassador was en route to Turkey.[27]

While awaiting Harbord's arrival, the English community in Turkey enjoyed the interregnum. Mr. Coke presided over a most harmonious "commonwealth." Only one source of misunderstanding troubled its peace. Jakob Coyler had been entrusted by William with the extra obligation of representing the English Crown in any business having to do with the mediation which might arise in the interim between Hussey's death and Harbord's arrival in Turkey. He was armed with the appropriate letters in due course, and on the basis of this restricted commission he began to act as if he were the Ambassador of the King of England -- it was heaven-sent opportunity to interfere in the purely internal affairs of the English colony. the long-established rivalry between English and Dutch merchants in Turkey was sufficient cause for trouble, but an additional source of irritation had been created by the difficulties the English as a people experienced in adjusting themselves to the fact that they were now allies of the Dutch and had a member of the House of Orange as their King. Coke was particularly sensitive to Dutch arrogance, and he bridled quite plainly at the orders he occasionally received from Coyler.[28] But further complication was added to this picture when Count Marsigli, who had returned to Adrianople and then to Pera upon his recovery, circulated the report that he was the official representative of the King of England, on the specious pretext that he had not been merely Hussey's secretary but the secretary of the embassy as well. Coyler and Coke combined temporarily to repel this intruder, and they made short work of his pretensions. The young Italian was reduced to complicating a *Description of the Fish in the Bosphorus.*[29]

It was foolhardy to predict what kind of a reception would be accorded Harbord by the Dutch Ambassador, but of on one point all the parties to this disgraceful controversy could be agreed. The Turks had been treated to the spectacle of disagreement between professed allies, and this could not fail to cause doubts in their minds as to the value and dependability of Anglo-Dutch offers of mediation. The absence of a united front was too obvious to be overlooked, and the French Ambassador was making full use of this situation in his drive to prevent any further contact between the Emperor and the Turks. English complaints had little effect on Whitehall or the Dutch even when they bordered on the ironic -- "Our King has more public Ministers here, or those that pretend to be so, than all the other Christian Princes beside and are of all degrees and sizes like a nest of boxes."[30]

Mr. Harbord's tempo and enthusiasm had been substantially reduced by an attack of the gout and the severe winter weather, and he even expressed the hope that he would be able to return to England in a year's time.[31] His experiences in Vienna were an exact repetition of Hussey's, but in his case illness was added to the infuriating indecision of the Austrian ministers. It was May before he was able to leave Vienna with proposals which were probably similar to those which Hussey had carried with him the year before.[32] Ali Pasha of Diyabekr, the Grand Vizir, informed Coyler in July that he was leaving for Belgrade and that he would be ready to receive any proposals there that Harbord might submit to him.[33] But this meeting which might have led to a resumption of negotiations never took place. "Our Ambassadors," complained Thomas Coke, "pick the true season of the dogdays to take their journeys into bad airs," and the malignant fever, which had killed Sir William Hussey the year before, acted swiftly to release Harbord from the mission he had been so anxious to undertake.[34] Death came at Belgrade just as the Grand Vizir was expected to arrive, and Harbord was buried in the Greek Church. The Grand Vizir despatched a letter to William III in which he offered his condolences. The sincerity of the King's friendly feelings for the Turks could not be denied. His desire to mediate in the war with the Emperor was a most laudable one, but two English Ambassadors had perished in attempting to carry out their master's wishes, and the Grand Vizir was now inclined to be pessimistic about the chances of peace. "When it shall please God that this peace be treated, He will find the means to accomplish it, else what his divine Majesty has predestinated must be."[35] And for once this fatalism of the Turkish mind was to find an echo in English and Dutch reactions. Harbord's death, following as it did by an interval of one year the events surrounding the death of Hussey, could not be simply regarded as an accident. Forces beyond human control seemed to be conspiring against the efforts at mediation made by the Maritime Powers. Coke, whose many years of residence in Turkey may have converted him to a belief in *kismet*, was of the opinion that Harbord's death "may well end all hope of peace."

In Vienna the mood, as far as the representatives of William were concerned, remained one of optimism. It was clear that they were working against time, but there was still the chance that the Grand Vizir, if approached before the end of the year, might be willing to accept the latest set of proposals. Paget had been mentioned before as a possible candidate for the post of English Ambassador to Turkey and it did not require prolonged deliberation on the King's part to name him to succeed Harbord.[36]   Since Paget was on leave in England when his appointment was made, it was decided that his Dutch colleague Van Heemskerck should undertake a temporary mission to Belgrade that would preserve a continuity in the negotiations with the Turks.

Van Heemskerck had the mistaken notion that he was being sent "to conclude a treaty so far managed and successfully carried on, that it needed only the help of an active Agent to bring it to the desired end."[37]   Van Heemskerck did not completely exclude the possibility of failure, but he tended to take this mission rather lightly as a pleasant foray into Serbia which might result in the capture of a most important diplomatic prize. If the negotiations were prolonged into the winter months, he expected that Paget and Coyler would relieve him of his responsibility and allow him to return to Vienna. He was most concerned about the financial arrangements; the cost of such a venture was high -- ten thousand Dutch dollars would be needed for the costs of the trip alone. Jakob Jan Hamel Bruynincx, Van Heemskerck's secretary, was to temporarily represent the interests of the United Provinces in Vienna, and this gave Van Heemskerck the assurance that Dutch affairs would be in good hands while he was gone.[38] He was convinced that his habitual method of speedy and decisive negotiation would be sufficient to assure him success where so many others had failed. Such impetuous pride was natural in the novice, and he would have abundant opportunity in any case to realize how mistaken he had been about the disposition of the Turks to peace.

He arrived in Belgrade on October 11, 1692, and was promptly received in audience by the Grand Vizir on the very next day. On the following day, he had an opportunity to present his complete set of peace proposals to Ali Pasha. Unofficial conversations, following on these meetings, were held with Mavrokordatos, who had recently resumed his post as Grand Dragoman on his return from his long stay in Austria and Hungary. The Greek was an unfortunate choice, as far as Van Heemskerck was concerned, for a partner in these discussions, since he was known to be in a vengeful mood after his experiences with the Austrians. The talks dragged on, and the Grand Vizir neglected to give Van Heemskerck an answer to the proposals. It was apparent now that the brief trip to Belgrade would not be so brief after all.[39]

Van Heemskerck's mistake at the very beginning of his talks was his premature presentation of the complete text of the Imperial proposals.[40] The Turks had reiterated their interest in peace and their wish to receive proposals from the Emperor, but the moment hey were faced with detailed articles and conditions (they had not had such a concrete offer for four years) they were reduced to silence. The articles were unexceptional enough, and Mavrokordatos must have been well aware of their likeness to the Imperial offer he and Sulfikar Effendi had received. This time there was no mention of the ancient claims of the Kingdom of Hungary, though the admission of the fundamental principle of *Uti possidetis* would involve the loss of Transylvanian independence under Turkish suzerainty, a recognition at this date of a *fait accompli*. The other articles were concerned as usual with the regulation of the frontiers, diplomatic and trade relations, and the exchange of captives. The treaty was to remain in effect for thirty years, and for a period of one year after its ratification, full satisfaction by the Turks of the demands of the remaining members of the Holy League (Russia's participation was mentioned for the first time) would provide the opportunity for the conclusion of a general peace.[41]

The Imperial Court was convinced that Van Heemskerck had erred in leaving nothing to Turkish imagination, and Leopold, in a letter to Lord Paget on the occasion of the latter's departure for Constantinople, advised him to pursue a more moderate line with the Turks. It was sufficient to win agreement on the fundamental principle of *Uti possidetis*; the rest of the points at dispute should be entrusted to the decisions of a peace congress. Paget found it ridiculously easy to regard any policy of Van Heemskerck's as a mistaken one, but there was in this case good reason for his complaint that the Dutch Ambassador's precipitate action had tied his own hands; he was "barely reduced to the proposition of Uti possidetis .... his way of proceeding has straightened mine."[42]

It was long past the annual deadline for peace negotiations when Paget presented himself to Ali Pasha. He had not taken Van Heemskerck's advice to hurry on ahead of his party with the utmost despatch, and the uncooperative attitude of the Turkish officials along the way and the unfavorable weather conditions had made his progress painfully slow. It was the end of February, 1693, before he was able to present to Ali Pasha his credentials and King William's letters to the Sultan and the Grand Vizir. The King informed the Turks that he was most anxious to assist in the establishment of peaceful negotiations between the Emperor and the Sultan, and he made a formal offer of his mediation. Lord Paget produced his proposition of *Uti possidetis* in the course of his remarks, and on the strength of this, he was asked by the Grand Vizir to submit proposals in writing. Paget quickly complied with this request. Although the written proposals had little to add to his initial suggestion, he did lay down the fundamental principle as the basis for the treaties that should be concluded with the Emperor, Venice, and Poland -- the Polish demand for the cession of Kaminiec was the sole exception to the general rule.

The Grand Vizir was doubtless having his little joke at the expense of the latest English emissary of good will when he pressed Paget for additional proposals. The wayward humour of Ali Pasha was to find a further outlet in a meeting he arranged with the three ambassadors. Van Heemskerck had followed the Grand Vizir to Adrianople in the hope that he might receive an answer to his proposals there, and under the mask of Turkish politeness he could see the iron determination to have him expiate the crime of the long interment of the Turkish envoys by the Austrians. Paget was surprised by the great gathering of Turkish ministers and their retainers at the Grand Vizir's residence, but even more surprising was the fact that the Grand Vizir read to the assembled multitude Van Heemskerck's articles instead of Paget's -- a maneuver which distressed Paget greatly since he felt quite rightly that the Dutch Ambassador's proposals had not figured in his own discussions with the Grand Vizir.

The foreign envoys were then dismissed, and the crowd which had had the peace proposals read to it was told that this was what the "pretended friends" of the Porte had offered in the way of peace terms. Did the Turks want peace on such terms? The crowd was unanimous, of course, in its refusal to accept such proposals. The Grand Vizir then asked if he might accept reasonable terms, and this evoked a favorable response. Paget by some intuitive process known only to himself concluded from the report of this 'spontaneous demonstration' that his own proposals (he evidently judged them to be reasonable) had pleased the Turkish ministers. The other "unhappy paper" had been read only to encourage the Turks at the outset of a new campaign, for on the very night of the meeting orders were issued by the Grand Vizir to bring the army together at Adrianople.[43]

Paget had no intention of being put off by such a shabby device as the Grand Vizir's meeting for morale purposes, and he immediately demanded an audience of Ali Pasha for March 17. On the appointed day his prize once more eluded him; Ali Pasha had been deposed. It was March, to be sure, that fateful month in the years 1692 to 1695, when an annual change was made of Grand Vizirs. Paget's written proposals were presented instead to Mustapha Pasha, the new Vizir, but the English Ambassador was becoming depressed with the sombre picture of the prospects for peace. The continued presence, or captivity, of Van Heemskerck in Adrianople disturbed him. He felt that his Dutch colleague had made fateful mistakes at a crucial point in the negotiation, but he himself was having no better luck in securing a reaction from the Turks to his offer.

Failing in this direction, he turned his attention to the benefits which might be derived from contacts of an unofficial nature with prominent Turkish officials. The Mufti, the Aga of janissaries, the Reis Effendi, the local Kaimakams received him courteously enough, but they were unable to give him much encouragement in the hopeful period of the beginning of a new campaign. The Kaimakam of Adrianople, Osman Pasha, was particularly patient with Paget, and he had need to be, for Paget treated him to a long and learned lecture on the differences between a Peace and a Treaty, and the usefulness of this last diplomatic form, to which were added some reflections of mediation as a diplomatic activity. Paget thought that the Turks were even ignorant of the meaning of *Uti possidetis*; but in fact they were by now well aware of the nature of such key phrases in Europe's diplomatic vocabulary, and *Uti possidetis* might indeed be regarded as one of their contributions to European diplomatic discourse. Osman Pasha seemed a likely pupil even when he was engaged in learning things he already knew, and Paget inclined to place all his deciding hopes on this man.[44]   But at the beginning of December, death intervened once more, and Osman Pasha was lost to the cause.[45]

Stalemate at Adrianople almost automatically involved a spirited resumption of Allied diplomatic activity in Vienna, and George Stepney, a poet whose diplomatic talents were easily more striking than his literary attainments, had been sent by Whitehall to act as Secretary at Vienna until such time as an Ambassador was appointed, and was the focus, for a brief period, of further negotiations.[46] This was Stepney's first visit to the city in which he would spend most of the most valuable years of his career, and his first impressions -- they were to be decisive -- were not favorable ones. He lamented that "Mirth and Muses are quite forgott" in the Austrian lands, and his Whiggish Protestantism suffered a constant series of shocks when confronted with the baroque piety of the Emperor's court.[47] He was heard to complain in an ironic fashion that the great pilgrimage of the Emperor to the shrine of Mariazell should have been undertaken sooner, for then a "Miracle" would have occurred at an earlier and more opportune moment. Moreover, Leopold's acts of devotion were wastefully expensive, particularly when there seemed to be no practical consequences.[48] And the *stoicus* in Leopold annoyed him. When the report reached Vienna of the failure of the Austrian siege of Belgrade in 1693, Stepney was amazed to see how this great defeat was born with a truly Christian resignation.

> When the Empress asked him (the Emperor) of news? He answered coldly Das Spiel ist suss (the game is at an end) and away he went to Chapell as if he would thank God for it.[49]

Shortly after his arrival at Vienna, Stepney, too, began to feel the lure of a mission to Turkey, and William III sent him rather vague instructions to place himself in readiness for a trip to Turkey or for a prolonged stay in Vienna, according to the pleasure of the Emperor. Stepney reported to Mr. Secretary Vernon that he was well prepared for any mission the Emperor might give him to Lord Paget or Van Heemskerck, and as he would have no opportunity to receive further orders, he wished to prepare Vernon for the report that he had gone to visit the "Musulman." One great qualification that he possessed was his good health (this was bound to strike a responsive chord at Whitehall), and he admitted that he knew no fear when he could be of service to his King -- exceedingly good qualifications all in all for a role in such a mortally dangerous undertaking as these negotiations with the Turks had been.[50] The chance to participate in the Mediation would be an excellent opportunity to improve his prospects, and Turkey may well have attracted him as a needed change from the monotonous round of German courts to which he had been exposed.

Count Kinsky now began to sound Stepney out on the subject of his new offer of assistance. Doubtless this was only another source of puzzlement to the ever cautious Minister of an even more cautious monarch. Stepney could obviously say nothing more than that he was at His Imperial Majesty's disposition. In the meantime, he made himself useful by despatching copies of the recent French peace feelers to Paget and Van Heemskerck, so that the Turks might discover upon perusing them that Louis XIV was seriously contemplating abandoning the Turks to their fate.[51]

By the middle of September, 1693, Stepney's proposed trip had to be abandoned, as the Emperor could foresee no need for a special mission of this kind. Kinsky once more felt the wrath of an English diplomat, for in his reports to London, Stepney camouflaged his disappointment with an attack on Kinsky's policy.

> For Count Kinsky is of such a Jesuiticall persecuting principle that I believe he had rather the War shou'd last a year or 2 longer, than that poor Count Teckely shou'd escape with Estate or life.[52]

But in this particular case the Emperor and Count Kinsky were wiser than the latest English speculator in Mediation futures. Lord Paget had abandoned his post at Adrianople for the further discomfort of Pera (the Levant Company made his life miserable there), and Van Heemskerck was certainly in no position to receive further proposals when his original efforts had not been favored with an answer. The rumour circulated in Adrianople -- it was most probably a hasty French improvisation -- that the impetuous Dutchman was in reality a German spy. There is no doubt that he was being treated as if he were actually the agent of a power with which the Porte was at war.[53] Revenge was certainly being exacted for the bitter experience of the Turkish embassy, and he had the misfortune to be the first diplomat on whom the Turks could use such tactics -- his diplomatic status was imprecise enough from their standpoint to allow for unfortunate mistakes. In The Hague, Their High Mightinesses began to grow impatient. Official notification was given to the Turks by Coyler that Van Heemskerck had been recalled to his post in Vienna, but beyond that announcement they found it unnecessary and unwise to go in their circumspect efforts to free Van Heemskerck from his confinement.[54]

A wintry hope revived with the return of Ali Pasha to Adrianople at the end of the year, but the Grand Vizir and his advisers were at such odds over their reply that Van Heemskerck was compelled to wait once more. It was only in the following March (1694) that he was received in an *audience de congé*, and the answer -- it was barren of all meaning at this point -- was given to him that his "proposals were not found to be acceptable and consonant with the dignity and grandeur of the Sublime Porte."[55] Van Heemskerck did not tarry for second thoughts or comments; he wasted no time in beginning his journey, despite the unusually cold winter, to Vienna by way of Belgrade.

But in Belgrade further disappointment awaited him. The annual shakeup had taken place in Adrianople just after his precipitate departure, and in view of the fall of Mustapha Pasha and his replacement by Ali Pasha "the Defterdar," the Pasha of Belgrade thought it politic to keep the Dutch party at Belgrade until the newly-appointed Grand Vizir arrived there, in the expectation that a decision might be made to renew discussions with an envoy about to depart for Vienna. The Turks may also have thought that Van Heemskerck, in a desperate effort to secure his release, might concede a point or two. He soon found himself forced to enter upon new discussions with the Grand Vizir and his old nemesis Mavrokordatos, but he did not fail to point out the absurdity of these talks; he had been so long out of touch with both Turkish and Austrian developments that he was unable to say anything of value to the propositions which the Grand Vizir might put to him. His 'captors' finally decided that they, too, had had enough of this affair, and he was eventually allowed to continue his trip to Vienna, which he reached in December, 1694. His "temporary" mission to Belgrade had lasted more than twenty-six months.[56]

With his safe arrival in Vienna a most distressing chapter in the history of this Mediation was closed. Its significance is not entirely clear, and any satisfactory solution of the mystery must wait upon the study of the relevant Turkish documents. It is possible to regard it as the consequence of a number of long-standing Turkish diplomatic practices rather than as an expression of any active Turkish policy in regard to peace with the Emperor. There was, first of all, the desire to pay the Emperor back in his own coin, and second the notion that it was good to have Van Heemskerck on hand in the event that a sudden change of affairs made peace more attractive, and finally the atavistic love of secrecy which was expressed in the effort to conceal from him as much as possible the true state of Turkish affairs, so that on his return to Vienna he would not be able to provide the Imperial ministers with information which could only whet their appetites for further expansion.[57] In this last area -- that of up-to-date knowledge of Turkish affairs -- the Turkish maneuver was a failure.

One of Van Heemskerck's first official acts on reaching Vienna was to present to the Imperial government a lengthy report on affairs in Turkey. He consoled himself for his failure and his humiliating confinement with his expert knowledge of affairs in the territories of the Grand Signor, and he presented himself to the Emperor as a person well-qualified on the basis of a long and bitter experience to advise him on the policy vis-à-vis Turkey to be pursued in the future.[58] But though he had been converted to a firm belief in the declining power of the Turks (he announced his finding as if it were a discovery) and had come to the conclusion that this weakness of his hereditary enemy made it possible for the Emperor to continue with war on two fronts, he tended quite naturally, for a representative of the Maritime Powers, to the position that the war on the Eastern front should be continued on a more moderate scale. Suggestions to this effect were despatched to William III, and in a report of January 12, 1695, he promised the King that "to the extent that I shall find a hearing at this Court for my recently acquired knowledge of Turkish affairs, they will no longer overexert themselves in continuing the war, since Turkey is not able to make a powerful diversion in favor of France."[59]

All through the period of his confinement, Paget and Coyler had carefully observed a previously concerted line of affecting disinterest in anything relating to mediation. Occasions on which they would have formerly raised their embarrassing question were allowed to pass without any reference to the desired peace between the Emperor and the Turks. Events in Adrianople reinforced the wisdom of this policy. Lord Paget had received permission to go to Adrianople in December, 1694, and there was the unexpressed hope in his mind that the Grand Vizir would make some reference to his original proposals. But the death of Sultan Ahmed II on the very eve of his audience with the Grand Vizir acted as an effective damper to any flickering embers of Turkish interest in peace. The Sultan Mustafa II was as yet an unknown quantity, though he gave promise of being more "stirring, vigorous, and resolute in affairs than many of his predecessors have been, and is likely to make great alteration in the Empire."[60] His youthful arrogance would doubtless incline him to war rather than to peace, and if Paget in his letters concurred with his erstwhile Dutch rival on the striking evidence of Turkish decline, he could see with equal clarity that the Turks' *amour propre* would make it virtually impossible for them to comprehend the exact degree of danger inherent in their truly parlous situation. It was a restrained and almost philosophical Paget, for a change, who concluded at the middle of 1695 that there was no immediate chance for peace and requested permission to return to England.[61]

But this was only after he and Coyler had had another series of talks with the Grand Vizir in February. The dangerous influence of Châteauneuf appeared to be wanting. Every report of Louis XIV's ill-conceived secret negotiations with the members of the Grand Alliance weakened the French Ambassador's influence, for he had the unenviable task of presenting these negotiations to the Turks under the guise of a French ruse to break up the alliance. The Grand Vizir in a two hour audience which he granted to Coyler listened with perceptible interest to the Dutch Ambassador's warning that France was no longer able to provide sufficient diversion to the Emperor's forces on the Western front. Upon receiving the customary offers of mediation, the Grand Vizir declared that a permanent peace settlement was an impossibility, but that a truce might well be arranged. It was agreed that he would urge the acceptance of this feasible plan in his discussions with the young Sultan; the Ambassadors were expected to produce the plan itself and wisely include, if possible, some face-saving concessions to Turkish pride, so that the bellicose young ruler would find it less humiliating to give his consent.[63]

This suggestion struck Coyler as an unimposing, if hopeful, start, but he discovered on conferring with his English colleague that Paget was fully determined to wait for an answer to the proposals which he had presented three years before. A basic difference over the policy to be pursued was evident here. Coyler was ready to avail himself of the slightest chance for a resumption of peace negotiations, while Paget was beginning to feel that English honor and prestige were being continually weakened by this excessive and demanding interest in a peace at any price. The consequent 'loss of face' by the Mediation reduced, as far as Paget was concerned, its effectiveness in assisting in the conclusion of a durable peace in Eastern Europe. It was another instance of the curious competition between the Dutch *empressement* and English restraint; the victory on this occasion went to Paget. The Dutch Ambassador, since he could not possibly repose much confidence in the value of the Grand Vizir's suggestion and since he wished to maintain a united front in the Mediation, gave way to Paget and did not press his point. They agreed once more to allow matters to follow their course and to make no further mention of their willingness to mediate until the Turks reopened the question.[64]

The year 1696 ended for them on that note of resignation. The war seemed quite literally endless (it had already lasted thirteen years), and if it was no longer prodigal of victories it continued to impose a crushing burden on all the countries concerned and particularly for those unfortunates in Hungary and the Balkans who resided in the *sedis belli*. And for a diplomat like Paget who found life in Turkey easier to bear when there was a diplomatic coup in the offing, the disappointment and frustration were doubly hard to bear, and the thought of Beaudesert Hall was the only thing to which he could look forward with any anticipation.

But at the very moment of deepest gloom and most complete stalemate the situation in Eastern Europe received a rude shock from rapid and decisive changes which had taken place in the West. Louis XIV was finally ready to make such concessions as were required by the English and the Dutch and to concede to the Emperor and the Empire the bare minimum which could not fail to disappoint Vienna but which seem sufficient from the standpoint of the Maritime Powers, and thus effectively preclude the resumption of the war by the Grand Alliance. The Congress which met in Holland at the little castle of Rijswijk was a success as far as the French and the Maritime Powers were concerned, but the Emperor's tardy and grudging acceptance of a virtual *fait accompli* was literally forced upon him by allies who showed little interest in his claim to Strassburg and his claim to the Spanish succession.[65] The Grand Alliance was, for all practical purposes, at an end, and a fluidity appeared for a brief period in the relations of the European powers.[66] The way was open for the conclusion of William III and Louis XIV of the Partition Treaties which could only be regarded in Vienna as fresh defeats for Leopold's Spanish and Italian policies. By the very process, however, of this growing estrangement between Austria and the Maritime Powers over their objectives in Eastern Europe became possible: the Mediation's work there suddenly became much easier. The Emperor was now deeply concerned that he would have to defend his family's interests in Spain without the support of his Western allies, and the opportunity provided for him by the Grand Alliance to fight both the French and the Turks no longer existed. He was ready, as he had never been to quite such a degree before, to treat with the Turks and happy to call once more on the mediating offices of Paget and Coyler.

But Rijswijk was not to be the only harbinger of change. Barely ten days before the English and Dutch plenipotentiaries had put their signatures on the formal instrument of that treaty, a great Austrian general had made another and perhaps more striking contribution to a peace settlement in Eastern Europe. Eugene of Savoy had been finally provided with an opportunity to bring his military genius to bear on the Turks; on this occasion he was not required to serve under commanders whose dynastic ties and financial contributions to the war chest were more noteworthy than their military gifts. Eugene's army had caught up with the retiring Turkish army at Zenta on September 11, 1697, and had achieved the most striking victory for Austria since Szlankamen. The bellicose young Sultan ignominiously escaped the general slaughter with a handful of guards, but the Grand Vizir and numbers of high officials together with the best of Turkey's experienced officers and troops perished. Zenta was a sign that not even Turkish arrogance could mistake; Eugene had finally "beaten them into passable good manners and made them not unwilling to talk of peace."[67]

The man who was to embody the Ottoman desire for peace was Hussein Köprülü, the fourth member of the great family to serve as Grand Vizir; he had been entrusted by the Sultan with the dangerous task of making peace with the Holy League. The aged and valetudinarian Köprülü made the expected first move: he asked Lord Paget at the beginning of December, 1697, to come to Adrianople to discuss with him outstanding difficulties in Anglo-Turkish relations, matters relating to England's Levant trade for the most part. Paget was naturally pleased with the invitation, for he expected that this was evidence that the Turks were now disposed to listen to him on his favorite subject: peace with the Emperor. Before his departure for Adrianople he conferred with Jacob Coyler and gave the Dutch Ambassador his assurance "*en foi de gentilhomme*" that he would keep Coyler informed of any negotiations which might take place.[68]

His arrival at Adrianople coincided most auspiciously with the receipt by the Grand Vizir of a printed copy of the Treaty of Rijswijk, and he immediately received a visit from Mavrokordatos, who inquired in the name of the new Grand Vizir if Paget was "the person who had formerly brought some overtures for Peace between the two Empires?" Paget had no intention of making it any easier for the Turks to adjust to the new situation, and he brusquely reminded Mavrokordatos, if his memory needed any jogging, that the Dragoman knew very well that he was the same person.[69] At his audience with the Grand Vizir Paget followed up this question of the Dragoman with a vigorous plea for the acceptance by the Turks of the offer of mediation by William III, to which no answer had been vouchsafed for over four years. He was willing to admit that radical changes had taken place since the time of the initial offer and the specific proposals were probably obsolete, but a favorable Turkish answer would constitute the basis for further negotiations. Mavrokordatos paid him another visit; this time with assurances that the Turks were quite capable of continuing the war, but Paget would not listen -- "I told him, that having been here so long, I was not to learn anything from such topicks." Paget was evidently not endowed with the conventional diplomatic virtues of patience and dissimulation. He was as bored with Turkish posturings as Lord Lexington was in Vienna with extravagant Austrian claims, and he made no secret of it.[70]

Their next encounter must have reminded Mavrokordatos of the initial discussions in Vienna in 1689. He told Paget that the Sultan would require the principle of *Uti possidetis*, but since the Emperor had been so well favored by fortune in the course of the war, the Turks would expect him to demonstrate his moderation by restoring the *status quo* in Transylvania. Paget did not trouble to conceal his displeasure with this demand. He warned the Greek that such a suggestion had been so uniformly rejected by the Emperor (this was not entirely true, of course), and that its incursion now in the Turkish proposals would only prejudice the whole negotiation at the very outset.

In their almost frequent meetings which extended through January, the English Ambassador and the Grand Dragoman managed to go over a lot of well-worn ground again. The Turks were reminded that they would also be expected to make satisfaction to the Emperor's Allies. The Turks countered with a display of their accustomed interest in the fate of fortresses held by the Emperor in the vicinity of the proposed boundary line: they demanded the demolition of forts like PeterVárad, Illock, and Essek. Once again Paget left little doubt in their minds as to the reception such a proposal would receive in Vienna.

The traditionally accepted view of mediation -- it was still open to a number of interpretations in practice -- was that it was confined to the exchange by neutral powers of projected peace terms and additional communications between belligerents and impartial efforts by the intermediaries to secure agreement on disputed points. In January and in the following months Paget and Coyler would far exceed these limits, and Paget, in particular, was conscious that he was mediating with a difference.

> I repeated what I had before say'd against this notion, and then told him, that as Ambassador from a Mediator, I was not to councel or advise anything but only to receive what should be given to me, but that speaking with him, not as a Minister, but familiarly as a privat person, it would, I thought, connduce towards the facilitation of affairs, that wee might have liberty to discourse and examine them, to dispose things so that they might have a likelihood of succeeding.[71]

Paget was soon able to inform the Turkish government that he had received instructions from his sovereign which assured him that the Emperor had agreed that, in the event a Turkish peace offer was made to him, commissioners would be appointed to settle matters, with the great likelihood that peace would be finally achieved. Relevant portions of the King's letters were shown privately to Mavrokordatos to convince him and the Grand Vizir of the sincerity of Paget's offer.

The air of secrecy was a natural by-product of the only stages of such a negotiation; the Turkish officials were unwilling to make public their desire for peace until they had assurances that the Emperor would not reject their latest peace feeler out of hand, and Paget was well inclined, after years of bitter experience, to humor them at this point. There were other good reasons for his preservation of the air of secrecy: the peculiar character of his simultaneous negotiations "as a Minister and ... as a privat person" and his puzzling attempt to keep Coyler, who was still in Pera, in the dark about the amazing turn affairs had taken in Adrianople. Paget's explanations for his failure to honor his gentleman's promise are not completely candid, least of all when he defended the wisdom of his attitude for the benefit of Whitehall.

> First because he (Coyler) has not (as I know) offer'd his offices here, since Signor Heemskerck went away; secondly Because he is not here; Thirdly because the Discours with the Vesier, and the Transactions upon it, were accidentall and suddain, and I had not time nor convenience to advise with him, so that what it said in the Vesier's letter about the States, relates to former overtures, and not to what has pas'd now, but I shall be proceed henceforward, as His Majestie shall be pleased to command me, when all else is disposed to carry on the business ....[72]

The Dutch Ambassador's suspicions about Paget's activities would have been confirmed if he had seen the letter.

Paget was not above trying to monopolize the affair (the great prize was at last in sight), but it is difficult to judge what chance he thought he had of succeeding in carrying off such an obvious coup. William III would never allow it, since he expected the English and Dutch diplomats (they were all servants of the one master) to cooperate as a matter of course in Vienna and Adrianople. The very best for which Paget may have hoped was that he would be accorded a position of pre-eminence in the negotiations and that any prestige which might follow upon the successful conclusion of peace would be largely his. Rumor had it -- though it was never substantiated -- that he had bribed the Turks with 50,000 ecus for the privilege of the direction of the Mediation.[73] A sum as large as that would have had to come from his own pocket, since no Secretary of State would ever allow him to pursue a policy at variance with the expected cooperation with the envoy of the States-General.

In the course of January the Grand Vizir and his advisers had prepared on the basis of the Dragoman's conversations with Paget an answer to William's offer which Paget had presented to the Porte years before and, in addition, a set of proposals which would serve to make the Turkish position clear in any forthcoming exchange of views. The Grand Vizir's letter lamented the fact that the Turks had been unable to accept his offer of *Uti possidetis* in 1693; they had, moreover, not been convinced that the Emperor was inclined to a just and honorable peace. But at the present juncture they were ready to formally accept once more the Mediation of the King of England and of the States-General, though his acceptance had not lapsed since 1693, in the hope that an agreement could now be reached with the Emperor and his Allies. The proposals revealed that Paget's advice had had some effect: the Turks were ready to make peace on the basis of *Uti possidetis* with the Emperor, Venice and Poland. The Emperor would be required to demolish or evacuate a number of fortresses on the Danube-Sava-Unna line; Poland would be required to demolish Kaminiec and to evacuate Moldavia; Venice would have to agree on a number of evacuations and demolitions of fortresses along the proposed Veneto-Turkish frontier. The main obstacle to a peace with the Emperor had been retained: the Emperor was to withdraw his troops from Transylvania and permit the re-establishment of a semi-independent principality there.[74]

Paget had hoped for something better than this, but he did not allow himself to be pessimistic. The unfortunate demand for the restoration of the *status quo* in Transylvania would not, he felt, be insisted on violently enough to necessitate a complete rupture of the negotiations, and he expected that a similar elasticity would be displayed by the Turks in the demolitions question, though here some concessions by the Emperor would be necessary. Confirmation of Turkish tractability had been given by the Grand Vizir when Paget had asked him if the Turkish government would concede some points in negotiating on the basis of the articles which it had prepared, and Köprülü had assured him that the Turks had recommended their proposals to the King of England's consideration "not only as a Mediator but even as a Plenipotentiary" and that what his Ambassadors did would be acceptable to the Porte.[75] The Vizir's reliance on the Mediation was now as strong as was his desire for peace, but he could also reasonably expect that the Mediators would use their influence to secure a peace for the Turks which would be the best possible in the light of Turkey's present depressing state. England and Holland, as he was well aware, were vitally concerned by their Levant trade, and on more than one occasion this hidden Turkish sanction had prevented the Maritime Powers from throwing their weight behind a forceful anti-Turkish policy in the Near East.

But if the Austrians appeared to hold a great advantage over the Turks, the advantage was certainly more apparent than real. The financial strain of the war had produced a state of complete chaos in Imperial finances, and the officials responsible in virtue of their positions for remedying the situation were far from equal to the task. Distinguished Austrian statesmen who had graced this Court with their brief experience and powers of intellect in 1693 were gone for the most part. The outspoken advice of the Marques de Borgomanero, the Spanish Ambassador, had terminated with his death in 1695 -- a blow that was deeply felt by Leopold and his ministers and by the Allied diplomats with whom he had championed the cause of peace with the Turks. The Western-oriented wing of the Imperial ministry had been seriously weakened by the deaths of Count Stratmann (1693) and Count Windischgrätz (1695). Their happily Imperial breadth of view, however dated might be its primary attachment to the interests of the *Reich*, would be missed; they had been first-rate statesmen and diplomats and they could not be easily replaced. One younger man showed promise, Count Dominik Kaunitz, who owed his ever-widening influence to his proven talent in negotiation and to the support of the Empress and the Neuburg party, but he was clearly not of the stature of Stratmann and

Windischgrätz. He and Count Kinsky, both of them leading members of the Bohemian aristocracy, were in the natural process of Court politics fated to be rivals, but their incipient rivalry was not pronounced enough to prevent them from working fairly amicably together.

Jacob Hop, returning to Vienna once more as Dutch envoy at the beginning of 1698, found Kinsky a sickly and deeply disappointed man.[76] He had aged strikingly in appearance; he was troubled by the gout -- it now prevented him as it had formerly prevented Königsegg from attending crucial meetings of the *Conferenz*, but beyond the strain on his physical energies which a blindly devoted service to the Emperor had entailed and the traditional pattern of life of the Viennese aristocrat had only furthered, there was his immense disappointment that Leopold had preferred another minister to him in filling the recently vacated post of *Oberhofmeister*, the post of primacy of dignity, if not in political influence, among the ministers. Leopold's old crony Count Ferdinand Boniventure Harrach had been given that post on his return from a none too successful mission in Madrid. The appointment was, however, as much an indication of Leopold's concentration almost exclusively on questions relating to the Spanish succession as it was a testimony to his lifelong affection for Harrach. The 'Austrian' tendency which Kinsky continually espoused, with its possible corollary of an accommodation with Catholic France, no longer inspired the confidence as it had in 1689 and 1691.[77] The interests of his House now demanded that he secure its Spanish heritage at all costs, and growing Habsburg responsibilities in Eastern Europe would literally have to wait their turn. The direction of the impending negotiations with the Turks was turned over quite logically to Kinsky. He was the most experienced in these matters (there was no one else competent to do the job), but Paget was pessimistic:

> But I fear the Delays of the Court of Vienna (with which your Honor is well acquainted) and I apprehend the scrupulous, irresolute temper of Count Kinsky (tho'

otherwise a very able, understanding Minister) will endanger the spoiling all; for I know he can't obtain from his self, or be prevailed with by any body else, to expedite business and nothing can disappoint and Prejudice this but speculative delays and put offs, for the Turks are in this business like Women, Quicquid volunt, valde volunt.[78]

This fear of the havoc that could be wrought by Kinsky's scrupulous, irresolute temper" was particularly marked in the case of Robert Sutton. Sutton, the newly appointed British Minister, had succeeded his cousin Lord Lexington, whose secretary he had been for the past four years; his position required him to be in close touch with all the complicated aspects of Imperial policy and particularly with the confused picture of the relations of the members of the Holy League. And for this very reason, he could not be as sanguine as Paget had been, for he saw little chance of anything decisive being accomplished until the campaign of 1698 (just then in its preparatory stages) had ended.[79] It would take endless amounts of time for the Austrians to consult with Warsaw, Venice, and Moscow. With the last Leopold had concluded an offensive alliance in February, 1697, which specifically bound him to the conclusion of peace with the Turks in concert with his Ally.[80] Sutton soon found himself actively engaged in furthering the work of the Mediation in Vienna. He normally forwarded all of Paget's reports to London, and at the same time he informed Paget on the state of affairs at Vienna. He was the first to give official confirmation of the Turkish inclination to peace, and he was surprised at their reaction, which was far more favorable than he had expected. The clerical party and Count Kinsky could still be expected to set obstacles in the way, but the overwhelming majority of the Emperor's ministers were favorable to peace in 1698 as they had been in 1689.[81]

Mr. George Schreyer, Paget's secretary, who had carried the Turkish letter to London, brought the long-awaited English reaction to the Vizir's letter and proposals on his return to Constantinople on April 30. Secretary Vernon reported on the decisions which had been taken by a Cabinet Council that had discussed the Turkish proposals. Paget was to continue on as the English Ambassador to the Sublime Porte; he was the man with the widest experience of both interpretation of the role of the Mediator; any difficulty on this score, from the Turkish at least, had been removed by his acknowledged role as "Plenipotentiary." And since both England and the States-General were to be associated in the present Mediation, as they had been "from the beginning," Whitehall expected that Paget and Coyler would work together. Paget's diversionary action had been short-lived.[82]

The Austrians were meanwhile surprising Europe with a most unusual show of decision. The lingering shadow that was poor Carlos II -- all of Europe's attention seemed focused on his tenuous existence -- inspired even Count Kinsky to a rash of activity. In this he was acting upon the promptings of the Emperor, for Leopold, as Louis XIV had been quick to note, was most anxious to conclude a peace with the Turks.. And while deep-seated English and Dutch suspicions to the contrary would never be at rest until a treaty was signed, Kinsky and the Cavaliere Carlo Ruzzini, the Venetian Ambassador at Vienna, took a step in the right direction by formally agreeing on June 23, 1698, that *Uti possidetis* was accepted by their governments as the basis for negotiation with the Turks.[83] This necessary prelude to further talks -- it quite pointedly did not refer to Turkish efforts to limit its application -- was despatched to Paget and Coyler with George Schreyer who was travelling once again to Constantinople with *pleinpouvoirs* for the two Ambassadors.

The Austrians and Venetians had for once not set obstacles in the way of peace negotiation, while the Turks gave no indication of changing their minds. The hopes of the Mediators began to rise, though there were still two outstanding problems which were important enough to postpone agreement for another year. The Grand Vizir's inclusion of Poland in his offer to William III had not been favored with a response from Warsaw, and there was the additional minor difficulty that there was absolutely no indication that the Poles would accept an Anglo-Dutch mediation. The customary couriers had been despatched by the Austrians to Warsaw, but the length of time consumed in waiting for a reply might prove fatal. The Turks, as Paget said, were like women, and what they wanted they wanted right away. But even more threatening to the peace settlement was the Russian enigma. There had been no reference in the Turkish statement to Russia, and in the course of his discussions with the Turkish officials Paget had received no indication of their intentions in respect to Russia. Paget and Coyler tried belatedly to remedy this deficiency, and after a number of further conferences with Mavrokordatos and the Grand Vizir, they succeeded in securing from the Turks the concession "that the Moscovite may be included in the Treaty upon the same termes as shall be agreed with the other Allies."[84]

But the Moscovite, who was in the very midst of his first Grand Tour, seemed in no mood to agree to such terms. The suggestion was made to Tsar Peter during the Spring by his English and Dutch hosts that it was now high time for a peace settlement in Eastern Europe, but the Tsar's reactions were so violently negative that they were forced to abandon such a painful subject. This was a matter to be regulated when he and his Ally the Emperor conferred during his projected visit to Vienna.[85] Peter's arrival there in July coincided with the return of Schreyer from Constantinople. Paget's secretary carried despatches from the Mediators which requested further instructions from the Imperial ministers on the course of action they were to follow. The preliminary negotiations were by now well advanced, and it was up to the Austrians to come to terms somehow with their awesome guest.

Count Kinsky was the natural, if not the wisest, choice for the difficult task of winning the Tsar over to the Austrian position. The two men were possessed of temperaments and views which could not be more diametrically opposed, but Kinsky managed to have a fairly amicable discussion with the Tsar. He did not fail to weigh all the implications of the possible courses of action, but he managed in doing this to introduce a sufficient amount of practical politics to please Peter. Peter was annoyed with what he felt was a premature acceptance by his Allies, the Emperor and Venice, of the principle of

Uti possidetis, this would certainly be prejudicial to the negotiations that he and Augustus of Poland might conduct with the Turks, for it would be wellnigh impossible to demand anything more sweeping from the Turks than the Emperor and Venice had done. His own expenditures in the recent campaigns had been very large, and he had not yet achieved those gains which he could reasonably expect as a result of that investment. The Emperor's position was understandable: his main concern that the Spanish Empire remain a Habsburg possession and the compelling need for a free hand in the event of Carlos II's death. But Peter was of the view that the gains which could be made in Eastern Europe at that very moment were more valuable than any hypothetical expansion of Western Europe. The Turks were momentarily in a difficult position, and they were naturally eager to secure the easiest way out. If the Emperor came to terms with them now he would discover that the Turks would not honor their pledges but would attack him from the rear in the event that he went to war with France. And in such a circumstance, Leopold would find it difficult to renew his alliances in Eastern Europe -- this was an implied threat of Russian and Polish neutrality in a future war between the Emperor and the Turks, if he abandoned his Allies now.

Kinsky replied with great tact to the numerous objections made by Peter. It was true that the Emperor had agreed that the possession of the territories occupied by the belligerent powers at the date of the conclusion of the treaty was to be the basis for negotiation. But that did not prevent Russia and Poland from making good some of their plans in the months that would pass before the treaty was signed. Kinsky had not yet received sufficient assurances that the Turks were ready to agree to *Uti possidetis* without any strings attached, and, if they were not ready to do so, there obviously could be no peace settlement. But in the event that the Turks did abide by the principle, it would be virtually impossible to refuse their offer. All of Europe desperately needed peace, and the Emperor had no wish to bear the onus for the continuation of the war.

The reference to the peace loving powers of Europe aroused all of the developing sense of Realpolitik in the Tsar. He could understand why the Emperor and Spain would want such a peace (their reasons were obvious enough), but the mention of England and Holland could not pass without some particularly memorable and characteristically Eastern European reflections on his part on the value of the Emperor's alliance with the Maritime Powers and on the real significance of Anglo-Dutch Mediation.

> The Emperor is well aware on the basis of his experience in the recent war with France of what he can expect from the loyalty and dependability of those powers. He was simply abandoned by them and was forced, as a result, to make peace. One just can't trust them. They are only interested in what is of value to their rade; everything else, even the wishes of their Allies, are not even considered.

Peter was to learn from his own bitter experience that the Maritime Powers had no monopoly on such political shortsightedness. The very Emperor who had been deserted by England and France at Rijswijk would not scruple to desert him in the course of the crucial talks at Carlowitz. But perhaps Kinsky was preparing him for such an eventuality by reminding him that Russia had only recently entered the lists against the Turks; the Emperor and his forces had had to bear the major burden of the conflict for the past fifteen years.[86]

The uprising of the *streltsi* in Moscow required Peter's immediate departure from Vienna and prevented further exchanges of views between the Tsar and Kinsky, but before he left the Austrian capital he submitted his own proposals -- they included a demand for the cession to him by the Turks of Kertch -- to the Emperor. The sole and ambiguous result of the talks was his agreement grudgingly given to participate in the forthcoming Peace Congress.[87]

While these necessary preliminaries were posing great problems for the Austrian ministers, the Turkish Army began its annual march to the front, but what had been so long a custom did not fail to underline the necessity for speed in the subsequent discussions. The Grand Vizir admitted to Coyler that it had cost him an "unbelievable effort" to secure the Sultan's consent to the peace negotiation, and the slightest hopeful sign in the military situation would probably result in a collapse of the whole project. But Hussein Köprülü was still personally convinced of Turkey's pressing need for peace, and he urged the Ambassadors to join him at his camp near Belgrade as soon as possible so that all would be in readiness for the Congress.[88]

There had been a definite change in the official Turkish attitude to the envoys of the Maritime Powers. The great lapse in Turkish courtesy in Van Heemskerck's case was forgotten, and the trip of the Mediators was something of an excursion. The two diplomats began their preparations in a really festive mood this time. Their competitive instinct was displayed in the size and the magnificence of their retinues; Coyler travelled with a company of one hundred and forty people -- he was particularly delighted with his two trumpeters. Paget may have envied him that extra flourish, but he was consoled by the knowledge that the size of his own party was quite equal to that of Coyler. It was petty, perhaps, this love of ceremonial and pageantry, but it was one of the things that would make the next few months bearable. The expense of such a show was enormous, and the States-General was quick to complain about the extravagance of its Ambassador. His excuse was airtight: he had to keep up with the English, for otherwise Dutch honor and prestige would be seriously weakened in the eyes of the Turks.[89] The Turks made their own distinctive contribution to the festivities by providing impressive escorts for the trip and in displaying the full resources of Turkish hospitality on the road from Adrianople to Belgrade. The journey was necessarily slow; it took nearly a month to cover the distance between Adrianople and Sophia. It was there that Paget's secretary rejoined the party, and on the strength of the despatches he carried, including the joint declaration of the Emperor and Venice, the Grand Vizir was able to proceed to the selection of the Sultan's plenipotentiaries at the Peace Congress.[90]

The chief Turkish representative was Mohammed Pasha, the Reis-Effendi, a man well-fitted for this difficult assignment. Endowed with more natural talent than the generality of Turkish diplomats, he was regarded as an able negotiator by European observers, though in moments of crisis his stubborn Turkish pride often caused a scene, which the other diplomats took to be an unavoidable indication of his admittedly barbarian nature.[91] His assistant, as might have been expected, was to be the Grand Dragoman Alexander Mavrokordatos, who was now at the very height of his career. His talent for negotiation would serve him in better stead on this occasion than it had in the years of alternate confinement and negotiation in Austria. The Turks reiterated their acceptance of *Uti possidetis* and their demands for the demolitions and withdrawals of Imperial troops, but these were uttered in a far less militant tone. The whole adventure, and adventure it certainly was, was placed under the care of the Mediation of His Britannic Majesty and Their High Mightinesses.[92]

After another wearisome journey the small army of diplomats and their retinues camped before Belgrade on August 12, 1698, and waited for a decision to be made on the site of the Congress meetings. The Austrians had at first proposed Vienna (there were traditional grounds for this, since two previous Austro-Turkish treaties had been concluded there), and if this proved unacceptable, and the fiasco of 1689 made this very likely, Debrecen. The Turks, for their part, showed little desire to negotiate on enemy soil, and they held out for the even more customary practice of negotiating on the front line. This simplified matters of protocol, and if the negotiations failed the armies encamped nearby could then seek a solution of a different order without delay. Turkish pride could not hear of Szlankamen, but they declared that they were agreeable to any location in the area in the immediate vicinity of Petervárad and Putak that the Mediators would designate. The area in question had the added advantage of being in the no man's land between the Austrian and the Turkish lines. The final choice was the Mediators', and it was an eminently unfortunate one. Carlowitz could boast of little more than a decaying monastery, a set of ruins which these men would not possibly find to their taste, and a complement of migratory Serbian peasants. The terrain was marshy and desolate; it would be muddy in September and icy in December, and in addition to these merits the locale rejoiced in bandits who would not be overawed for a moment by the rank of the visitors or the presence of the escorting contingents of Austrian and Turkish troops.[93]

The sole obstacle to the meeting was the reluctance of Poland to participate. Tsar Peter had had a meeting at Cracow with Poland's newly crowned King Augustus of Saxony on his trip home, and while the two monarchs were primarily concerned with their future plans for the Baltic area, they took up the question of the Turkish peace offer. Augustus was, if anything, more opposed to the settlement which had been offered to the Holy League than the Tsar had been. Poland's contribution to the common cause had not been an impressive one in the years after Sobieski's aid in raising the siege of Vienna, but the new King, who had thoroughly enjoyed his role as an Imperial field marshal in the recent campaigns, wished to cast new glory upon himself and the Republic by redoubling Polish efforts on the Eastern front. His view was not shared by the majority of Polish leaders. The French party in the years when Louis XIV had hoped that Poland would conclude a separate peace treaty with the Turks and thus to add to the Emperor's difficulties, that even when the situation was reversed it could not find it in its heart to enthuse for the crusade.

The recently-converted Augustus turned to the patron and guarantor of the Holy League, Pope Innocent XII, and begged him to support Poland's position at the Court of Vienna. This was to be the one occasion on which the role of the Pope was mentioned in these negotiations. Since the much lamented passing of Innocent XI, papal influence and contributions had declined, and there was little of practical value that Augustus could expect to receive from such an appeal. His graphic picture of the injustice being done to Poland was calculated to elicit a paternal response from the Supreme Pontiff: "some were rejoicing; others (i.e. the Poles) were weeping," but it would have little effect on the Emperor, to whom a similar appeal had been sent on August 21.[94] Polish dissatisfaction with the action taken by the Emperor in violating the terms of the Holy League in fact if not in principle was keen enough, but Polish complaints could not possibly halt the negotiations at this point. Leopold was sincerely distressed at the Polish reaction to his declaration, but his reasons for negotiating were so important that he had to run the risk of a deterioration of his relations with Poland. He had, it is true, the excuse that he had kept the Poles informed, and they had a brief respite in which to make additional gains before the treaty was formally concluded. Moreover, the Polish plenipotentiary to the Congress was at perfect liberty to require specific concessions from the Turks which did not fall under the head of *Uti possidetis*.

Growing diplomatic tension in Northern Europe distracted the King of Poland's attention just at this time: he and the Elector of Brandenburg Frederick III were involved in a lively dispute over the fate of Elbing. And so, still complaining to his Allies of the shabby treatment he had received, Augustus despatched the Palatine of Poznan, Stanislaus Malachowski, to the Congress. It was a most uncongenial prospect that this Polish envoy faced; he had to walk the narrow line between the refusal to accept the basic principle and the mediation of England and Holland and abstention from the deliberation of the Congress. He soon found himself making use of both the *Uti possidetis* and the Mediation without for a time admitting that he was doing so. This ready-made dilemma was only further complicated by his embarrassment at the shabbiness of his party; it produced a diplomatic inferiority complex that forced him to compensate by creating *contretemps* over minor matters of protocol.[95]

In the course of that summer the Emperor had been engaged in the worrisome business of picking his own representatives for the Congress. Most of the likely candidates would have been willing to travel as far as Buda of Debrecen, but, when it became increasingly clear that they might be required to spend an unspecified period of time in a "pestiferous place" on the Danube, the honor held no further attraction for them, and one by one they politely declined. Count Kaunitz had been one of this group. He had distinguished himself at the Congress of Rijswijk, and it was only because of poor health that he missed the unusual opportunity of figuring in the history of the earlier Congress' Eastern European pendant -- the Congress of Carlowitz.[96]

Almost on the eve of he appointed time for the departure of the Imperial representatives, Leopold secured the acceptance of this mission by his President of the Imperial Aulic Council, Count Wolfgang von Ottingen-Walderstein. This was a man of seventy-one years who had spent his whole adult life in the Imperial service and was yet in spite of it a "perfect original." Incurably rustic in his manner and eccentric in his views, his single-minded devotion to his judicial responsibilities had limited his intellectual horizons and had certainly not prepared him for negotiation at Carlowitz, though he customarily attended the more important ministerial conferences which had to do with the Turkish war.[97] His rank and status added éclat to the delegation, but the burden of the diplomatic tourney would have to be borne by others. Count Leopold von Schlick was chosen with that in mind. He was young and ambitious, his connection with Kinsky was very close, and his military career was an additional point in his favor, for the discussions would revolve for the most part about the minutia of the demolition or evacuation of military installations along the proposed frontier. Schlick's education was broader than most, and his Italian was to be particularly useful, since the bulk of the conferences would be concluded in that language.[98]

No affair of this kind would, of course, have been complete without the presence of that gentleman adventurer and walking encyclopedia Count Marsigli, and he was duly appointed to serve as an assistant to the Imperial Ambassadors, particularly as a consulting engineer and cartographer, an appointment which qualifies him for the honor of being one of the first experts called in to assist the puzzled diplomats in the long history of European peace conferences. But his activities would not be confined to a demonstration of his detailed knowledge of the frontier zone which found enduring and aesthetically pleasing expression in the map of Hungary, Transylvania, Croatia and Slavonia which he prepared for the Congress.[99] For he made himself quite as useful in the deliberations of the Imperial delegation on the day-to-day policies, and, in addition, the Ambassadors were happy to make use of his influence with Count Kinsky. Both Schlick and Marsigli carried on private correspondences with Kinsky in the course of the negotiations which are precious sources for the inner history of the Congress at Carlowitz.

With the naming of the Imperial plenipotentiaries and their assistants, everything seemed ready at last for the actual encounters, though there was the usual under-current of complaint in Turkish circles about the delaying tactics of the Austrians and their Allies, and fears were expressed by the Mediators that the Grand Vizir would not remain in office much longer. One slight storm of another sort did appear on the horizon, and for a brief moment it seriously disturbed the now serene course of preparations for the Congress.

Hector Marquis de Villars, Louis XIV's Ambassador to the Court of Vienna since the conclusion of the Treaty of Rijswijk, made one last minute attempt to delay the meetings by offering the mediation of the Most Christian King to the Emperor. This would have certainly made for an embarrassment of riches as far as mediation was concerned, but the French offer struck Kinsky as being very suspect indeed, for Villars had bolstered his proposal with the assurance that the Turks were particularly anxious to have the mediation of France. Kinsky sent off a query on this point to Lord Paget, who inured as he was to French intrigues, was not seriously alarmed. After some cursory investigation of the problem, he reported at the end of August that the story of Turkish interest in French mediation was pure fabrication. It was true that the Marquis de Châteauneuf had approached Hussein Pasha shortly after the latter had been made Grand Vizir with the suggestion that the King of France might assist the Turks in arriving at a peace treat with the Austrians. In Köprülü's reply there was evidence enough of his dissatisfaction with the recent desertion of France and more particularly his annoyance at the constant maneuvering of Châteauneuf. "You are so recently reconciled with the Emperor that you would do well to strengthen your position there before you offer your good services to others." He reminded the French Ambassador that the Mediators had been working toward the conclusion of such a peace for many years, and if the Porte did decide to make peace it would call upon the Mediation of the Maritime Powers. French intervention at this point had the added disadvantage of being unacceptable to the Emperor; the Turks had no doubts about that.[100]

Châteauneuf happened to be at Belgrade when the affair of French mediation came to a head, and his presence only occasioned further alarm in the minds of the uninitiated observers, but the French maneuver was effectively foiled by Paget and Kinsky just in time. Defeated on that score, Châteauneuf now suggested to the Turks that they would do well to delay until the death of the King of Spain, whose departure from this life was expected momentarily. For then the war in the West would be certain to break out again almost immediately, and the Turks would be able to secure better conditions than those they were likely to accept at this time.[101] But since neither the Grand Vizir nor the Emperor showed any interest in further delay of what they took to be the inevitable treaty of peace, the Congress was permitted to get down to business.

[1]Colyer reported on "de fransche tentatives om met de Porta eene defensive en offensive alliancie te sluyten, onder het Duytache Rijck geen vreede soude maecken voor ende sler de Ottomanische Porta volkomen satisfaotie hadde becommen.", Letter to Griffier, January 31, 1689, quoted in *Hora Siccama*, 74.

[2]*Ibid.*, 75-78.

[3]*Ibid.*

[4]*Ibid.*, 79-80; "...nademae, Sijne Keyserl. Maj'. door voorslagen van schandeleuse en onaennemelijcke condition de onderhandelinge tot een Vreede off Treves heef believen affesnijden, den Grooten Heer gresolveert was alle doenlijcke machten te samen te rucken, om sijn vijaden tot reden te brengen.", Letter of Coyer to Their High Mightinesses, May 3, 1690, quoted by *Hora Siccama*. 81.

[5]"Den 9[en] Mei wa hij daar terug. Nu restte hem niets meer dan den afloop af te wachten van den veldtochte, waartoe de Porte besloten was, en die ook door eene ter elfder ure aangeboden bemiddeling van konig Willem III niet kon worden verhinderd.", *Hora Siccama*, 81-82.

[6]Daniel de Hochepied, the Dutch Consul at Smyrna, reported that Sir William Trumbull had received an instruction from William III to offer his Mediation to the Porte so that peace might be speedily concluded between the Turks and the Holy League; *ibid.*, 82n.

[7]"But as to your proposal for our petitioning his Majesty to give you order to be assistant in bringing a peace to a conclusion, it being a matter of State, and not relating to trade ... we do not think it convenient for us to proceed to partitioning unless some intimation be given from us above so to do ... ", Levant Company to Sir William Trumball, Oct. 13, 1688., *Downshire MSS* (Hist. MSS. Comm.-1924) 1, 302.

[8]Sir William Hussey to Sir William Trumbull, Feb. 1, 1689/90, *ibid.*, 336.

[9]Sir William Trumbull to Lord Paget, Constantinople, May 5/15, 1690, *Add. MSS.* 8880 (British Museum), 199.

[10]Cf. *British Diploamtic Representatives 1689-1789*, 150 (there is to my knowledge no article on Sir William in the *Dictionary of National Biography*).

[11]Lord Paget to Daniel, Earl of Nottingham, Vienna, May 25, 1690, *S.P.F.*, 80, #17, 61.

[12]Paget to Nottingham, Vienna, March 19, 1690/91, *S.P.F.*, 80, #17, 187.

[13]Sir William Hussey to Nottingham, Vienna, Jan. 8, 1690/1, *S.P.F.*, 80, #17, 169.

[14]C. van Heemskerck to the Griffier, February 15, 1691, *W. G.*, 482: "Eyndelijck heef de Gr, van Kinsky niet langer tegen kunnen houden het accepteren *in forma* van de mediatie van den Con. van England ende de Staet. 't is drie a vier maenden geleden, dat desele mij seer bits in d'atichambre van den Keyser seyde: dat S. M. de vrede op sijn manier noch tot geene mediateurs waeren aengenomen, maar alleen geaccepteert voor officiën. Ik antwoorde, *dat officiën ter wederzijde sengenomen, van sijn selve mediatie wierde*...(Italics my own)"; Van Heemskerck to Anthonie Heinius, 1691, in Heim, *Het archief*, 1, 125.

[15]A fairly complete report of the meeting of the Conferenz which drew up these terms is to be found in Van Heemskerck's letter to the Griffier, April 1, 1691, *W.G.*, 484-486.

[16]C. van Heemskerck to the Griffier, July 1, 1691, *W.G.*, 491.; a brief but interesting characterization of Count Marsigli is to be found in a note of Oswald Redlich, *Geschichte Osterreichs* (Huber-Redlich, Bd. 6) (Gotha-1921), 348. There is certainly no more interesting figure in this period, and it is a great misfortune that there is no critical modern biography.

[17]This account of the audience granted by the Grand Vizir to William Hussey must unfortunately rest on the notoriously suspect "Relae der audientie van der heer Engelschen Ambassadeur bij den P^mo Vizier tot Adrianopolen", an enclosure in a letter of Coyler to the Griffier, June 30, 1691, in *Hora Siccama*, 87-88. Suspect because Hora Siccama believes that this relation of the event was written by Marsigli himself. Its value as a source must then remain very much in doubt, but it is to be feared that further research in the archival materials will not produce a more satisfactory version.

[18]C. Van Heemskerck to the Griffier, July 5, 1691, *W.G.*, 491-492.

[19]Thomas Coke to Nottingham, Constantinople, Feb. 18/28, 1691/2, *S.P.F.*, 97, #20, 237.

[20]"Daerby komt een tweede fataliteyt, te waten dat den Grave van Maraigly gequest ende den Turcksen Chiaus, die deseive versiede ende tot afspraek van de praeliminaris in 't leeger van den Prince van Baden is geweest, door de Ratzen doodgeslaegen ende voormelte Marsigly binnen Lippa, om genesen te werden, is gebracht. Men sal 't werck vcvan de vrede daerom wei niet t' eenamael opgeven, dock deese interruptie is seer groot ende nadeligh, ende wie wet, wat deel de Frasche corruptiën daerin niet gehad hebben.", C. van Heemskerck to the Griffier, Octover 25, 1691, *W. G.*, 493.

[21]"The Count (Marsigli) comes hither, but in lieu of procuring that Power, he (with Count Kinski) contrived a way to attempt the business, without the Ambassadors Mediation, or without using his Majesty's or the States offices; it was, to persuade the Port to send Ambassadors to Prince Louis of Baden ... to negotiate the Matter, that occurred (without saying any thing to his Majesty's Ambassador or mee of it) Count Marsigli went from Adrianople, with a Chiaus ... they were encountered by a Party of Rascians. This Accident (and not Sir William's death) has delayed, if not wholly defeated this plot; of which the Emperor had no knowledge nor I (til lately) tho' not from the managers of this secret) ...", Lord Paget to Viscount Sidney, Oct. 25, 1691, N.S., *S.P.F.* 80, #17, 214.

[22]Paget to Sidney, Feb. 14, 1692 N.S., *S.P.F.*, 80, #17, 251.

[23]The section on the sudden reversal of Turkish fortunes and the death of Hussey and Coyler's sickness are based on *Hora Siccama*, 91-94. It is interesting to note that the rumor reached Western Europe that Hussey had died of poisoning; Huygens, for example, in his journal reported that "boision seyde gehoort te hebbien dat den Engelschen Envoye sen de Porta schielijk gestorven was en den onsen oock (this was a false report of Coyler's death), ende dat men meende dat Frans werck was." in his entry for November 7, 1691, quoted by *Hora Siccama*, 92n. However tortuous French policy may have been, it clearly did not have to go to such extremes, since the malignant fever worked quite as well. Disease was to be one of the great allies of France in defeating the efforts of the Anglo-Dutch Mediation.

[24]Letter of Paget to Sidney, October 25, 1691, N.S., *S.P.F.*, 80, #17, 215.

[25]Letter of Coyler to William III, Adrianople, Dec. 14, 1691, in English translation in *S.P.F.*, 97, #20, 242.

[26]C. van Heemskerck to the Griffier, December 30, 1691, *W.G.*, 499.

[27]A brief biography of Mr. William Harbord is to be found in the *Dictionary of National Biography*; cf. also the listing in *British Diplomatic Representatives 1689-1789.*, 151.

[28]A long and rambling report by Coke of his "difference with the Dutch Ambassador" is contained in his letter to Nottingham, Constantinople, August 4, 1692, *S.P.F.*, 97. #20, 252-253.

[29]J. Evans to Sir William Trumbull, Galata, March 3, 1691/2 O.S., *Downshire MSS.* 1, 399.

[30]Letter of Per. Whitcombe to Sir William Trumbull, Galata, March 26, 1692, *ibid.*, 1, 402.

[31]"Mr. Harbord is stopped with his gout and the snow a day's journey on his side Lintz. We have no reason to imagine his negotiations can succeed this season, and if he keeps himself warm I believe that is all that can be required of him.", Matthew Prior to Sir William Trumbull, The Hague, Feb. 19, 1691/2, *ibid.*, 1, 386.

[32]C. van Heemskerck, June 5, 1692, *W.G.*, 511.

[33]*Hora Siccama*, 97-98.

[34]Thomas Coke to Nottingham, Constantinople, Oct. 9/19, 1692, *S.P.F.*, 97, #20, 254.

[35]Letter of the Grand Vizir to William III, August 12, 1692, *Downshire MSS*, 1, 415.

[36]*British Diplomatic Representatives 1689-1789*, 151.

[37]An interesting characterization of Van Heemskerck's mission is included in the summary of the negotiations which Lord Paget sent to Nottingham in his letter of Oct. 13/23, *S.P.F.*, 97, #20, 279-280.

[38]Paget recommended J.J. Hamel Bruynincx in the warmest terms in a letter to the Secretary for the Northern Department, Vienna, Nov. 19, 1692 N.S., *S.P.F.*, 80, #17, 305.

[39]*Hora Siccama*, 103 ff.

[40]Paget to Nottingham, Adrianople, March 9/19, 1693, *S.P.F.*, 97, #20, 261 ff.

[41]The Latin text of the proposals exist in a copy in *S.P.F.*, 97, #20, 269.

[42]Leopold in his instrucktion to Paget of Nov. 6, 4692, had referred to Van Heemskerck's experience as a mnonitory example: "...sed cum merito dubitem, an haec adhbita testinatio calcer ad pacem an stimilos potius innatae ferociae et insolentis superbiae Turcis additura sit, mihi pafcem incliinatos, vel ad esdem adverson, prius espresset, quam nostros praemature patefacis set, praesertim cum meo nomine ea proposuerit, quae cum fundamento Uti possidetis nix sint, vix vilam tractandi materiam reliquunt in congressu, sine quo, ut ipsimet facile perspicietis, nec limites utriusque Imperli, per tractatus pacis ab invicem separandi, rite decide, nec foederatorum causa tractatui... obnoxis discuti;", *S. P. F.*, 91, #20, 269.; Paget to Nottingham, Adrianople, March 9/19, 1693, *ibid.*, 262.

[43]Paget provided Whitehall with an exceedingly detailed account of his audience with the Grand Vizir and the curious meeting at the Grand Vizir's house, see his letter to Nottingham, Adrianople, March 29, 1693 O.S., *S.P.F.*, 97, #20, 271-272.

[44]Paget to Nottingham, Adrianople, August 1, 1693 N.S., *S.P.F.*, 97, #20,275.

[45]Paget to Nottingham, December 15, 1693, *S.P.F.*, 97, #20, 283.

[46]*British Diplomatic Representatives 1689-1789*, 28.

[47]"I am to add my thanks for the good Song you sent me, the rather since I am in a Country where the Mirth and Muses are quite forgott.", Stepney to James Vernon, Vienna, Aug. 2/12, 1693, *S.P.F.*, 80, #17, 330.; his report of an incident in which a footman in the retinue of the Swedish Ambassador refused to kneel

when the sacred host was being carried by is typical:" ... and the Gentry at this bigotted Court make strange superstitious reflexions.", Stepney to James Vernon, Vienna, June 20, 1693, *S.P.F.*, 80, #17, 316.

[48]Stepney to Vernon, Vienna, Sept. 9/19, 1693, *S.P.F.*, 80, #17, 344.

[49]Stepney to Vernon, Vienna, Sept. 8/18, 1693, *S.P.F.*, 80, #17, 352.

[50]Stepney to Vernon, August 5, 1693 N.S., *S.P.F.*, 80, #17, 322.

[51]Stepney to Mr. Blathwayt, Vienna, Aug. 16/26, 1693, *S.P.F.*, 80, #17, 336.

[52]Stepney to Vernon, Vienna, Sept. 12, 1693, *S.P.F.*, 80, #17, 343; Stepney to Mr. Blathwayt, Vienna, Sept. 8/18, 1693, *S.P.F.*, 80, #17, 353.

[53]Van Heemskerck's desire to negotiate with the Turks survived his enforced stay in Turkey. On one occasion he told the Caimacam of Adrianople that "whenever he pleased, (he was ready) to conclude a Peace in four and twenty houers." The Turkish official in reporting this offer to Paget had been much amused; he felt that the time specified was far too brief for "so much work"., Paget to Nottingham, Constantinople, Oct. 13/23, 1693, *S.P.F.*, 80, #17, 281.; *Hora Siccama*, 102-17 *passim.*, is the basis for the discussion of the Dutch envoy's plight.

[54]*Ibid.*, 108.

[55]"...dat de voorslangen tot vrede gehoort ende daerop gedlibereer sijnde, deselve niet acceptabel ende overeekomende met het respect ende hoogheyt van de Porte gevonden werden, sonder zich wijder te expliceren...in der Constantinople, March 1694, quoted in *ibid.*, 113.

[56]*Ibid.*, 114-116; C. van Heemskerck to the Raadpensionaris, December 18, 1694, *W.G.*, 579-580.

[57]For the Van Heemskerck affair as a "represaille", cf. *Hora Siccama*, 117.; "... and (as I formerly supposed) will keep him in ignorance; and have him in reserve in case of necessity.", Stepeney to Mr. Blathwayt, Vienna, Aug. 2/12,

1693, *S.P.F.*, 80, #17, 329.

[58]*Ibid.*

[59]*Ibid.*

[60]"I had reason from severall circumstances to hope it would be favourable, when Sunday the 27th instant, I had notice that the Grand Signior was dead.", Paget to Sir John Trenchard, Adrianople, January 29, 1695 N.S., *S.P.F.*, 97, #20, 285.

[61]"... this Empire wants men, mony, and able Officers, and it is not in a condition to carry on a War vigorously, tho' the Emperor will not hear of Peace; I have seen so many hopefull likely opportunitites to make it, miscarried, that I am persuaded, 'tis not now to be obtained, and I humbly entreat His Majesties leave to return home, since my endeavours to serve him heer have not succeeded to my desire; I don't think any other business can make my stay desirable.", Lord Paget to Charles, Duke of Shrewsbury, Adrianople, July 25, 1695, *S.P.F.*, 97, #20, 305.

[62]Letter of Coyler to the Griffier, Adrianople, April 11, 1695, quoted extensively in *Hora Siccama*, 121.

[63]*Ibid.*, 122 ff.

[64]For a full account of the preliminary negotiations leading to the Congress of Rijswijk and an account of Congress deliberations, see Heinrich Ritter von Srbik, *Wien und Versailles 1692-1697: Zur Geschichte von Strassburg, Elsass und Lothringen* (Munchen-1944), particularlry pp. 192-316.

[65]*Ibid.*

[66]Lord Paget to Lord Lexington at Vienna, Adrianople, December 29, 1697, *S.P.F.*, 97, #20, 391.

[67]Coyler to Gysbert Cuper, Pera, December 27, 1697, published in M. Bosscha ....; "Enfin den Lord Paget soeckt, terwijl ick stil moet sitten, in troebel water te visschen, omme natie (in de Levant resideerende) te bedingen.", Letter of Coyler to Cuper, Pera, Feb. 28, 1698, published in Bosscha, 76.

[68]The following description of the preliminary meetings between Paget and the Turks is based on the detailed account which Paget sent to the Duke of Shrewsbury, Adrianople, Jan. 23, 1697/8 O.S., *S.P.F*, 97, #21, 4-13.

[69]Lord Lexington to Mr. Ellis, Vienna, August 27, 1697, *Ellis Papers*, Add. MSS. (British Museum) 28899, 424.

[70]Paget to Shrewsbury, Jan., 23, 1697/8, *S.P.F.*, 97, #21, 6-7.

[71]*Ibid.*, 7.

[72]"Paget, welcher seine Hofe die Ehre der Vermittelung um füngsigtausend Thaler erkauff hatte, und darauf um so mehr rechnete, als der französische Bothschaffer, nicht so viel biethen durfte...", Hammer-Purgstall, *op. cit.*, VI, 648-649. No source is cited for this transaction, and I was moved to investigate the matter further. A manuscript of Hammer's study *Die Geschichte der diplomatischen verhältnisse österreichs mit der hohen Pforte vom Beginn des XVI bis zum Ende des XVIII jahrhuderts* is preserved in the collection *Turkel* of the *Haus-, Hof- und Stattsarchiv*, Vienna. The section relating to this problem is even more puzzling: "england und Frankriech stritten sich und der Pforte um die Eher Vermittlungi/i, und der englische Bofschaffer Lord Paget erkauffe dieseibe mit 500.000 Thalern beym Ministerium der Pforte...", II, 432. This is even more unbelievable, and it is at this point that the mystery of Hammer's suggestion that Paget bribed the Turks so that England might hve the honor of the Mediation must stand. No mention of this situation is to found in *State Papers Foreign, Turkey*.

[73]The Latin translation of the Grand Vizir's letter to King William III, Adrianople, March 6, 1697/9 is in *S.P.F.*, 97, #21, 10-11.

[74]Paget to Schrewsbury, *vide supra*.

[75]J. Hop to Griffier, Vienna, January 13, 1698, *W.G.*, 11, 17.

[76]"Nicht ohne Grund wurde Kinsky bezichtigt, er neige dem Frieden mit Frankrich, sei es auch auf Kosten des politischen deutschen Gesamtkörpers, zu un er verschleppe die Beendigung des Turkenkrieges, um dem Raumgewinn Habsburgs im Osten in dem Katholischen Kreuzzug gegen den Mohammedanismus die Bahn offen zu halte.", Srbik, *Wien und Versailles*, 34.

[77]Paget to Shrewsbury, *S.P.F.*, 97, #21, 17.

[78]R. Sutton to James Vernon, Vienna, Feb. 5, 1698, *S.P.F.*, 80, #17, 423.

[79]The text of Russia's treaty of alliance with the Emperor is in Hurmuzaki, *Documente*, V/1, 478-479.

[80]"... I already discover, that this Court has a greater inclination to a Peace with the Turk, then I could imagine, and that t*hey would be glad to have their hands free to deal with France* upon another occasion, they lying yet under great apprehension from her (italics my own).", Sutton to James Vernon, Feb. 8, 1698, S.P.F., 80, #17, 424.

[81]James Vernon to Paget, London, August 16, 1698, *S.P.F.*, 97, #21, 29.

[82]"...onde si stabili di formar un Instrumento solenne di Freliminare, firmato sotto li 23 Giugno 98 con espresse Plenipotenze dal Chinschi per Cesare; da me per v^{ra}. Ser^{fa}.;" Vienna di Sr. Carlo Ruzini, Venice, Dec. 19, 1699, *Die Relationen der Botschaffer Vendigs*, hrsg. Joseph Fiedler 9(FRA, II, 27) (Wien-1867), II, 351.

[83]Paget to James Vernon, Adrianople, May 9, 1698, *S.P.F.*, 97, #21, 17.

[84]*Hora Siccama*, 130-131.

[85]The protocol of the meeting of the Tsar and Count Kinsky is in Hurmuzaki, *Documente*, V/1, 487-490.

[86]Hammer-Purgstall, *op. cit.*, VI, 655-656.

[87]*Hora Siccama*, 142.

[88]*Ibid.*, 144n.

[89]*Ibid.*, 144-145.

[90]Cf. Ruzzini's characterization in his *Relazione, loc. cit.*, 376.

[91]"...omme d'onderhandelinge tot een Vreede op het Congres in qualiteyt als Ext^s. Ambassadeurs ende Plenipotentiarissen van 't Ottomannische Rijk, op den

voet van "Uti possidetis" niet slleen voort te setten, maer ook te sluyten ende teykenen, mitsgaders alle andere differenten van overgift, wisselen ende demolitien van plaetsen, onder de mediatie van hoochstgedachte Sijn Majesteyt van Groot-Brittanien ende Haer Hoog. Mog. te vereffenen."; Colyer to the Griffier from the Turkish Camp before Belgrade, August 13, 1698, quoted in *Hora Siccama*, 145.

[92]Hammer-Purgstall, *op. cit.*, VI, 656.

[93]The negotiation of the Imperial ministry and the Polish Minister and the letters of Augustus II to Leopold and Pope Innocent XII are in Hurmuzaki, *Documente*, V/I, 502-509.

[94]Cf. Ruzzini to the Palatine in his *Relazione, loc. cit.*, 378.

[95]J. Hop to William III, Vienna, Sept. 13, 1698, *W.G.*, II, 6.

[96]"Count Ottingen is a perfect original; so singular he is in all his ways and actions. No man understands justice better or practices it so uncorruptly, but he is so unhewn in his manner and behaviour, and rigid in his principles that Cato and Timon of Athens were good-natured in comparison with him. His righteousness gives him great liberty in commending himself and making severe reflections upon others, and (he) has a wife of impertinent virtue. He is ever oppreating the Emperor with his honesty and the very knavery of his neighbors. I have near a hundred histories of his adventures, which might be good entertainment in discourse, but they are too tedious to be committed to writing. He keeps close to his charge, which he executes with great dilligence, and is capable of being anything but a dissembler and a courtier.", Stepney to Sir John Trenchard, Vienna, Oct. 20, 1693, *Bath MSS.*, II, 13

[97]Ruzzini, *loc. cit.*, II, 377.

[98]The *Kriegsarchiv* in Vienna has an impressive collection of maps prepared by Count Marsigli for the use of the Congress and his own work in the Boundary Commission that was established by the treaty between the Emperor and the Turks, cf. under file B IX C, numbers 99-1, 743, 829, 830, 832.

[99]"Votre Excellence (Count Kinsky) me mande de m'informer sur ce que le M. de Villars a Prone de la Volonte de cette cour a vouloir introduire la Mediation de Sa Majeste Tres Chretienne pour conduire le present Traite, et je puis de

[99]"Votre Excellence (Count Kinsky) me mande de m'informer sur ce que le M. de Villars a Prone de la Volonte de cette cour a vouloir introduire la Mediation de Sa Majeste Tres Chretienne pour conduire le present Traite, et je puis de science certaine l'assurer que c'est un conte, in verite, et sans fondement; il est vrai que, tot apres que le present Grand Vizir fut eleve a cette Dignite, l'Amb[f]. de France lui proposa l'entremise du Roi T. C., pour pourchaser la Paix a Vienne; a quoi, le G. Vizir repondit, Vous ete des nouveaux reconciglies qui devrais lacher d'affermir vos interet la, avant d'offrir Vos Offices a d'autres, quand on veut traiter la Paix, nous avons icy des Ambassadeurs Mediateurs de Sa M. Britannique et des Etats des Pais Bas, Qui sont approuves des Deux Parties, qui ont longtems travaille avec application pour y unir about, c'est leur Meditation que nous employeriouns, la votre n'etant, peut etre, pas fort agreable...", Paget to Kinsky, Sept .4, 1698, *Turcica (Haus-, Hof- und Staatsarchiv*, Vienna), I, 166, 60.

[100]*Ibid.*

[101]*Ibid.*

Chaper 4

The Congress at Carlowitz

"I hope in a little time we shall have a Peace, for we are here no longer able to carry on the war."

Lord Lexington

The significance of the Congress at Carlowitz was out of all proportion to its obscure location and to its checkered origins.[1] For the historians of a later day there would always be something momentous about it. They would undertake the congenial task of cataloguing its important results and of enumerating the 'firsts' in Europe's diplomatic history which occurred there. It was certainly the beginning of a new chapter in the history of the relations of the Ottoman Empire with the European powers. Peace at the conclusion of a war with Turkey was no longer in the free gift of the Sultan; it was arrived at by the negotiation of equals with all the attendant conveniences and inconveniences of standard European diplomatic practice. Turkey had, for the first time, initiated the peace talks at Vienna and Carlowitz, and the traditional reliance on the *Uti possidetis* clause was slowly giving way to a more sophisticated interest in the *fractione panis* which even that summary principle involved. The presence of an Anglo-Dutch Mediation lent further novelty and importance to the proceedings. For observers with the gift of historical hindsight, the essence of the work of the Congress was its formal recognition of Turkish decline: the high water mark of Turkish expansion in Europe had been reached at the beginning of the war; the conclusion of the hostilities made it clear that continual contraction of the Ottoman Empire in Europe was to be regarded as a matter of course. It was at the Congress house at Carlowitz that

Turkey made its first appearance in the uncongenial role of the "Sick man of Europe"; students of the ensuing period of the patient's history would be content to chart the course and the ravages of the disease.[2]

But the Congress was something quite different to its participants, who alternately suffered from the inclemency of the weather and rejoiced in the pageantry, and something quite different to their principals, who followed the proceedings, now with satisfaction, now with unconcealed displeasure. The acquired taste for the momentousness and novelty of the proceedings was missing, and this was not simply due to the tendency of people deeply involved in an historical event to miss some of the larger implications of their activity. Close as they were to it, they could not fail to see how ramshackle much of the settlement was and to what degree it bore the marks of hasty improvisation in the face of Congress crises. For their minds were troubled by the prospect of an almost immediate resumption of hostilities in the West that would almost automatically entail a renewal of war in this area. The novelty of the Congress was lost on most of the participants, for they had been connected with its prehistory for so many years that the unusual had simply become the habitual. The tired, sickly Kinsky reverted to the alternating currents of hope and pessimism as he had done ten years before; the Mediators had been too often cheated of their prize, and they could not be certain that it awaited them in the desolation of Sirmium; and Mavrokordatos, threading his way as usual through the labyrinth of Turkish politics, knew better than anyone else how a sudden change of favorites in Adrianople, any increase of influence for the Mufti and the War party surrounding him, could suddenly relieve him of the frightening responsibility of securing from four enemy strikes a peace with a modicum of honor.

As for the "Sick man," if he was somewhat the worse for the wear of sixteen campaigns, he was surprisingly jaunty for someone believed to be in an invalid state; he continued to give very definite signs of life. Turkish defeat was not regarded by either side as final, and the increased involvement of the members of the Holy League in the pressing concerns of Western and Northern Europe made it highly probable that the Sultan would be able in the near future to make a powerful bid for the recapture of the territories he was about to cede formally in the treaties of peace. The *Uti possidetis* could only underline the ephemeral character of any agreement reached here, and it was the result of developments quite unforeseen by the diplomats of Carlowitz that their improvisation was transformed, as far as the Ottoman and Habsburg empires were concerned, into the fairly permanent settlement that it became.

The actual work of the Congress, since it was so largely concerned with the details of demolitions and evacuations, was extremely complicated, but the major events and achievements fall quite simply (and this is true chronologically as well) into four recognizable parts. There was the painful preliminaries which had to do with differences over protocol to which were added the inclemencies of the weather and certain obscurities in the relations of the members of the Holy League and the Mediators. The second period followed upon the solution of these difficulties: in a brief span of time agreement was achieved by the Emperor's representatives and the Turks on the main contested points in their treaty. Once the ranking member of the League had been satisfied, there was another brief period in which the initially reluctant plenipotentiaries of the Tsar and the King of Poland were suddenly transformed into most devoted partisans of quick and decisive negotiation -- a miraculous transformation which scored a great success in terms of the treaty and armistice which were concluded with the Turks. The last two months of the Congress were taken up with the obscure position of Venice. The readiness of Carlo Ruzzini to agree with Kinsky on the framing of the joint declaration in June was now replaced by a series of prolix delaying tactics which alienated friend and foe alike. It seemed on a number of occasions that the whole existence of the Congress was in jeopardy, and the compromise which finally brought the ponderous discussions to their festive conclusion was as much the work of the

Imperial Ambassadors, gravely concerned at the thought of a failure to achieve a peace settlement, as it was that of the Mediators.

* * * *

Futak, a small settlement across the Danube from Petervárad, had been designed by the representatives chosen for the Congress by the Holy League as the place of rendezvous. There they would await the promulgation of the necessary armistice for the immediate area of the Congress deliberations and the preparation of the actual site itself for the distinguished visitors. Ruzzini was the first to arrive at the rendezvous on October 13; two days later his Austrian and Russian colleagues made their appearance. Prokop Bogdanovich Voznitsin, a Knight of St. George, was very much of a puzzle to the Westerners, and Peter's representative made little effort to dispel the mystery, for after a brief stay at Putak, he moved to Petervárad, a place of more considerable size and comfort, in open defiance of the agreement to wait at Futak. The Polish delegate, the Palatine of Poznan, appeared at even this early stage to be engaged in a competition with the Russian, and he, too, hurried on from Futak to Petervárad without stopping to exchange the accustomed ceremonial visits. Indeed, it was not until October 18, that the two men condescended to send official notification to the Ambassadors at Futak that they had arrived.[3]

The armistice for the Congress area had by now been proclaimed at Belgrade (for the Turkish side) and at Petervárad (for the Imperial forces). Contact between Futak and the Mediators, who were travelling with the Turkish party, was lively at this point, and Austrian engineers had been despatched to Carlowitz to survey the area for a likely place of encampment. As the Turks were already quite close to their destination, the Mediators, fearing that further delays on the other side might be misunderstood, urged representatives of the Holy League to speed up their progress to the Congress site.[4] The engineers returned to Futak with the report that a likely site had been chosen, and markers had been left to denote the proposed place for the Austrian tents. The apparently innocent placing of the markers was the cause of the first display of Slavic temperament. The Russian Ambassador was overly anxious to occupy the place of honor on the right of the Austrian tents, and he managed to establish his party there before the Poles and the Venetians arrived on the scene. The report that Voznitsin had occupied the site which the Pole, Malachowski, had chosen to be his -- one of his servants who had been guarding this prize had been rudely ejected by the Russians -- led to his refusing to leave his boat until satisfaction had been made.[5]

The Imperial Ambassadors arrived on the next day with an impressive military escort and to the accompaniment of salvos from the forts which they had passed in their progress along the riverbank. They were immediately confronted with the dispute over the positions of the various parties. The Mediation provided them with a solution in proposing a change of location for the Allied encampment, and this alteration in plans made it possible for the Imperial Ambassadors to square the diplomatic circle by arranging for a rectangular camping area at the new site. They were of the opinion that the mere choice of such a geometrical form would eliminate any further difficulties over precedence. But they were mistaken: the new arrangement could not possibly remove every source of conflict. While the Austrian, Venetian, and Russian parties were establishing themselves at the new site, the servants of the Polish envoy, arriving somewhat later than the others, perhaps inadvertently proceeded to set up their main tent a mere fifty feet in front of that of the Cavaliere Ruzzini. Marsigli was then despatched to the Polish envoy with the request that the Poles remove to themselves to the side of the square reserved for them. The Venetian Ambassador was not slow to produce a variety of protests, and Voznitsin now offered his Venetian Colleague the support of his retainers in the very likely event that the Polish and Venetian parties came to blows. His was only a prelude to more intensified negotiation, and appeals were presented to the Polish envoy from all sides, urging him to occupy the place reserved for him; this common front strengthened the corporate spirit of the Allies and prevented another "Scandalo." The Palatine realized that he must concede the point, but he continued for a time, for appearances sake at least, to be reluctant to move.[6]

It was at this point that the Mediators made their first appearance *in corpore*, and such was the display that attention was diverted for a time from the vagaries of the Russians and the Poles. Milord Paget's appearance struck his Imperial hosts as odd: his European hat and wig seemed incongruous in combination with his Turkish clothes, and the great mustache which he now sported did even more to change his appearance.[7] His change of costume may have been due to a well-meaning effort to reproduce his function as a mediator in his mixed dress, but it was more probable that he was considering his own comfort and making, in addition, a slight concession to the customs of the country to which he was accredited. This adoption of Turkish customs was even more apparent at the Mediators' camp. When the Austrians returned the visit, they discovered that the quarters of Paget and Coyler were far more luxurious than their own, and they were treated to the standard Turkish fare of coffee, sherbet, and rose water.[8]

The appearance of the Mediators made actual the question of their role in the forthcoming discussions, and on the very next day, October 28, a tentative beginning was made of Congress business. The Mediation urged that the Allied powers accept their role and agree on the fundamental principle; the Turks, it was explained, were to make their formal ratification the next day. All but Voznitsin found themselves able to respond to this invitation. The Russian replied that as far as the Mediation was concerned he could not accept it, because, as he put it, "the Mediators had not adopted him as a son, and he had not adopted them as parents."[9] But his refusal to cooperate was short-lived, and if he did not bring himself to recognize the work of the Mediation, he managed on the next morning to transmit to the Imperial ambassadors his *pleinpouvoir* to treat with the Turks. This was the last, if somewhat partial, acceptance of the system of negotiation which was to be followed at the Congress.[10] The Mediators were to be by common agreement at the very center of Congress activities; their good offices were often to exceed the limits prescribed by the nascent diplomatic practice, but objections to this practice, when they did appear, were concerned not so much with the nature of their contribution as with its failure in specific instances to satisfy the parties concerned. On November 1, after prolonged discussion with the Imperial Ambassadors who were now required to be something of mediators in the Allied camp, the Polish party finally moved to the spot which had been originally reserved for its use.[11]

It had been a trying period, this period of acclimatization for as if by the working out of a physical law, the first contacts of so many delegations had resulted in minor explosions, but these had had the merit of clearing the diplomatic atmosphere, and all the participants could feel happier now that their positions in these disputes, explained at tiresome length to their governments and to the other parties, had been vindicated in one way or another. Only the poor Palatine had been forced to make serious concessions, but he had done this with good grace at last, and the notoriety he created for himself in those early weeks at Carlowitz must have consoled him for his shabby equipage and the anomalous role he was required to play in Congress deliberations.

The exchange of papers could now begin in earnest, and the propositions which had been prepared by the Allied diplomats on the basis of their instructions and their informal discussions with the Mediators were now formally submitted to Lord Paget and Mijnheer Coyler. The Mediators decided that it would be wiser on this occasion not to submit them immediately to the Turks, but to allow their contents to be revealed more naturally when the actual discussions commenced. A practical difficulty rose in the matter of the building which was to house these meetings. Erected as the joint product of Austrian and Turkish labor and materials, its progress in construction was so slow that for the first month of the talks tents had to be used.[12]

Diplomatic storms had now been followed by inclement weather. On the afternoon of November 8, a storm of hurricane proportions hit the three camps, destroying a large number of the tents and making conditions so uncomfortable that the Russian and Polish envoys seriously considered retiring to the relative comfort of commandeered houses at Petervárad.[13] This was the first hint that the unfortunate choice of the Congress site might be responsible for slowing down and even halting negotiations completely. Communication between the camps was tenuous enough and had been established only after prolonged negotiation; the Turks were in no mood to acquiesce in changes at this late date, since they customarily regarded them as indications that their enemies only wished to "amuse" them and had no intention of concluding peace.

In the course of the visit which Voznitsin had made to Öttingen and Schlick the day after the storm, he had protested strongly against Mediation, and had announced his intention of carrying on his whole negotiation without any further interference from that source. For this purpose he required a pass from the Imperial Ambassadors so that he might communicate directly with the Turks. The Austrians attempted to reason with him but with little success, and they were forced to consult Vienna for further instructions. That very evening another storm struck the camps, and their condition on the following morning was really a most pitiable one. The Russians and the Poles, far less well-equipped than the other parties, withdrew for a time to Petervárad.[14] The Imperial Ambassadors could only feel that their luck was suddenly changing, when on the very day after the second storm they met with the Turkish party for the first time. The ceremonial of the first encounter had been meticulously prepared beforehand; the tempi of the arrivals and withdrawals were minutely coordinated. The strain involved was, however, for once sufficient to make it seem advisable in view of the long hours of discussion to reduce ceremony to a bare minimum.[15]

Even before these first meetings of the Imperial and Turkish Ambassadors took place the major obstacle to the conclusion of their peace treaty had been removed. The Turkish proposals which had been handed to the Mediators in October had listed the return of Transylvania to its *status quo* as one of the most pressing Turkish demands. The Mediators had once more made it clear to the Turks that such a requirement was contrary to the fundamental principle and had absolutely no chance of winning Imperial agreement; when it was formally communicated to Öttingen and Schlick, the expectations of the Mediators were confirmed by a summary refusal on the part of the Austrians.[16] But the Turks were not to be put off by this refusal, and they returned the suggestion that the Emperor might have Transylvania on the condition that the annual tribute traditionally paid by that Principality to the Sultan henceforth would be presented as a gift. The Reis-Effendi and Mavrokordatos, moved virtually to tears by the gravity of their own responsibility, pleaded with the Mediators to prevail upon the Austrians to make some kind of face-saving concession to Turkish pride which they might take back with them as a proof of their powers as negotiators to the Sultan and the Grand Vizir. Moreover, any concessions at this time would 'ensure' perpetual friendship between the two Empires.

This was a theme which had figured prominently in the talks in 1689, but it had as little chance for evoking a favorable Austrian response at Carlowitz as it had in Vienna in 1689. Count Schlick was of the opinion that at this decisive stage in the negotiations no concessions should be made to the Turks: any show of compromise would be interpreted by the Turks as a show of weakness and they would be encouraged to become more extravagant in their other demands.[17] So their second and more moderate proposal on Transylvania was flatly refused as well, but not before the Mediators, whose credit with the Turks had suffered somewhat in the course of these preliminary interchanges because of the failure to secure any concessions from the Imperial Ambassadors, were given a delay of twenty four hours by the Austrians, so that the impression might be created in the Turkish camp that the Mediators had argued long and violently in support of the second Turkish proposal.[18]

Repulsed on two occasions by the Ambassador, the Turks now decided to make a direct appeal to the Imperial ministers in Vienna. Paget and Coyler were approached with the request that they transmit to Count Kinsky (a singularly unfortunate choice) a last minute Turkish appeal for something in the way of a concession. The Mediation now found itself in a quandary. It seemed to them that the crucial point of the whole Peace Congress had been reached, and this before the actual discussions had begun. Their good offices as Mediators were threatened at the very outset by the unrelenting position of the Austrians and the understandable refusal of the Turks to return to Adrianople empty-handed. For a brief time, they seriously considered allowing the Turks to go over the heads of the Imperial delegates and communicate directly with Kinsky. But they realized almost immediately that such an extraordinary understanding was condemned to failure from the start -- their knowledge of Kinsky could suggest no other outcome -- and such a departure from the normal course of negotiation would only weaken the prestige of Öttingen and Schlick in subsequent talks with the Turks. The Mediation's refusal to cooperate in this matter was communicated to the Turks, who, once they had been required to abandon all pretensions to a tie with Transylvania, accepted the inevitable with what grace they could manage.[19] Schlick's policy of steadfast adhesion to the Uti possidetis had proved a great success, but Schlick did not simply possess the ability to stand pat in his repertory as a diplomat; he would reveal unexpected talents in driving shrewd bargains and in conceding unimportant points to the Turks when the occasion seemed to demand it.

This final laying to rest of the spectre of Transylvania coincided with the first meetings in the Conference tent and with the departure of the Grand Vizir for Adrianople. This traditional move into winter quarters should not have caused the Austrians any difficulty, but coming as it did so closely on the failure of the Turkish negotiators to win any concessions in the matter of Transylvania, it occurred to the Imperial Ambassadors that the Grand Vizir might well have changed his mind about making peace with the Holy League. No clear indication of his alleged *amor pacis* had reached them in the time they had been in camp at Carlowitz, and it was not out of the question that Hussein Pasha, like so many of his predecessors, had decided that his own personal survival was more important to him than any peace, however necessary it appeared to be, between the Sultan and the Emperor.[20] Powerful interests at Adrianople were working against him and his peace policy (they had already secured a minor victory in bringing about the deposition of one of the Grand Vizir's supporters) and, in addition, the old man's health was by no means good.

The last but one of the Köprülü Vizirs would have touched by the knowledge that the Mediators and the Imperial Ambassadors as well were prayerfully concerned about the state of his health and most anxious that his possession of the Vizirate would last out the negotiations at Carlowitz. He did not depart without leaving some indication of his continued interest in a peace treaty: five thousand Tartars were left behind at his camp before Belgrade with orders to wait there until a peace was concluded, and a sum of money was despatched to Mavrokordatos for his support during the Congress deliberations. But throughout the remaining months of the Congress the spectre of the death of the deposition of Hussein Pasha was something which no one could overlook, and it was this which encouraged the Austrians to display more alacrity in negotiation than was usual with them.[21]

The two delegations now began a point-by-point discussion of the Imperial proposals, which in their final form were the work of Count Öttingen and Count Schlick. They were based on the instructions which had been given to the two Ambassadors before they left Vienna, and they bore a striking resemblance to the detailed proposals which had figured in the peace negotiations of 1689 and 1691. This similarity was largely due to the fact that the emissaries had been provided with copies of all the state papers which had been exchanged in the whole course of the infinitely complicated negotiations which had preceded Carlowitz, but the instructions revealed an amazing continuity in Austrian demands as well. The proposed boundary line was to follow the Danube-Sava-Unna line in general; more specifically, the Banat of Temesvar was to remain a Turkish possession, the Bacska was to be Austrian, and Petervárad was to remain an Imperial stronghold. The ministers in Vienna had wisely suggested a *modus operandi* for Öttingen and Schlick: they were to advance in their talks from areas whose possession was not in question to areas where there was doubt, and they were to adhere *simpliciter* to the fundamental principle until the Turks raised the question of demolitions and evacuations.

The preparation of the instructions had been a difficult task for the Imperial ministry. When the problem had first been discussed early in the summer, a wide difference of opinion was evident. Kinsky had urged the Emperor to abandon the fundamental principle to the extent that the Turks be offered the demolition of Petervárad in exchange for the cession to the Emperor of the Banat. Leopold had requested the written opinions of Count Starhemberg, Count Buccelini, and Prince Eugene to assist him in coming to a decision in this matter, and the three men had quite naturally concentrated their attention on the Banat and Petervárad alternatives.[22] Starhemberg, the aging hero of the siege of Vienna, without wishing to brag about the fact that he had "more science and experience *in militaribus*" than Count Kinsky found the proposal to acquire the Banat an unacceptable one. For one thing, it was a striking contradiction to the *Uti possidetis*, and might have as a consequence the presentation of strong Turkish demands in the case of Transylvania. But what was uppermost in his mind in making his decision -- and in this he was in agreement with his colleagues -- was the strong possibility that the war which was imminent in the West might involve a resumption of hostilities with the Turks in the very near future.   In such an eventually, his instinctive attachment to a defensive conception of Austrian military power on the southern frontier convinced Starhemberg that Petervárad would be immeasurably valuable as an obstacle to the Turkish attack, since it would prevent the Turks from resorting to their usual point.   Count Buccelini, the Austrian Court Chancellor, agreed with this view for reasons more axiomatic than experiential.   He argued that the Danube line was of providential importance to the house of Austria, and the demolition of the fortress would weaken that line at a crucial point and would remove in effect any possibility of an Imperial attack against Belgrade.   In the event of war the road to Buda and the very heart of the recently reconquered Kingdom of Hungary would be open to the Turks.

These two men were of the older generation, married by long and painful experience to the policy of survival and acutely sensitive at the moment to the empty Imperial treasury and the immediacy of the French threat in Western Europe, and it came as no surprise that Eugene of Savoy did not agree with them.   Since his victory at Zenta, he had won the right to a respectful hearing of his opinions on the part of the Emperor and the older ministers, but his position was still that of a talented subordinate.   He had been recently engaged in fighting the Turks in the very area in question, and he suggested that the swap which Kinsky had proposed might be a wise move.   The rationalization of the frontier would be immeasurably advanced, he thought, and the establishment of a new fortress at Illock would secure the section of the line weakened by Petervárad's demolition. Eugene revealed signs of a developing political talent when he recognized the possibility of such violent Turkish opposition to this solution that the peace negotiations would again enter the stalemate stage.   When all these *vota* had been duly considered, Kinsky's proposal, which had found support only from Eugene and in a tentative way at that, was rejected, and the all important fundamental principle was rescued once more from the toils of devious diplomatic bargaining.

The remainder of the Imperial proposals was devoted to the mechanisms for regulating and maintaining peace on the common frontier, establishing orderly diplomatic and trade relations, and ratifying and supplementing, if the need arose, a proposed general peace of thirty years' duration. An article which required the surrender of Count Thököly made its reappearance together with the demand that the Franciscans be allowed to retain their control of the Holy Places in Palestine. There was one novelty in this list, the establishment of independence for the city state of Dubrovnik with the right to trade freely with both empires; Dubrovnik was to be placed under the joint protection of the Emperor and the Sultan.

A comparison of these proposals with the articles in the final draft of the treaty reveals the great degree of success which Öttingen and Schlick had in transforming their desiderata into reality. For only the three special provisions did not appear intact. No mention was made of Dubrovnik and the Holy Places (they were in the hands of the Roman Catholics at the moment in any case); and the Sultan agreed to keep Thököly and his followers at a safe distance from the frontier. Moreover, any of these Hungarian exiles who continued to live in Turkey would be regarded in the future as Turkish citizens.[23]

Difficulties arose only in matters of doubtful possession, and the amount of ignorance displayed by both the Austrians and the Turks in this area was not always feigned. Öttingen and Schlick were quick to report their first successes in transferring disputed territories into the category of Austrian possessions to the Emperor and the Ministers in Vienna. Schlick, on whose shoulders almost all of the actual negotiation fell, showed great virtuosity in detailed work of this kind. He even vaunted his ability to acquire territory by ruse if necessary, and he reported with understandable pride the success he had had in maneuvering Mavrokordatos into ceding to the Austrians control of the confluence of the Tisza and the Sava. It would have been impossible to make such a demand at the beginning of the talks; he had managed the trick by waiting for a favorable opportunity.[24] But there were other doubtful cases, especially along the Unna, which brought forth stiffened Turkish resistance, and here he had far less success than had been expected in Vienna. Indeed, a change in the reaction to the Ambassador's efforts was soon so obvious that Schlick felt it necessary to present Kinsky with an apologia for the policies he had pursued.

There had been a radical change in the Turkish attitude, for one thing, and the demands which they were now submitting were more like "conditions than articles." What he and Öttingen had been able to manage in the past week, he was careful to explain to the home office, seemed to them the very best that could be gained from the Turks. He denied that they had exceeded their instructions through any carelessness; they had been faced with a choice between two alternatives. "Caught between two extremities: to allow matters to deteriorate to such an extent that the harm would be irreparable and a rupture in the negotiations would result or to carry on by making concessions which were not absolutely essential, we thought it necessary to choose the second course."[25] The hard-pressed diplomats turned in their predicament to utilizing the influence which Marsigli had with Kinsky, and the general factotum was sent to Vienna with their dispatches and the instructions to report orally to the Emperor and the Bohemian Chancellor on the recent developments.

These extensive explanations and excuses had their desired effect, and Marsigli returned to Carlowitz with fresh instructions for the Ambassadors which contained a recognition by the ministry of the crucial stage which the Austro-Turkish talks had now entered upon and bestowed Imperial approval on the tactics which Schlick had been pursuing. This was an all too familiar case of the age old disparity of views held by officials charged with the formation of a general policy and the diplomats responsible for achieving the possible within that pre-established framework at a peace conference. But the Imperial Ambassadors at Carlowitz had more difficult principals to deal with than most, and it was only natural that the Emperor and Count Kinsky began to have their doubts about the wisdom of the day-to-day policies of their representatives at the peace congress.

The Emperor, writing to Kinsky on December 22, 1698, showed signs of discontentment with the way things were proceeding to the point of considering anew whether it should be peace or war.

> In the meantime, I find myself becoming increasingly disturbed when I see how the Turks interpret the principle of Uti possidetis in demanding that I restore places to them which are actually in my possession. Things seem to have reached the point where, as the saying would have it, "The bird eats or it dies."[26]

But Leopold's anxious mediations on the practical applications of the fundamental principle were still far short of occasioning a break in the talks. Actually there was a tone of unreality about his observations, for, as he wrote to Kinsky, Schlick and Öttingen, quiet and unperturbed, were putting the finishing touches to the treaty.

The Imperial delegation could now experience a certain amount of *Schadenfreude* as they turned from concentrating on their own perplexities to the picture presented by te analogous exertions of the other diplomats at the Congress. The Mediation, which had customarily followed a course of 'most favored nation' in the case of Austria, now found itself under attack from that very quarter. Count Schlick complained in one of his early secret reports to Kinsky about the general weakness of the Mediation. He was Kinsky about the general weakness of the Mediation. He was quick to excuse Lord Paget, since the Englishman conducted his part of the business with wisdom and moderation, but Coyler he dismissed as "so poor and sterile" that little was to be expected from his efforts. In his view, it was by reason of this weakness in one of its members that the Mediation was forced to bear with all manner of complaints and insults from the Turks without being able to retaliate in kind.[27]

Schlick's judgment was not entirely devoid of value. There is little doubt that Paget was the more eminent member of the Mediation duet. His age and wide experience of the world gave him a tremendous initial advantage, and his interventions in the course of the closely-argued discussions were far more frequent and a good deal more helpful to the achievement of an agreement. A close study of the protocol of the Mediation, the most detailed record extant of the conversations held in the presence of the Mediators, indicates that Paget, Mavrokordatos, and Schlick were the three most influential figures at the Congress. But something of Paget's vaunted wisdom and moderation was due to his tendency to see things more eye to eye with Schlick than Coyler did. If he could not be accused of being a violent partisan of the *Domus Austriae*, he was far less sympathetic to the Turks than Coyler had shown himself to be; it was natural for him to remember that the Emperor nominally at least was King William's ally and that the two rulers might shortly be engaged in another common struggle against the French.

Coyler had spent all of his life in Turkey, and in his mastery of the Turkish language and his open attachment to Turkish customs he was almost more Oriental than European. He could have a pardonable pride in the great gap that extended between his profound knowledge of the mysterious entity that was Turkey and Lord Paget's superficial acquaintance. The two men had so many reasons for disagreement; the unrelenting memory of personal slights, the unambiguous tensions established by commercial rivalry in the Levant, the legitimate differences over the tactics to be adopted in the course of their long and enforced collaboration, and, not least, the predisposition of Paget to favor the Austrian version of the controverted points, while Coyler was obviously more anxious for his Turks to secure the best possible terms.

Schlick's complaint (it had been uttered in utmost confidence in a secret report to Kinsky) was soon after, to his great confusion, brought to public notice. Count Kinsky took advantage of an interview he had with Jacob Hop to complain to the Dutch envoy that the Mediators were failing in their responsibilities; they had not spoken up to the Turks, for instance, in the question of the demolitions demanded by the Turks in the Tisza and Maros river area. Such a specific complaint could not fail to be interpreted as an indication of a more general and widespread dissatisfaction with the Mediation in Viennese circles, and it was precisely in such terms that it was communicated by Hop to Coyler. The reaction to this bit of news was immediate. The English and Dutch Ambassadors, who had been gravely wounded in their honor as diplomat and *honnêtes gens*, managed to convey in the most tactful way possible to Öttingen and Schlick their keen disappointment at the way they had been ill-used by the Austrians, particularly since cowardice was one of the charges in Kinsky's indictment of their behavior. Schlick could only be distressed that his original observation -- an effort probably to put a great part of the responsibility for concessions on his part to the Turks at the door of the Mediation -- had been transformed by the tactless Kinsky into the material for a minor diplomatic contretemps.[28] Kinsky was suffering from overwork, and his state of irritation was only exacerbated by his ever more serious illness; in such a state it was relatively easy for him to make diplomatic blunders. But the possibility exists that this was one of the few devices by which Kinsky could inform the Mediation of his desire for a more overtly pro-Austrian direction to their good office. When writing to Paget, he was customarily bond to say things he did not mean. A faux pas was regrettable, but it would provide a moment of truth, and in this particular case Kinsky was lucky -- the Mediation gave no signs of allowing its hurt feelings to disturb the great work which it had undertaken to perform at Carlowitz.

Once that the Imperial Ambassadors were convinced that their own treaty was well under way, they could devote a large part of their attention to seeing that their Allies were similarly well served by the Turks. The possibility seemed remote of achieving a general peace that would satisfy the four allied powers, and Schlick, who had been treated to the tasteless spectacle of the petty squabbling and the sudden reversals of character on the part of the Polish and Russian envoys, felt that such a peace "could not be anything else than a miracle of heaven."[29] He and his colleague were bound of course to assist the Allies to the best of their abilities, but their degree of commitment and the character of the services they were supposed to render varied to the extent that the Emperor felt himself bound to oblige each ally. Despite all the outward signs of his recently concluded solemn alliance with Tsar Peter, Leopold did not believe that he was required to do more than make certain that the Russians received such concessions from the Turks as could be considered equitable and adequate in the judgment of the members of the League. This clearly wavering sense of loyalty to the Russian tie cannot, however, be construed in any way as an activity anti-Russian policy. The stern demands of power politics required that Leopold make peace, and, while he had no wish to alienate his recent Russian guest, he could not indefinitely suspend his own treaty negotiations to satisfy the whims of his Russian ally.

His sense of obligation to Poland was more striking. He could not forget that it had been the initial Austro-Polish alliance which had saved Vienna from the Turks and which had provided the nucleus for the great crusading campaigns of the 1680's. But the Polish demands at the moment were excessive: Kaminiec and Moldavia were not actually in Polish hands and in exceeding the limits imposed by the fundamental principle Poland had placed herself in a position where his support could not possibly extend to the extreme of breaking off Congress deliberations. Poland's recent performance had been poor enough to further reduce her claim on the Emperor's gratitude and her expectation that Leopold, as an ally, would not make peace without her. All too frequently Poland had flirted with a separate peace with the Turks, and only the miraculous intervention of providence had favored the Habsburgs by thwarting French intrigues which had had such a separate peace as their object. The Poles had remained nominally faithful to the League, even though their contributions of manpower to the common struggle had fallen far short of the treaty stipulation. On more than one occasion Leopold's forces had found themselves in a dire predicament because no diversion had been provided by the Poles. It was his intention to consider Polish interests carefully, but to make peace without Poland if it came to that extremity.

Only with the Venetians was Leopold aware of a really binding obligation. To make peace without the concurrence of the Republic would be enormously difficult, indeed such a drastic step that prolonged assessment of the risks involved would have to be made by the Austrians before embarking in such a course. The Venetians were well aware of the Emperor's attitude; Ruzzini even assured Schlick at one point -- "I really believe that the Emperor doesn't have the heart to make peace without us."[30]

This depressing, if realistic, canvas of the responsibilities of the Imperial delegation was further darkened by the feeling that the Russians and the Poles had not come with the express purpose of making peace but with the intention of sowing further discord and eventually of ruining the whole great Congress effort. The Austrians described them quite simply as *renitent* and prepared themselves for the worst: the abandonment of all hope of concerted action by the Allies and the assumption by the Austrians of an attitude of indifference to the fate of Russian and Polish negotiations. Their sense of relief was understandable when at the beginning of November, the Palatine and his Russian colleague suddenly gave every sign of a sincere desire to conclude their agreements with the Turks without further delay. Couriers recently arrived at the Congress site from Poland and Russia were doubtless responsible for this most unusual tractability, but the weather may have been its contribution to the new attitude. The Palatine arranged almost immediately for his first face-to-face encounter with the Turks. Thanks to the continued assistance of the Mediation, he managed to acquire Kaminiec intact for Poland, though in doing so he had to abandon Polish claims to Moldavia. This was a most important concession for the Turks to make and the strong representations of the Mediators had much to do with it. Malachowski appeared at Öttingen's tent on the evening of November 18 (he was in the best of moods now) and announced that his treaty was for all practical purposes concluded, and that he wished to express his gratitude for the assistance of the Emperor's Ambassadors and the Mediators in making this possible.[31]

Russo-Turkish discussions did not fail, however, to follow a more eccentric pattern. Prokop Voznitsin had never formally accepted the Mediation or the fundamental principle, but he agreed to make use of the friendly offices of Paget and Coyler, and two meetings actually did take place after the manner established by Congress protocol. His blunt demand for the cession of Kertch, which was in Turkish hands, and his listing of the demolitions required by the Tsar on the Turkish side of the common frontier consumed the greater part of these meetings by reason of the violent Turkish opposition which developed. Apparently despairing of success in pursuing this line, he abruptly suggested that the two Powers should conclude an armistice of two years' duration on the basis of *Uti possidetis.* Towards the expiration date of that period a Russian embassy would in due course appear at Constantinople to negotiate there directly with the Turks.

His imprecision about the details of this treaty postponement puzzled the Turks, but it irritated Paget, who took it to be a Russian maneuver to postpone indefinitely any agreement, a stratagem which had the added malice of depriving the Mediators of any glory that might accompany the signing of a treaty between the Tsar and the Sultan at Carlowitz. Paget was known to explode in a most undiplomatic manner, when he was angry, and on this particular occasion he so far forgot himself as to accuse the Russian of not acting in good faith in promising the despatch of an emissary in two years' time to Constantinople. Paget demanded that the Tsar make his intentions known within three months' time; if he failed to do this, the Mediation intended to resume its own efforts to bring about a peace settlement between the two belligerents. This outburst of Paget's only further convinced the Russian envoy that any meetings he might have with the Turks in the presence of the Mediators were doomed to failure, and he resorted thereafter to the expedient of sending his physician Hanse to private nocturnal discussions with

Mavrokordatos. These talks proved eminently successful from his point of view; Turkish agreement to his armistice proposal was obtained without much further difficulty.[32]

Russia had chosen to play the role of "apostate" at the Congress by brashly disregarding the normal methods of procedure and by finally concluding not a treaty of peace but merely an armistice for two years. The Russian envoy set the tone for all subsequent Russian reaction to the work of the Congress by placing the blame for his failure to achieve anything more substantial squarely at the doors of the Austrians and the Mediators who had abandoned him to such an extent that he had been forced "to finally agree to a truce ...." Paget was soon informed of the Russian's view, and it was with a natural desire to defend himself that he gave his version of the Russian negotiations to Count Kaunitz. According to Paget's account, it was in the course of the second meeting between Voznitsin and the Turks on November 12, that the Russian had proposed a "shortcut" -- leaving it up to the Turks whether they would accept it or not. Voznitsin, and not the Imperial Ambassadors and the Mediation, bore full responsibility for the offer of an armistice and for all the other private conferences with the Turks that followed. If one was to speak of abandonment at the Congress, it was the Russian envoy who, acting certainly on instructions from the Tsar, had deserted the common cause of the Allies.[33] Paget fails to make mention of the fact that the Russians correctly surmised that none of the Allies was ready to endanger the success of the Congress by supporting the Russians in their intransigent position. But the report of the Austrian-English decision to isolate the Russian delegate at that early stage in the discussions has no foundation in fact. What Austro-English complicity could not achieve was an easy task for the roughshod manners of untrained Russian diplomats. Russian xenophobia would find it easy to blame the failure of Voznitsin on the deviousness of the Tsar's alleged allies and friends in Western and Eastern Europe, and it would be a perilously easy charge for a Russian historian to repeat in our own day when the Soviet Union finds herself constantly at loggerheads with Western Europe.

The last phase of Congress activity consisted of two months of difficult and almost hopeless Veneto-Turkish negotiations. The Cavaliere Ruzzini had been quick enough to agree with Count Kinsky when the latter had proposed in June a joint declaration of willingness to treat on the basis of the fundamental principle *simpliciter*, but his readiness to cooperate on that high level was not to be matched when the particulars of disputed possession were aired. Ruzzini, who brought with him to the Congress the reputation of a most distinguished and experienced diplomat in the great Venetian tradition, quickly realized that his success depended not so much on sweeping declarations of this kind but on his ability to haggle in specific disputed questions. The method he adopted was anything but diplomatic, and the Venetian proposals were presented to the Turks with the stipulation that they were to be treated as a whole and not point by point as the Turks had been accustomed to do in other negotiations. This virtual ultimatum was necessary, according to Ruzzini, because he did not possess any authority to alter his proposals in detail without the express consent of the Venetian Senate, and this would involve the time-consuming process of consulting with Venice.[34] This announcement struck his colleagues as being a most unusual way of conducting business at a Congress of this kind, and any value it possessed would, as they expected, be a very limited one. The air of dictated conditions was unfortunate, and both the Mediators and the Imperial Ambassadors complained that in effect the Venetian Ambassador was setting himself up as the arbiter of the destinies of the Ottoman Empire.[35] The attitude of the Turks began to stiffen noticeably as the discussions developed without achieving any agreement; Ruzzini's arguments were endlessly monotonous, and his "torrent of eloquence" soon became one of the wonders of a Congress which had its share of the strange and the exotic.[36]

The major source of disagreement was the frontier line to be established between Venetian and Turkish possessions in Greece and

Dalmatia. The Turks stipulated that the Hexamille be regarded as the boundary line of the Morea, which was to remain in Venetian hands, and on the *Terra firma* north of the Isthmus of Corinth the fortresses of Prevesa, Lepanto and Rumelia were to be demolished by the Venetians and ceded with all the land in their immediate vicinity to the Turks. The Venetians had a more generous view of their territory in the Morea; they declared that a chain of mountains beyond the Isthmus in the *Terra firma* was the boundary line, and this view required the cession of a considerable amount of territory by the Turks to Venice. The relative vagueness of the two sets of proposals was not simply due to the desire to maneuver for the best position; there was on both sides a woeful lack of information on the extent of their possessions in this critical area. The obscurities which became apparent in the discussion of the Dalmatian line were even more numerous, but they did not provide the grounds for obstruction and delay that the Morea question did.[37]

Ruzzini was finally prevailed upon by the Mediation and the Austrians to send a courier to Venice for further instructions from the Senate on these disputed points. In the three weeks it took for the completion of the courier's trip, the Imperial Ambassadors availed themselves of every opportunity to delay their own work of polishing up the details of their treaty so that the Turks would not become restive and begin to threaten to suspend the Congress negotiations.[38] Ruzzini found himself in a most unenviable position. The diplomats of the other powers had virtually concluded their business, and Venice was left to treat with the Turks in an atmosphere of isolation. But he was able to console himself with the notion that a strong Venetian position, maintained in the very teeth of Turkish "severe dealing" and of appeals for compromise on Venice's part from the impatient Mediators and the Austrians, would be finally successful in calling the Turks' bluff. He refused to believe that the Emperor was ready to abandon his Venetian ally to her own devices. To make doubly certain of this, he had frequent recourse to Father Menegatti, the Emperor's influential Jesuit confessor, whose sympathies for his fellow Italians might be enlisted now in support of Venice. Schlick soon discovered the existence of this correspondence and alerted Count Kinsky; that minister and Menegatti had already had a falling out in the course of the secret negotiations leading up to the Treaty of Rijswijk, and Ruzzini's appeal to the Jesuit on this occasion would only weaken his position as far as Kinsky was concerned, for in addition to his well-known disapproval of clerical interference in political matters he was now more than usually jealous of his prerogatives *in Turcisis*.[39]

An intrigue with the Emperor's confessor was not the only charge made against Ruzzini. The Austrian diplomats in growing alarm at his stubborn refusal to make any concessions to the Turks -- this was a *tour de force* which could send them all home empty-handed -- began to suspect the presence of the evil machinations of the French. Though they did not actually accuse him of being a tool of the French, they knew that Venice's sympathies for France had a long history. Moreover, Ruzzini's doctor had been for most of his life a pensioner of the King of France, and the Austrians knew that the physician had recently received communications from a "creature" of the Marquis de Chateauneuf. Schlick had an unhappy inspiration of breaking the present deadlock by a sudden realignment of the Allies: the Austrians would combine with the Pole and the Russian, thus assuring a clear majority of votes for peace. This illusory proposal received no response from Vienna.[40]

The reappearance of the Venetian courier was taken to be a hopeful sign, and Paget was assured by Ruzzini that he was now able to facilitate matters on the eve of a new series of conferences with the Turks. But the sessions themselves revealed no change, however slight, in the Venetian position; the stalemate was still very much in effect. At this juncture, the Turks gave notice that they required "a positive answer to their requisitions, and that they might have it within a very few daies, that they might take their measures accordingly, either for Peace or war."[41]

The moment of crisis was suddenly upon the Congress (it coincided with the approach of Christmas): this was a threat to the successful completion of Congress business that far eclipsed the dispute over the fate of Transylvania. The Mediation appealed immediately to Vienna for help, and both Sutton and Hop were soon doing their very best to procure Venetian compliance through the intervention of the Emperor. Sutton called on Ruzzini's successor as Venetian Ambassador in Vienna, Francesco Loredan found Ruzzini's conduct at the Congress most unfortunate and that he would urge more moderation in his stand. In an interview that Sutton had with Kinsky he underlined the need for immediate action. Both men were well aware of that this was the time of year in which the Turks actually began to think about the next campaign. Kinsky could only give him assurances that the Imperial government would take steps to secure Venetian cooperation at Carlowitz. But Sutton could see little hope of this happy issue unless very real pressure was brought to bear on the *Serenissima*. Kinsky's response was not calculated to put Sutton's fears to rest. "L'Empereur ne peut rien commander à une Puissance souveraine. Nous avons cherché et taché à procurer quelque temperament, mais à l'avenir nous ferons quelque chose d'avantage."[42]

Only one possible course of action remained for the Austrians. The Emperor must conclude his own treaty with the Turks on schedule, and the Venetians would be grated an extra period of time in which to accept such conditions as might be reasonably arranged for them by other hands at the Congress. Kinsky seemed ready for that eventuality on Sutton's next visit. It was clear that Venice could not be ordered about, but if she did not allow herself to be persuaded, the Emperor would be literally forced to take such measures.[43] And this was what in fact did happen, and the Imperial Ambassadors found themselves the very center of a novel and unlooked for set of negotiations. they now assumed for all practical purposes the direction of the Venetian talks with the Turks -- Ruzzini was reduced to a grudging agreement with the arrangements they made in his name. With the full cooperation of the mediation and the Turks they were soon able to settle all outstanding differences. Their method could not fail to succeed; they made very certain beforehand of just what the Turks would allow and then in the actual discussions they were careful to accept Turkish suggestions without proposing any modifications.[44] In the dispute over the Morea the original Turkish proposals were accepted as being "the more reasonable," and the Venetian claim to the strip of *Terra firma* bounded by the line of mountains was allowed to lapse. This was dealing with Venice's interests in a most highhanded manner, but no one was in any mood to take much thought of Venetian feelings at this point; the winter was becoming an ever greater inducement to finishing up the work of the Congress.[45] The treaties were to be formally signed on January 26, 1699, and if Ruzzini had received a favorable reply from Venice by that time it was expected that he would sign his treaty as well. In the event that no such orders had arrived from Venice he was to be allowed an additional period of time in which to put his hand to the Veneto-Turkish treaty.

There was pronounced relief on all sides that this last great obstacle had been removed however summarily, and the diplomats impatiently awaited the day which would put the finishing touches to their work. On January 24, Voznitsin signed his Armistice and made a farewell call on the Austrians; he was a strange figure to the very last in his picturesque and often amusing choice of costume and his swiftly changing moods. He seemed for the moment satisfied with what he had been able to accomplish, and in good Orthodox fashion he set off on a tour of the local Serbian monasteries before he actually began the long trip back to Moscow.[46]

On the great day itself, there was a brilliant display of the ceremonial which had been allowed by common consent to be in abeyance during the actual deliberations. Impressively large escorts of cavalry and infantry accompanied the diplomats, who were now in *gala*, and immense care was taken with the details of the ceremony of signing the treaties. The afternoon had been chosen by the Turks as being more propitious, and it was then that the Imperial Ambassadors, Malachowski, the Mediators, and the Turks gathered in the Congress House. The texts of the treaties between the Emperor and the Sultan and between the Republic of Poland and the Sultan were checked over for the last time by the ambassadors concerned, and then the three Allied representatives performed a similar operation on the articles which they were about to accept for Venice.

The doors of the Congress House were then thrown open to admit a large and motley crowd of soldiers and local inhabitants which flooded into the small apartments of the building to witness the actual signing. The press was so great that the ambassadors experienced great difficulty in performing this task, though the diplomats did not appear to mind very much. The rest of the day was spent in celebration; Paget had five thousand guests to dinner. This festive note was sustained during the next few days, and visits were at last exchanged between the Turks and their erstwhile enemies. Gifts were exchanged as well, and in an atmosphere of well-deserved recreation the various parties made their preparations to depart for more comfortable climes.[47] The desolate waste of Carlowitz was allowed to return to its native state, enriched by the fame that attached itself to the place that had given its name to a great peace in the year 1699 between Christendom and the Turks, and enriched in a more tangible way by the survival of the Congress House as a Franciscan chapel -- a pious memento of the workings of Divine Providence in those difficult months of negotiation.[48]

The conversation of the scene of so much rancorous debate and callous bargaining into a chapel was an undeniably characteristic Congress of Carlowitz touch. The diplomats, who had figured so prominently in those long and wearisome sessions, were not certainly extraordinary in their piety or marked by an optimistic faith in the dictates of Divine Providence. They had come to this Congress possessed of the very limited objective of gaining some tangible increment for their own country in power and prestige. That all the Powers would manage to achieve something in the way of satisfaction of their claims seems an improbable if not impossible outcome. And Congress and the Peace that had been concluded at Carlowitz had been a genuine surprise in the unexpected success they had had in presenting Europe, which fond itself on the very eve of another great conflagration, with a peace settlement in Eastern Europe. Even the most hardened diplomat felt the mysterious influences of the Almighty in the glorious achievement of January 26. Ruzzini, in whom a sense of *raison d'état* of a most extreme variety was an ingrained Venetian trait, felt called upon to recognize the work of God in all of this, for only by referring to the Creato was he able to explain the relatively speedy transition from a decade of military and diplomatic stalemate to the happy denouement at Carlowitz.[49] It was not a perfect peace settlement that had been concocted there; there was too much of the casually improvised to permit it to endure for long. In its creation there had been moments indeed, when the whole enterprise could have foundered completely, as so many preliminaries had done. Yet accommodation had come at the eleventh hour, and even Ruzzini had to be grateful for that.

Their marked feelings of gratitude to God were combined in the minds of the Allied diplomats with a sense of appreciation for the work of the Mediation. The contributions, however unequal they might seem from different vantage points, of Paget and Coyler had been very real. On numbers of occasions they had intervened in the interests of what their by then well-developed sense of the possible told them might be effectively achieved. They were not innocent of the charge of favoritism; the Emperor, the Turks and the Venetians could complain with some justice that the impartiality of the Mediation had failed it on one or more occasions. But there was no complaint about Paget and Coyler's conception of their task. Paget's much vaunted 'method' would have scandalized even a contemporary stickler for the niceties of diplomatic practice, but it had the merit of being hammered out by long and painful experience. It was elastic enough and sufficiently sensitive to the degree of importance each successive problem possessed to allow the diplomats to carry on with the essential business of the Congress.

The Mediators returned to their posts in Pera, feted and praised on all sides (the Turks made of their entrance into Belgrade a virtual triumph) and bearing with them the responsibility of mediating any minor disputes which might result from the practical applications of the peace agreements. The chequered career of the newly-established Austro-Turkish boundary commission would soon require their attention: the troublesome Count Marsigli and the cooperative Turkish representative Ibrahim Effendi made a most ill-suited pair, and disputes developed almost immediately.[50]

The Emperor evinced a good deal of gratitude in rewarding the labors of the Ambassador-Mediators; the English Milord and the stoutly bourgeois Dutch Mijnheer were presented at his command with diplomas testifying to the fact that he had raised them to the dignity of Counts of the Holy Roman Empire and of the Kingdom of Hungary as well.[51] Their new honors might exist in uneasy combination with their accustomed rank and perquisites (the picture of Jacob Coyler reveling in his newly-acquired distinctions in his Embassy in Pera is one that excites the historian's imagination without any hope of discovering just what the Hollander's reactions were in fact), but it was a sincere tribute none the less and bore the mark of a graciousness that was not alien to the Emperor's character. One additional consequence of their ennoblement in the Holy Roman Empire was that they now found themselves to be the undoubted peers of Kinsky and Kaunitz. But this would be of little practical assistance to them, for Kinsky died the month after the signing of the treaties, and Kaunitz would have little opportunity to treat with them in the years following upon the conclusion of their great work.

It is possible to sum up at this point, to ponder the import of their experience and the value of the Anglo-Dutch Mediation as a whole. Never before in the history of Eastern Europe had the Maritime Powers played such a significant and sustained role. Virtually a whole generation of Dutch and English statesmen and diplomats had grown accustomed to the consideration of events taking place in that area and had become acclimated to the business of offering their services (and did not exclude real intervention -- the natives would call it 'interference' -- in the internal affairs of an Ally and, again, a friendly state) to effecting an accord between the Emperor and the Sublime Porte. The interest of these men was compounded of a desire to free Imperial troops for action in concert with their own forces against the French in Western Europe and of a worthy solicitude to maintain and develop commercial contacts between their countries and the Levant.

There will always be free play for debate on the degree to which political and economic factors influenced their policies. In tracing the chequered history of the negotiations that led to Carlowitz we have concentrated quite naturally on considerations arising out of high politics. This was a conscious decision on the basis of the assumption that the political relationships in this story were the most important and, in a very real sense, decisive. This may well come as a disappointment to the students of economic history and in an even profounder way to the partisans of the economic interpretation of historical events. But the sources themselves encourage such a view; they provide no real basis, as far as they are presently known, for an economic history of the Peace of Carlowitz.

Both William III and the States-General were forthright enough in alluding to economic interests when they dispatched instructions to their representatives; they were anxious, particularly in the case of Turkey, that a general peace in that area would redound to the commercial benefit of Dutch and English merchants. But it would be a hazardous course indeed to view their more insistent declarations of a desire for peace that would ease the strain in Western Europe as mere camouflage for deeper economic commitments. On the basis of present knowledge of the affair, it is possible to establish the fact that commercial considerations played a part in sustaining Dutch and English eagerness to mediate. Further exploration of the history of both Levant Companies may reveal that the commercial rivalry that existed between the two countries frequently played a limiting role on the well-meaning efforts of the diplomats. We have seen something of this in the tensions that existed between the English community in Turkey and the Dutch Ambassador, and we have suggested that this sad state of affairs may have had real repercussions on Turkish official opinion. The impression that does survive is one of paramouncy of political interests.

One interesting development had certainly occurred in the course of the Mediation, and that was a shift in the center of gravity diplomatically speaking from the Dutch to the English. The Mediation began under Dutch auspices, and it remained pretty much of a Dutch monopoly until the period immediately following upon the breakdown of the peace conference in Vienna in 1689. It was then that English diplomats were entrusted for the first time with a measure of responsibility in the common cause, and the increasingly important contribution of Lord Paget was a token that England was moving towards a senior partnership in the firm. The torments of Van Heemskerck found no equivalent in English experience; the fatalities of Hussey and Harbord were historical accidents in the craft's sense of the word.

It is possible on the basis of this drift from Holland to England to regard the story of the Anglo-Dutch Mediation at Carlowitz as one of the early chapters in the decline of Dutch power and Prestige in European affairs. The traditional date for this event has usually been assigned to the closing years of the War of the Spanish Succession, but it would not be simply a case of the extreme use of the historical hindsight to note the signs of that trend in this remote area of Anglo-Dutch friendly rivalry. Something of this tendency may be due to the personalities involved (Paget was by all accounts a more impressive fellow than Coyler); part of it may be traced to accidents of time and place: it was much easier for a series of English Ambassadors to make new tentatives towards peace than it was for the all too familiar and stationary Coyler who had little opportunity to make use of the element of surprise, such an infallible weapon in diplomatic negotiation. But the fact of the trend is too obvious to be mistaken for a composite of circumstances; the process had begun under the very watchful eye of William III and it would increase in momentum in the period after his death.

The work of the Mediation had had its effect on official circles in Vienna. The traditional antipathy to the heretics was transformed into an ambivalent feeling that provided scope for gratitude as well as for suspicion that the good offices of the Maritime Powers were simply due to their crass political and economic interests. Certainly this was an improvement, though not very much, on the older view, and it represented a definite modernization of Austrian reactions to her Allies. This was but part and parcel of the secularization of politics that was then making itself felt at the Court of Vienna; even in the pious atmosphere that surrounded Leopold a revolution in political emphasis was making itself felt. The ecclesiastical party had celebrated its last great triumph in the accomplishment of the Hungarian *reconquista*. Leopold had leaned heavily on the advice of his confessors and his court theologians, but their theology did not preclude association, even alliance, with Protestant states. His successor the short-lived Joseph would carry on the work with an air of being quite conscious of what was involved, and it was he who would provide Christendom with the curious spectacle of the final military conflict between a Holy Roman Emperor and the Pope.

The continued presence in Vienna of diplomats from the politically more advanced states like England and Holland had contributed to the breaking down of a more narrowly Catholic view -- in political terms -- of Austria's role as a power. The paramount importance of Spain gradually yielded place to the more discordant representations of the English and the Dutch. The death of the Marques de Borgomanero was the end of an era; all that remained was the dream of the Spanish inheritance and with the loss of much of that to the Bourbons the influence of Spain was doomed to lose its effectiveness. Austrian official opinion slowly adjusted to the new situation; it had little enthusiasm on occasion for its work, but it could not discount the signs, as it could not overlook the subsidies that appeared from time to time from London and Amsterdam bankers.

Old Hamel Bruynincx and Lord Paget had added a new tone to the Viennese atmosphere; they did their work far better than they themselves perhaps realized. For it became the habit of Austrian statesmen to conduct their negotiations with London and The Hague through the English and Dutch representatives in Vienna rather than entrusting it to the Austrian diplomats in London and The Hague. This development in the history of the international relations of the European states at this crucial point is a more pedestrian tale than that of the appearance on the scene, as members of the European community, of Russia and Turkey, but it clearly deserves more attention than it has so far received. European states were called upon at the turn of the eighteenth century to take into account the activities of states which had hitherto been geographically and psychologically remote. The Anglo-Dutch Mediation at Carlowitz was a chapter in the history of that growing consciousness of the indivisible character of Europe's political concerns.

Notes to Chapter 4

[1]My intention in this chapter was to make a substantial advance in the way of presenting a detailed and nuanced picture of the work of the Congress of Carlowitz. There have been a number of attempts in this direction (cf. note 1 to Chapter Two), but they have usually fallen far wide of the mark, since they failed to make any more than a cursory examination of the extensive source collections. The *Turcica*, preserved in the *Haus-, Hof- und Staatsarchiv*, Vienna, is extraordinarily rich in materials relating to the preliminaries of the Congress and the actual Congress negotiations. Included in this collection is the secret correspondence of Count Kinsky with Count Schlick, and this is certainly the best source for an understanding of Austrian *Realpolitik* at the Congress. In addition, I made use of the *Diarium et Ceremoniale Tractatis Pacis Carlovicensis de annis 1698 et 1699*, the best running account of the activities of the Allied diplomats and the Mediation. The relations of the Imperial Ambassadors are a rich source; they have been used here to supplement the Kinsky-Schlick correspondence. An extensive use of these relations would have required the expansion of the present chapter into a book.

A most valuable addition was the collection of the letters of Lord Paget and Robert Sutton, for this allowed me to make a fairly close study of the work of the Mediation at the Congress. *Hora Siccama* was also of some help, but since his attention was largely focused on Jacob Coyler, his study was not as important for an understanding of the work of the Mediation, as it as for the earlier period when the Dutch had the lead in mediation efforts. The published materials in Hurmuzaki, *Documente*, V/2, and the final relation of Cavaliere Carlo Ruzzini (published in the *Fontes rerum austriacarum*) were also helpful.

The study of the sources, though care was taken to include large amounts of material that had not been studied before, cannot pretend to be exhaustive. A secret correspondence between Count Kinsky and Count Marsigli is also to be found in the *Turcica*, but I did not believe it was as important a source as the Kinsky-Schlick letters. The most precious single source of all, the *Protocolle de la Mediation*, which was an attempt to preserve a verbatim account of the actual Congress negotiations, was used only occasionally by Hammer-Purgstall; it certainly deserves closer attention than I was able to give it. For in this way it would be possible to come to more accurate judgments on the contributions of Lord Paget, Mavrokordatos, and Schlick.

Needless to say, I did not find it possible to study the published materials on the participation of Poland and Russia in the work of the Congress. I have discussed the activities of Malachowski and Voznitsin only in so far as they affected certainly remains to be done in this extraordinarily complicated field of diplomatic relations in Eastern Europe at the end of the seventeenth century -- the archives still preserve many secrets and a bewildering number of historical literatures remain to be worked through and collated; I can only hope that this chapter marks an awakening of interest in that immensely interesting and infernally difficult field.

[2]The most striking description of the significance of Carlowitz is to be found in Hammer-Purgstall, *op. cit.*, v.

[3]The entries in the *Diarium et Cerimoniele Tractatus Pacis Carlovicensis de Anni 1698 et 1699, Turcica*, I, 170 (hereafter the *Diarium*), for October 16, 17, and 18.

[4]Letter of Jakob Colyer to the Imperial Plenipotentiaries, Turkish Camp at Belgrade, October 10, 1698, *Turcica*, I, 167, 30; Kinsky blamed the delays on teh representatives of the Allies: "...Sa Majeste Imperiale auroit bien souhaitee d'avancer les choses necessaires au Congres pour en hater l'assemblage, et ny Votre Excellence ny les Turcs n'y avoient rien a souhaiter, si les choses n'avoient dependues d'elle seule parce qu'elle tire sincerement a la paix mais comme le concert se devoit y prendre indispensablement avec plusieurs des ses Alliez les choses ont este retardiez bien malgre ses sentiments...", Kinsky to Paget, Vienna, Oct. 18, 1698, *ibid.*, 54.

[5]The *Diarium*, Oct. 23, 1698.

[6]*Ibid.*, the entries for October 25 and 26, 1698. An extensive report on the incident was sent to Vienna in *Relation Nr. 4, Turcica*, I, 167, 212.

[7]"Mylord Pagett selbsten durch zwey seiner Leüth geführet selbsten anfangs mit bedeckter, hernach aber entblöster Haupt biss zu den antritt entgegen kome. Seine Tracht möcht denen fremden sowohl etwas wunderlich anzusehen gewesen seye, den dass Turkische ware durch den Christlichen Hut undt Perruquia teperiret; die gestalt iedoch ist mehr durch die grosste moustachen als anderwertige zufälle verändert.", *Diarium*, Octover 27, 1698.

[8]As far as the Impreial Ambassadors were concerned, Colyer had won the prize for the magnificence of his quarters: "Bey den Holländischen fanden wir nicht allein eine gleichmassige schöne ordtung, sondern mit wahrheit in vielen noch einen grössern pracht.", *Diarium*, Oct. 27, 1698.

[9]"...der Mocoviter aber bedeüten lassen, er könte es nicht Ihnen, ursachen die Mediatores ihm nach vor keinen Sohn, und er Sie vor keinen Vätter angenoben hatte.", *Diarium*, Octover 29, 1698.

[10]"Morgents überschukte der Moscoviter, wo man sich dessen gar nicht vermuthet, seiner vohero geweigarter Vollmacht an die Kayerlichen;", *Diarium*, October 30, 1698.

[11]"...als nach so villen mühesamben undt verdrüsslichen abhandlungen endlichen die von Kay. *Mediation* zu satisfaction des Pohlnischen Gesandten verfasst, undt von den Venetianer such unterschribene erklärung überraicht, undt placidirt worden...undt solche mit den überrest seiner Compendiosen bagage an dass ihme anfangs zugewidmete orth übersezen;", *Diarium*, November 1, 1698.

[12]"Les Assemblees puliques du premier abord ne sont pas de leur (i.e. the Mediation) gout a cause du naturel farouche et hautain de nos adversaires, et il vaut mieux eroient-ils se donner le premier choc par la plume. Tout comme les plein-pouvoirs des alliez leur furent delivre par nos mains ils nous ont remis sussi avec ceux des Turcs, et toute cette premiere ouverture se fait sous les auspices de Sa Majeste Imperiale.", Count Schlick to Count Kinsky, Carlowitz, October 30, 1698, *Turcica*, I, 167, 208-209; the early progress of the *Conferenz-Haus* is described in the *Diarium*, particularly on November 4 and 13, 1698.

[13]"...dass den nachmittag über angehaltene groosse gewölck ist bey der nbachten ein so grausambes gewitter von donner, bliz, und sturm-windt ausgebrochen, dass nicht allein in den Christlich, Türkisch undt Mediatorn Lager kong einziges zelt nit stehen bleiben, sondern auch von theils der holzeren häueser die dächer abgerissen, undt etliche derley gar zu boden geworffen worden. Die Moscoviter undt Pohlnische Gesandter haben sich darüber so verunlustiget, dass Sie allbereith die gedanken fassen ich nacher Peterwarden retriren zu wollen.", *Diarium*, November 8, 1698.

[14]*Diarium*, November 9 and 11, 1698.

[15]"Enlich und endlich hat der güttifg und ungüttiger himmel es also geschicket dass denen solang Erwünschten gepflogener dreystundiger unterredung wurde behebet der schluss prothocollieren zu lassen der Session so forth ein endt gemacht, undt von allen seithen vergleich, dass sogar in denen zusammen

künfften forderes hin auch alles Ceramoniale ausgehebt werden, undt man sich ganz bertraulich begegne solle;", *Diarium* , November 13, 1698.

[16]Letter of Schlick to Kinsky, Carlowitz, Nov. 13, 1698, *Turcica*, I, 167, 284.

[17]Lord Paget had urged the Turkish Ambassadors to abandon any hope of an Austirian concession in the matter of Transylvania, but "toutes ses plus chaud remonstrances et protestations sur la honte meme,...ne les en avoient pas pu faire desister, et que tous les deux en larmes, Mauro Cordato se laissa a la fin aller a ces parole: Li Signori Mediatori per l'amor di Dio vedino, cerchino e persuadino, che qualche cosa sisa concesso all'amicitia e consolatione del Sultano ed alle nostre instanze, accioche non siamo obligati di ritonarene colla pace piagendo.", Achlick to Kinsky, Nov. 8, 1698, *ibid.*, 169.

[18]"J'avais public de dire a Votre Excellence, que c'es a dessein d'accrediter les Mediateurs de plus au plus aupres les Turcs qu'on a donne un tour a le'entree de la response comme s'ils nous eussent parle avec beaucoup d'empressement en faveur de la proposition.", the postscript to Schlick's en faveur de la proposition.", the postscript to Schlick's letter ot Kinsky, Carlowitz, November 8, 1698, *ibid.*, 169.

[19]"Le dernier recours furt aux Mediateurs, lesquels par des importunites et bassesses, qu'on auroit de la peine a aux Ministres de Sa Majeste Imperiale. Ceux-ci y avoient a demi consenti; Mais nous autres croiants que c'etoit revoquer en doute et choquer directement notre caractere, que clea pourroit tourner en mauvaise consequence pour la suite, et ces delais ne donnants que trop occasion de soupconner il etoit necessaire de se mettre au clair, nous nous y sommes oppose, iusques a parler un peu haut. J'y ai pousse d'sutant plus librement, qui ie suis persuade qu'il y a des recontres ou il faut etre fire et qu'il n'y a rien de tel pour se delivrer d'un querelleur que de lui mettre la marche en main. Nous avons reussi. Ils ont abandonnee la Transilvanie avec droits et presents...", Schlick to Kinsky, Carlowitz, Nov. 13, 1698, *ibid.*, 284-285.

[20]Schlick had predicted this move in a letter to Kinsky, Carlowitz, October 30, 1698, *ibid.*, 210.

[21]"Du resete les Francais barcent le diable a la Cour du Grand Signior. Ils ont fait des efforts pour perdre Reis-Effendi et Mauro Cordato. Ils s'attachent au parti de Mufti qui est contraire a la paix,. On pourroit ie croi en fort bonne conscience prier Dieu pour la conversation du Vezir.", Schlick to Kinsky,

Carlowitz, Nov. 5, 1698, *ibid.*, 45; the departure of the Grand Vizir did give the Austrians pause: "...ob nit selbiger alle friedens gedancken abgethan, und sich anders *resolvirt* haven mögte; in deme Wir von Ihme seith Unserem dahier sein nicht den geringsten antrit zu den nTractaten verapürenm, oder sonse hoffnung vernoben, wasgestalten derselbe noch fünff Tausendt Tartarn in der gegendt Belgrad bis zu auswarthung des friedens zuruck gelassen, der Mauro Coradato auch noch drey Tausendt *zicchin* zu seinem *subsistenz* von Belgrad bekommen habe.", Relation Nr. 7, Nov. 12, 1698, *Turcica*, I, 168, 262.

[22]The instructions and the acts of the previous negotiations with the Turks which were furnished to Ottingen and Schlick are in the *Turcica*, I, 167; the *Gustachen* of Count Buccelini and Count Starhemberg, *ibid.*, August 20 and 21, 1698, while the opinion of Eugene of Savoy has been published in

[23]The text of the treaty is in Hurmuzaki, *Documente*, V/2, 329-335.

[24]"Nous avons pris Mauro-Cordato a un moment be berger et obtenu sussi que la ligne dee Tivisque vers la Save sera tiree de la pointe du rivage en dela. Nous restons, ainsi le maitres du confluant; mais l'auroit ete une chose commencement. Il faut un certain tour aux paroles, prendre des biais et en un mot beaucoup de delicatesse pour venir a bout de ces gens-la. Ils temoignent n'etre pas mal satisfait de nos manieres, et une espece de contentment de se trouvee avec nous." Schlick to Kinsky, Carlowitz, Nov. 23, 1698, *Turcica*, I, 168, 162-163.

[25]Schlick to Kinsky, Carlowitz, December 2, 1698, *Turcica*, I, 169, 16.

[26]"Interes fateor me esse perturbatum, cum videam Turcas punctum "uti possidetis" non bene explicent et multa a me restitui velint. quae actu in mea sunt possessione. Et vere videatur remo eo venire, ut dici possit: "Vogel friess oder stirb."" Leopold to Kinsky, December 22, 1698, *Grosse Korrespondenz*, 63 II, folder 1698, fol. 1083.

[27]"La Mediation de Milor Pget est conduite avec sagesse et moderation; mais soit vous dit sous un dernier secret, du'un autre cote si pauvre et si sterile, qu'elle nous sert de fort peu de chose. Ils souffrent insultes, reproches et menaces sans oser piper devant ces Messieurs la.", Schlick to Kinscy, Carlowitz, November 18, 1698, *Turcica*, I, 168, 309.

[28]Jakob Hop had reported to the Mediators tha the Austrian ministers were dissatisfied with the showing of the Mediation in the much disputed question fo demolitions along Maros and the Tisza. The Mediators quite naturally protested to the Imperial Ambassadors. "Ils nous l'ont reproche a la verite avec beaucoup de modestie, mais touiours donnant lieu de connoitre le resentiment que les honnetes gens doivent avoir loraqu'ila sont accusez d'un manque de devoir et de poltronneria. Votre Excellence se peut figurer l'embarras et la confusion ou nous avons ete reduits. Il est vrai que nous en avons touche quleque chose dan notre relation a Sa Majesta mais par forme de recit comme on est oblige a faire, sans nous plaindre directement et ce mot semble sous le voile d'un tres grand secret.", Schlick to Kinsky, Carlowitz, December 2, 1698, *Turcica*, I, 169, 94.

[29]"Car comme une bonne paix pour les interst de Notre Auguste Maitre sera votre ouvrage, un contentment universel de tous les Alliez ne pourra etre qu'un miracle du Ciel....", Schlick to Kinsky, Carlowitz, October 30, 1698, *Turcica*, I, 167, 211.

[30]"...il sera necassaire de sonder et nous avertir a tams des intentions, instructions, et de ce qu'au cas le pis de tous l'Abassadeur de Venise y boudra ou pourra faire, car de Compagnie avec luy on pourrot franchir le pas fait a la paix sans la Pologn' et la Moscovie mais le faire sans Venise, la chosse seroit plus difficile et meriteroit plus de consideration...", Kinsky to Schlick, Vienna, November 9, 1698, *Turcica*, I, 168, 188. An Imperia, Rescript which had been sent on the day before to the Ambassadors repeated customary gradations of commitment which the Emperor felt he had to his Allies: The tie with the Tsar was the weakest, the Poles had a claim on him, but they had been notoriously ineffective in recent years. Only in the case of Venice did the Emperor have a sense of obligation in the light of the *sacrum foedus.*, Imperial Rescript, Vienna, November 8, 1698, *ibid.*, 128.; Ruzzini had told Schlick at the end of a long and disagreeable conference that "io veramente credo che l'Imperatore non ha il cuore di concludere ala pace senza di noi.", Schlick to Kinsky, Carlowitz, November 27, 16398, *ibid.*, 236.

[31]Schlick to Kinsky, Carlowitz, December 18, 1698, *Trucica*, I, 19, 126.

[32]L. A. Nikiforov, *Russko-angliiskie otnoshentis pri Petre I* (Moscow, 1950), 18-19; "Der Moscoviter agiret nunmehro seine geschäften directe mit H. Mauro Cordato, undt gebraucht sich keiner andern Mediation mehr als seines Medici welcher sich fast täglich bey jenem einfindet dahero dan ein geheimbe verfassung des projectirten Stillstandts Instrumtri gemuthmasset, undt Er

Mocoviter als ein von denen übringen Allyrten abtrünnig gewordener angesehen wirdt.", *Diarium*, December 26, 1698.

[33]An extensive report on the Mediation's relations with Voznitsin is to be found in Paget's letter to Count Kaunitz, Pera, July 18, 1699, *Turcica*, I, 172, 77: Paget answers the Russian charge that the Austrians and the Mediation were responsible for Russia's 'mauvais succez' at Carlowitz by describing the early history of Russo-Turkish negotiations at the Congress: "Ce bon gentilhomme oublie peut etre, que la premiere audience qu'il eut avec les Abassadeurs Turcs a Carloviz, etoit mercredi le 9e. de Novembre 1698, dans la quelle on ne fit rien; la seconde fut sasmedi le 12e Novebre. Ou d'abord il dit ' que si les Turcsa bouloient parler de demolition, il en demanderoit aussi, mais *qu'il propseroit un moyen tout court, pour parvenir ala fin, laissant aux Turcs la liberte de bouloir l'accepter, ou non*, ewt apres quelques digressions de peu d'importance, il declara ce qui suit (comme on l'a pris de sa bouche, et registre dans le Portocolle: *Legatus Moscovitarum assertive pronuntiait, velle se armistitium inter Ecelaum Ottomannum ac Czarum Moscobiae, ut intra terinum hujus armistity difficultates omnes amoveantur, et Pax coalescat, atque posse reliquos Dominos Plenipotentiareios, sejunctim a Moscovitis, id est, excluss ab his Tractativus Moscobia, concludere tractatus suos.*) Vous observez, que cette proposition fut faite par luy meme, et dans la seconde conference, et sans etre alors acceptee des Turcs."; Nikiforov believes that the Austrians and the Mediation were responsible for Russia's isolation at the Congress, 34, *op. cit.*, 19ff.

[34]Schlick had urged Ruzzini to follow his method of negotiating with the Turks -- "de n'entrer en sucune prolixite dex discours et de reculer quelqu fois pour ensuite mieux sauter; lui alleguant pour example un changement de methode en nous-meme diferente de celle que nous avions cru devoir emploier au commmencement." But all the good advice was in vain; Schlick to Kinsky, Carlowitz, November 23, 1698, *Turcica*, I, 168, 164-165.

[35]"The Venetian Ambassador condemned Sigr Ruzzini's conduct in this matter and promised to write to him to persuade him to alter it....", Sutton to James Vernon, Vienna, Jan. 10, 1699, S. P. F. 80, 17, 462; "Mais l'ambassadeur n'a pas le puvoir de changer, a ce qu'il dit, un mot bien loing d'admettre aucune limitation ux articles prescrits par le Senat meme. Chose bien extraordinaire par ma foi que ces Messieurs s'erigent en dictateurs a l'efard de la puissance Ottomane.", Schlick to Kinsky, Carlowitz, November 23, 1698, *Turcica*, i, 168, 164-165.

[36]"La torrent de son eloquence l'a neanmoin emporte et Mauro-Cordato s'en piquant aussi pour son part ils se sont si fort brouille que ni les uns ni les autres ne scavent proprement pas de quoi il est question, et qui pis est y ont fait entrer un peu d'aversion personelle.", Schlick to Kinsky, Carlowitz, November 23, 1698, *Turcica*, I, 168, 164.

[37]Schlick to Kinsky, Carlowitz, November 27, 1698, *ibid.*, 246-248; "He still insists to have uncertain Mountains allowed him by name, for a Confine to Morea .... Strange! that he should be so obstinately persist in this, when the Turks have often declared and protested that they know nothing of such mountains, and he tells me himself he does not know where they are, and yet have them he must, without suffering the business to be examined by Commissaries; the only way to ascertain things.", Paget to Sutton, Carlowitz, December 23, 1698 O.S., *S.P.F.*, 80, #17, 457.

[38]Schlick to Kinsky, Carlowitz, November 27, 1698, *Trucica*, I, 168, 250-251.

[39]"J'ai cru devoir a Votre Excellnce, mais a'vec las reserve de ce billet separe, que l'ambassadeur de Venise entratient une correspondence fort reugliere avec le R. Pere Menegatti...La regle de bonne prcaution couloit que nous veillassions au commerce des lettres de M. l'Abassadeur. Celles qu'il aviot remis au dernier ordinaire pouvoient avoir de quoi nous eclaircir; mais comme cet eclaircissement ne vous pouvoit encore etre si utile qu'a la cour-meme, qui doit prendre les resolution, ie vous les addresse, Monseigneur. Vous vous en serviez, s'il voius plait et a tout cas il sera fort aise de les faire rentrer au bureau des postes.", Schlick to Kinsky, Carlowitz, November 25, 1698, *ibid.*, 236-237; for the rivalry between Count Kinsky and Father Menegatti se Srbik, *Wien un Versailles*, 245-250.

[40]"Ainsi cetta condute du Ministre de Venise nous est suspecte. Nous croions y avoir envisager de mistere pour ne pas interesser la prudence et prevoiance du Senat a des faits si lourdes, qui seroient: un pouvoir si serre a son Ambassadeur dans la conioncture et saison ou nous sommes, et une prescription de plusieurs autres demarches et du fond de leur interet. Le Medcin Juif qui toute sa vie a ete un pensionnaire de France: la dernier lettre a Nicolosi en chiffre venus de quelque creature de l'ambassadeur Chateau-neuf;"; Schlick goes on to discuss the possible economic reasons for Venitian indifference at the Congress; Schlick to Kinsky, Carlowitz, November 27, 1698, *Turcica*, I 168, 249-251.

[41]"Before he (the Venetian Ambassador) went to Conference, he came to me to let me know that by his Messenger returned from Venise, he had a lattitude allowed him, which he did not question would serve to facillitate the business; but at the Congresse he declared himself otherwise, stumbling and slipping at the same tone that hindered his going forward before, so that no more was concluded in this than in the former Conferences;", Paget to Sutton, Carlowitz, December 23, 1698 O.S., *S.P.F.*, 80, #17, 457; Ruzzini had made things so difficult for the Turks that "they desired his Excellency to give them a positive answer to their requisitions, and that they might have it within a very few daies, that they might take their measures accordingly, either for Peace or war. I hope that we may obtain from them, as much time as will be necessary to have an Answer to these letters, if by then wee have not positive orders from the Imperial Court to agree and sign the Treaties, I am afraid the war will be continued, and we shall have the dissatisfaction of returning back to Adrianople without doing anything, tho' the Article with the Imperialists and Pole are concluded.", Paget to Sutton, Carlowitz, Dec. 25, 1698 O.S., *ibid.*, 449.

[42]Sutton to Vernon, Vienna, January 10, 1698 O.S., *S.P.F*, 80, #17, 463 ff.

[43]"...there was but one way left, which was that His Imperial Majesty should order the signing of his Treaty, and leave the Venetians a certain term, within which they may accept of the conditions, that may be obtained and stipulated for them; That this would not be abandoning them to the mercy of the Turks, but obliging them to what is reasonable; That the Design of the league was not, that the war should never be ended, and that the abuse and perversion of the intent thereof would justify the necessity of a remedy." Kinsky's reply, as reported by Sutton, sounded a note of agreement : "L'Empereur ne peut pas commander a la Repulique, mais si elle ne veut pas se laisser persuader, il prendra ses measures.", Sutton to Vernon, Vienna, Jan. 14, 1698 O. S., *S. P. F.*, 80, #17, 466.

[44]Paget was soon able to report that peace was "in a fair way of being very speedily concluded. the Imperial Ambassadors have been forced to handle the interests of Venice, and settle their limits for them, in doing which they have taken a very good Method; for, inducing the Turks by means of the Mediation to explain themselves about the Bounds of Dalmatia, and to passe their words before the Mediation, that they would desire no alteration nor make any new difficulty about them, they the Imperialists have begun to regulate the possession of the Morea and the Terra Firma, wherein they comply (as it was

found necessary) with the positive Demands of the Turks, which indeed may be judged very excusable.", Paget to Sutton, January 12, 1699, *S.P.F.*, 80, #17, 470.

[45]The rigors of winter emboldened lawless elements in the neighborhood to raid the three camps, cf. the *Diarium*, January 20, 1699.

[46]*Diarium*, January 25, 1699; the Austrians were much amused by Voznitsin's appearance: "Er war dieses mahl ganz *galant* in Einen Verbrämten rock mit alle andere zugehör, so gar auch einer scharpe bekeidet, undt gewiss lächerlich anzusehen."

[47]A detailed account of the actual signing of the treaties and of the ceremonial visits and festivities that followed is to be found in the *Ceremoniale*, January 26-30, 1699.

[48]

[49]"Dai decreti del Cielo era riservata all'anno presente la gloria di farli veder coronati, e finiti; mentre puodirai, che non una; ma piu cause si sian congionte a produr efficace, a propitio l'influsso sopra la sorte d'un tanto negotio.", Carlo ruzzini, *Finalrelation* (FRA), 350.

[50]Lord Paget to Count Kaunitz, Adrianople, July 18, 1699, *Turcica*, I, 172, 78ff.

[51]*Hora Siccama*, 182.

An Epilogue:

The Affair of The *Boursillo Secret*

"Il ne laissa pas péricliter l'empire ottoman, il ne vendit pas sa dignité, il ne marchanda pas sa parole, comme l'ont prétendu, sans preuves, quelquesuns de ses détracteurs, mais il jugea qu'il pourrait tirer quelques avantages pour sa religion et pour sa race des victoires des impériuaux sans laisser aux Allemands at aux étrangers les moyens de s'implanteur, comme il arrive aujourd'hui, au coeur de la péninsule balkanique, dont il savait l'ame hellénique ancestrale opposée aux Germains et aux Slaves autant qu'aux Turcs."

Alexandre Stourdza on Mavrokordatos

For the student of the diplomatic history of Eastern Europe at the time of the Peace of Carlowitz who has a taste, in addition, for modern detective fiction, the aftermath of that Peace provides one interesting puzzle by way of a bonus. A most unimportant postscript, it might be argued, to the work of the Peace Congress, but one that none the less deserves elucidation. New leads have come to light, and this new impetus, combined with a judicious use of the 'little grey cells', may help to clear up a case that has remained unsolved for over two centuries -- one which incidentally casts a good deal of light on the atmosphere of the East-West diplomatic struggle at the beginning of the eighteenth century.

Lord Paget, when he returned to Pera, had a number of diplomatic odds and ends on his mind, but there was one item which had a very pressing claim on his attention because he was personally involved and was, in a sense, responsible for its settlement. In the course of the difficult period of negotiation at the recent Peace

Congress between Austria and Turkey the Imperial Ambassadors had promised a large sum of money to the Reis-Effendi and his Greek colleague, if they would pursue a line more favorable to Austrian interests, particularly in the boundaries question.[1]

It is impossible to determine just who was responsible for this inspiration on the part of the Austrians. Paget may well have given them a hint; he had had sufficient opportunity to observe the success of French diplomacy when it had been armed with such inducements. But the Austrians may have come to this conclusion on the basis of their own views of the ways and means of negotiating with the Turks. In any event, the Ambassadors had concluded even before the negotiations began that they would require an expense account for such a purpose: Count Schlick had informed Kinsky on October 18, 1698, that he was of the considered opinion that "un boursillo secret" would be of absolute necessity in insuring the success of the Austrian delegation's work at the Congress. It would be most unfortunate, he felt, if really choice opportunities were allowed to pass by simply because five hundred ducats were lacking.[2] This sum must be taken as a figure of speech; it was far too modest to obtain concessions of any magnitude. A good deal more than five hundred ducats would be necessary to subvert the two top Turkish envoys, though a sum like that might be perfectly reasonable in the course of talks with Turkish authorities at the local level.

Paget was informed of the plan of the Austrians to offer a token of their appreciation to the Turks. As Mediator, he would be expected to make arrangements in a delicate case of this kind, as he would be expected to see that the conditions of the agreement would be observed and that the money was paid out according to plan. His own view of the matter was far more grandiose than that of the Austrians, and he asked Count Schlick point-blank if the Imperial envoys had received instructions to renew the promise of a gift of two hundred thousand florins which had been entrusted on an earlier occasion to Sir William Hussey.[3] The Austrians seemed to be unaware of such an offer; all they had to o on was the assurances of

Kinsky that if Austrian gold could be of any assistance to their endeavors there must be no thought of being sparing in its use. Kinsky was particularly anxious that funds of this kind should be used to make certain that the members of the Holy League would conclude a peace with the Turks en masse. Austrian gulden would apparently help to make good the deficiencies of Imperial and Allied diplomacy. The *Hofkammer* would presumably take a dim view of this secret weapon, and Kinsky assured the diplomats that he would make certain of its cooperation.[4]

Paget appeared to be content with developments, since he told Kinsky in one of his letters that he was confident that any promises made by the Austrians to the Turks in this way would be carried out. And he was quite content that the details of the arrangements be left to the discretion of the Imperial Ambassadors.[5] Their discretion was extreme for this period, for we have no traces in the documents of the time and place of the secret agreement and of the size of the sum which was promised to the Turks. Even more mysterious, if that be possible, is the extent of the concessions to which the Turkish envoys bound themselves.

The transfer of a large sum of money from the Imperial camp to that of the Turks would certainly have excited comment -- French spies were active at the Congress and the Austrians were well aware of this menace -- and it is doubtful, in any case, that Ottingen and Schlick had the requisite funds at their disposal. The secret undertaking undoubtedly specified that full payment hinged on Turkish performance in the immediate aftermath of the Congress. In March, 1699, the *Hofkriegsrat* asked the *Hofkammer* to make arrangements for a supply of presents for the use of Count Marsigli in his work on the boundary commission. Here was clear proof that the military men were convinced of the wisdom of these bribes; they were almost patronizing in assuring the officials of the Treasury that even inexpensive presents often could do wonders in negotiations of this sort. They specifically requested, too, that Marsigli be provided by this *Kammer* with a sum in cash and a *Kammer* official to supervise the financial activities of Marsigli's group.[6] The *Kammer* may have been reluctant to part with the money, for early in May, the Emperor found it necessary to prod it by issuing a directive that *Hofzahlamtsoffizier* Carl Deissbacher should accompany Marsigli with a sum of seven thousand gulden and a collection of pistols, clocks, and silver plates.[7]

It was not until the Great Embassy of Count Ottingen to Constantinople the following year (this was for the purpose of putting the ceremonial finishing touches on the work of the Peace Congress) that an opportunity was provided for honoring the Austrian promise to the Turkish diplomats. A great number of presents was routine for missions of this kind -- the Turks customarily gauged their importance and not infrequently their success by the value and the diversion provided by the mementos left behind -- and it is interesting to observe the care with which Ottingen prepared his stock in trade. On one occasion, he was moved to complain to the *Kammer* that his supply of gifts would be insufficient.[8] These gifts were, of course, of an official variety; they would be duly presented to the Sultan and his advisers and would be scrutinized by delighted women of the Harem, but the worthy and most incorruptible Ottingen also was to carry with him a gift destined for two men alone. The Emperor had only complicated matters by giving instructions that the *boursillo* was not to leave the bands if his Ambassador until the intended recipients had given proof of their compliancy in assuring that the Austrian demands in the case of the Novi would be met.[9]

The choice of Ottingen for the mission was logical enough; it was but a continuation of the thinking that had gone into his appointment originally to head the Imperial delegation at Carlowitz. But he was the worst of all possible candidates for the delicate work of paying off a bribe. His rude sense of justice did honor to his official capacity as President of the Imperial Aulic Council, the highest judicial body of the Holy Roman Empire, but it did strike observers as being eccentric even by Austrian standards. It would be a wonder to behold and a positive scandal to the Turks in indulgent Constantinople. The fortunes of the *boursillo* in his hands would constitute one of the few amusing moments in the long and difficult course of Austro-Turkish relations.[10]

Ottingen made an almost triumphal entry into Constantinople and his mission appeared to be a great success, but he made little effort to convey the contents of one of his chests to the waiting Reis-Effendi and Grand Dragoman. Paget soon learned of the Imperial Ambassador's hesitancy, and he reacted rather violently, since he felt, rightly or wrongly, that his good name as Mediator was at stake. He had put the full weight of his enhanced prestige as a successful go-between behind the Imperial promise; he was convinced that the Turks had observed their part of the bargain and he was anxious to see the Austrians honor their promise. A series of polite inquiries and calls on Count Ottingen seemed to make little impression. Ottingen declared that the persistence of difficulties over Novi bound his hands in the matter. Paget became ever more importunate, and finally the interested parties themselves evinced an interest in the whereabouts of their gift. But this particular Imperial Ambassador was not the man to be rattled by an English lord and two prominent Turkish officials, and he only appeared to waver when Paget suggested that the money be kept in the English Embassy until such a time as the Emperor was satisfied that his conclusions had been carried out by the Turks.

This suggestion was much to the point, since Ottingen was in the process of packing up for the trip back to Vienna. There was the unexpressed fear in the minds of Paget and the Turks that he would simply take the money home with him. And he finally did announce that his packing was so far advanced that it would be literally impossible for him to leave the funds with Paget. It would certainly cause comment if a wagon belonging to the Imperial Ambassador was suddenly lightened of a strongbox at the very moment of departure. Ottingen feared that the excitable common people would catch wind of this suspicious operation and connect it with the ministers, who were most unpopular because of their role in bringing about the ignominious Peace of Carlowitz.   The Turkish officials added unconscious comedy to the situation by admitting the wisdom of his opinion, and it was finally decided that the *boursillo* should return to Vienna to await there the next favorable occasion for its transfer to Turkish hands.

Ottingen's role in this chapter of the Affair of the *boursillo* is puzzling to say the least. His action was certainly not a part of an independent policy, and yet the very detailed character of his explanations to the Emperor suggests that he was conscious of having adhered too closely to the letter of the law.   The return of his Ambassador with the bribery money must have convinced some Austrian officials that Ottingen was indeed unique. The Emperor had a diplomat who was above suspicion, and, as for the *boursillo*, it had taken a round trip to Constantinople.

But this was not quite the end of the affair. For on May 9, 1701, the *Hofkriegsrat* informed the *Kammer* that the "Donativ-Gelder" which Ottingen had taken to Constantinople and had been unable to the Turks in secret should now be transferred from its place of safekeeping in the *Kammer* to the *Hofkriegszahlamt*, a section of the *Hofkriegsrat*, so that a certain Baron Fingaufs (?), recently appointed Imperial Internuncio at the Sublime Porte, should be able to take it with him when he left for Turkey. The sum -- its quantity was specified on the occasion -- was fifty-five thousand dollars; somewhat short perhaps of the magnificence of Hussey's figure but a most reputable sum in any case.[11] By Turkish standards it was a princely gift for the two men. The usual gratuity for ordinary figures was two bags of gold coin (reckoned by the Austrians as being worth one thousand dollars), and this meant that the two men would receive the equivalent of fifty such bags apiece.

The affair had no such happy ending; indeed, it had no proper ending at all. The existence and the activities of Baron Fingaufs remain matters of mystery, and it is impossible to say whether or not the good work of Mehmed Effendi and Mavrokordatos was ever actually rewarded by the Austrians.[12]

The detective may trace the *boursillo* finally to the *Kammer* and discover that the trail becomes cold there. But the historian whose purposes are vastly different in such an inquiry considers the evidence sufficient (*pace* Stourdza) to state that Mavrokordatos was bribed by the Austrian envoys at Carlowitz. The historian can have no special brief for human weakness, but he must approach it with particular attention to the particular light it throws on events under consideration. The interest in following the fortunes of a bribe must not focus on the guilty party but on the question of the degree to which the kind of settlement achieved at Carlowitz was due to the existence of a variable of this kind. It is a great misfortune that it will always be difficult to answer that kind of question, especially since the sources provide us with only a few scattered hints.

The Affair of the *boursillo* might well provide the starting point for prolonged meditation on the state of relations obtaining between the Austrians and the Turks at this time. Turkish proclivities as far as money was concerned were well-known. The West had made use of this device in the days of Turkish greatness to appease the menacing wrath of the Sultan, and it continued to exploit such a system to the real disadvantage of the Turks in the era of their decline. It was a relatively easy matter, considering the primitive state of geographical information prevailing on both sides of the frontier, to cover up concessions made in this fashion. A Grand Vizir might suspect that his representatives were coming to special agreements with the Europeans, but there was little possibility of catching them red-handed. And even inn that event, moral indignation did not exist for the Turks, as their public morality made no difference on this score. The fate of a 'few fortress on the Turkish frontier' had only a limited hold on both the Austrian and Turkish official imaginations at a time when great territories were changing hands with unexpected rapidity. The role of a Mavrokordatos in this Affair cannot fail to detract from his stature as the reputed statesman of the political revival of Greece under the protecting cover of the *Pax Ottomanica*, but his interest in money was no more striking than that of a Kaunitz or a Windischgrätz, men who could be approached at such a level. His misfortune was that his concessions represented the permanent alienation from the Turkish Empire of the territories which had long been under its control. The subsequent history of Turkey had thus worked to magnify the guilt of the culprit rather than, as is more generally the case, to diminish his responsibility.

Notes to the Epilogue

[1]The puzzle of the *boursillo secret* was first called to my attention by the Kinsky-Schlick correspondence, and I have come to regard it as one of the most interesting problems in historical detection in this period. I was naturally most surprised to discover that Alexandre A.C. Stourdza in his *L'Europe orientale et le role historique des Maurocordato: 1660-1830* (avec un appendice contenant des acts et documents historiques et diplomatiques inédits) (Paris, 1913), 63, was convinced that Mavrokordatos "ne marchanda pas sa parole, comme l'ont prétendu, sans preuves, quelques-uns de ses tracteurs ...." My search for clues in this case eventually widened out to take in a number of collections of documents in the *Hofkammerarchiv*, Vienna, particularly the collection of *Reichsakten* and the *Hoffinanz, Ungarn*.

I can't pretend to have proven that the *Donativ-Gelder* ever actually passed into the possession of the Reis-Effendi and Mavrokordatos, but there can be little doubt that they accepted the offer of an Austrian present for services rendered at the Congress of Carlowitz.

[2]"Nous avons esperé un boursillo secret et à parler en fidel serviteur de Sa Majesté ie le croirois absolument necessaire. Il seroit à plaindre s'il falloit laisser échaper un gros avantage pour n'étre pas en etat de paier cinq cents ducats.", Schlick to Kinsky, Futak, October 18, 1698, *Turcica*, I, 166, 63; Kinsky's answer: "Pour ce qu'est dell' boursillo secreto, quoy qu'il aye grande disette, il faundra tacher d'en trouver, et vous en remettre quelque chose au premier ....", Kinsky to Schlick, Vienna, October 25, 1698, *ibid.*, 151.

[3]"Milord nous a fait sonder aussi, si nous n'avions pas ordre ou povoir de renouveller les promesses d'un present de deux cens mil florins permises jadis au Chevalier Houssey.", Schlick to Kinsky, Carlowitz, October 30, 1698, *ibid.*, 209; "Je lui (Milord) ai répondu que l'avois remarqué beaucoup de bonnes dispositions pour cela et nommement de la part de Votre Excellence quand il y auroit un coup d'état à faire. Il me demanda s'il en pouvoit etre seur? Je lui ai reliqué que la recompense naturellement suivant la service il pouroit entre-tems faire esperer ....", Schlick to Kinsky, Carlowitz, November 5, 1698, *Turcica*, I, 168, 44-45.

[4]"... si par notr'argent ils e pourroit faire quelqu' avantage aux Alliez, il n'y faut pas l'eparggner en ce cas, important que tous ensemble sortent de cette guerre,", Kinsky to Schlick, Vienna November 9, 1698, *Turcica*, I, 168, 189.

[5]"Touchant la distribution des largesses Imperiales, dont Votre Excellence fait mention, la discretion et prudence des Ambassadeurs Plenipotentiaires de Sa

Majesté Imperiale est cette que sans direction ils en disposeront sans doute trés à propos, selon les intentions genereuses de Sa Majesté Imperiale.", Paget to Kinsky, Carlowitz, December 20, 1698 O.S., *Turcica*, I, 169, 178.

[6]"Zugleich such wegen bestraittung anderer vorfallender noturften absonderlichen falls (wie bekant, dass die Türckhen interessirt seyn, und von ihne durch geringe schänckhungen in geld, manicher Vortheill in negotiis zuerhalten) durch einig wenige schänckhung zu nutzen ihro K.M. diensten bey diser commission etwass ausszuwürckhen were, ihme ein fundus und, zu berechnung dessen, ein Cameral-oficier mitgegeben werde.", *Hofkriegsrat to the Hofkammer,* March 10, 1699, *Reichsakten,* 193, 360-361.

[7]Leopold to the *Hofkammer,* May 2, 1699, *Reichsakten,* 194, 361-362.

[8]December, 1699, *Hoffinanz, Ungarn,* 403.

[9]Bosanski Novi had ben recognized as a possession of the Emperor by the Turks, "tho the retention of the Castle was acknowledged (by the Turks) as contrary to the Articles of Peace.", Robert Sutton to Lord Manchester, Pera, March 20, 1701 O.S., *S.P.F.*, 97, #21, 92.

[10]"Neben-relation desz H. Gr. v. Oettingen vom 24, 8-ber 1700, so herabgekomben den 24. 9-ber.", Hurmuzaki, *Documente,* VI, 6-10.

[11]The Emperor had ordered that "die jenige sogennante Donativ-Gelder, welcher H. Gr. Oetting in Konstantinopel mithatte in einer summa von fünffundfünffzig tausend thaller in goldt ...., daselbst aber zue vorgehabter gewissen heimblichen aussgaab nit aussgelegt, sondern mit sich zurukhgebracht undt dem Hofkriegszahlamt wieder zurueckgegeben hat, anietzo dem nechst nach der Ottomanischen Porthen abschickhenden und aldorten nach allergnedigstem special befelch angewendet werden sollen.", *Hofkreigsrat* to the *Hofkammer,* May 9, 1701, *Hoffinanz, Ungarn,* 412, 355-356.

[12]There is no mention of a Baron Fingaufs in the list of Austrian diplomatic representatives to Turkey in the *Repertorium diplomatischen Vertreter aller Länder seit dem Westfälischen Friede,* ed. Ludwig Bittner, Lothar Gross, I, 172.

Part Two

Hungary *Conquista et Neo-Acquistica*: 1697-1703

e ursach oder ursprung dieses aufruehr seye haubtsachlich die grosse contribution von 4

lionen... die andere der Ragozi der grossen anhang fündet, undt keine teutsche truppen in

ngarn."

- Count Ferdinand Bonaventura Harrach

Introduction

The formal exchange of the ratifications of the treaty concluded by the Emperor and the Sultan at Carlowitz officially initiated the first period of peace that the lands of the Emperor Leopold had enjoyed for sixteen years. This peace on all fronts had come none too soon; the strain of the war had been enormous. The cost in men and material had dwarfed any previous expenditure, and the Hereditary Lands which had borne the burden of the twofold fight to defend the Empire against French aggression and to restore Hungary to Christendom under Habsburg auspices had reached the point of complete exhaustion.

The condition of the Imperial army was most depressing. Both officers and men had been long unpaid (they were hungry and clothed only in the decomposed remnants of uniforms), and it was only natural that these desperate men were responsible for an ever increasing number of outrages against the civilian populations. Since the great bulk of this army was quartered in Hungary, its Hungarian 'hosts' were learning through bitter experience once again the unchanging truth of the traditional Hungarian axiom -- 'Do not trust the German.'

The Imperial treasury was, if possible, in an even more desperate condition. The perennial lack of funds now extended virtually to the point of bankruptcy, and the men of the Hofkammer were forced to resort to desperate measures and to a whole range of stop-gap devices to maintain solvency on a day-to-day basis. Certainly a prolonged period of recuperation would be required to make good the great losses incurred by the war and to provide an opportunity for the release of the creative energies of these varied lands and peoples held in abeyance by nearly two decades of war. And with this chance to bind up the wounds would be vouchsafed an occasion for catching up on a problem that had been in moratorium for as many years.

For peace on all fronts meant that the Austrian official mind could turn from its almost exclusive involvement in European power politics to a consideration of the crisis of Austrian internal affairs. This malaise had only become more virulent under the strain of the war effort, but its treatment had been constantly postponed due to the war emergency. But now there would be time to take the measure of the disease and to think of remedies. It might even be possible to carry out a sweeping reorganization of the governmental apparatus and in doing so to pay fitting tribute, in the face of aging men and valetudinarian institutions, to the challenges imposed by expansion and change. The simple truth of the matter was that the governmental apparatus of the Habsburg lands was no longer equal to its recently-acquired Great Power status. This young giant was certainly hampered by the usual growing pains, but there was, in addition, a strong likelihood that, suffering as it did from such a serious constitutional weakness, Austria might never attain to full maturity.

But if this was in a very real sense the basic problem on which al other questions hinged, there was only a wan hope that it would now be examined in any detailed and unhurried way. The mentality of the ministers was opposed, as we have seen on more than one occasion, to a theoretical discussion of the assumptions on which the Austrian system was based, and this condition of mind found support at the moment from the presence of a goodly number of more obvious and immediate problems. How large an army should the Emperor maintain? Where was he to find the money to pay his troops? What measures were to be taken to insure the collection of such necessary funds? What was to be the position of Hungary as far as the Imperial ministry was concerned?

Moreover, there was little time for this weighty consideration; the ministers were well aware that the days of peace were numbered. The spectre of Carlos II could not let them pause for long; his shadowy figure seemed closer to its final resting place in the Escorial with every passing day. It was the anticipation of this crucial eventually which had furnished an unaccustomed haste and decisiveness to Austrian diplomats in their efforts to make peace with the Turks, and this same impatience was to be evident in the official deliberations on taxes, on the optimum size of a peacetime army which had to reckon with an almost immediate resumption of hostilities, and on the measures to be taken to restore order in Hungary.

These three areas of discussion were naturally, even fatally, linked to one another and to the great constitutional problem itself. It was virtually impossible to speak of one without almost immediately raising a discussion of the others. And if the puzzle of the form of government best suited to the Habsburg lands was most often treated under the guise of financial, military, and Hungarian considerations, it was none the less this essential weakness of the whole system which would be present in this breathing period to thwart, to confuse, in some cases to render impotent the most solemn of Imperial resolutions, the most gifted of Imperial ministers.

This interrelated character of the important questions troubling the Austrian ministers in the closing years of the seventeenth century and of the policies developed to meet these situations has not received the attention it deserves. The tendency to operate exclusively within the limits of political, institutional, and economic history has robbed the appraisal of these policies of a good deal of depth and penetration. I cannot hope to reverse such a well-established tendency, but a real service can be performed, I believe, by insisting on the very real connecting links between the various dimensions of Austrian political activity.

Again, virtually all of the previous historical accounts have sinned by reason of the nationalistic commitments present at their base. It is easy work to point out *Grossdeutch* and Hungarian treatments. The present account, while it cannot hope to be free of bias, will at least be free of those particular myopias. On one point, however, the warring factions did approach agreement, and that was in the matter of describing the view taken in Austrian official circles to Hungary. They are generally accused of an anti-Hungarian animus, as being violently opposed to the retention by Hungary of its feudal rights and privileges. According to this composite picture which is by now so well-established as to be regarded as certain, this feeling was applied to Hungarians as individuals, and the lives of Hungarians who were most devoted to the House of Austria were perpetually troubled by this prejudice. Vienna's interest in its Hungarian possession is regarded as largely selfish in nature, and a picture has grown up of statesmen who were committed to a policy of using Hungary for the aggrandizement of Habsburg power without troubling to consult the Hungarians as to their wishes in the matter. This narrow-minded policy required a drastic Gleichschaltung of Hungary with the Hereditary Lands; it was to become a kind of experimental farm for the development of a hardy strain of Austrian absolutism of the Leopoldinian variety.

This is a standard interpretation which is by now so much a commonplace of historical writing that it is difficult to foresee much in the way or revision. The cliché is in any event quite often in accord with the facts. The Austrian ministers' tragic ignorance of Hungarian history and affairs must certainly be admitted, and with it their unfailing tactlessness in their dealings with all too sensitive Hungarian magnates and prelates. Instances can be cited in which they revealed a good deal of cynicism in handling the most sacred institutions of Hungary and the most solemn promises made by Habsburg kings to their Hungarian subjects. Suspicion certainly did exist as to the loyalty of the Hungarians; Austrians had all too frequently discovered that when one scratched a Hungarian one found a rebel.

But this is not the whole story (one might say even on the basis if *a priori* argument that it simply could not be that simple and forthright), and our advancing knowledge of Viennese court circles must inevitably lead to a more balanced picture of the views current in responsible quarters as regards Hungary. Any modern reconstruction of the topography of Austro-Hungarian relations circa 1700 will thus provide a gentle and helpful corrective to the usual view.

The present attempt at reconstruction will fall quite naturally into two parts. The fist chapter will treat the situation in light of the experiences of the Austrian officialdom. Attention will be focused particularly on the deliberations of a policy-making body the reputation, whose relatively brief span of life was often troubled by the Hungarian question. This will be an opportunity to observe important officials, who must have felt secure in the relative privacy of such a council meeting, discussing matters Hungarian with a franchise and a striking diversity of opinion that must come as some surprise to those accustomed to the traditional view. On the basis of my study -- the first to my knowledge -- of the protocols of the Deputation, the extent to which the Austrian ministers were inspired by anti-Hungarian feelings, their real intentions in the matter of the reorganization of Hungary , and the degree to which they were aware of positions like absolutism and particularism can now be described with a greater degree of accuracy.

A second chapter will present the situation from the Hungarian standpoint. Here a connection will be established between dissatisfaction with Austrian policy and Hungarian society as it existed at that time. The difficulties inherent in such an approach are eased appreciably by focusing on the figure of Prince Ferenc Rákóczi -- a precious source for the social as well as the political atmosphere of the period. This life, which has been studied with such an excess of *pietas* and an awesome love of detail by generations of Hungarian historians, has only infrequently been pressed into a service of this kind -- the illumination for a Western audience of a somewhat obscure chapter in the social history of Eastern Europe in early modern times. In instances where it has been felt that the pre-eminence of his princely rank and the rather special experiences of his early years might conceivably create a false impression of the lie of the collective, an appeal has been made to other sources. This chapter will perform two needed tasks: it will introduce the man and his society and it will follow the development of the revolutionary forces in Hungary don to the actual outbreak of the rebellion.

It may well be objected that an excessive amount of attention has thus been lavished in Part Two on the Rakoczi Rebellion and that the care for the preliminaries verges at times on that idolatry of origins of which Marc Bloch spoke so distrustfully, but in no other historical development of the magnitude of the Rakoczi Rebellion has such a disproportionate amount of time been spent on following the fortunes of the rebellion once it had appeared as an active and disturbing force on the European scene and so little care taken by comparison in studying the origins and causes of that force. This section is based on the belief that the study of the origins of this Rebellion is not in any sense of jejune undertaking but that it is very much of an open and actual question.

Chapter 1

The *Deputation des Status Publico-Oeconomico-Militaris*[1]

"Die lender sollen das eisserste zu thun bewogen werden"
- Leopold

"Ungarn könne man such nit bloss lassen. Scriberetur de conventiculis."
- Ernst Rüdiger von Starhemberg

The desperate straits in which his ministry found itself in 1696 and 1697, finally moved the all too conservative Leopold to establish a new top policy-making body to advise him on the measures which must be taken to avoid approaching disaster. There was a profound sense at last of the emergency -- the well-trained eye might discern a deepening of the traditional note of despair customary with the hard-pressed Austrian statesman -- and the existent councils had long since demonstrated their ineptitude in meeting emergencies quickly and decisively. The causes of this failure were apparent: these bodies were far too slow and tentative in their movements; their competencies had a way of becoming perpetually snarled, and working political figures were too variously mixed in their meetings with holders of high and prestigious Court offices who had no real political responsibility or influence. Leopold had inherited the Imperial Privy Council from his predecessors, but this institution had been superseded, as early as 1672, for all practical purposes by the smaller and more manageable *Geheime Conferenz*. This last had in time fallen prey to the common lot of such institutions in the faultiness of its operation and the excessive spread of its membership with the result that further limitation of the number of participants in the grand political conversation at the Court of Vienna became necessary as the century came to an end.[2]   It was in the frequently-used device of *ad hoc* deputations (*Deputierte Räte* had been known since the early part of the century), committees within the *Geheime Conferenz* charged with discussing specific situations and composed of admitted experts in the area under discussion, that Leopold found the solution to his difficulties, and on September 19, 1697, he issued an Imperial rescript which created the Deputation "*des Status publico-oeconomico-militaris*".[3]

Its name was an immediate indication that its scope would be broader than that of the usual deputation, while the formability of its creation indicated that it would enjoy a longer span of life than was usually the case.   Moreover, its name was a helpful guide to its composition. The habits of mind of the Viennese administrators habitually divided the broad area of governmental activity into smaller categories whose relative primitiveness had the apparent merit of simplifying (in theory at least) their handling of any problem. Discussion, when it occurred, immediately fell under the headings of *cameralia, militaria,* and *politica,* and by an extension of this principle of division all problems which were important enough to require deliberation at the very pinnacle of the administrative system were regarded as being "partly military, partly financial, partly logistical, and partly political."[4]

The practical consequence of this was that it required the presence in the Deputation of a representative of the *Hofkriegsrat* and the *Kriegscommissariat,* the offices charged with directing and supplying the Imperial military machine, and of the *Hofkammer,* the office which had the uncongenial task of paying the bills out of the Emperor's all too meager financial resources. The heading of *politica* was less straight-forward.[5] There existed a system of chancellories at Vienna which acted as intermediaries between the Emperor and his subjects in the Holy Roman Empire, his Hereditary Lands, Hungary, and Transylvania, but not all of these offices could be expected to participate in the meetings of the Deputation. It seemed more sensible to require the presence at the meetings, though this was in no sense a formal rule, of the Supreme Bohemian Chancellor Count Kinsky, the Imperial Vice-Chancellor Count Kaunitz, and the Austrian Court Chancellor Count Bucceleni. But the presence of an official was more often a function of his personal influence with the Emperor than the objective importance of the office which he held.[6] For it was quite naturally the Emperor and he alone who gave the Deputation the form and the power it would possess; he regulated its relations with existent bodies, and only he could give its conclusions the *placet* which would transmute them into Imperial resolutions.[7] In the infancy of the Deputation, the Emperor devoted much time and thought to it, the last and perhaps most promising of his experiments in administrative institutions, for he hoped that he would find real counsel and an organization powerful enough to take upon itself some of the frightening burden of state affairs without arrogating to itself, of course, any of the responsibility and authority that was uniquely his.[8]

The working formula was simple enough. Twice a week, once in town and once at the Sommerschloss of one of the members, the presidents of the collegially organized *Hofkriegsrat*, *Kriegs-commissariat*, and *Hofkammer* met with the chancellors in a concentrated effort to hammer out a compromise policy acceptable to all the parties involved. The meetings were presided over by a *praeses* and were attended as well by high-ranking officials from the participating agencies, who assisted their chiefs by providing a continuity and making it fairly certain that the practical implications of the suggested solutions would not escape the Olympian view of the more distinguished and more socially eminent presidents and chancellors.

The position of the *praeses* of the Deputation was one of extreme importance, and the Emperor Leopold showed great interest in providing the office with the maximum in power and prestige so as to simulate as best he could the presence of the Emperor. The *praeses* was charged with the preparation and the announcement of the agenda for the meetings, the direction of the discussions towards the goal of working agreement, the summation of the results of the meeting in the *conclusa*, and, what was most important of all, the securing of the Emperor's approval for the recommendations which the meeting had made.[9]   The fate of the Deputation was thus intimately tied to the person of its *praeses*, and in its formative period the Deputation was fortunate to have Count Kinsky as its first *praeses*.   As Supreme Bohemian Chancellor, Kinsky would have been virtually an *ex officio* member in any case, but his almost paramount role in the political scene at the time made his possession of the presidency a certainty, for thus it was made absolutely certain that the decisions of the Deputation would be acted upon favorably by the Emperor simply on the grounds of the confidence he had in his minister.[10]

On Kinsky's death on February 27, 1699, something of the influence of the Deputation passed with him. His less gifted rival Count Harrach became his successor. Harrach's personal ties with the Emperor were closer than any other minister's had been, but the Emperor was not as dependent on his political wisdom, which was not particularly compelling in any case.[11] The Deputation could trace the remainder of authority that it possessed to the presence of Count Dominik Kaunitz, who frequently served as the acting praeses, and of Count Gundacker von Starhemberg.[12]

The roster of the membership of the Deputation at the moment of its origin will cause little surprise.   Count Ernst Rüdiger von Starhemberg represented the War Office, and when he was unable to be present (ill-health and pique seemed to head the reasons for his absences) Fieldmarshal Count Aeneas Caprara appeared in his stead. Count Siegfried Ereuner, who had presided in recent years over the *Hofkammer* without noticeable success, appeared in his capacity as the director of the *Kriegscommissariat*, while the *Hofkammer*, temporarily without a president, was represented by its acting president Gundacker von Starhemberg, a younger half-brother of Ernst Rüdiger and a man whose talent as an administrator, particularly in financial matters, was rare in that period. His position was not particularly well-established in the Deputation as yet; his often heedless impulse to get things done quickly set him in opposition to the senior member of the group.

In addition to Kinsky, Kaunitz, and Bucceleni in the *politica* wing of the Deputation, Leopold Cardinal Kollonitsch served as a regular member. Neither the Hungarian Palatine nor the Hungarian Chancellor were members of the Deputation, and their exclusion from such an important council and one which would be so intimately concerned with Hungarian affairs had all the appearance of being but another application of the Emperor's standing practice of barring to Hungarians positions of real importance in his government. But Leopold and Austrian officials generally might well have countered with the assertion that it was the Cardinal-Archbishop of Esztergom and Primate of Hungary who was in precedence and in reality the only sensible choice for the role of representing Hungarian interests in the new body.[13]

There were reasons enough for such a position. As a member of a Hungarian noble family (albeit of Croatian origin), Kollonitsch could lay claim to ties of blood with the Hungarian nation.[14] Moreover, he had served as the president of the Hungarian *Hofkammer* as early as 1672, and in the course of hi ecclesiastical career he had been ordinary of a series of Hungarian dioceses until he was finally raised to the primatial see on the death of Archbishop George Széchényi in 1695. But for all his origin and his long experience of Hungarian affairs, there would always be the suspicion that in the deepest recesses of his heart His Eminence was not truly Hungarian. The impression had been created -- it was not without foundation -- that he was above all a representative of the Universal Church and a devoted adherent to the ideology of the supranational monarchy so characteristic of the Counter-Reformation in the

Habsburg dominions. His pronounced and unflinching zeal in the interests of the Roman Church, whose cardinalitial dignity he bore, and his extreme loyalty to the Emperor could not fail him in the eyes of Hungarian public opinion.

But such a judgment of Cardinal Kollonitsch, particularly in the versions current in Hungarian historiography in the nineteenth century, is not entirely fair; its animus was too often inspire by anachronistic judgments on past events and personalities implicit in the though world of modern nationalism.[15] Without possessing anything like the sheer spiritual distinction of Pazmany, or the vigorous, homely and undeniably Hungarian virtues of the Archbishops of Szelepchenyi and Széchényi, his immediate predecessors in the see of Esztergom, Kollonitsch possessed a lofty conception of his role: "As the Pope has the responsibility for all Christendom, so do I, as Primate, have to answer to for all the souls in Hungary."[16] And this was said as a reminder to his colleagues in the Deputation that he would be required in view of his position as the patron of Hungarian interests and as the Mediator between Vienna and Pozsony. In Pozsony the Palatine presided over the remnants of Hungarian autonomy. Through his coordination, the system of *comitats*, based on their *congregations* of magnates and gentry, carried on the business of collecting taxes, providing for local defense, and administering justice. The present Palatine was the enormously wealthy Prince Pál Esterházy, and he was responsible according to constitutional practice for mediating between the King and the whole nation. But Esterházy was too pliant a man to wish to exert his prerogative, and the work of mediation had passed by default to the Primate, who now felt called upon to resist any policy which was manifestly unfair to the Hungarian 'souls' in his keeping. His conception of unfairness is clearly the point at issue, but it is important to remember that he could on occasion defend his Hungarian charges against the extreme measures of his Austrian and Bohemian colleagues.

That he was accustomed to follow a devotedly pro-Habsburg line, there could be little doubt, but he might well have defended his position by underlining the undoubted fact that the exact nature of the best interests of the Kingdom of St. Stephen was far less certain in 1698, than it had been at almost any other crucial point in Hungarian history. He might have pointed to the existence of other prominent Hungarians who were anxious to establish a new *modus vivendi* between Hungary and the Hereditary Lands by reconciling as best they could the legacy of the past with the necessities of the present. The Primate's greatest crime in the eyes of Hungarians was his refusal to assume that the Hungary that had gone down to disaster at Mohács was an eternal and unchanging political absolute -- the only possible criterion of all further political development. This skepticism placed him immediately at variance with the feudal and particularistic interests of the Hungarian nobility and gentry who found the necessary ideological support for their extremely privileged position in an idyllic fantasy of pre-Mohács Hungary,

It was in his *Einrichtungswerk* (1688) that Cardinal Kollonitsch presented a fairly nuanced statement of his compromise position and in doing so made the most substantial contribution of the period to the literature of Habsburg planning for the future of Hungary.[17] His plan did not contain anything in the way of general axioms to govern future Austrian policy; it hugged the more mundane path of administrative reforms on Hungary, with some reference to legal and ecclesiastical questions as well. The plan leaned rather far in the direction of a Catholic centralism in the Habsburg dominions, Hungary included, and this tendency was supported by arguments drawn from the latest versions of Natural Law theory and Austrian mercantilism.

But for all this apparent modernity, it assumed the peaceful co-existence of Austrian absolutism and Hungarian feudalism; once the more outstanding areas of disagreement had been removed. Hungary, whose constitutional and social organization was far more traditional than that of the neighboring Habsburg lands, was to be admitted to the Austrian 'family of nations' without first undergoing any radical modifications in its social and political form, though it was clear from the plan that any effort on the part of the Hungarians to preserve a *Ständestaat*, that political system in which the Estates of the realm were in control, in full panapoly would have to be abandoned. This was particularly true as far as the freedom of the Hungarian nobles from taxation was concerned. Since the nobles were no longer required to join the Apostolic King with their feudal retinues on the field of battle, Kollonitsch believed that they should contribute to the maintenance of the Habsburg administration in Hungary and thus assume a fairly large proportion of the costs of the Imperial military machine. There was nothing excessively Germanizing or anti-Hungarian in a suggestion of this kind, but it ran into the most reassured privileges of the Hungarian ruling classes, and revealed in this the Cardinal's easy disregard of one of the most prominent obstacles to any accommodation between Vienna and the Hungarians.

The balance of the plan considered means of modernizing Hungarian judicial, financial, and ecclesiastical organization. The judges were to be made independent of the administration, and a greater equality before the law was to be assured for all classes of Hungarians. The obligation of the peasants to work the lands of the landowners was limited to three days a week in the hope that the condition of the peasantry might thus be improved. The Catholic Church was to undergo a great tightening up of its parochial and diocesan administration: the period of Turkish occupation had resulted in a great number of abuses in ecclesiastical practice.

For all its omissions and its cavalier manner with obvious points of contention, his plan was certainly a thoughtful proposal by a well-intentioned man whose experience of administrative chaos had been a long one, but this variety of political education had limited his view of the whole Hungarian horizon to questions of administrative practice and the readjustments of financial responsibilities. That this proposal was proof of the high degree of culture in social, political and economic affairs possessed by Leopoldinian statesmen is doubtful.[18] The absence of any great current of political intelligence at the Court of Leopold 1 is only further emphasized by such a document. The *Einrichtungswerk* was condemned, it must be admitted, to remain largely a plan, but even as a work of political creativity it cannot bear comparison to with the military genius of Eugene of Savoy and the architectural achievements of Fischer von Erlach. Again, in Cardinal Kollinitsch there can be no question of a devious Machiavellian who took a Richelieu or a Marazin for his models with the aim, in this casse, of destroying a nation's existence rather than of developing it. Here was an aged and not overly gifted prelate and administrator whose best moments had always been in the role of the crusader, who had the gift for apprehending the presence of human misery and misfortune without being able o do very much to remove the deeper sources of the trouble. His contributions to the work of the Deputation would be a further indication of the invariable honesty of the man and of the pathos of his political position.

An outstanding omission from the list of membership was the victor of Zenta.[19] Count Kinsky had asked the Emperor at the very outset whether or not Prince Eugene might not be called upon to participate, but Leopold's reply left little room for further discussion: when it was necessary to have Eugene there, he would summon him.[20] This occasion never arose, and when Eugene finally did come to a position of real prominence in 1703, the Deputation had succumbed to the usual fate of such institutions and had entered into that twilight existence from which it was summoned only rarely to advise the Emperor.

It would be a great error to overlook the presence at these meetings of men like Weber, Palm, von Mayern, Albrechtsberg and others whose names do not survive -- men who figured in the Deputation as *referendarii* for their offices or as secretaries of the *praeses*. The three offices of military and financial affairs (the *Hofkriegsrat*, the *Kriegscommissariat*, and the *Hofkammer*) were required to send, in addition to their presiding officer, the head of their chanceries, the *Kanzleidirektor*. These were responsible career bureaucrats who would be most able to report to the Deputation on all the minutiae and the latest developments of any case, since they were charged with the supervision of incoming and outgoing mail. In their capacity as *referendarii*, they kept minutes of the meetings which they attended, and these protocols were used as reference works by their chiefs and their offices. Occasionally, they provided the basis for the detailed reports on the meetings that were submitted to the Emperor. These professionals were not confined to the passive role of observers; they were permitted to pronounce on matters under consideration particularly when they fell within their competency. The extent to which they were able to influence a decision of the Deputation must remain a mystery.[21]

But one of these men, the official who acted as secretary to the *praeses*, was to play a very special role in the history of the Deputation. Unfortunately there are at the moment no clues to his identity (though further research may eventually solve this minor mystery), and we must be content to refer to him simply as the 'Secretary.' He was probably one of the private secretaries (*Secretarii secreti*) of the Emperor, and, in addition to his usual task of keeping the minutes of the meetings of the *Geheime Conferenz* and preparing the *Vorträge*, the traditional form in which these minutes were presented to the Emperor, he was charged with performing the same function for the Deputation.[22] Though it was clearly impossible for him to cover all of the meetings, a great percentage of the surviving minutes of the meetings of the Deputation are his work, and they are, for all their maddening paleographical obscurities, minor masterpieces of reporting. Since he was present as an assistant to the praeses, he played the role of a neutral observer whose position as a close collaborator of the Emperor himself afforded him the best of vantage points from which o follow the proceedings. As a consequence of this, he was not merely content to transmit the bare outline of the Deputation *vota* and *conclusa*; he considered it part of his job to inform the Emperor on the whole range of the Deputation's activity. He was careful to report on factional and personal disputes (a subject of great interest to his Imperial master); he was content to hint at their existence, when they were still largely hidden from view, but when they burst into the open he reported on them tersely and yet dramatically enough to leave no doubts in Leopold's mind as to the nature of the disagreements.

The Secretary was not without his own personal feelings; they occasionally figured in his protocols (Count Breuner, the President of the Kriegscommissariat, was a particular *bête noire* of his), but a fair amount of objectivity in his reporting was assured in that he had no commitment to one of the participating offices and thus did not labor under the disadvantage of having to support a particular point of view.[23] His actual contribution to the work of the Deputation must have been a most respectable one, but the historian of the period can be excused for regarding this activity as paling into insignificance when compared with his authorship of these precious sources for the history of the Deputation. The historian of the period will always be very much in his debt, since he will always be fated to follow the dramatic events in the Deputation through the eyes of the nameless Secretary.[24]

The specific problem with the Deputation had been called into being to solve was this: what was the best working compromise that could be struck between the urgent needs of the Imperial military establishment, requirements which continued to be enormous in light of the impending resumption of hostilities in the West and the additional menace of a Turkish attack at any time, and the amount of tax revenue to be collected in the hereditary Lands, Hungary, and Transylvania? Two limiting considerations on any official solution of the conundrum were obvious enough: first that the army must not be reduced below the point of immediate effectiveness in the case of attack, and second that the various components of the Habsburg system should not be reduced by excessive demands on the Hofkammer to despair and ruin.[25] But once any discussion advanced, as it must, beyond those generally accepted verities, real differences developed easily enough on questions of practice, and full play was thus provided for the abrasive action of the conflicting competencies and personal antagonisms present in the Deputation.

It was difficult, for instance, to secure general agreement on the precise number of troops that would be required to maintain the Austrian lands in a respectable position of defense, and quite as difficult to determine just what sections of the population should be required to bear the major brunt of the tax burden that had been set on the previous basis of military needs. Our small circle of men was well aware that a simple mathematical relation was at the very center of their problem. It was an ironclad equation in which any increase or decrease in military strength had to be immediately adjusted for in the tax bill, or if one cared to approach it from the other side of the equation any variation in the amount of revenue would have immediate repercussions on the size of the armed forces.[26]

The majority of the Deputation appeared to favor approaching the problem from a financial *point de départ*. Long and bitter experience had taught the older men that official optimism on the amounts of money that might be raised must not be allowed to run far in advance of the realizable tax income; the Emperor, they felt, should take account of his financial resources and should then conduct his foreign and military policy on that basis. An interesting case occurred here of statesmen acting contrary to the selfish interests of their offices. The President of the *Hofkriegsrat*, at one point, declared his support for a policy of retrenchment which would reduce the army to a more manageable size; there were good military grounds for his proposal: he found it difficult to be responsible for hordes of unpaid, riotous and mutinous troops, whose contribution to the success of any future campaign would probably be slight in any event.[27]   The spokesman for the *Hofkammer*, his half-brother Gundacker, on the other hand, opposed such retrenchment on the grounds of a principle self-evident to him "that a monarch should not regulate his expenditures according to his income but rather should levy taxes according to his budgetary needs."[28]

In line with this position which had all the marks of a revolution in *nuce* as far as administrative thinking was concerned, Gundacker von Starhemberg favored a sweeping reform of the whole financial administration and of the entire tax system. The Emperor had customarily depended for his funds on indirect taxes and money from regalia and royal monopolies, and the direct taxes (*contributiones*) which required the express consent of the Estates of the various kingdoms and provinces, and obtaining this consent was a lengthy and often disappointing procedure. The introduction of a universal income tax was one of Gundacker von Starhemberg's most radical suggestions; it naturally encountered heavy opposition from the older generation in the Deputation, and even when approaching disaster moved the body to propose it finally as a last-ditch measure to the Emperor, it was some time before Leopold could be brought o give his assent to a measure that was do at variance with the constitutional structure of his domains.[29] The directness of the younger Starhemberg's approach as well as its direction were, as we will see in some detail, isolated instances; the habits of administration acquired in years of permanent chaos had convinced most Austrian ministers and bureaucrats that "everything hinges upon the money" -- the counsel, obviously, of the pessimist and the pusillanimous.

It was no accident that the Great Enigma facing the Deputation was discussed in its first year at least largely in its Hungarian aspects. The link between the Kingdom of Hungary and the Deputation was clear: Hungary had been largely responsible for the creation of this special council, and it would be the failure of the Deputation to solve the Hungarian question that would make virtually certain the Hungarians' recourse to rebellion when a favorable opportunity presented itself. The recently-completed conquest of Hungary was in large measure responsible for the woeful state of Imperial finances and for the astonishing degree of exhaustion evident in the Hereditary Lands; it was this state of affairs, coupled with the constat tension between the top administrative offices, that had occasioned the Emperor's creation of the Deputation. It was in Hungary, too, that the great bulk of the army whose peacetime strength was to occasion such frequent debate in the Deputation was stationed, and it was Hungary, too, that constituted for these anxious bureaucrats the sole wan help of relief for Austria's financial difficulties -- Hungary might yet manage the *salto mortale* of quartering most of the army, of maintaining a large cameral administration in the recently-acquired areas of the country, the *neoacquistica*, and of providing hitherto untapped sources of income, the veritable bonanza that was needed to avert bankruptcy. That this was the expectation of normally cautious and painfully realistic men only increases the pathos of their faith in Hungary, for Hungary could not fail to disappoint them.

For this was a country that had spent the long decades of Turkish rule in stagnation and economic decline. Large areas of the richest areas agriculturally were bare now of men and crops; where once medieval Hungarians had flourished there was now a melancholy collection of ruins, deserts, and swamps. What had survived in the way of manpower and economic resources had been further tried by the long series of recent campaigns on Hungarian soil, and the Austrian officials were well aware that Hungary, liberated now and enjoying a nominal peace, was exposed to the exactions of disorderly German troops and marauding bands of Serbian volunteers. These military formations were established in that country as a dubious warranty for its security and as a punishment in some cases for its political indiscretions whether real or imaginary. All the best will (and it was difficulty to see how there could be much of that in Hungarian circles) of the Palatine and his subordinates in the *comitats* would never be able to bring off the miracle which the men of the Deputation needed so desperately.[30]

If there was something illusory in this expectation in Vienna of the great Hungarian bonanza, there can be no illusion about the nature of their motives in pressing for a change in the Hungarian tax system. There was nothing very pretty or inspiring about this desire to shift a good deal of the burden of the *contribution* to Hungarian shoulders; it had little to do with any anti-Hungarian spirit, any calculated effort to establish an absolutistic and centralized uniformity in the Kingdom of Hungary, or any desire to experiment along the lines suggested by the mercantilists. The sheer need for funds was so great and so actual that the Austrian ministers could not afford to be at all punctilious in their tapping of Hungarian sources of revenue. The specter of imminent bankruptcy was a more potent force in their minds than any brand of ideological planning for Hungary's future. The grim chase that developed in which the Viennese government would play the role of hunter and Hungary would act as the quarry filled many pages of the deliberations of the Deputation.[31] With the expert assistance of the observant Secretary it will be possible to abandon the usual macroscopic view of this tragic situation -- an attitude based in equal parts on a relative scarcity of sources and on the presence of fairly coherent preconceptions as to the configuration and relative degree of responsibility of the forces at work -- for a microscopic approach in which an effort is made conscientiously to follow the actual course of the chase as carefully and minutely s possible and with only the bare minimum of theoretical aids.

Hungarian affairs had begun to assume a sufficiently ominous form even before the Deputation was established; they were, as we have seen, largely responsible for its existence. The last decade of the seventeenth century was a transitional period in the relations of Hungary and its Habsburg king: the old order was evidently in question, and there was even talk in some Viennese quarters about the existence of a state of political and constitutional vacuum in Hungary, that *tabula rasa* which would permit of a new order of relationships solely at the behest of the Emperor. But the official discussions in the *Conferenz* were less revolutionary in tone; they had created a pattern of conversations *in Hungaricis*, based on a constant dialogue between Vienna and Pozsony, that was to be carried over with little change into the meetings of the Deputation.

In a meeting of the *Conferenz* on August 21, 1696, with six high officials present who would later figure prominently in the

Deputation, the reactions of the Hungarians to the suggested tax assessment for the coming year and to the somewhat mysterious reform project for Hungary fathered by Count Auersperg, an Austrian military bigwig who had long been stationed in Hungary, were reported on and discussed. The memorial presented by the Hungarians was blunt enough: "The kingdom will not even hear of the four million (gulden) and the Auersperg project."[32] Once the door had been so summarily closed on those two possibilities, the Hungarians seemed tractable enough in expressing their willingness to discuss a figure in the neighborhood of two million, and they made a tentative request that they be consulted in the drawing up of the *repartition*, the itemized tax schedule which broke down the direct tax by classes and counties. To these important points was added a selection of the customary *gravamina*: military excesses in Hungary, the enormous burden of quartering the army, and the present state of subordination of local Hungarian officials to the agents of the military government. This memorial gave every indication that the great struggle would take place on the question of the amount of the tax -- the sum of four million was exactly one-third of the total for the Habsburg lands -- and secondly on the method of collection, since this would presumably determine just what sections of the Hungarian population would bear the brunt of the steep tax bill.

A year later when the Deputation initiated its own discussions of Imperial finances, it confined itself logically enough at first to the same two questions of *quantum* and *quale*? It had to determine the amount of the optimum sum (the *fundus*) and once this had been decided upon the means for raising the sum had to be determined. Twelve million florins continued to be the figure mentioned for the *fundus*, and there were members present who optimistically felt that the money could in fact be raised. Time alone was in short supply, and it might well be that the twelve millions would be finally collected long after the crisis had been reached. The pressing character of their obligation, as members of the Deputation, to assist the Emperor in establishing some kind of order in his finances did not prevent the whole group from indulging in the fine old Viennese custom of prolonged discussion. Kinsky was very much in character when he expressed the opinion that the Deputation must proceed with great care and arrive at a decision only after all the possibilities had been canvased.[33]

But in the course of these preliminary discussions three specific proposals were made with regard to Hungary: First, that the clergy, the magnates and the nobles, the cities and the peasants were to receive fair treatment, based on their ability to pay; second, that the excise system in operation in the Hereditary Lands should be introduced into Hungary; third, that the *repartition* was to be prepared as quickly as possible so that it could be forwarded to Pozsony and then to the *comitats*, and that a date for the expiration of payments should be set. A further suggestion was made that the presence in Pozsony of Cardinal Kollonitsch would be of great assistance in expediting this procedure.[34] It was important to be expeditious in this affair because the rigors of the winter were already depleting the ranks of the taxpayers in Hungary -- a goodly number was seeking refuge from the weather and the tax collectors in the more easygoing atmosphere of the Turkish Empire. The Deputation noted in passing that the Hungarians were not the only problem children; the Austrians had been showing increasing reluctance in paying their taxes in full; even the grudging *Bewilligung* of the Austrian Diets did not encourage them to pay up in full.[35]

On February 20, 1698, the Deputation returned to the knotty question of the most efficient system of direct and indirect taxes for Hungary. Kollonitsch expressed his doubts about the utility of his trip to Pozsony; it was pointless, he felt, to argue first and then wait expectantly for the money -- only when the gulden were flowing into the *Hofkammer* would it be time to discuss matters of such moment with the Hungarian leaders. He inclined to believe that Hungary's share of one-third of the total was excessive, but since there appeared to be no disposition in official quarters to compromise on the *quantum*, he had a contribution to make towards the solution of the problem in *quale*. Two million gulden should be paid by the *misera plebs contribuens* and the royal cities, and the remaining two millions by the upper estates, the clergy, the magnates, and the gentry. The Deputation was in substantial agreement on these points, and it was especially anxious that His Eminence should assume personal charge of the whole affair; the members were afraid that if the matter were left to the Hungarian administration, the privileged classes of Hungarian society would evade their unquestioned responsibility by simply not paying their portion. The Cardinal ha no illusions about the consequences of his programme; the assistance of the military would certainly be required to encourage and to compel payment if need be, and a small army of Kammer and Commissariat officials would be required to make certain that all segments of Hungarian society were doing their share.[36]

When word of this new policy reached Pozsony, the Palatine was quick to appeal to the Deputation. The reports that had reached him of the latest plans for Hungary were certainly not calculated to ease an already difficult situation. His present objections were limited for the moment to the problem of the *repartition*; he could only protest against the radical change involve in taxing the privileged classes. But the Deputation continued to be adamant. It declared that any resistance to its recent directives would not be consistent with loyalty to the Emperor who had approved its work, and reiterated its position that all segments of Hungarian society must now contribute their share. Special care would be taken, in addition, to make certain that "the weight of the tax load was not transferred to the weaker by the stronger." The Hungarians were promised a visit from the Primate -- an event even less likely to calm apprehensive Hungarian magnates -- in the meantime the Deputation expected that the Palatine would carry out the *repartition* along the lines which had been established.[37]

The expected visit of the Cardinal of Pozsony did take place, but it is clear that the prelate made little impression on official circles there. For early in May, 1698, the Deputation received a personal visit from the Palatine, and the delicate matter of the "remaining two millions" (this was a Hungarian euphemism for the amount which the Hungarians felt was in excess of the sum they could be reasonably expected to pay) was discussed once more. The Palatine, acting in his official capacity but more immediately on this occasion as the spokesman for the Hungarian magnates resident in Vienna and for a number of other magnates who had been moved to visit the capital on learning of the Deputation's tax policy, wisely restricted himself at the outset to technical problems consequent on that decision, but he was clearly interested in securing some relaxation in the programme and, in particular, obtaining permission for a conference of delegates from the *comitats* to meet and discuss the whole question in Vienna.[38]

While the Palatine was sounding out the Deputation, the Primate was meeting with the Hungarian leaders, who were present in Vienna. Somewhat reluctantly they conceded him the point of the four million gulden; they even went to length of being willing to have that money collected, if need be, by the extreme device of *execution*, a brutally confiscatory process carried out by the military. But one of the magnates found a sufficient courage to warn the Cardinal that the present policy would most certainly lead to a general rebellion in Hungary. His Eminence's serenity was not to be disturbed, however; he discounted any talk of the danger of rebellion.[39]

The very next session of the Deputation was taken up with the consideration of a formal statement submitted to it by the Hungarian representatives. One of the members voiced the suspicion that the two millions would never be forthcoming whatever the agreement with the Hungarians now or ever in the near future. The *Secretrius* put his usual footnotes to the discussion, and it was pessimistic enough: "The *Kammer* will never put its eyes on the sum in question." He didn't doubt for a moment that the Hungarians had the wherewithal to pay the tax -- all Hungarian denials had obviously failed to convince him, but he was much alive to the fact (he felt that this was beyond doubt) that in forcing through its programme the Imperial government made insurrection virtually inevitable.[40] For if the pen of the Secretary moved too quickly to allude to it, he was obviously aware of that other iron law of Hungarian politics with which the members of the Deputation must surely reckon: any increase in the financial strain imposed on Hungary would be reflected in a proportional increment of the danger of revolt.

Recent events in Hungary, the unsuccessful rising of Ferenc Tokay and his peasant followers the previous summer for example, only further established the validity of this fateful proposition. The only practical consideration remaining, then, was to establish the point of no return where a Hungary *in tormentis* went over to open revolt against Hungarian rule. The relentless nature of their financial obligations made it virtually impossible for the ministers to be overly delicate in this matter of crossing the Hungarian's pain threshold, and thier Viennese insouciance, however understandable under the circumstances, would prove finally disastrous.

But at the moment, a difference of opinion on just how real the danger of insurrection was could still be maintained. His Eminence was not worried, though the Secretary certainly was. His Imperial Majesty in replying to the latest Hungarian petition appeared to be unaffected by such weighty considerations. He was in no mood to quibble with the Hungarians and he declared with all the accents of an irrevocable decision that he could not possibly relax anything of his demand for the full sum of four million gulden. His decision was presented in terms that must have given even the members of the Deputation grounds for amusement: "His Sacred Majesty accepts with a grateful heart the undertaking of the lords, the Primate, the Palatine, and the magnates to raise the full sum in the space of twelve months."[41] The Palatine continued to hope that even the ingenuous Imperial resolution did not close the door on further negotiation, but he was privately assured that this was indeed Leopold's "last word".[42]

The next stage in this complex and bitterly fought dispute was reached in June, when the Palatine submitted a memorial which confined itself to the question of the *repartition*. It now appeared that he had made up his mind to accept the Deputation's programme as a *fait accompli*, but it was easy enough to suppose that his administrative apparatus would now throw obstacles in the way of any policy of fulfillment. Cardinal Kollonitsch, realizing immediately that the question had evolved to this point, was anxious to have the records of the *comitat* tax recorders (the *perceptores*) sent on to Vienna so that it might be possible in considering the *repartition* to have all the relevant facts on hand. But it was objected that it would consume a long period of time to bring these records to Vienna and that it would slow down the preparation of the *repartition*. No one doubted that it was an excellent suggestion on the part of the Cardinal to keep the closest possible watch on what the local administration in Hungary did, but time was so pressing, that any checkup of this kind would have to be postponed.[43]

The Deputation moved on to a consideration of the equally difficult situation in the Hereditary Lands, and here a wide difference of opinion was evident. Officials who had a close working tie with the local administrations found much to complain about in the proposal that there should be no preferential treatment of any one of the Hereditary Lands. In the course of the debate on this point, ministerial tempers, which had been under a great strain throughout the course of the negotiations with the Hungarians, began to reveal themselves in no uncertain way. The indecisive Kinsky found himself in the uncongenial position of urging the members of the Deputation to abide by its previous determination to insure equal treatment of the lands and provinces; he felt that it was dangerous practice to reopen time and time again debate on questions which had been regarded as decided. In his dual role as Supreme Bohemian Chancellor and *praeses*, he begged his colleagues to adhere to the policies they had laid down. A quick interchange with Count Bucceleni developed, and Kinsky so far forgot himself as to observe that the Buccelinis had always been a troublesome lot.[44]

This contretemps may have had the effect of clearing the atmosphere, for Kinsky then went on about the business of concluding the meeting as if nothing had happened. The Deputation was responsible for the Imperial decision to treat the Hereditary Lands on terms of equality. And this system, once it had been established, must be maintained as a standing practice. Any changes and exceptions to the *fundus* would cause irreparable harm to and would only lead to a further deterioration of the financial sitation, the very eventuality which the Deputation was seeking to avoid. As far as the *quale* of the *contribution* was concerned, there were to be no admitted differences between the components of the *Ländercomplex*, though in practice Kinsky admitted that there might be concessions to local conditions.[45] Equality and a respect for local conditions were strange partners indeed. As Kinsky envisioned it, there was to be a mystical harmony established between the Emperor's obligation to treat all of his subjects as equals and the Emperor's sacred responsibility to maintain local privileges.

The Emperor ratified Kinsky's position in the subsequent resolution, but he did not involve himself in his minister's niceties of reasoning. As the father of his people, Leopold could not permit any inequality to exist, especially in the present grave situation. As far as the how of the tax system was concerned, he was prepared to follow local practice as long as the funds were forthcoming. Kinsky had reported that, while Hungary had not actually figured in this discussion of the division of the direct taxes for the Hereditary Lands, it was now assumed that the Hungarians would go ahead with their *repartition*. "No one shall be exempted, though the manner of collection may be left to the *comitats*."[46] The Emperor wished to bring Hungary into line with the overall policy for his dominions; this was a move that was eminently understandable from his point of view but one which would be regarded as catastrophic in Pozsony.

At the end of June, the Deputation suddenly returned to the suggestion of the Palatine that delegates from the Hungarian counties be summoned to Vienna to discuss the whole matter of taxes with the Imperial ministers. Cardinal Kollonitsch reiterated his belief that such a meeting would be to little purpose. It would be a costly business, or one thing, and it was condemned from the start to be at cross-purposes because each *comitat* had its own peculiar customs in collecting the taxes. Kinsky informed the Deputation that the Emperor had decided that the Hungarians should be called to Vienna; this would be an application in the case of Hungary of his practice of calling the *capli* of the *Länder* to Vienna for exploratory talks on the amount they would be expected to secure from their diets. Once the Imperial will had been made known, there was an end to further discussion.[47] A silence reigned so complete that the Deputation gave no hint that it was willing to provide the ministry with a concerted plan for its discussions with the Hungarians. This may have been a consequence of the particular nature of the Deputation as an administrative agency -- it existed as a method of achieving compromise solutions rather than of initiating policies, or the silence may have been produced by the feeling that the forthcoming talks would be of little practical value, and the men of the Deputation would still be expected to perform a minor financial miracle once the talks had failed.

In any event, the summer of 1698 was consumed in the discussion of other aspects of the great overall problem of finances. Transylvania, whose situation also approached disaster, occupied the foreground.[48] But at a meeting on September 18, 1698, the Deputation received a memorial from the Palatine once more. Prince Eszterházy had arrived in Vienna to oversee the preparations for the conference, and his statement to the Deputation had clearly been composed under the influence of the conversations he had had with the first wave of Hungarian visitors. The representatives of the *comitats* had encouraged the usually malleable Palatine and his close advisors to adopt a more intransigent position. He was now arguing that in accord with the ancient laws and privileges of the Kingdom which had been duly sanctioned by its Habsburg kings, matters of exclusively Hungarian interest could not be decided upon outside the Kingdom's borders, and thus the present question of taxes must be referred to the Hungarian administration at Pozsony and to the deliberations of a Hungarian Diet (the Diet was not mentioned but it was clearly implied by the preamble to Eszterházy's statement).

The Deputation was quite unmoved by Ezsterházy's insistence on the antiquity of these laws. The members felt that much could have happened in one hundred and fifty years to change conditions. Moreover, the Hungarians had previously shown slight interest in these particular laws. It was the Hungarians who had requested this Viennese meeting, and for the past two years they had been submitting proposals to the ministers which had made no reference to the illegality of any decision which the ministers might make. The mood of the Deputation was not a propitious one for the successful outcome of the talks. The replies to the Hungarian arguments were makeshift and evinced little desire on the part of the members to preserve equality and particularly at one and the same time. But the members were aware that the explanation for these most recent Hungarian demands was to be sought in the selfish attitude of the Hungarian upper classes; they simply did not wish to pay taxes, and the pious talk about ancient privileges was mere smokescreen. It would be simple for them to cover up their iniquitous behavior if the whole question was referred to Pozsony.[49]

The hint that had been made about the calling of a Hungarian Diet ran into solid opposition in the Deputation; the members were in complete agreement -- there was to be no Diet. If Kinsky in his *conclusa* adopted a more moderate tone it was because he fully expected that his conclusions would be used as a rough draft for the Imperial answer to the Hungarians. Representations must be made, he felt, to the Hungarians that the recently-adopted tax programme bypassed the normal Hungarian channels only out of sheer necessity.[50] His Majesty in his subsequent resolution declared that he had no intention of assailing the privileges of the Hungarian Estates. There was no more interested than he in restoring the Kingdom of Hungary to the full possession of its lawful rights and privileges. "*Salus populi suprema lex*"; there was a good chance that Leopold was entirely sincere about this.

But in his present concern about the desperate state of finances there had seemed no other way of expediting matters than to summon representatives of the Hungarian counties to Vienna. Since the Hungarians themselves had so often expressed the wish to be treated on an equal footing with his Hereditary Lands, he had availed himself of a device which had been frequently used in their cases and which had in no way weakened the fundamental laws of those provinces. This was a fairly complete restatement of the ministerial position; it was not entirely free from an undercurrent of the disingenuous, but it had the merit of coherence and vigor in argumentation. The sense of emergency which it conveyed had been even more insistent; the Emperor expected that his *deputirte ministerium* would quickly put an end to the present imbroglio by coming to agreement with the Hungarian. If it failed in this undertaking, the Emperor would be literally forced to make other arrangements.[51]

Further negotiations produced little that was new in the way of talking points and little that could be helpful in bringing about an agreement. There was a constant flow of grievances and complaints from the Hungarian side and quite as steady a flow of admonitions from the Deputation. The members continued to abide by their decision that there were to be no exceptions in the *repartition*, that all in sundry were to assist in carrying the enormous burden "according to their means." The Hungarians were also given to understand that their convocation could not be adjourned until the question of the obligation of the various classes had been raised and settled -- presumably in line with the expressed wishes of the Deputation. Imperial patience continued to be in short supply, and the Emperor almost peevishly pressed the two parties to reach an agreement.[52]

Weeks passed by without any modification in the two positions; the most that could be said was that the matter was still under consideration. Cardinal Kollonitsch reported to the Deputation on October 20, 1698, that Pál Széchényi, the Archbishop of Kalocsa, had visited him the day before, and speaking for the entire group of

Hungarians present in Vienna, he declared that the delegates found themselves unable to agree to the *postulata* of the Emperor without the official sanction of the Hungarian Diet.[53] This meeting was confronted with even more disquieting news; reports had reached the older Starhemberg of an uprising near Munkács that appeared to be aimed not so much at the Emperor and his German soldiery as at the Hungarian landowners themselves.[54] This was a pointed comment from the *misera plebs* on the conversations in Vienna, but the news gave little comfort to the Austrian ministers; it seemed only further reason for concluding an agreement with the Hungarians.

The condition of the military had never been quite so desperate, and one member of the Deputation urged that a *repartition*, whether legally justified or not, should be prepared in Vienna and submitted as soon as possible to the inspection of the three interested parties: the *Hofkammer*, the *Hofkriegsrat*, and the *Kriegscommissariat.* The pressing need to make decisions on winter quarters for the troops demanded an almost immediate forecasting of the amounts that could be expected from the Hungarians.[55]

A Hungarian plan of *repartition* did exist. but Palm, the *referendarius* for the *Kammer*, declared that it was quite unacceptable. It was decided then to compare it with another version which had been tentatively prepared by the *Commissariat.* One further point seemed even more laden with direful effects for the Hungarians. The Deputation was of the opinion that the whole responsibility for the continued state of indecision rested with the Hungarians. A not entirely unfounded suspicion was present in the minds of the ministers that the Hungarians had been using a wide variety of delaying tactics. This condemnation of the Hungarians was certainly too factious to be very convincing, but the renewed sense of annoyance was something which even the neutral observer might appreciate. But following immediately on the heels of this broadside came the first hint of approaching compromise: the Deputation gave the Hungarians to understand that the peasants were to bear two-thirds of the tax and the upper classes the remaining third. Cardinal

Kollonitsch, who was in constant communication with the Hungarian delegates in his thankless role as go-between, was instructed to convey this latest proportion to the Hungarians. The Deputation expected that the magnates would revise the Hungarian draft of the *repartition* on this basis.[56]

A week later, the Deputation amplified its directive to include the Hungarian cities; they were to contribute one-sixteenth of the four millions. Count Kaunitz, now that an initial concession had been made, came forward as an exponent of a policy of moderation vis-a-vis the Hungarian privileged classes; he feared that the nobility and clergy would become disaffected if pressed too far. He suggested that repeated assurances be given to their representatives that the present plan was only valid for one year; in was in essence an emergency measure.[57] The Deputation agreed with him that everything possible must be done to quiet the fears expressed in Hungarian circles that this allegedly temporary measure would become customary practice. The burden of responsibility was thrust once more on the Hungarians, but this time the turn of phrase was novel: "....the present system will remain until they (the Hungarians) suggest a more suitable one." As Austrian officials began to tire of the chase, they became less careful in the expression of their opinion. The ministers had come to realize at last that the nobility and clergy would do everything in their power (and this power was not to be easily brushed aside), and that the means would be found to shift their obligations to the already overburdened peasantry. Injustice would evoke further injustice; force would be required to carry out the tax collections. The members of the Deputation turned from prospects such as these to echo the pious hopes that a close watch would be maintained on the *comitats* during the period of tax collection.[58]

The Deputation might be excused for feeling that it had said the last word on the subject -- the word was 'force', but on November 12, the Palatine returned to the attack with a memorial that revealed how little progress had been made. Eszterházy now had his turn to be disingenuous; he had "understood that a third of the contribution would have to be paid by the clergy and the nobility, and he hoped that it was not the wish of His Majesty that the Hungarian nobility should perish." He followed this with a depressing picture of the conditions in Hungary. Barely eight of the fifty-two *comitats* were in anything approaching a normal state; the flight of taxpayers to a low tax haven in the Turkish Empire continued; the nobility faced a ruin quite as complete as did the common people. He reminded the Deputation that the Kingdom of Hungary had chosen a Habsburg king of its own free will and that could not have reasonably expected treatment of the kind it was receiving. He requested that another system of taxation be established -- "it would be a simple matter to discover one" -- and suggested that a special commission be formed to restudy the whole problem.[59]

The Deputation reacted in a most surprising way to this latest Hungarian gambit. The members sounded for once as if they had been impressed by the Palatine's arguments. They looked for a time into the very center of the general chaos then prevailing in Hungary and had emerged from the experience chastened and more reasonable men. It might be wiser after all to proceed with sweet reason than with violence, and the Deputation declared that it was ready to receive the Palatine in person on the very next day.[60]

The Palatine appeared at the appointed time, supported by Archbishop Széchényi, the Hungarian Chancellor, and two secretaries from the Chancellory. The little delegation was assured at the very outset by Count Kinsky that it owed its day in court to the gracious resolution of the Emperor that the case of the Hungarians should be heard once more. In the meantime, it was given to understand that all the previous directives of the Deputation retained their full legal force.[61] The Hungarians' feelings of gratitude were difficult to measure, since they went about their accustomed business of airing grievances with the same tiresome insistence. But one point they did make with great solemnity: that it was quite impossible for the clergy and the nobility to pay one-third of the Kingdom's direct taxes. Archbishop Széchényi sought to illustrate this point by his own experience: he received only eighty gulden from his holdings and yet he would be required, according to the present ruling, to pay forty thousand in taxes. His injustice was repeated through the whole gamut of Hungarian taxpayers; the peasants, for example, were now required to pay the *Kammer* three times the taxes they had paid under the Turks, and they were expected to provide food and quarters for the Emperor's soldiers as well. Taking another tack for a moment (any argument on the basis of comparison with the Hereditary Lands was always a dangerous line of argumentation for the Hungarians to adopt), the Archbishop reminded his hearers that the nobility and the clergy in the Hereditary Lands had never been required to pay as much as one-third of the *contribution*. At this point, the discussion was broken off, and the Hungarians were told to return the next day for further conversations.[62]

The Palatine probably felt that an appeal to the existing practices in the Hereditary Lands was more calculated to arouse a feeling of compassion in the members of the Deputation than prolonged references to the ancient laws of the Kingdom of St. Stephen. And so on the next day, he reminded the Cardinal that the Hungarians had always prepared their own *repartition* and that they felt it to be the only right, according to the customs of their country, that they retain this power in their hands. Once he had made this point, he got down to cases. The cities were now prepared to pay a sixteenth of the 4,000,000 gulden, and the upper Estates approved this plan. he then produced his surprise of the day for the Deputation: the nobility and the clergy was ready to contribute one-thirtieth of the total -- a sum of 133,333 gulden.[63] At this crucial moment, the Hungarian delegation was asked to withdraw, and the Deputation was left to consider what its next step should be.

It could be certain of a quarter of a million florins from the Hungarian royal cities and now 133,333 florins from the three upper Estates; that left 3,616,667 (the very enormity of this latest turn of events led to some arithmetical fumbling) that had to be found, and there was, of course, only one possibility.[64] The members found it convenient to confine the debate to facts and figures without caring now about the moral issues involved, and this strengthened the hand of the forces at work in the meeting who were interested in making concessions to the Hungarians. It was Kaunitz's opinion that the demand for one-third would never work. Twice the figure that was to be contributed by the cities seemed reasonable -- an eighth or 500,000 gulden would probably be the best solution. The Secretary was at his corrosive best in marvelling at the suddenness of the jump from a third to a thirtieth; the nobles, he reminded his listeners, had never yet made any contribution at all. It was their sacred duty to do something to alleviate the burdens of the *misera plebs* and the cities; if ever there had been an opportunity to do just that it was now.[65] But his pointed remarks no longer found much in the way of response; the members were content that the discussion should continue in an aimless fashion on the question of the figure to be set. Five hundred thousand gulden -- the figure mentioned originally by Count Kaunitz -- was finally adopted without much show of enthusiasm.[66]

But even this concession was not sufficient, and on November 17, 1698, the Hungarians gave notice that the only solution was to establish the figure at one-twenty-fourth or 166,666 gulden.[67] This bargaining operation continued down to the very end of the year 1698, and it was terminated only when the Emperor intervened with another show of decision and established the sum of 250,000 gulden as the final figure. The Deputation might wonder how *der arme mann* would ever be able to raise as much as three and a half million gulden, but a salve to its conscience was provided by the well-meaning promise that a measure of relief would be given to the common people by reducing the levels on food for the soldiers quartered in Hungary.[68]

The first part of the year 1699 was devoted to a consideration of the problems arising out of the implementation of the *repartition* which had been finally agreed upon after so many months of negotiation. It was soon evident that the most flagrant abuses were common in the *comitats*; funds were not forthcoming with the speed and in the abundance that had been expected, and this most inequitable of tax programmes was undergoing the addition of further impurities at the local level. A whole series of complaints from the *comitats* began to clog the Deputation's agendas. Surprise, indignation, and then a sense of frustration, the whole armory of emotions at the disposal of a harried and virtually powerless bureaucracy, were in increasing evidence there. The Deputation loyally moved that each and every case should be submitted to an investigation and that alleviation, wherever it seemed just, should be allowed in individual cases. But as far as the *fundus* itself was concerned and the division of responsibility along class lines, there no concession could be made.[69] In the early months of 1699, the Deputation was still unwilling to advise the Emperor to collect his taxes by force; it might be wiser to see what the Palatine and his subordinates could achieve in their own way. However they managed their eccentric behavior, the important thing was that the money be collected. Never had the contradictions at the base of Austrian 'absolutism' in this period been made quite so manifest.[70]

But by the middle of the summer, the ministers were forced to abandon that ambiguous position for the brutal and unequivocal appeal to force. The support of the military would now be necessary to carry out the *execution*, and it was soon a not uncommon occurrence for soldiers to whom their pay had been owed for months to receive the few gulden directly from the taxpayers without having any recourse to the intermediary offices of the *Kriegscommisariat* and *Hofkammer*.[71]

The assembly of Hungarian notables was convened on November 10, 1698.[72] The ministry attempted from the very beginning to secure agreement on the question of the taxation of the nobility. But since freedom from taxation was the dearest and perhaps most fundamental privilege of the Hungarian nobility, the government encountered a tremendous amount of resistance to its proposal. An instance of the reaction of the magnates is to be found in the account of the assembly written many years afterwards by Prince Ferenc Rákóczi. He reports that the delegates were informed that the ministry was determined to abolish the existing Hungarian laws, remove the remnant of the privileges of the nobility and the free cities, and establish a permanent appropriation, a *contributio continua*, that would release the ministry from the necessity of bargaining on the tax question each year with Hungarian leaders. One can doubt that this is an accurate description of the ministry's goals in the convocation. But Rákóczi was convinced that there was a plot against the traditional Hungarian liberties and privileges at the bottom of every ministerial proposal, and in his account, therefore, supposition has been transformed into fact.

A high point of the convocation was the interview which Archbishop Széchényi had with Emperor Leopold. Acting as a representative of the notables, the Archbishop told the Emperor that they were unwilling to make any binding commitments without the formal approval of the Hungarian Diet. In Rákóczi's version of the meeting, the Emperor was moved on hearing this to inform the Archbishop that he fully agreed with him but that "his ministers had assured him that they could succeed by following the path they had taken; he only wished to let them do this to see what the outcome would be." It is questionable that the Emperor would disavow his ministers so sweepingly, though Leopold may have been guilty here of the old Venetian practice of trying to make the best of a difficult situation by offering boundless assurances of goodwill. On the following day, the Hungarian delegates demonstrated so violently for the calling of the Diet, that the meetings of the convocation had to be prorogued. The Emperor provided the Hungarian leaders, who were in the process of returning to their *comitats*, with a signal expression of his displeasure. In an Imperial Rescript of December 24, 1698, he complained of the attitude of the nobility and declared that he had no intention of permitting the nobility to evade its tax obligation.

The spirits of the delegates to the convocation were not obviously depressed by their sudden dismissal and the Emperor's manifest displeasure. They had no intention of yielding the field permanently to the so-called 'temporary expedients' of the Deputation, and distance permitted them to indulge themselves in renewed thought about the ancient constitution of Hungary. The fact that peace had been formally concluded with the Turks gave them another opportunity to agitate for the re-establishment of the old order in its pristine form. The Palatine and the *Brevia brevium*, the highest Hungarian tribunal, reflected this feeling in a set of proposals relative to the return to the status quo that were presented to the Emperor for his consideration.

This latest memorial was discussed, as was customary in the case of problems arising out of more properly constitutional situations by the *Conferenz*, rather than by the Deputation, and at an important meeting of that council on March 31, 1699, the current atmosphere of Austrian official opinion was displayed in some detail.[73] Since the members of the *Conferenz* present at this meeting were with one exception -- the Supreme Chamberlain Count Waldstein -- members of the Deputation as well, the opinions expressed on this occasion provide us with a continuation and an amplification of the evolving opinion in the latter body. One important figure was absent (Count Kinsky had died the month before), and the great political conversation had narrowed, as far as its participants were concerned, to the Cardinal, Count Harrach, Count Kaunitz, the warrior Starhemberg, and Count Bucceleni.

The Hungarians specifically requested the calling of a Hungarian Diet, the reuniting of Hungary and Transylvania, and a reduction in the number of troops stationed in Hungary, and in the amount of the *contribution*. Kaunitz, Bucceleni, Starhemberg, and the Cardinal in their *vota* united in opposing the calling of the Hungarian Diet. They made no difficulty on the grounds of principle, though there was enough in their remarks to indicate that they feared that the Hungarians might exceed the bounds of political good taste, if they were allowed to meet in Diet without having first given full assurances that nothing untoward would occur in the course of the meetings. The activities of the Vienna conference were too recent a disaster to permit the ministers to contemplate the spectacle of a full Diet at Pozsony. In addition, both the Imperial Vice-Chancellor and the Primate were suspicious of the role of the *Brevia brevium* in helping to formulate these proposals; it was well known that courts of this kind had frequently been sources of revolutionary activity in the past. The *Conferenz* urged the Emperor to tell the Hungarians that he was completely occupied at the moment with other problems (this was true enough in that the problem of the Spanish Succession was absorbing more and more of his attention) and that he would submit to them, when a favorable opportunity presented itself, a plan for the best reorganization of the Kingdom of Hungary.

Opposition to the union of Hungary and Transylvania assumed a milder form. The Emperor had in his *Diploma Leopoldinum* of 1691 formally sanctioned the continuation of Transylvanian autonomy and its separation from Hungary, and Kinsky's policy of separating the two which had been embodied in the *Diploma* continued to puzzle at least one of the members -- the Supreme Chamberlain. Thought the *Diploma* as it stood clearly militated against a reunion of the two countries, it was not in any sense irrevocable. Starhemberg based his opposition to reunion on his belief that the political traditions of the two lands were at this stage so much at variance that any fusion would automatically result in a rebellion on the part of the Transylvanians. The Primate's opposition was largely on religious grounds. The union of Hungary and Transylvania would furnish non-Catholics, who were prominent in the politics of tolerant Transylvania, a chance to play a similarly important role in Hungarian politics (this because the chancellories would have to merge as well), and he had no wish to see the Transylvanian system introduced into Hungary. For the moment, delay seemed the wisest course of action. The usual consolations would be offered to the Hungarians; they might be promised that there would be a reduction in the number of troops stationed in Hungary consistent with the security requirements of the Emperor's dominions. But this was a dim hope; any very drastic diminution of the military establishment of the Emperor was doomed at this point to receive the veto of the men who were responsible for the conduct of Austrian foreign affairs.

While the Deputation was still hesitating to ask the Emperor for a full-scale military execution in Hungary, Cardinal Kollonitsch attempted to provide a good example by a rigorous inspection of the tax registers of the *comitat* of Pozsony, and he reported to the Deputation that, while seventeen hundred individuals had paid their taxes, seven hundred were still in default. His loving care was offered to the emulation of both sets of officials, but in the face of the growing desperation evidenced by the Viennese financial circles there seemed little point to worrying about the legal and moral niceties of the *repartition*.[74]

The Secretary in his usual oracular manner expressed his opinion that it was precisely on the outcome of its most ambitious undertaking, the recent *repartition*, that the Deputation would stand or fall. "The Deputation should order another execution or it will prove itself to be of absolutely no value whatsoever -- which is in fact the case."[75] This view of the Deputation's efforts was not general, though the increasing number of absences of important members gave support for the suspicion that others were fairly close to the Secretary's conclusion. His testimony deserves close attention, since it is the completely spontaneous reaction of a well-qualified observer of Austrian politics. He was quick to note the ease with which the officials in the Deputation fell back into the hallowed ruts which had been laid down by the indecision of the emperor and Count Kinsky, though he was careful, of course, not to mention them by name.

But the spirit of reform when it occasionally manifested itself evoked almost similar misgivings. This was certainly the case when the Secretary commented on the proposal of Gundacker von Starhemberg that the tax system should be given a greater degree of permanency, since the *Kammer* found it increasingly difficult to be able to rely on annual appropriations by the Diet. In a particularly revealing *nota bene* the Secretary disclosed the extent of his commitments to the old system and, by implication, to a particularistic conception of the government of the Habsburg lands. "Everything depends on the Bewilligung of the local diet."[76] This was to his mind a foundation stone of Austrian political life which not even the Emperor could afford to jeopardize. If for any reason, and he was well aware that the present emergency might be considered reason enough, the Emperor were to by-pass this system, he would be guilty of a great error, and there was no chance that he would gain from such a transgression -- "indeed it would produce just as little as had been secured before."[77]

Our Secretary's ultimate comment on the Deputation is almost lost amidst his hurried hieroglyphs. When the chances of raising ten million gulden in 1700 were being discussed, he turned from the world of official imagination to the most pessimistic of mediations on the ways and means of this government. "We won't get the money even if we command it with ..."[78] The sentence trailed off as if the Secretary realized that he was composing the Deputation's obituary. Bankruptcy and/or a general insurrection in Hungary were clearly the most likely consequences of the Deputation's demise. The Secretary's melancholy conclusion can be critically appraised only after further research in the records of the *Hofkammer* receipts from Hungary for these years. The protocols of the Deputation, while they give no comprehensive picture of the actual tax returns, suggest that reality was always far short of the Deputation's ideal.

Even a cursory examination of the negotiations in the matter of the Hungarian *repartition* for 1700 that were carried on at the end of 1699, adds further weight to this pessimistic picture. That October the Emperor sent the Hungarian Chancellor to Count Harrach, the *praeses*, with the report that the Palatine had intended to draw up the next *repartition* with the assistance of a number of Hungarian magnates who were in Vienna at the time, but these men had refused to cooperate because they wished to avoid any further responsibility in the tax question that might involve an unfavorable reaction from their countrymen. In lieu of this improvised body, they suggested that the six parts of the kingdom of Hungary, namely Croatia, Slavonia, Transdanubia, Cisdanubia, Upper Hungary, and the Transtibiscan region should be empowered to send representatives to Vienna for a conference on the *repartition*.[79] The unblinking inclusion of Croatia and Slavonia was not to be wondered at, since, it was the Hungarian view that the extents of the past century and a half not modified the territorial limits of the Kingdom; the Austrian officials, though they did not immediately protest, were by no means so certain of the legal status of these areas. Cardinal Kollonitsch remembered the unpleasant experiences he had had with the meeting of the year before and naturally wished to avoid any repetition of that debacle. The Deputation parried the Hungarian thrust eventually by sending the proposals back to the Palatine with the suggestion that the Palatine, the Hungarian Chancellor, and the resident magnates should confer on this matter.[80]

The Palatine forwarded yet another Hungarian memorial to the Deputation. The Hungarians had hoped that the return of peace would bring with it the need of emergency measures and the re-establishment of the rights and privileges of their Kingdom, particularly in the case of the exemption of the nobles from taxation, and now they were shocked to note that the Palatine was once again going about the business of parcelling out the taxes in what they could only interpret as the transformation of an emergency wartime measure into standard fiscal practice. They understood their misgivings about the legality of taxing the nobility "as if it belonged to the common herd."[81] Once this most important of all points had been driven home, the memorial asked that Croatia, Slavonia, and those countries in the *Neoacquistica* which had not figured in the previous *repartition* should be included in the one that was under consideration.

The remaining proposals took serious issue with the current practice of selling estates in the newly-acquired territory (the *Hofkammer* had been doing this on a fairly extensive scale) or of making presents of such properties to deserving ministers and generals, even to the Palatine himself, as the Hungarian Chancellory had been doing. The memorial expressed the wish that these estates should be returned to those individuals who could legally establish their ownership.[82] The impression created by such a document was that the Hungarians were only providing a further variation of an all too familiar theme -- the demand that the Austrians should permit the continuation in Hungary of the favored position of the clergy, the magnates, and the gentry.

The *vota* of the Deputation on the points raised in this memorial were not particularly impressive. Croatia, they allowed, did fall under the historic jurisdiction of the Kingdom of Hungary, but the members seemed unwilling to come to any practical conclusions on that ground. As for the remaining points, they were willing only to promise that they would discuss the other questions at a later date.[83]

The remainder of the negotiations for the *repartition* closely followed the desultory pattern which had been established in 1698. There was the usual set of definitive decisions on the part of the Deputation and protests on the part of the Hungarians. Eventually Hungary was required to pay three million gulden out of a total of ten million gulden. The actual finale of the affair was an even more striking repetition of the proceedings of the year before. In the midst of the Court's extensive preparations for Christmas, the Deputation set the figure as final, commissioned the Palatine to see the details, and comforted the Hungarians with the assurance that everyone concerned would be happier if His Imperial Majesty could afford to be more permissive in such manners but his financial difficulties left him no alternative. The reports from Madrid were more disquieting with the arrival of every courier, and Hungary was exhorted to continue patience and promised that it would receive concessions, unspecified of course, in other areas.[84]

It is possible at this point to total up the achievements and failures of the Deputation in its two years of exceedingly close involvement with the Hungarian question. In both these years the *quantum* of the tax bill had been established, if only at the eleventh hour, and on both occasions the Hungarians had been forced to accept this figure as final. But the experience of the Deputation in attempting to alleviate the pressures on the *misera plebs* had been less satisfactory. At the very beginning of its activities, it had sought to introduce a rough degree of equality in the tax obligations of Hungary's classes. The decision that the privileged should pay half and the peasants should pay half seemed eminently sensible at the first sight, but it was to prove a most utopian measure when the prevailing forces in Hungary, even in the state of advanced disorganization in which that Kingdom had found itself, began to defend their privileged position.

Slowly and reluctantly the Deputation was required to sacrifice its humane principle to the uncomfortable realities of Hungarian social life. The empty treasury in Vienna required that the Austrians make concessions to the established order in Hungary. The balance that was achieved in the course of these two years was a most precarious one. There was no decision that could ever be regarded as final in this struggle between the ministers and the Hungarians, and positions which had been espoused and then ostensibly abandoned by the Hungarians had a curious and annoying habit of reappearing: the demand for a Hungarian Diet, the demand for the complete exemption of the upper Estates, the request that areas like Croatia, Slavonia, and Transylvania should be reunited with Hungary and thus enabled to contribute their share of Hungary's obligations to the *Kammer*.

Certainly in its central problem of finding the means to pay and feed the great Imperial army in Hungary the Deputation had drawn a blank. But the opportunity -- it was rare enough -- to produce order where there was only chaos had passed as surely and as finally as the chosen moment to establish a more advanced form of government in Hungary. The experiences of the Deputation left the Emperor facing a dilemma in regard to Hungary; he could not permit the traditional system to continue there on the same footing and yet he could not bring himself to initiate any real reform.[85] His tendency and that of his advisers was to solve the problem by avoiding it; the collective sense of inadequacy in the face of the dilemma eventually forced the Austrians to drive it deep into the administration's subconscious.

The Deputation survived is failure, though it now devoted the majority of its deliberations to smaller items of business which developed out of the growing tensions on the European scene. When it did touch rather gingerly on Hungarian affairs in the crucial period between the outbreak of the War of the Spanish Succession in Italy and the raising of Rákóczi's standard in the foothill of the Carpathians in the spring of 1703, it confined itself as if by choice to lists of grievances from the *comitats*.[86] Case after case in sickening succession of military brutalities, thefts, corrupt practices, and mutinies were brought to its attention. And even if the old Starhemberg might sniff and grumble with a reminder to the members that 'soldiers are not monks,' there was an impressive display of an outraged sense of justice on their part.

The primate, much maligned for the alleged Hungarophobia, made a manly effort within the admittedly circumscribed limits of his view of injustice to make amends to Hungarians who had suffered as a result of these excesses and to make certain that the guilty parties of whatever rank would be punidhed. In one case involving an officer, both he and the Secretary insisted that the good name of the Emperor was at stake in this affair and that any convenience in a miscarriage of justice on the part of influential Austrian officials would have a most profound and disastrous effect on the affection which the Hungarians had for their King.[87] And then there was the tragi-comic Affair of the Cow's Feet. An officer, quartered on a family of German farmers in Hungary, had developed late one evening a sudden appetite for baked calf's foot. He had demanded that his host should provide him with this delicacy, and when the latter objected that he was unable to do so, the officer had dispatched his orderly to the barn with orders to chop off the pedal extremities of the German's cows. A very real indignation was expressed at this report in the Deputation; compensation was ordered, and the non-military members went to great lengths to complain that the military was simply indulging in pointless enormities of all kinds.[88] This particularly senseless act was but one of many.

That a body of the importance of the Deputation should spend its precious time adjudicating on the Affair of the Cow's Feet was a sufficient indication that the members could be moved by injustice, but it was also a sure index of the body's decline as an effective instrument for administrative trouble-shooting. It had taken refuge in minutiae, and there it was destined to remain for the balance of its existence.

The failure to face up to the great questions posed by such a critical period in the history of the Danubian lands was due in part to the awareness of the mechanisms of war and rebellion that were beginning to operate in Hungary. If the presence of taxes, the quartering of soldiers, and the disorders continued at a constant, and a number of the better regiments were removed, rebellion would be the logical consequence. As early as 1698, allusion had been made to this process -- ".... soldiers are always an absolute necessity in Hungary ... it takes only a small band of rebels to set the whole country into motion."[89] The danger increased, of course, when the Emperor began to make preparations in earnest for securing the Spanish Succession for the Archduke Charles; this would necessarily involve the transfer of regiment from Hungary to the Italian front. Towards the end of 1700, old Count von Starhemberg reported that "in Hungary everything points to a rebellion and so we can't possibly denude the country of troops."[90] The crisis of 1683 seemed perilously to close once more; this time the outlook was even bleaker.[91] The members of the Deputation were well aware of the danger of explosion at any moment in Hungary, and when the rebellion did come in 1703, it can hardly have come as a surprise.

The infuriating lack of interest with which these Austrian officials responded to the first reports of rebel activity and their criminal inertia in devising means with which to remove the danger must be traced on the basis of these previous discussions in the Deputation not to their being caught off guard but to the fatalistic feeling that matters had reached such a state that any official intervention was condemned to failure.[92] This tragic loss of faith in the government's effectiveness was fairly widespread as far as the Hungarian Rebellion was concerned; the ministers acted as though they had already made their peace with the inevitable, in this case the uprising. They would put their aged heads together, discuss minute details with a pedantic relish that even a real state of emergency could not dim, and then transmit their directives, condemned as they must have known to remain largely dead letters, to the appropriate government agencies. Another generation would describe this process as that of 'passing the buck'; whatever the terminology, there can be no question that the members of the Deputation were past masters of this art. "Ad cameram denique"; this was to be the swan song of the Deputation and of the older generation of ministers which had made of that body in its declining years a sounding board.[93]

The Deputation in its brief career followed the evolution common to institutions of its kind. There was the halcyon period of its first fifteen months. The Emperor was full of hope and solicitude then, inspired by the belief that the Deputation was the answer to his prayers, and it was at this time, too, that the device worked fairly well. There was even a spaciousness in the atmosphere in the early days that permitted discussion verging on a complete theoretical examination of the financial state of the Habsburg lands, but the bias of these Austrian officials was too pronounced in the direction of a casuistry of politics to allow for a high degree of abstraction.

The death of Kinsky was the first serious blow to the hopeful progress of the Deputation, and it was to be a setback from which that body never really recovered. For one thing, it was to be the sign for the advance to the foreground in the meetings of the Emperor's old cronies, men like Harrach, Mansfield, Salburg, and Bucceleni. The tender spirit if reform personified by the younger Starhemberg was less evident, and from the beginning of 1701 he was replaced by the incompetent Salburg; the death of his brother at about the same time was also a great loss. There followed a period of roughly two years in which Austria was governed by the most unfortunate combination of officials in its long history, and this regime of incompetents was in power during the gestation of the Rákóczi Rebellion.[94] The Deputation continued to exist; we can be certain that it survived until 1706, but the history of its last years is so shadowy that any discussion of its final chapter would be a work of imagination rather than of historical description.[95]

Before any conclusions can be reached about the work of the Deputation, it will be necessary to survey the whole horizon of 'parties' and political points of view which figured in the meetings. A close reading of the Deputation protocols does not produce a picture of great unity and coherence as far as the factions are concerned. Both groups and individuals oscillated too frequently to allow for easy labelling. They were often too subject to their immediate reactions to events and too ambivalent in their feelings to allow them to follow at all closely a particular line. But the conclusion can be made on the basis of this evidence: the conventional picture of Austrian absolutism circa 1700 must be modified in the light of the off-the-record views expressed by the members of the Deputation.

The complex life of factions had been so characteristic of the beginning of the decade, was not reflected in the Deputation. The reason is to be sought in the character of the Deputation's work: matters of finance and administration were central here, and foreign policy was not touched on as a rule, though from time to time it appeared as a factor which could decisively influence the size of the army and the size of the budget. The parties that existed at the beginning of the Nineties had at their core divergent conceptions of what policy the Habsburgs should pursue in the European power politics of the period. In the domains of finance and administration the political horizon was necessarily less complicated; here the debate focused about the polarities of particularistic *status quo* and centralized reform. But it would be an over-simplification to divide the field rigidly between the conservative wing and the reform wing. For most of the conservative members of the Deputation had agreed that there should be a *fundus* established for the Hereditary Lands and Hungary, and this was clearly a move in the direction of financial reorganization. It would be closer to the truth to say that there were actually four easily discernible orientations which figured in the Deputation's debates.

Of the original group in the Deputation, Kaunitz, Cardinal Kollonitsch, and Gundacker von Starhemberg displayed an interest in reform along the lines of rationalization and centralization. But there were noticeable differences in emphasis in their positions. Count Kaunitz (he was to be joined later by Count Czernin, the Bohemian Chancellor) can be said to have represented the 'Bohemian' orientation. He believed that the component parts of the Emperor's dominions should all be treated alike in the hope that Bohemia which, they felt, had been doing more than could be rightfully expected of it in a financial way might assume its proper place in the Habsburg system.

But the insistence with which these Bohemian magnates reiterated their slogan of 'Each land should be treated like the others' was not accompanied by any detailed suggestions as to how this treatment was to operate in practice. They appeared to be content with a crudely proportional division of the tax burden and which the general recognition in official quarters that there were no favorites as far as the relations of the Emperor and his *Länder* were concerned. It is doubtful that this set of nostrums represented in any sense a radical policy of centralization or of Germanization. The slogan had a negative rather than positive force; it put a limitation on the tractability of the Imperial administration in making concessions to local interests, but it failed to be specific on what line of policy was to be followed in a positive way.[96]

The Primate of Hungary had its own 'Hungarian' version of the Bohemians' programme. He was convinced that Hungary must do its part in assuming the responsibility for the great Habsburg development in central and eastern Europe; it was to be brought into line with the new situation without being made to feel that it was the ugly duckling of the variegated collection of Habsburg progeny. His professed interest in equal treatment for the Hungarians carried with it the perhaps nullifying codicil that a full measure of respect must be shown for local conditions -- "God did not make Styria flat."[97] In practice, this meant that he acted as the watchdog for the interests of the *arme mann*; indeed, the Hungarian peasant had no more persuasive an advocate in Vienna than his much maligned Primate.

Kollonitsch extended the principal of equality to the various classes composing Hungarian society, for only by a fair division of the taxes among these classes and by a close supervision of the tax collection by the Viennese administration would the status of the peasant be improved. The Primate felt that there were eminently practical grounds for this proposed official intervention on behalf of the peasants: a few thousand could do incalculably more harm to the government than individual noblemen.[98] He, too, took issue on a number of occasions with the view that the Austrian lands (and this in the narrow denotation of the term) were to be given special treatment.[99] In its broadest extension the position of Cardinal Kollonitsch failed in great measure to approach the pole of centralization. It wavered to a far greater degree than did the Bohemian party between the two alternatives, but in a way that was strikingly similar it sought to avail itself of the slogan of equality to ameliorate the conditions in a particular part of the monarchy. In his case it was Hungary; in their case, Bohemia.

The young Gundacker von Starhemberg was the only individual who possessed the interest and the inspiration requisite for a forthright policy of centralization of the Habsburg lands. His views were unfortunately never set down in any logical and developed form (in this at least he was typical member of the Viennese Auliker of his time), but his well-founded sense of urgency, based on his observations of the deepening financial crisis, forced him to make a stand for the rationalization of the Imperial finances and, as a necessary corollary to such a move, the strengthening of the powers of the Viennese administration. We have seen him urging upon his colleagues a policy of determining the amount of taxes to be raised on the basis of the probable expenses for any fiscal year; he had also supported the introduction of a universal income tax and the establishment of a system of long-term credits from the Diets of the Länder which would give more freedom and more certainty to the activities of the policy-making offices in Vienna.[100]

The desire for reform closely paralleled the pattern that was followed generally in the European countries of the time. The financing of the wars of the last half of the seventeenth century had proved too much of a burden on outmoded cameral and constitutional arrangements; empty treasuries had driven harassed administrators of willy-nilly into reform programs of varying degrees of intensity. Necessity had been the unquestioned parent of these 'progressive' notions of the younger Starhemberg. The great weakness of his programme was that it had developed too narrowly as a response to virtually permanent financial crisis with the predictable result that it was manifestly unpolitical in nature.[101] It was reasonable enough within the limits of purely fiscal considerations, but it made little effort to approximate those views of reality, quite respectable in their way, of the members of the Deputation who directed the Emperor's foreign policy and who represented the taxpayers.

At moments of real crisis, it was possible for Starhemberg to achieve a grudging acceptance of parts of his programme, as, for example, in the case of the adoption by the Emperor of the device of income tax in the very face of complete bankruptcy. The specter of disaster might jog old and indecisive men into a posture of modernity, but they had little enthusiasm for their work. But there were personal reasons for the opposition to his ideals as well. In the eyes of the members of the Deputation, his views were inextricably linked with his junior position and his youth, and there was, moreover, the notoriously bad example he had been giving by allowing his luxury-loving mode of life to impose even further burdens on the *Kammer* he was so interested in reforming. Special grants were made by the Emperor to cover his debts, and this was enough to evoke the complaints of old Otting and the envy of the Palatine, whose appetite for money and property was quite as strong as Starhemberg's.[102]

The balance of the Deputation tended to be fairly consistent in their defense of the complicated web of local customs and privileges in the Hereditary Lands. These men were Austrians from above and below the Enns, for the most part, and their exceedingly close connection with the Emperor and their intimate knowledge of his affairs had produced in them the belief that the old system was always the best. They made statements to this effect in the Deputation which were quite as programmatic as the slogans of equality. "The constitutions of the *Länder* are not the same, and it would be quite impossible to alter them in any way." If such a truly revolutionary course were followed they were convinced that the Emperor would be guilty of breaking his sacred word to his subjects and that he would be responsible for involving himself and his dynasty in the subsequent general ruin.[103] It might be expected that this group of traditionalists would, as if by extrapolation of their principles, be particularly sensitive to the damage being done to the old order in Hungary, but this was obviously not the case. They were more tolerant of change in the case of Hungary perhaps because the pretensions of the Upper Estates there seemed outmoded even by their standards. They could explain their obtuseness, too, by alleging that the state of emergency required that exceptions be made to ancient rules of conduct, and they could argue with some foundation that Hungary was not the only victim of this official recourse to temporary expedients.

It was only natural that their devotion to the letter of the law and their recognition of the needs of the moment involved them in maneuvers which sought to preserve legal appearances in the very midst of actual modification of government practices. This kind of ambiguity was antipathetic to them, and it required only time for their sense of guilt to assert itself, an occasion that was made even more inevitable by the failure of the timidly reforming policies that had been adopted by the Deputation in the early ardors of its youthful enthusiasm. It was at this juncture that the attack was pressed home with great vigor on the party of equality -- the party of the innovators. Count Mansfield acted as their spokesman when, at the meeting of the *Conferenz*, he summed up the reactions of the older generation to the policies of their opponents:

> They have placed far too much trust in their twelve millions, hoping in this way for miracles and realizing only after some time had passed that their plan was simply not practical. The proponents of such measures wish to imitate France without first deciding whether or not that system is possible, indeed practical here. It is their novelties that are responsible for the fact that the old ways have been completely abandoned and that the military is in a state of complete ruin.[104]

This was an obvious overstatement of the case of the gerontocrats, but it is interesting that Mansfield attempted to establish guilt of the innovators by a process of association. The Emperor would be quick to react to the suggestion that policies pursued by his government were French in their inspiration. While it was true that French absolutism was certainly à la mode at this time, it is wellnigh impossible to determine its influence on the thinking of the innovators; once again it was largely a question of the development of similar modes of thinking purely on the basis of local conditions. Leopold only added further complication to this internal debate in the Deputation by favoring, now the innovators, now his old cronies. He would admit the need for reform and even go to the length of encouraging its proponents in the development of a detailed programme, and, then, when faced with the practical consequences of such a policy, he would customarily permit it to be emasculated by those close collaborators of his who shared his need for the security afforded by the 'old ways'.

Any analysis of the political opinion in the Deputation must necessarily be given further substance by a discussion of the social context in which its members moved. The ranking members of this body were members of the *Auliker* class, and their lives almost without exception followed that small set's pattern of thought and behavior. Living as they did at the very pinnacle of society, the men and women of this group were thrown into continuous close contact. Intermarriage was exceedingly common, and political loyalties customarily followed familial connection. Political differences were quite often based on personal animosities, and these were deep and lasting enough to involve antagonists in activity most unbecoming loyal and devoted servants of a common sovereign. But for the most part it was a life characterized by a striking homogeneity; the courtiers shared the ennui of the Spanish court ceremonial and the unchanging daily schedule of notoriously brief periods of work in their offices, punctuated by long hours of hunting, card playing, banqueting, and devotions.[105]

Their exceedingly privileged role was not often on a par with their individual gifts as soldiers or statesmen, and one can imagine that the *ressentiment* of less socially distinguished subordinates (we have fleeting traces of this feeling in the *obiter dicta* of the Secretary) was widespread. If it was possible on occasion for these great landowners to interest themselves in the lot of the common man, as in the case of the Deputation's discussions of the Hungarian question, was far from removed from their immediate purview.[106] And when it appeared that a political policy which they had initiated verged on a programme of social reform, they drew back quite naturally from these unexpected consequences of their handiwork. A Christian interest in one's fellow man was not to be confused in their minds with radical modifications of the social structure (even in Hungary) in favor of the *Pöbel*. As nobles, whether Auliker or Hungarian magnates, they had much more in common as a class than any Starhemberg might have had with a Viennese sugarbaker or an Eszterhazy with a long-suffering *jobbágy* on one of his estates.

It was this awareness of being *Standesgenossen* -- fortunately they did not use the term -- that was a constant undercurrent in the formally political discussions in the meetings of the Deputation.

When a Count Csaky, for instance, was granted a reduction in his tax bill, the members found this quite understandable; he was after all "of an ancient family."[107]   Again, the striking solicitude of Count Dominik Kaunitz for the morale of the Upper Estates in Hungary was a natural projection of his own fierce care for his holdings in Bohemia and his sense of the inviolable character of the nobility's economic and social, as distinguished from their political, privileges.

This group of men lived in a period that was characterized by the transition from the world of the *Ständestaat* to the rationalized state of the Enlightened despot, and their loyalty to their Emperor not infrequently ran counter to their loyalty to their class. Any resolution of a conflict of such depth and complexity was bound to be ephemeral; it was possible largely because the actors in this drama were often so blissfully unaware of the ambiguities of their situation. Even the Emperor to whom they owed a primary allegiance acted as if he were a member of their circle, with necessary variations in view of his unique political authority and responsibility, but his mental horizons were hardly broader or more advanced than theirs. And if he did not sense that loyalty to him and to the dynasty might involve his associates in disloyalty to their class they can be excused for their insensitiveness to the imponderables at stake.

In addition to these areas of political commitment and class loyalty, there was a psychological ground within which the Deputation operated, an atmosphere possibly more central to its history than any of its financial brainstorms or its consensus on the social *status quo*. A phenomenology of the Viennese consciousness in its historical development deserves to be written by some future Husserl; he would be struck in the course of his research by the similarities between the traits displayed by the ministers in the Deputation and those which are considered to be typical of the modern inhabitants of Vienna. The Western observer might describe it quite indiscriminantly as 'Viennese charm', but closer study reveals a number of clearly defined categories within that broad classification. The most obvious of these is the insouciance of these men, their love of improvisation, and the very negligence with which the most serious problems were frequently handled. This mood was something more than the possession of a particular class; it was, as we have noted, the expression of the whole culture. The Englishman or the Dutchman might sniff and say that these people were basically not serious; they would be as close to the enigma as the modern who describes this as being Catholic or Baroque. The Western diplomats were congenitally incapable of convincing these Austrians that their attitude was one of egregious error, for the testimony of the Westerner struck the Austrians as being without real relevance to the historical role Austria was called upon to play in Central Europe. They would not have expressed it in that fashion, but they had reason enough for their skepticism of a Marlborough or a Heinsius 'bearing gifts'.

The Austrian ministers had grown up in a state of permanent emergency, and chaos was for that reason more familiar to them than order. They delighted in it when it appeared in the form of a tangled mass of medieval customs, and they regarded it as the staple diet of international relations. It was not that the men of the Deputation were irrationalists *avant la loi*; they enjoyed the processes of reasoning as much as Western statesmen, but they differed in being aware of the ineffectiveness of such reasoning to do much in the way of solving the burning issues of their day. Negligence came of necessity to be paired with a concentrated desire to survive this crisis at all costs. "*Uberstehen ist alles*" a Rilke would say, and the Viennese dialect would express the tendency in the word '*wurschfeln*', muddling through in the face of the most frightening odds.

These traits of spirit do not complete the collection. When the official mind could no longer tolerate the alarming abyss between its optimistic professions and its small accomplishments, it sought refuge in humor, in a corrosive irony which often approached the realm of religious and political sacrilege.[108] While these Viennese officials cannot be accused of participating in that broad movement which Paul Hazard has called the *crise de la conscience* they reveal a great precocity in the process of demythologizing the most beloved symbols in their possession at the very moment when they were most anxious to preserve them. Little practical purpose was served by such a practice, but it did reduce a pressure which had built up, though in doing so it consumed large quantities of mental and psychic energy which might have been better turned to other uses.

When severity was called for, another distinguishing trait put in its appearance. When a Draconian tax policy was decided upon for Hungary, the natural delicacy of the Viennese temperament found it essential to sugarcoat the bitter pill. The ministers realized that their policy involved terrible demands on the Hungarians, but there was little that could be done to alleviate their distress. And to the Deputation made the best of an embarrassing business -- and salved its conscience in the meantime -- by giving its assurances to the 'good Hungarians' that next year things would be different or that concessions (they failed to be specific) would be made to them on other counts. The charming trifler, the inveterate cliffhanger, the satirist, and the pious fraud; these are recognizable stock types in the tragicomedy of the Viennese spirit at the end of the seventeenth century. In combination or in sequence they provided an undeniable tone to the deliberations of the Deputation, a tone which survives into the present day to puzzle, to irritate, and, finally, to convert the avowedly more pragmatic and rational Westerners.

But no degree of charm or of a complementary readiness to forgive and forget can entirely dispense us from the obligation of analyzing the Deputation's failure. The fact of its inadequacy has been established and the symbiotic relationship by which its failure in one area of its responsibility. e.g. financial affairs, had the most fatal consequences in such a closely-related matter as the status of the Kingdom of Hungary. Certainly, a clear and demonstrable connection exists between the place of the Deputation in the history of Austrian administrative institutions and the coming of the Rákóczi Rebellion. For as its attempts to grapple with its main complexus of problems became ever weaker and more spasmodic, Hungary moved by an ineluctable process to that very rebellion with the Ministerial Deputation had been clairvoyant enough to foresee; with every soldier transferred in the period 1701-1703 from Hungary to the Western front, particularly to Italy, the outbreak of the rebellion came that much closer and the degree of initial success it might expect became that much greater.

'Failure' may be too strong a word to use in such context; it would certainly be a hazardous affair to place on just administrative agency all the blame for what happened in the years following. But an analysis of its inability to meet the great challenges it faced is undertaken, not in an effort to situate responsibility, as a jurist might care to do, but from a desire to comprehend just how this came about, as the historian is inevitably required to d.

The first reason that comes to mind is the *modus operandi* of the Deputation itself. Its work was limited for the most part to the business of bringing about a compromise between existing poles of opinion rather than of initiating a programme of its own. It was expected to act as a mediator in an *ad hoc* manner in disputes that developed between any of the offices which were represented in its midst. In the midst of the Emperor there may have been the expectation that it would produce a higher synthesis, but its decisions were certainly not remarkable in this way. Even in the case of Hungary, where there was room for experimentation, the Deputation, after embarking bravely on its own policy, had learned that it must negotiate with the Hungarians. It discovered that the Hungarians, too, had wishes that must be respected, and it soon found itself modifying its original position so as to prove more accommodating to those interests in Hungary upon which it was forced in such large measure to reply.

Weakness was tied to the personalities who had a prominent place in the work of the Deputation. A startling look of leadership was evident, since no one man seemed ready to hold the council to a definite course and to derive the maximum benefit from its useful role as a shortcut through administrative red tape. The Emperor's contribution was passive cooperation, and Kinsky, the one possibility in the way of furnishing direction, lacked both the great talent and the decisiveness that were necessary. Moreover, he was sick, overworked, and disappointed man at this time, and, while he was able to use his personal influence with the Emperor to insure the ratification of the *conclusa*, he was unable to maintain a continuity of policy and any assurances of administrative compliance once decisions had been reached. This *primus inter pares* lectured the members, even begged for unity at times, but neither he nor anyone else was capable of doing the work that was so desperately needed.

Furthermore, it is in the decline and fall of an older generation of Austrian statesmen and soldiers that is mirrored so accurately in the career of the Deputation. The best days of these men had coincided with the raising of the Siege of Vienna and the reconquista of Hungary that had followed. By 1700, the force of that movement had spent itself militarily and ideologically (even the victory of Zenta had not been their triumph as it represented the promise of the next generation); the men themselves were tired, and those who had survived the perils of seventeenth-century living were far from being the most gifted of their generation. The belief in the cooperation of Divine Providence with the best interests of the House of Austria formed an uneasy combination in their minds with a defeatism that had grown out of their knowledge of individuals and collective failure.

The rich growth of factionalism which had flourished at the Court of Vienna some years before had been reduced by the wear and tear of the endless war to a 'two party system'; their party, which consisted of the aged friends and associates of the Emperor, and the party of young hopefuls clustered about the heir apparent, the King of the Romans. The old men blindly relied on tradition and prophesied doom if innovations were introduced; the young men dreamed of reform without caring to be too specific about the details. The old could not transmit the dread knowledge they had acquired in long years of maintaining such a ramshackle system, while the young could not infuse their seniors with something of their optimism. The Emperor's quite natural reliance on the men of his generation (they were all sexagenarians now) had been reasonable enough in 1683, when they were in their prime; in the crisis of the Imperial finances and the seedtime of Hungarian rebellion from 1697 to 1703, it was little short of criminal folly, and the Deputation, which he had felt to be such a hopeful sign, was one of the most important victims of this policy.

It is notoriously easy to dismiss these men and the Deputation in which they served as failures, when they are viewed from the Olympian heights of the twentieth century, and it is well to remember just how tentative any analysis of the work of the Deputation must be at the present time. Even the best intentioned effort to recreate its situation runs into the obstacle of deficiencies in sources and in their interpretation. The study of this particular institution is only in its infancy, and great difficulties will be encountered in searching out other protocols and in deciphering them. The student is further handicapped by the absence of theoretical tools with which to approach such a study, though Otto Hintze did open great vistas for further investigation by his comparative study of administrative institutions in Austria and Prussia. But a really compelling study of institutions of this kind, as they existed in the major European countries of the period, must wait on the further publication of sources, and it is to be feared that serious lacunae will always exist here -- the silences of England and France are cases in point. Only *felix Austria* had the good sense to preserve the records of the deliberations of its ministerial councils at that particular stage of their evolution. What is needed here is an approach that will take full account of the uniqueness of the Habsburg monarchy's role in European history and will yet be of a sufficient degree of abstraction to provide further insights into the meaning of the Deputation's experience.

Additional and more cogent grounds for humility in discussing the 'failure' of the generation of '83 are provided by the deeper limitations of any historical inquiry. It can be established on the basis of present evidence that the Deputation did not achieve any noteworthy measure of success in solving the great problems which had been the reasons for its establishment in the first place. But it may well be that those problems were in any case insoluble. The historian has no very satisfactory method of determining this, since the existence of other lines of development and historical possibilities can only be surmised. The challenge may have been too great; the collective sense of impotence in the face of war and rebellion suggest that this was the reaction of the actual participants. As for the men of the generation of '83, it is well to remember that any variation in perspective involves a striking change in the interpretation of their contribution to Austrian history. The longer view in time furnishes us with a picture of its success in other conjunctures of the period's history. They had the misfortune as a group to live on past their *acme* in responsible posts; they lived in their later years in the seedtime of the Rákóczi Rebellion and in the bankruptcy of Austrian finances, but these are episodes, it must be pointed out, in a period which is now regarded as the time of the coming of age as a Great Power of the Habsburg monarchy in Central Europe.

Notes to Chapter 1

[1]The present chapter should be regarded as a preliminary study of the Deputation as an International institution; I hope to be able in the near future to make it the subject of a monograph after the manner of Professor Henry Schwartz's study of the Imperial privy council in the seventeenth century. As it stands, it is the first extensive treatment of this institution on the basis of a close study of the most important sources. Mention has occasionally been made in the standard treatments of Austrian institutional history of the existence of the Deputation and of its interests in financial matters (the only treatment worthy of note is to be found in Thomas Fellner, *Dieösterreichische Zentralverwaltung*, I, 3 Bd. (Wien-1907), but since such treatments were not based on a study of the protocols of the Deputation, much is shadowy andmuch erroneous in their discussion of this institution. I have thought it wiser, then, not to refer to mistaken positions in each and every case in the previous scholarship but to begin from zero ans to construct slowly and wwith all the requisite care a picture of the Deputation's career that is to be obtained by the all too precious traces it left behind it.

The main difficulty in studying the Deputation has always been the state of the protocols themselves. Lothar Gross in *Die Geschichte der deutschen Reichshofkanzlei von 1559 bis 1806* (inventare des Wiener Haus-, Hof- und Staatsarchiv, V) (Wien-1933), 247, underlined the importance of the *Konferenzvota* for any understanding of the history of the Austrian lands and of Germany in the seventeenth century, and he lamented the fact that they had not been studied or published in any detail. But it was difficult for him to be optimistic about the chances of such projects, since the handwriting and the actual conditiion of the protocols -- may forever defy even the most ingenious paleographers. But thanks to the interest and assistance of the personnel of the *Haus-, Hof- und Staatsarchiv* and to the minor miracles performed by Dr. Walter Leitsch of the *Institut für Osteuropäische Geschichte und Südostforschung* of the University of Vienna, I have been able to follow the development of the Deputation with some assurance. A brief discussion of the collection in which these protocols are preserved and the nature of the protocols themselves will be found in the Bibliography; a *Kostprobe* with accompanying photostats will be found in Appendix One. Since my main interest in the present chapter is to concentrate on the role of the Deputation in Hungarian affairs, some worthwhile material relevant to other aspects of Austrian internal policy had to be omitted. It was thought sufficient for the moment to provide as commplete an account of the instituttion itself before discussing in detail its negatiations with the Hungarians in 1698 and 1699.

Since this is relatively uncharted country, I have decided to include as much quotation in the notes as possible; the reader will have the consolation that these are not to be found in any published work. The quotations will certainly convey the 'living presence' of the meetings of the Deputation without unduly cluttttering up the actual discussion.

[2]This process has been given a definitive treatment in Henry F. Schwartz, *The Imperial Privy Council in the Seventeenth Century* (Harvard historical studies, LIII) (Harvard - 1943).

[3]A deliberative body, similar to the Deputation in form, which confined itself exclusively to financial mattters is known to have existed in 1695; its protocols are partially preserved in the collection of the *Vorträge*, Fasz. 35, folder July-December 1695, fol. 107-185. The *Instruktion* of Emperor Leopold has been published by Fellner, *op. cit.*, 1, 4, 24-39. The Deputation actually met for the first time on December 12, 1697: -"Deputation den 27. Feb. 1698. Seither dess 12. Dezembris 1697 ist man haeut dass 23ichste mahl beysammen.", *Vorträge*, Fasz. 36, folder 1696-98, fol. III.

[4]"Quoad puncta partim ibi militaria, partim cameralia, partim commissarialia, partim politica.", *Konferenz* session of August 21, 1696, *Vorträge*, Fasz. 36, folder 1696 (VIII-XII), fol. 195.

[5]Leopold simply referred to the presence of the chancellories without being specific ("... die cantzleyan auch seynt ...") in a passage in which he expressed his hope that their presence would assure the carrying out of the decisions of the Deputation; *Hoffinanz* (a collection preserved in the *Hofkammerarchiv*, Vienna), *Ungarn*, Fasz. 388, March-June 1698, March, 1698, fol. 74-87.

[6]Leopold to Kinsky, December 9, 1697, *Grosse Korrespondenz*, Fasz. 63 II, fol. 878-880.

[7]Leopold declared that the Deputation did not stand above the normal offices but rather "diese vereinend ergänzt"; *Hoffinanz*, *Ungarn*, Fasz. 388, March-June 1698, March, 1698, fol. 74-87. On another occasion, Leopold ordered that a dispute between the *Hofkriegsrat* and the Austrian *Hofkanziel* be mediated in the Deputation (this was certainly but one of the many such instances) and that he be informed of the result; *Hoffinanz*, *Ungarn*, Fasz. 403, November-December 1699, December 12, 1699, fol. 98.

[8]The Emperor's hopeful attitude was expressed in one instance in a letter to

Kinsky, February 17, 1698, *Grosse Korrespondenz*, Fasz. 63 II, fol. 938-939.

[9]A sense of the operating practice of the Deputation can be gained largely from the protocols of the meetings themselves, and it is difficult to pinpoint such observations as these on the role of the *praeses*. That the *praeses* had real powers of decision on the agenda is clear from Leopold's statement that Kinsky could make his own decision on a matter or submit it to the Deputation; Leopold to Kinsky, April 6, 1698, *Grosse Korrespondenz*, Fasz. 63 II, fol. 973.

[10]The daily exchange of letters between the Emperor and Kinsky reveal that the Emperor regarded the Deputation as the most important body and that he was particularly interested in having Kinsky direct it ("... ut tu praefatae Depuationi non solum adsis, sed etiam ut praeses dirigas.") Kinsky was discharged from some of his responsibilities as Supreme Bohemian Chancellor so that he might have more time for his work in the Deputation. The Emperor's complete confidence in his *praeses* is expressed in his promise to let Kinsky do pretty much as he wished and in the additional promise to ignore any calumnies that might be made against him; *Grosse Korrespondenz*, Fasz. 63 II, Dec. 11, 1697, fol. 870-873.

[11]Count Harrach's appearance as novus praeses on March 9, 1699, is mentioned in the *Deputationsprotokoll*, in the *Vorträge*, Fasz. 37, 1699-1700, folder I (1699), II v. There is far less evidence of his participation than there was in the case of Kinsky, and the attention of the Deputation moves from the big questions to smaller considerations, as if the chiefs of the offices had decided to settle matters outside the Depuation. Harrach's absences were quite frequent; he was absent on both December 7 and 10, 1699; *Vorträge*, Fasz. 37, 1699-1700, folder I (1699), 68 v.-70.

[12]Leopold advised an ailing Kinsky to allow the Deputation to meet with Count Kaunitz presiding; Leopold to Kinsky, May 30, 1698, *Grosse Korrespondenz*, Fasz. 63, II, fol. 1001.

[13]"Quod ecclesiastica et civilia gehöre alles unter den herrn cardinalen; esset metropolitanus et supremus comes."; Session of April 2, 1699, *Vorträge*, Fasz. 37, 1699-1700, folder I (1699), fol. 19.

[14]Cardinal Kollonitsch has not been the subject of a modern biography; the work of the Austrian church historian Joseph Maurer, *Cardinal Leopold Graf Kollonitsch, Primas von Ungarn: Sein Leben und Wirken* (Innsbruck --1887)

suffers from the regrettable tendency of many products of Austrian historians in that day to be ill-digested collections of source materials. His work is a mine of information, but it fails notably to present a compelling picture of this interesting and all too neglected firgure.

[15]This unfavorable judgment can be traced back to Ferenc Rákóczi in his *Histoire des Revolutions de Hongrie* (La Haye-1738), 1 ff.

[16]"Er hette die verandwortung aller seelen; hoc in Ungaria, quod pontifex in christianitate, et primas regni."; Cardinal Kollonitsch in a meeting of the *Conferenz* in 1696 (the exact date is not known), *Vorträge*, Fasz. 36, folder 1696, fol. 192.

[17]The *Einrichtungswerk* has unfortunately never received the complete treatment it so well deserves from a Hungarian historian; it forms the basis of the study of Theodor Mayer, *Verwaltungsreform in Ungarn nach der Türkenzeit* (Wien, 1911); the complete text of the *Einrichtungswerk* is printed in the *Anhang*, pp. I-XLV, of Mayer's book.

[18] "Andreersets aber beweist das E. W. wiederum, dass der Wiener Hof in seinen sozialen, wirtschaftlichen und kulturellen Ansichten ausserorde3ntilich hock stand...."*, ibid.*, 80.

[19]It is wellnigh impossible to determine just what role this important omission played in the eventual decline and fall of the Deputation.

[20]The problem of Eugene of Savoy's participation is mentioned by the Emperor in his letter to Count Kinsky, December 9, 1697, *Grosse Korrespondenz*, Fasz. 63 II, folder 1697, fol. 880. Leopold's final decision two days later was "sobald ich für nötig ansene. werde ich ihn rufen.", *ibid.*, fol. 883.

[21]Palm, a *Hofkammerat* and *Kanzleidirektor,* wrote the protocols for his office; he was praised for his exertions in the course of the meeting on November 13, 1699; *Vorträge,* Fasz. 37, 1699-1700, folder I (1699), fol. 62 v. Palm also acted as messenger; "Herr Palm solle dem Palatino sagen, man werde ihn hören, ut cras veniant."; Session of November 12, 1698, *Depuationsprotokoll 1698,* fol. 242 v., *Vorträge*, Fasz. 36 (1696-1698), folder 1696-98, fol. 63-256. (Hereafter cited simply as *Deputationsprotokoll 1698.*)

[22]A comparison of the handwriting proves that the same man wrote many of the protocols of the Conferentia Secreta as well as the protocols of the Deputation.

A remark like "Hora II ^{a} venit d. Kinsky *et non aspexit Caprara.*" illustrates his position. The Emperor would be interested to learn of the tension existing between the two men. The Secretary added the section about Caprara in cipher to preserve the utmost secrecy about his work as an observer for the Emperor. A dispute between Count Breuner and Count von Starhemberg was reported on at some length and without the aid of cipher in the protocols of the sessions of June 30, and July 3, 1699, *Vorträge,* Fasz. 37, 1699-1700, foler I (1699), fol. 34-35.

[23]Breuner read an opinion that was "*satis fusum*" (cipher) and on another occasion, "Dominus Comes Breuner nihil *vult scire.*"; *Vorträge,* Fasz. 37, 1699-1700, folder I (1699), fol. 34; *ibid.,* fol. 65)

[24]Further research will undoubtedly establish the Secretary's identity.

[25] "Magna contraria. Minarentur nobis belli. Deesenet media. Das geglament werde nicht gehalten. Necessarium die sach also einzurichten, das man trouppen halte, die man zahlen könne, alias nil nisi praedae et ruina provinciarum"; Session of October 22, 1699, *Vorträge,* Fasz. 37, 1699-1700, folder I (1699), fol. 56.

[26]For example, in the *conclusio* of the Session of June 30, 1699, "Was für eine armada zu halten, dependire von den mitteln. 100.000 mann wären zu wünschen; halte man disciplin und gebe dem Soldaten nichts, gehe er zugrunde."; *ibid.,* fol. 33; on another occasion Cardinal Kollonitsch had declared that it was possible to maintain an army of one hundred thousand men, and Count Czernin replied, "Das wären pia desideria, da die Mittel nicht da sind. Man soll mustern und ein kleineres aber gutes Heer aufstellen.", *Konferenz* session of November 11, 1699, *Vorträge,* Fasz. 37, 1699-1700, folder II (January-November 1699), fol. 207.

[27]Session of October 20, 1698, *Deputationsprotokoll 1698,* fol. 231 r.

[28]"D. comes Gundacarus: Bey einen monarchen müsse man nicht die aussgaben nach denen einleuffen nemmen, sondern die reditus nach denen ausssgaben reguliren."; Session of October 16, 1699, *Vorträge,* Fasz. 37, 1699-1700, folder I (1699), fol. 53.

[29]Session of the Deputation of September 23, 1699; *Vorträge,* Fasz. 37, 1699-1700, folder II (January-November, 1699), fol. 141; further discussion at a

session of the *Konferenz,* July 29, 1700, *Vorträge,* Fasz. 37, 1700, folder III (January-October, 1700), fol. 52-53.; the members of the Konferenz were aware that the Emperor opposed the income tax; this was the reason for constant delay in coming to a decision; Session of November 3, 1700, *Vorträge,* Fasz. 37, 1700, folder IV (XI-XII, 1700), fol. 12-13. The Emperor finally gave way to the view that the critical finacial situation made necessary the introduction of the tax; *Konferenz* session of January 7, 1701, *Vorträge,* Fasz. 37, 1699-1700, folder IV (Dep. Protokoll), fol. 133.

[30]For a brilliant picture of the state of Hungary in this period, see Gyula Szekfü's chapter "Bécsi kisérlet az uj berendezésre", *Magyar történtet,* VI, 5-44.

[31]"Geld müesse man haben."; Session of Feb. 14, 1698, *Deputationsprotokoll 1698,* fol. 99 r.

[32]"Conferentia super Hargaricis, 21. August 1696, apud pricipem Dietrichstain. Praesentibus comitibus Starenberg, Breiner, Bucelleni. Secretariis Mayer, Eyllers, Bechin, Palm."; *Vorträge,* Fasz. 36, 1696-1698, folder 1696 (VIII-XII), fol. 67; "Von den 4 millionen undt deme Auerspergschen project will regnum nichts hören."; This memorial consisted of twenty-one points. Another memorial submitted to the Conferentia Secreta on Nov. 4, 1696, contained only ten points, but it was obviously a continuation of the list of *gravamina* in the first one; *ibid.,* fol. 137-138.

[33] "Conclusum: Ihr May. vorzustellen, das heut von zwey haubtpunkten tractirt: Primo de stabillendo fundo der 12 millionen. Secundo die mittel zur anticipation zu finden. Ad primum quia fundus 12 millionen ex puris tributis provinciarum conflueret, den ietzigen standt des contributionswesens in iedem landt zu überlegen und zu sehen, wo es haffte, durch wass mittel und wege es zu stabiliren."; Session of Feb. 14, 1698, *Deputationsprotokoll* 1698, fol. 100-101.

[34] "Ratione Hungariae dess bisherigen unbilligen modi, quod in tribus consistat, befunden: 1. Dass in dass ocntrigbutionswesen clerus, magnas, nobilis, civis et subaccisen eingeführet. 3. Die repartition ehistens verfertiget, anhero gesendet und das verflossene monath assignirt werde."; "Weillen man vermeinet, das des herrn Cardinalen anwesenheit zu Pressburg einen grossen vorschub geben würde, requisitus fuisset, sich dorthin zu verfügen und authoritate sua dass werckh stabiliren zu helffen."; Session of Feb. 14, 1698, *ibid.,* fol. 100 v.

[35] "idque sine mora, quia forte ab remissum frigus subditi fugerent et repartitio

una cum 4 millionibus posset impossibilitari."; "Respectu Ossterriechischer landen seye in facto nichts gezeigt; wohl aber, das es in conatu et fieri bestehe, gezeiget worden. Die erkhlärung nock hit vorhanden. Die Zeit werde lehren, wie selbe lauthen würde."; same Session, *ibid.*, fol. 101 r.

[36] "Herr Cardinal: in Ungarn zu gehen seyue umbonsonst, si non habeamus pecuniam. Dixisset mense Malo, das man vorhero das geld haben müesse...*Ungarn thue mehr, alss es versprochen, unterhalte die gantze armada* (italics my own). Zwey mi.llionen wären auff die pauern und die stettische repartirt. Zwey solle man auff den clerum und die nobiles schlagen."; that the Cardinal saw that the collection of the taxes would have to be carried out *vi et armis* is seen from another remark at that particular session; "Putaret Sua Eminetia, dass sie mit verweilung der militz und commissariats dahin zu gehen, die repartition zu erweingen. Item zur einfreibung des benöthingtren sich gebrauchen könten."; Session of February 20, 1698, *ibid.*, fol. 103 v.-106 *passim.*

[37] "Legitur memoriale domini Palatini....;1. Repartitio. 2. Reglement. 3. Glechnheit der contribtion; Concluditur: Rescribendum Palatino, dass dergleichen mit Ihr May. Dienst nicht bestehen (könne), die comitatus cum omnibus incolis sive sit clerus sive nobilis sive rusticus sive civis in ein gleiches mitleiden zu ziehen und zu beobackten, das *der schwechere von dem sterckheren übertragen werde* (italics my own). Herr Cardinal werde mit nechsten hinunterkhommen. Unterdessen solle der Platinus ihme angelegen sein lassen, die notturfften und repartition zusammenzubringen, ne plus temporis consumatur."; Session in early March, 1698, *ibid.*, fol. 117-118 r.

[38] "Respondit dominus Palatinus, quod regnicolae viderint se impares residuiis 2 millionibus et speraverint relaxationem."; "Dominus Palatinus: Praestaret hic Viennaeillos convenire et delibverare de omnibus puctis, quorum copiam petunt."; Session of May 6, 1698, *ibid.*, fol. 153 r.

[39] "Ihr Eminenz: Die Ungarn wären den 6. nachmittags beysammengewesen und (hätten) geschlossen, man solle die vorige 2 millionene dopplet anlegen und per executionem einbringen. Budiani putasset, ess würde einen auffstand veruhrsachen. Dominus Cardinalis etiam iudicassset iniquum."; Session of May 9, 1698, *ibid.*, fol. 153 v.

[40] "*Votum meum* (cipher): Modo apparet, dass man weder die 2 millionen noch die 800.000 fl. haven werde.... Allengant impossibilitatem; an haec possit

superari, me latet. Interea timendi magni motus. Tentandum tamen."; the same Session; *ibid.,* fol. 154 v.

[41] "Legitur resolution Caesarea ad Ungaros: Quod nihil potuerit relaxari de 4 millionibus et nullas amplius relicas admittere velit. Legitur dass Kay. billet, lauth dessen Ihr. May. dem auffsatz der resolution, welche denen Ungarn zu eröfnen, appropirt. NB: Est ibi his verbis: Acceptare Suam Sanctam Mtem grato animo, quod praefati domini, Primas, Palatinus et magates 4 milliones spatio 12 mensium integre persolvendos susceperint etc. etc."; Session 46, probably in the middle of May, 1698; *ibid.,* 156 v.

[42] "Palatinus interrogat, an non velimus communicare resolutionem, ut desuper possint colloqui. Respondetur esse ultimam resolutionem."; the same Session, *ibid.,* fol. 457 r.

[43] "Dominus Cardinalis dicit, es werde der arme man doppelt belegt, wan die perceptores ihre register nicht einschickehen theten, dass man sehe, wer contribuire und wer nicht contribuire, werde man nicht auff den grund kommen." This *votum* is followed by that of the Secretary: "Zuzuwarthen bis particulariter alles ex comitatiubus komme, brauchte viehl zeit. Registra ex comitatibus komme, würde gar zu lang hergehen."; Session of June 2, 1698, *ibid.,* fol. 162 r.

[44] "Herr graff con Stahrenberg resentit hoc, item donmus Aulae Cancellarius Khamen hart an einander. Dominus Kinsky inquit insurgens, die Bucceleni wären bissig."; Session of June 2, 1698, *ibid.,* fol. 162 v.

[45]"Intuitu dessen Ihr May. saepius ex parte Deputationis repraesentirt, wie nöthigen betrag zu den 12 millionen zu propotioniren und gleich zu halten, quae petitio reiteraretur, quia essetad conservandum scepter und cron, landt und leuth...ita etiam respectu qualis kein unterschied inter provincias. Die bewilligung wäre Ihr May. aigens gueth: die modi administrandi rem propriam iutxa convenientiam zu bestellen, und seye es an deme, das Ihr May. von diese Ihrer gerechtigkeit ohne praeiuditz ihrer höchsten authoritet darvon nit weichen konte."; same Session, *ibid.,* fol. 163 v.

[46]"Resolutio Caesarea: Was dass con meinem erbländern begehrte quantum anlanget, werde ich fest darob halten, dass solches auff ein oder andere weis oder weg von jedem landt eingehen solle. Indeme ich in meinen ländern keine ungleichheit Ulassen kan."; Dominus Kinsky: Nemo deberet esse exemptus;

modus collectandi autemdenen comitatibus gelassen."; Session of June 6, 1698, *ibid.*, fol. 164 r.

[47]"Dominus Kinsky proposuit de conventu Hungarorum, so dahier sein solle. Dominus Cardinalis: Frustra hic conveniret. Werde viehl kosten. Der modus contribuendi seye nicht in einem comitatu wie in den anderen. Respondetur, Caesarem vellle, ut conveniant."; Session of June 23, *ibid.*, fol. 175 r.

[48]A Session of the Deputation discussed at some length a report on conditions in Translyvania. The report had been submitted on August 17, 1698; the exact date of the meeting is unknown; *ibid.*, fol. 204 v.-205.

[49]"Legatur memoriale Palatini et procerum Hungariae, quo petunt, cum leges statuant, ut negotia regni non tractentur extra renum, ut deliveratio super communicata puncta remittatur Posonium...Propositiones renum concernentes tractandae per modum diatae allegant decreta von 150 jahren her, die vielleicht in einen anderen standt gerathen. Sie haben sich selbst eingelassen und propositiones übergeben. Nuper interrogaverunt, quorsum registra. *Ansam huius postulati dabit, quod magnates non contribuetrint, imo eingenommen* (italics my own). Si remittatur Posoniam, nihil fiet."; Session of September 18, 1698, *ibid.*, fol. 216 r.

[50]"Dominus comes Kinsky conludit: Man solle denen Ungarn repraesentiren, das die materia ex necessitate per compendium tractirt werden müesse. Es hetten Ihr May. kein intention, Ungariae status in ihren privilegiis zu khräcken, wohl aber dem ex discordia regni leidenden königreich zu einer gleichheit zu Verhelffen."; the same Session, *ibid.*, fol. 216 v.

[51]"Status ipsimet desiderarent cum caeteris provinciis sequaliter tractari. Unde etiam vocarentur ad aulam provinciales salvis tamen legibus fundamentalibus."; "Alias Caesar ipsemet cogeretur disponers."; Session of September 18, 1698, *ibid.*, fol. 217 r.

[52]"Deinde nullam exemptionem cuiuscunque personae commodum in regno parcipientis inveniendum, sed omnes et singulos pro qualitate facultatum in sustentationis onus trahendos. Dicendum etiam, dass man sie vor erörterung dieser sachen nit weglassen werde...omnia itaque haec cum ministerio Suae Mtis. Proinde opus esse, ut ipsimet omnia accelerent."; Session of September 22, 1698, *ibid.*, fol. 218 v.

[53]The Session of October 20, 1698, *ibid.,* fol. 230 v.

[54]"Starenberg: Die rebellen, so nach Monkatz kommen, non conquerentur contra Caesarem, non contra militem Germanum, sed contra dominos."; the same Session, *ibid.,* fol. 231 v.

[55]This opinion was in all probability that of the Secretary; the same Session, *ibid.,* 231 v.

[56]"Dominus Palm: Die Hungarn hetten eine geldrepartition gemacht, die nit richtig. Dicit Palm dass geld müesse de sein."; Ad memorialem Palati (sic/) dicendum, das auff ihnen die schuld ligge, das man kein ordnung gehalten habe...Das contributions quantum also auszutheilen, das 2/3 auff den unterthanen und 1/3 auff den herrn zu legen."; the same Session, *ibid.,* fol. 232 r.

[57]"Dominus Kaunitz: Cum incerta pax, wären die leuth noch zu behalten...Man solle doch die obere stände nicht disgustiren: Nur von diesem jar zu sagen."; Session of October 27, 1698, *ibid.,* fol. 233 v.

[58]"Etiam videndum, dass man ihnen metum perpetuitatis benemme und sage, der modus werde bleiben, bis sie einen besseren an die hand geben."; "Wass da wohl auffgesetzt, werde sine vi coactiva nit ad effectum zu bringen sein. Et sicut absque hoc modo non apud provinciam, ita etiam non sine vi apud militiam."; the *conlusum* of the Session of October 27, 1698, *ibid.,* fol. 234 v.-235 r.

[59]"Palatini memoriale: Quod intellexerit tertiam partem solvendam esse a clero et nobilitate. Non speraret intentionem hanc esse Suae Mtis., ut nobilitas pereat...Vix octo comitatus integros mansisse in Ungaria ab anno1662, dum Turca Varadinum occupassent. A quo tempore Turca fugatus, nullum respirium affulsisset. Immensum contributionis onus impositum. Plebs et nobilis in eandem devolvarentur perditionem."; Session of November 12, 1698, *ibid.,* fol. 242 r.

[60]In the *conclusum* of the same Session: "Sunt argumenta tamen ad specialem (?) poderosa. Magnae calamitates in Ungaria ... Pontius suavitate quam per violentiam."; *ibid.,* fol. 242 v.

[61]"Dominus Kinsky: Placuisse quidem Suae Mti., ut audiantur. Interea standum prioribus decretis."; Session of November 13, 1698, *ibid.,* fol. 242 v.

[62]"Colozzensis:...ibse ex suis bonis tantum haberet octingentos florenos et iuxta nostram dispositionem deberet dare 40.000 fl. Subditi ibidem darent triplum Camerae, de quo simplum dedissent Turcis...Nunquam practicatum in aliis provinciis, ut nobilitas et clerus dederint terialitatem."; the same Session, *ibid.,* fol. 243 r.

[63]"Dominus Palatinus dicit, quod semper ipsi fecerint repartitionem...Quoad clerum et nobiles haec modalitas suaderetur, ut in trigesima parte concurrent -- essent 133,333 aut loco tricesimae de centum -- ex proventibus tres."; Session of November 14, 1698, *ibid.,* fol. 244 v.

[64]"Fit computum von denen 4 millionen:
     16. pars .... 250.000 fl.
     30. pars .... 133.333 fl.
     manerent .... 3.061.666 fl.
(sic.), the figure should be 3.616.667 fl.; the same Session, *ibid.,* fol. 244 v.

[65]"Dominus Kaunitz:...Tertialitatem werde man nicht erhalten. Vermeinet das duplum, wass die stette geben. Nimirum octavem partem."; the *votum* of the Secretary (in part): "A tertia salant ad 30.; ist zu weith. Nihil unquam contribuerunt. Sancta intentio est meseram plebem et urbes sublevandi."; the same Session, fol. 246.

[66]Cf. the *conclusum* of the Session of November 14, 1698, *ibid.,* fol. 246 r.

[67]"Legitur memoriale dominorum Hungarorum contra octavalitatem: Petunt reduci ad 24. partem."; Session of November 17, 1698, *ibid.,* fol. 247 r.

[68]"Der arme man wirt die 3.500.000 fl. nicht geben können...Conclusum zu sagen, hic et nunc könne man es nicht ändern. Ess seye auff keine perpetuitet angesehen. Der gemeine man habe den last allein getragen. Mit dem brod wolle man doch dispensiren."; the same Session, *ibid.,* fol. 247 v.

[69]As, for example, the protests of Kassa, which were discussed at some length; the Session of January 2, 1699, *Vorträge,* Fasz. 37, 1699-1700, folder I (1699), fol. 2 r. (Hereafter, simply *Vorträge,* folder I).

[70]Cardinal Kollonitsch declared at the same Session that he could not advise the Emperor to order an *execution* in Upper Hungary; *ibid.,* fol. 3 r.

[71]"Commissariatus erindert, man solle den regimentern in Ungarn die quittung an die comitatus geben und ihre anweisungen selbst einbringen lassen."; Session of April 6, 1699, *ibid.*, fol. 21.

[72]The convocation of the Hungarian nobles remains shrouded for the most part in mystery. There are few events in this period which present so many difficulties in the way of establishing an accurate account of just what happened. Our only source for this meeting is Ferenc Rákóczi, *Histoire de Revolutions de Hongrie*, 140ff. The accuracy of his account (the Prince was probably not an eyewitness of the proceedings) has already been seriously challenged by Theodor Mayer, *op. cit.*, 113-115. One can only hope that more intensive research in the archival collections in Vienna and Budapest will lead to a solution of the mystery. At the moment, it is sufficient to note that the discussions of the Deputation's give further support to Mayer's claim that the Prince's account was not an accurate one. For it would be an unwarranted conclusion on the basis of this new evidence to ascribe a well-organized anti-Hungarian policy to the Austrian Ministry. The ministers were interested in introducing changes into the system of Hungarian tax collection, but this did not extend to the demolition of the entire framework of the Hungarian liberties and privileges.

Rákóczi was an elderly man when he recalled the events of 1698 for the *Histoire,* and his own experiences in the Rebellion, as well as the natural limitations of memory, may have subtly influenced his account. One small instance of innacuracy is his observation that Archbishop Széchényi's courageous stand was due in part to the disappointment of his hopes for the See of Esztergom; Prince Christian August of Sachsen-Zeitz had been preferred to him in naming a coadjutor to Cardinal Kollonitsch. Flathe in his article on the Wettin Prince (*Algemeine Deutsche Biographie*, IV, 178) states that Prince Christian became coadjutor in 1701.

[73]The discussion of the meeting of the Conferentia Secreta is based on the "*Protokoll einer Sittzung der Geheimen Konferenz ueber die Forderung der Ungarn, einen Reichstag abzuhalten, Siebenbuergen mit ungarn zu vereingen, die Zahl der in Ungarn Stationierten Truppen zu verringern und die steuern zu senken", Vorträge*, March 31, 1699. Fasz. 37, folder II (January-November, 1699), fol. 21-26. This protocol will be found in its entirety in Appendix Two.

[74]The Session of April 23, 1699, *Vorträge*, Fasz. 37, 1699-1700, folder I (1699), fol. 22 v.-24.

[75]"Der Deputation eine andere execution einzuräumen oder sie seye nichts nutz, quod *verum* (cipher) est.": the Secretary had delivered himself of this remark during the Session of January 29, 1699, *ibid.*, fol. 8.

[76]"Dominus Gundackher dicit, man müesse die tributa stabiliren NB: diss lasset sich da nit thun, *sie dependiren von der bewilligung.*"; Session of May 18, 1699, *ibid.*, fol. 27 r.

[77]In a marginal note to the remarks of Count Gundacker von Starhemberg: "Die postulata seint an die länder gebracht, was sie geben können oder geben werden, wirt man aus der erkhlärung vernemmen, da lasset sich derentwegen kein schluss machen. *Si per impositionem*, wirt es so wenig zu erreichen sein als.......(an illegible word, probably from the sense of the sentence'vorhin') (italics my own); the same Session, *ibid.*, fol. 27 v.

[78]"Non habimus (sic/), et si jubeamus mit........ (the rest of the senctence is illegible)"; Session of May 25, 1699, *Vorträge,* Fasz. 37, 166-1700, foleder l, fol. 29. It is unfortunate that this sentence -- one of the most epigrammatic comments on the trials and tribulations of Austrian absolutism -- is in such bad condition. Enough of it is legible to convey the writer's point and to remind the modern reader that even an allegedly absolutistic system of the kind that existed under Leopold I had very definite limits to its effectiveness.

[79]"Dominus Harrach refert, a sua Maeiestate seye der ungarische cantzler zu ihme verwiessen. Theils magaten wären dahier, der palatinus habe mit selbigen die repartition machen wollen, isti autem noluissent, sed -- sicuti essent 6 partes regni: 1° Croaten, 2do Sclavonien, 3° disseits der Donaw, 4to jesseits der Donaw, 5to Oberungarn, 6to wass überder Theyss -- man mögte rescribiren, ut singuli districtus mittant huc auos homines."; Session of October 16, 1699, ibid., fol. 53 v.-54 r.

[80]"Dominus Cardinalis dicit, ess werde lang hergehen, die zeit leide ess nicht; wären vorm jahr 3 mahl beysammen gewesen, et tantum clamassent," "Itaque domino cancellario et palatino dicendum, ut veniant una cum magnatibus, qui etiam adessent...(et) faciant repartitionem."; the same Session, *ibid.*, fol. 54 r.-55 r.

[81]"Deinde graviter conqueruntur, quod nobilitas subiiciatur tributis, *ac sis esset gregaria* (italics my own)."; Session of November 16, 1699, *ibid.*, fol. 63-64.

[82]"Volunt neoacquistos comitatus tanquam regni membra ad contibuendum immatriculari. Wollen Croaten und Sclavonien auch darbey haben...Dadditur etiam, die Cammer solle keine güter verkhauffen und die Ungarische Cantzley keine donationales aussfertigen, sondern Ihr May; die güter widergeben, ad quos antea pertinuissent."; the same Session, *ibid.*, fol. 64.

[83]"Croaten und Scavonien wären sub rubrica Ungarorum et cetera."; Session of November 19, 1699, *ibid.*, fol. 65 r.

[84]"Dominus Cardinalis dicit, 3 millionen 200.000 fl. wurden begehrt. Darob müesse man halten...Concludit: Ess wäre zu wünschen, das Ihr May: willfahren könten. Man habe aber die armada vonnöthen, könten also nit darvon nachlassen... derzeit geduld tragen, man werde sie in anderweeg consoliren. N. B.: Hoc omnibus dicitur, sed nihil servatur (this afterthought is undoubtedly the Secretary's work); Session of December 22, 1699, *ibid.*, fol. 74.

[85]"Die landtsverfassungen seint nit gleich , lassen sich nit übern hauffen werffen."; again, in the same session, "omnes haberent sua privilegia, non supponeret quod S. M. illa velit tollere. Richten Ihr M. diese länder einmahl zugrund, würden sie es nimmermehr bekhommen."; Session of May 18, 1699, *Vorträge*, folder l, fol. 28 r.

[86]The *Relatio Commissionis Posoniensis* was discussed in the Session of December 30, 1700, *Vorträge*, Fasz. 37, 1699-1700, folder IV(1700, Dep. Prot.), fol. 138.

[87]The sentiment was probably expressed by the Secretary: "Die statuirun eines exempels halte ich für nothwendig. Diese excess und grausamkeiten seint aller orthen publicirt, bringen Ihr May. um alle lieb; (die herren) gedenkhen nicht, quod maiestas et potentia consistat in affecta subditorum... Ess würde demselben eine grosse dissolation un ärgernus geben, wan da kein ausrichtung widerfahren und die justiz connivendo auff die seithen gesetzt solte."; Session of Sept. 16, 1700, *ibid.*, fol. 187.

[88]"Ein officier zu Trentschin ist bey einem Teutschen eingelegt; der (officier hat) um mitternacht gebachene kelberfuess begehrt und, alss der hausswirth keine gehabt, in den stall geschicket und denen khüen die füess abschneiden lassen. Concluditur: Der Kriegsrath werde remdiren und staffen. Dicerent semper se no habere solutionem; hae autam essent purae insolentiae."; Session of October 18, 1700, *ibid.*, fol. 192 vc.-193 r. The problem was raised again and

reparation ordered at the Session of November 12, 1700: "Emansi aliquoties propter pedem."; *ibid.*, fol. 196.

[89]"Dominus Cardinalis: Semper necessarius miles in Hungaria. Manipulus rebellium ferme totam turbasset."; Session of February 14, 1698, *Deputationsprotokoll* 1698, fol. 99.

[90]"Hofkriegrafspraesident: In Ungarn alles zum aufstand geneigt, also das landt nicht zu entblossen."; Session of October 26, 1700, *Vorträge*, Fasz. 37, 1700, folder III (1700, January-October), fol. 153-154. The previous spring the question had been raised of sending troops from Hungary to Bohemia, and the Deputation had decided against such a move, since "in Hungarn die gefahr (unspecified) allezeit vorhanden."; Session of May 4, 1700, *ibid.*, fol. 30-33.

[91]"Jörger: Periculum modo maius esset illo, quod fuisset anno 1683."; Session of January 7, 1701; *Vorträge*, Fasz. 37, 1699-1700, folder IV (1700, Dep. Prot.), fol. 130 v.- 131.

[92]"Es war begreiflich, doch von ernsten Folgen, dass... die Regierung in Wien diesem Unwesen eine Bedeutung nicht beimassen und die Gefahr unterschätzten.", Oswald Relich, *Das Werden einer Grossmacht: Osterreich von 1700 bis 1740* (Wien-1942), 162.

[93]"Conclusum: Man konne bey dieser session noch nichts stabiliren. Die ausgab übertreffe den empfang. Man seye such nit versichert, das die lander alles thun werden oder können. Consilium Bellicum diceret, man muste propter paricula eine armada haben. Camer diceret, es seye nit möglich; die contributiones wären ungewis und theten nit khlecken. Sehe also nit, wie auszukommen seye. Nemme man etwas für die creditores hinweg, entgehe es der militz. Ad cameram denique." -- this swan song had for its leitmotif the basic problem which had pursued the Deputation throughout its early days, and which in this moment of truth it admitted it could not solve; Session of May 20 1700, *Vorträge*, Fasz. 37, 1699-1700, folder IV (1700, Dep.-Prot.), fol. 173 v.

[94]Salsburg was decribed by Marshal Villars, the French Ambassador to the Court of Vienna, in his despatch of December 11, 1970, as "un parfait imbéile"; quoted by Max Braubach, "Prinz Eugen im Kampf um die Macht, 1701-1705", *Historisches Jarbuch* (LXIV), (1955), 300. The article document in some detail the general incompetency of the Emperor's ministers in this crucial period.

[95]A number of protocols of the Deputation are preseved for the years 1701-1706. In 1706, there were a few meetings that dealt largely with military problems; on occasion, they were held with Emperor Joseph I presiding ("sub Augustissima Praesentia"); *Vorträge*, Fasz. 39, 1703-1706, folder IV (1707). It is difficult to determine on the basis of these faint traces just what connection the Deputation under Joseph I had with the body that had flourished briefly under his father.

[96]"Herr graff von Kaunitz: *Man solle ein landt, wie das andere tractiren* (italics my own)....: Session of April 12, 1701, *Vorträge*, Fasz. 38, 1701-1702, folder III (1701-1702, March), fol. 13 v.; again, "Kaunitz: Die länder, es möge in Ungarn oder inanderen sein, wan sie renitent, solle man sie mit der execution belegen."; Session of September 13, 1699, *Vorträge*, Fasz. 37, 1699-1700, folder I (1699), fol. 27 v.-28 r. Count Czernin, for example, "Tschernin: Ess müesse eine geichheit zwischen denen ländern sein, sonsten würde denen Böhmischen hart geschehen."; Session of May 18, 1699, *ibid.*, 48 v.

[97]"Die länder wären nicht gleich. Gott habe Steyrmarck nicht eben gemacht. Man müesse das brod nehmben, wie es seye."; Konferenz session of September 19, 1697, *Vorträge*, Fasz. 36 (1697), fol. 83.

[98]"Moverem ego (the Secretary), wegen schwürigkeit dess adels: so er (Kardinal) widerlegt; man solle den adel nit förchten, mehrers 2,000 Bauern alss einen Edelmann."; Session of November 4, 1698, *Vortäge*, Fasz. 36 (1696-1698), fol. 237.

[99]The Cardinal was annoyed with Count Jörger, who had spoken up for special treatment of the Austrians at one session; the Primate felt that all the lands should be treated as equals and that the Austrians should not have special privileges; Session of January 7, 1701, *Vorträge*, Fasz. 37, 1699-1700, folder IV (1700, Dep. Prot.), fol. 131.

[100]"Dominus Gundagger: Wan die bewilligung stabiliert, wolle er geld aufbringen."; Session of May 18, 1699, *Vorträge*, Fasz. 37, 1699-1700, folder I (1699), fol. 28 r.

[101]"Il...conte die Staremberg, altro ministro della 'confereza segreta' dell' imperatore, e uomo di molto spirito e di grande penetrazione negli affari. E verstissimo nelle azlende dell finanze, ed applicato al suo officio. *Non passa pero per ministro grandemente instrutto degli affari di stato, massime stranieri."* (italics my own) in "Relazione della Corte di Vienna del conte San

Martino di Baldissero (1713)", *Relazioni di Ambasciatori Sabaudi, Genovesi e Veneti* (1693-1713), ed. Carlo Morondi (Bologna, 1935), I, 128.

[102]"Otting dicit, dominus Gundacker koste 200.000 fl. (cipher)"; Session of October 12, 1699, *Vorträge*, folder I, fol. 52 v.; the Palatine complained at the very end of 1699 that he had not received his salary as a general -- 30,000 gulden was owed to him. This was all the more annoying to him, since Count Gundacker "hätte so viehl und er so wenig."; Session of December 30, 1699, *Vorträge*, folder I, fol. 76 v.

[103]"Die Landtaverfassungen seint nit gleich, lassen sich nit übern hauffen werffen.", Session of May 18, 1699, *Vorträge*, Fasz. 37, 1699-1700, folder I (1699), fol. 27 v.

[104]"Man habe denen 12 millionen zu viel getrautet, mirabilia erhoffet, aber erfahren, dass es nicht practicirt werden könne. Quod voluerint authores imitari in Gallia, et non considerassent, an etiam in his locis sit possibile aut practicandum. Istae novitates fuissent in causa, ut ex hinc der alte fues umbgekheret und die militz ruiniret."; Session of the *Konferenz* of November 12, 1699, *Vorträge*, Fasz. 37, 1699-1700, folder II (1699, January-November), fol. 207-208.

[105]Probably the best description of the way of life (including the *horarium)* of the high officials of the Court of Vienna is that of the conte San Martino di Baldissero, Minister of the Duke of Savoy to the Court of Vienna at the beginning of the reign of Emperor Charles VI: "Li presidenti, vice presidenti, e conseglieri de 'suddeti tribunali e magistrati sono buona parte cavaglieri, che hanno studiato ben poco, e che, puoi doppo, non studiano; e quantunque vie siano in candun tribunale dottori, il numero pero di questi e il minore; ve ne e qualcuno che intende raggionevolemente, ma li più ne sanno poco.

Li più diligenti non si levano d'ordinaro dal letto che alls ore 8 della mattina, alle 9 vanno al conseglio, dove stanno sino a mezzogiorno, finito il conseglio vanno o alla corte o a apazzo, o a far qualche visita sino all' ora del pranzo, che per lo piu non e prima delle due ore doppo al mezzogiorno. Pranzano frequentemente fuori di casa, o in casa luoro, in compagnia. Il pranzo dura delle due e qualche volta delle tre ore. Doppo all pranzo, o dormono o guiocono. Indi vanno all' assemblea, e non vanno dormire che all mezzanotte, *in modo che non v' e tempo per l'applicarsi all' ufficio* (italics my own), e per lo piu vi dano la mattina della fest e dei giorni nei quali non intrano in conseglio, qual si tiene in tutti li giorni de lavoro, esclusi li mercoledi e sabbato a causa della posta. E quests e anche la vita, che in Vienna si fa dalli conselieri de statto, e dalli ministri della conferenza, eccettuatione il Conte Zailren (Seilern), qual non beve vino e fa una vita non men parca che retirate, e in continua applicazione."; Carlo Morandi, *op. cit.*, 114.

[106]Some indication of this was the complaint of the Deputation in the midst of the negotiations with the Hungarian magnates that "nemo hic, qui locutus pro uribus et plebe."; Session of Nov. 17, 1698, *Deputationsprotokoll 1698*, fol. 247 r.

[107]"... quia esset antiquae familiae."; Session of April 5, 1700, *Vorträge*, Fasz. 37, 1699-1700, folder IV (1700, Dep. Prot.), fol. 166.

[108]A good example of this characteristic "raunzen" is to be found in the occasional outburst of cynicism on the part of the high officials as regards the old traditions and privileges. In discussing, for example, the technical aspects of taxation in the mountain mining towns in Upper Hungary, it was concluded that "ob man es portas nenne order nicht, *dummodo habeamus pecuniam, wäre eben eins* (italics my own). Modo autem habere privilegia vel non, idem est."; Session of December 24, 1699, *Vorträge*, folder I, fol. 75.

Chapter 2

Ferenc Rákóczi's Hungary

"C'étoit (Rákóczi) un trés bon homme, et fort amiable, et commode pour le commerce; mais, après l'avoir vu de près, on demeuroit dans l'étonnement qu'il eut été chef d'un grand parti; et qu'il eut fait tant de bruit dans le monde."

- Duc de Saint-Simon

"Nos quando contra bellum per 84 annos gessimus, omne nostrum aurem et argentum in pecuniam conflavimus, vos autem in podice vestro gestatis."

- Hamel Bruynincx to Berscényi

The present chapter uses three distinct approaches in striving to come to grips with Hungarian society on the eve of the Rákóczi Rebellion: an impressionistic view that is based on a discussion of the Hungarian 'national character', a brief biographical essay on Rákóczi's career up to the beginning of the Rebellion, and a sociologically-oriented perspective on the cultural differences and the class structure. I have made no effort to introduce hitherto unknown material, but since a large part of the materials is virtually unknown outside of Hungary the chapter can lay claim to being a pioneering work in that sense. It must be noted in passing that a fair number of the standard Hungarian secondary works which relate to this problem do not exist in this country.[1]

We have generally assumed that the particular form of a culture has all-important consequences on the type of diplomatic, administrative, and broadly political activity in which that culture will engage. In tracing the background of the Peace of Carlowitz, we noted the fateful disparity in the cultures of the members of the Grand Alliance, as well as the degree to which the differences between the culture of the Austrian baroque and that of the Ottoman Empire influenced the course of the negotiations. In our last chapter, we related the life cycle of the Deputation to the atmosphere at the very heart of its discussions, and were struck by the similarities between that mood and the tonalities of modern Viennese culture. In the remaining chapters, since our attention will be focused on some of the more important aspects of the diplomatic history of the Rákóczi Rebellion, it will be absolutely necessary to describe the particular social and cultural context from which Hungarian diplomatic activity derived.

While an excursion into the phenomenology of the Viennese character may be regarded as a fruitful line of research, a discussion of Hungarian society at the time of Rákóczi in terms of the Hungarian 'national character' may well run into heavy opposition. For students of modern European history have become increasingly skeptical about the value of the category of national character as a means of understanding the great underlying currents of European history. The practice of comprehending the particular quality of a nation's experience in terms of its soul, its spirit, its character was once figured as the favorite intellectual exercise of European intellectuals. It first came into prominence at the beginning of the nineteenth century and became fairly common currency as the century progressed.. Cliché versions of the national characters of the leading European nations were established in the process; their very generality made it extremely unlikely that serious questions could ever be raised as to their value as a means of explanation. The historians of the period were not entirely unaffected by the general current of opinion; the natural interest in writing history within the framework of the European nation-states made it difficult to avoid occasional references to the national character. In our own day the use of such devices has become more and more problematical, and it is entirely possible that this category will disappear from the historian's vocabulary in the near future.

But in the period which we are studying, European observers were manifestly untroubled by the philosophical problems involved in the business of talking about the national characters. The diplomats, merchants, the scholars constantly dealt in such entities, though they avoided any implication that their phrases had a scientific foundation. An interest in the rich variety of national moods and cultural expressions served as a companion piece to the development of the nation in the political dimension, and at this particular stage in the development of the interrelations of the various European states, there was some warranty for an impressionistic use of the category of national character.

The Hungarians had been particularly successful in acquiring a collection of traits that were immediately recognizable to the cultivated European of the day. Indeed, it is true that the characteristic tone of the Hungarians was better known in Europe at the beginning of the eighteenth century than it is to the contemporaries of the October Revolution of 1956. The version of the Hungarian national character that had emerged had all the strengths and weaknesses of such portraiture. It was often embarrassingly close to the original, though on occasion the shadows and darker hues were more in evidence than they had need to be. For the study of national characters is frequently a more refined development of the custom of international name-calling, and it is often difficult to separate them. To say that this composite portrait of the Hungarians was everywhere the same or that it evoked the same general response would be to overstate the case. Yet the typed 'Hungarian' had such common currency that the Hungarians often adopted it when they had occasion to speak of their own countrymen.

"The Hungarians are a volatile people."[2] How often Western European observers would say something of this kind. The Hungarians had provided Europe with a great number of displays of temperament in the course of the seventeenth century. The storms had been sudden and unexpected, and they had customarily subsided as fast as they had appeared. There was clearly a mercurial streak in this nation's makeup. The frequent violent oscillations in Hungarian reactions did not commend themselves as an attractive characteristic, since they argued an absence of real depth and seriousness of disposition. And while this same absence of depth was evident in the Viennese character, the weakness did not proceed from the same source in both cases. Where the Viennese were cynical about the value of commitment as such, the Hungarian variations in spirit reflected the tragic imbalance between the ideal they cherished and the humiliating reality in which they were forced to live.

"The Hungarians have an exaggerated notion of their own importance." To this trait another was closely allied: the extraordinary love of liberty that Hungarians possessed. George Stepney, the English diplomat who vainly sought to mediate between the Emperor and the Hungarians, developed on this theme in an effort to explain to his superiors the peculiar nature of the Hungarians' position:

> 'Tis true they have hitherto been reputed a free people, who have neither lost their rights and liberties by conquest as Bohemia did, nor parted with them by concession as the provinces of Silesia and Moravia (who after the reduction of that Kingdom, submitted voluntarily to be annext, and governed by the same laws) But have preserved some greater degree of liberty, at least in appearance, than, the Emperor's other Dominions do enjoy, whereby the regal authority still continues circumscribed by certain laws and constitutions peculiar to the Hungarian nation. I remember formerly when I had an opportunity of discoursing with some of their chief men on this point, they offered to explain their meaning to me, by alledging the example of Scotland, which kingdom is annexed to the Imperial Crown of England, but not under that degree of dependency wherewith Ireland is subjected.[3]

The analogy was perhaps not entirely convincing in Stepney's mind, but it is an instance of the Hungarian case for special treatment, based upon the nation's invariable attachment to its liberty and expressed in terms which were thought to have meaning for an English observer. At a time when national feeling in Europe had not yet assumed an exaggerated hold on the popular consciousness, the Hungarians were already marked for their excessive devotion to Hungary, and in the course of diplomatic negotiations this would frequently come to be regarded as pathological in its obstinacy and overweening pride.

The attachment to the cause of liberty was a more attractive trait. Admittedly, the Hungarians understood liberty to mean specific liberties. As the cast of the Hungarian mind was still largely medieval, freedom inevitably referred to an itemized account of concrete rights and privileges. But even the word 'liberty', if enunciated with sufficient fervor in favorable circumstances, could set the Hungarian masses into revolutionary motion.[4] At once a useful emotional outlet and a ready focus for much of the Hungarian political rhetoric, the love of liberty had established its claim to being a national trait by the incontrovertible proof of the seven insurrections against the Habsburgs in the period from 1604 to 1703.[5] Even the Austrians were prepared to admit that this symbol had a tremendous hold on the Hungarians, but they customarily traced this state of affairs to the political immaturity and the inveterate quarrelsome nature of the Magyar.

"The Hungarians have a profound and unreasoning hatred of everything that is German." This well-known aversion owed its existence to the selfsame struggle with the Emperor and his attendant swarms of German soldiers, administrators, and ecclesiastics; the Hungarians had learned to resent the growing power and influence of Germans in every sector of the nation's life. The long and depressing history of national antipathies suggests that relatively few prizes can be awarded for distinction in this field, but the Hungarians of Rákóczi's time were clearly as extreme in their hatred of Germans as they were in the depth of their national loyalty. The words of the popular song "*Ne higyj a németek*" (Don't ever trust the Germans") were the automatic responsory of a generation that believed it was witnessing the last convulsive efforts to preserve Hungary from Germanization.[6]

"The Hungarians have a narrowly legalistic view of politics." This trait, too, was intimately connected with their love of liberty, but hampered them in the choice of tactics to be used in their negotiations. The pettifogging lawyer, rather than the astute practical politician, discovered that controversy with the Hungarians was his chosen domain. Viennese irritation in the face of the Hungarians' legal arguments only occasionally produced a decision to reply in kind. But the lists of grievances that arrived in a constant stream from Hungary were so clogged by the myriad references to laws that extended back to the earliest days of the Kingdom's existence that they reduced the

Austrian 'experts' to silence. The Emperor did have his own legal technicians -- there was nothing more truly frightening than Baron Seilern in the midst of his exegesis of an official document -- but the Hungarians were all Seilerns, and their manipulation of what the Austrians, and other outsiders as well, felt to be dead letters aroused more discomfiture than respect.

"The Hungarians are overmuch given to pomp and ceremony." The whole nation, however tragically divided by rigid social stratification and religious tensions, plainly enjoyed a good show. And the Rákóczi Rebellion provided it with opportunities for colorful display and self-dramatization that it had not had for years. The wearisome fastidiousness of Hungarian etiquette sprang from a general fear that carelessness in the use of titles and in the seating of guests, to mention only the more obvious instances where this came into play, might well proceed from a desire to slight the Hungarian nation in the persons of its leaders. Stepney's amazement as he observed the obvious care of Prince Rákóczi in availing himself of the social privileges of a sovereign prince was not unmixed with disapproval of such parvenu manners. And the solid and trustworthy J.J. Hamel Bruynincx was patently scandalized by the *luxe* of Count Bercsényi's establishment. A meal at the Count's residence was a feast by Dutch standards: the number of courses was immense; the dining room bulged with guests and innumerable lackeys, and the company consumed its meal with the assistance of an elaborate musical accompaniment. This was an independence movement whose airs and graces were in decided contrast to its actual situation. Bruynincx could not help but remember the great sacrifices of the Dutch in the course of their war of independence.[7]

Rákóczi sought to model the organization of his Court after the pattern of Versailles. His care in imitation revealed itself in the selection of his personal retainers, in the development of his bodyguard, and in the inducements offered to the sons of good Hungarian families to begin their careers as pages at the Court.[8] Court life for Rákóczi, as for Louis XIV and Leopold, constituted a school of practical experience that was absolutely essential to the development of the more privileged members of society. There aristocrats learned how to be courtiers. Even though the Hungarian imitation lost something in the absence of a permanent seat for the Court, it represented the fulfillment of a need to live on terms of equality with the other kingdoms of Europe. The modern observer has come to expect a spirit of austerity in his revolutions (and thus he would agree with Bruynincx's reservations), but in Eger, the occasional seat of this Court's manifold activities, it was possible to hunt through the days and dance through the evenings with the same singleminded interest in pleasure that one might find at Marly or at the Favorita.

"The Hungarians are protestants for the most part, and this explains their devotion to the cause of religious liberty." Stepney and his Dutch colleagues could never quite decide on just how many Protestants there were in Hungary. The estimates varied widely from two-thirds to seven-eighths of the total population, and in the default of reliable statistics it would be difficult to prove them wrong.[9] But the endeavors of the Counter Reformation had securely recaptured more ground than this, though it had not yet made of Hungary a predominantly Catholic nation. In the area of local politics there was not much evidence of Protestant feeling; the comitat congregations were heavily Calvinist in composition, while the Lutherans exerted powerful influence in the cities. The steadily-mounting drive to make the country Catholic evoked great sympathy for the oppressed Protestants throughout the Protestant areas of Europe. Needless to say, the feeling of a common bond with the Hungarian Protestants often failed to have any noticeable consequences in the domain of power politics.

"Hungarians do not make good soldiers, though they are brave enough as individuals." War had become a solemn technical exercise for most Europeans, and they naturally dismissed the military showing of the Hungarians as being most unmilitary. Hungarian fighters had little training and even less in the way of military supplies, but there was an admitted reluctance to adapt to military discipline. The peasant fought as a partisan in the open countryside with great stamina and occasional imagination, but he was a lamentable recruit. A constantly changing conglomerate of partisans acted, then, the part of the fighting force in this society, and the leaders of the Rákóczi Rebellion would be called upon to make of these marauders regular soldiers able to match the veterans of the Austrian army's Turkish campaigns. The Hungarian fighting men had the congenital drawback of becoming panic-stricken in the face of an enemy surprise attack. But happily for them, the Imperial armies moved like great ungainly beasts for whom surprise was impossible. Fearsome enough in its far-ranging expeditions deep into the Emperor's Hereditary Provinces, the Rebellion was doomed necessarily to fail, for reasons both practical and psychological, to meet any powerful thrust by the Austrians on the field of battle.[10]

Our litany of Hungarian traits cannot pretend to be exhaustive, but sufficient indication has been given to reproduce the tonality of European opinion of the Hungarians in general. This montage of personal observations, deepseated antipathies, and experiments in national caricature, combined as it is with a universal enthusiasm for Hungarian wines, assured the Hungarian society of the time a well-established niche in the European consciousness. A number of the alleged traits were not calculated to arouse sympathy, but Europe could be said to be favorably disposed.

But these views of Hungarian life and character that flourished in Europe at this time necessarily tell only a part of the story, for they remain far too external to the society itself. A care for objectivity requires that the Hungarians testify in their own behalf. A number of possibilities in this direction suggest themselves, but it is Ferenc Rákóczi who is clearly the best witness that Hungary can produce. A study of his career up to the very eve of the Rebellion affords an unusual perspective for an understanding of the nature of Hungarian society and its conflict with the Imperial government. Rákóczi has also furnished us with a large amount of penetrating observations on Hungary and its people. The testimony of his own life and his meditations on his social context, when combined with the recent findings of a number of the most distinguished representatives of Hungarian historiography, will round out our description of the social background of the Rebellion.

The life of an individual is a notoriously hazardous foundation on which to construct such a description, for the simple reason that the experience of a single man -- so matter how heroic its proportions -- cannot encompass the whole range of a society's possibilities. The natural contrast between the career of the great man and the humdrum existence of the average person, a dimension of particular importance for the student of social history, does not yield to easy solution. The life of Rákóczi, however, may constitute something of an exception to this general rule. For he expressed with unusual success the common needs and aspirations of his fellow Hungarians at all levels of society and his insight into the great social processes operating about him enabled him to comprehend much he could not know at first hand.

The forms his analysis took are at once usual and unusual. Rákóczi in his years of exile devoted much of his energy to setting the record straight in his *Memoires*. This book was to present the case for Hungarian freedom, and in so doing it would serve to stand as an apologia for Rákóczi's leadership in the Rebellion. It was not in the least surprising that a distinguished Hungarian exile should fight off ennui by recounting the moving events of which he had been the focus, but this exile possessed a touching desire to achieve the pinnacles of spiritual heroism as well. And this longing for sanctity found expression in his *Confessiones*, closely patterned on St. Augustine's work. This would be the autobiography of his soul, a detailed account of a spiritual odyssey that would take the place of the usual memoirs. In both these books he wrote with an eye to posterity, but the form of composition, the device of addressing all of his remarks to Almighty God, encouraged a candor and occasional eruption of dispassionate objectivity that is not usual in the reminiscence of exiles.[11]

The deeply spiritual character of these minor classics should not blind us to the fact that their subject had not always displayed leanings toward great purity of soul. To be sure, the young Rákóczi had had a finer grain to his makeup than did his associates, and even in the very midst of the great struggle he displayed a serenity of spirit which was outstanding. But only in his years of exile did he really discover in the quiet of the monastery of Grosbois a great attraction to the spiritual life. A Catholic by birth and education, he had given little indication heretofore that his views on religion and his religious practices differed from the median for Hungarian magnates. But defeat, that perennial midwife of reflection, came to him at a time when his fully developed powers, freed suddenly of the enormous strain induced by the Rebellion, sought new worlds to conquer. The great adventure would now transpire within his soul. Out of the new spiritual awareness of these years he produced a commentary on Hungarian society that is securely bedded in a series of meditations on the infinite goodness of God and the great sinfulness of Ferenc Rákóczi. The sensitive observer of the varieties of religious sentiment might well note the presence of Jansenism in these works (how clearly does Rákóczi require the illuminating services of a Bremond), but for our purposes it will be sufficient to remember that there were two Rákóczis, the youthful leader of the Rebellion and the pious exile of the *Confessiones*, and that the description of Hungarian society of the latter bears the imprint of an almost Jansenistic austerity.

The first few pages of the Confessiones convey the general trend of his whole life in a naive and disarming way. This was a man born to the purple, to a tradition of princely rule as a family occupation. "You, o my God ... were born in a stable; I was born in a palace."[12] Even in the shattering humility of a soul standing quite alone in the presence of God, it was difficult for Rákóczi to forget the wisdom of the Divine decree which brought him into the world as the heir of a great princely line. And if the ties of blood can be said to have meaning at all, the career of Ferenc Rákóczi was determined by heredity. He was born on March 27, 1676, at Borsi in northeastern Hungary. On his father's side, Rákóczi was the great-grandson of the Princes George I and George II of Transylvania, and through his personal paternal grandmother Zsófia Báthory, he could claim descent from that great Eastern European dynasty which had played an influential role in both Polish and Hungarian history. His mother, Ilona Zrinyi, was the daughter of Count Peter Zrinyi, one of the leaders of the abortive magnate conspiracy of

1671, who had been executed by the Austrians at Weiner-Neustadt. The Zrinyi name was one of the noblest in Hungary, but it had the additional distinction of having produced a great hero in the war against the Turks and a great poet who had written the epic of that struggle. Ferenc I Rákóczi, his father, had participated briefly in the conspiracy of 1671, but he had not followed Zrinyi to the scaffold. His death a few months after Ferenc's birth left the family in a particularly difficult position. Ferenc spent the first few weeks in the care of his mother and his grandmother at Munkács, a traditional family stronghold. The castle was redolent with memories of the Hungarian struggle for freedom, and the young boy quite unconsciously prepared himself for the family trade -- rebellion.[13]

The patriarchal character of the family's life at Munkács offered a wonderful sense of security to the young boy and his older sister Julia. But the idyllic life of those early years was abruptly terminated for him by his mother's marriage to Count Imre Thököly, the 'king of the *kurocok*', the anti-Habsburg irregulars. The suspicion was prevalent at Thököly's interest in the widowed Princess Rákóczi had much to do with her great landed wealth and the prestige of her name. Ferenc, in any case, never grew to like his step-father, who carried the mother and son with him into the harsh world of *kuruc* camps. The gentle Ferenc was literally allowed to seed in that most uncongenial atmosphere. In the course of his 'training', he developed a profound dislike for the Lutheranism of his step-father's circle, and a most reasonable distrust of the Turks and Tatars who were allied with the *kurucok*.[14]

These were the years of the Siege of Vienna and the first great Habsburg successes in Hungary. By the end of 1687, Ilona and her two children had been left to fend for themselves at Munkács, since the adverse fortunes of war required that Thököly participate in the general Turkish withdrawal from Hungary. A detachment of Austrian troops soon appeared under the walls of the fortress and demanded that the Countess surrender, but she displayed courage and foolhardiness in refusing to capitulate. She was unaware of the existence of any person, as she expressed it, who had the right to demand the possession of the fortress from her. Brave words indeed in those circumstances, but they could only help to postpone the inevitable. After a few months of resistance, she came to terms, and she and he children learned that they were to be removed to Vienna by the order of the Emperor. Ferenc now faced the prospect, deeply-felt for a boy of his age, of separation from his homeland. His boyhood in Hungary had come to a close, and many difficult years passed before he saw Hungary again.

While the Emperor pondered the fate of the Rákóczis, they were confined to a Viennese cloister. Leopold eventually commissioned Cardinal Kollonitsch, in virtue of his office as a Primate of Hungary, to act as the children's guardian. Their chances of flourishing under his aegis seemed slight indeed. Kollonitsch had a reputation for kindness to widows and orphans, but his zeal in the Emperor's cause made it constitutionally impossible for him to nurture the sprigs of such a damnably traitorous family tree. He sent Julia off in tears to the Ursulines and confined Ferenc to the quiet backwater provided by the Jesuit college at Neuhaus in Bohemia. The young Prince's isolation became even more intense when his Hungarian tutor left him on his arrival at Neuhaus; the last living contact with Hungary had been broken and he was completely reduced to the company of foreigners.[15]

The Jesuit Fathers took pity on the lonely boy and did everything to reconcile him to his new situation. One of the Jesuits left us a striking description of the boy on his first year at Neuhaus (1688). Though the lad was only twelve, he looked at least three or four years older. He had matured, both physically and intellectually, to a far greater degree than his classmates, who were usually the sons of Bohemian aristocrats. Occasional reminders of Hungary produced long bouts of depression, though he had finally agreed to learn German and to adopt the German custom of dress. On one occasion, he rebuked the good Jesuit for calling him 'Count'. "I am a Prince, and such as they (counts) serve me." The Jesuit had the presence of mind to tell Ferenc that the Fathers customarily called all the young nobles 'Count' until such time as they entered into the possession of their estates.[16] The Rákóczi domains were then being administered by the agents of

Cardinal Kollonitsch, and there appeared to be no expectation that Ferenc would take possession of them in the near future. It was even rumored that the Cardinal planned to encourage the young Rákóczis to devote their lives to the Church, so that on their deaths this vast property would pass into the hands of the orders to which they had belonged.[17]

Education at Neuhaus followed the directives laid down nearly a century before in the *Ratio studiorum*, the great classic of Jesuit pedagogical thought. The emphasis was heavily on classical languages and literatures, with some attention to rhetoric and the more elementary parts of scholastic philosophy. The Fathers lavished great care on the religious training of the boys, and the whole atmosphere took its tone from the school's baroque religious exercises. the Jesuit Fathers at Neuhaus could not be called exceptional men, but their kindness and humane attitude had a powerful effect on their students. The Jesuits had traditionally directed their attention to the elite of the societies in which they worked; in the case of Neuhaus, they had to do largely with members of the Bohemian aristocracy. These young men presented few problems. It was expected that they would marry well and then settle down to the business of administering their estates. Only rarely did this group produce a man of the eminence of a Kinsky or a Kaunitz; for the most part, it was content with the unchanging round of eating, drinking, hunting, and participating in the entertainments of their social equals. The Fathers were certainly aware of the probable future of their students; they gave evidence of this in their large tolerances of the weaknesses of their charges. The youthful Rákóczi was to discover that his intense realization of his sinfulness did not arouse undue alarm in his confessors, who seemed to attach little importance to the sins of the flesh. Moral laxity in a Catholic society like this was not the result of any lax moral theology espoused by the Jesuits.[18] Here as in so many other instances, human nature had had its way with religious rules and conduct. No one questioned their validity; they simply failed to take hold in everyday living. Rákóczi would look back in horror on the sins of his youth and the general conspiracy of silence which blunted the rigors of Catholic moral teaching. But the pathos involved in educating an elite of this variety was nowhere more noticeable than at Neuhaus. Its influence on Ferenc was slight; it was obviously not equipped to undertake the education of a prince.

After a brief sojourn in Prague at a house maintained there by the Fathers of Neuhaus for students attending the Charles University, Rákóczi took his appointed place in society. His sister Julia had recently married a Count Aspremont (much against Kollonitsch's wishes), and her husband took the young man under his wing. The first item on the agenda was the Grand Tour. In 1693, Rákóczi took a prolonged trip through Italy with the express approval of the Emperor. The state of war then prevailing in Europe forced him to confine his travelling in the years immediately before the Rebellion to Italy and Germany. In Italy he established contact with the living sources of Austria's baroque culture, and in Germany he looked for a wife. The question of his marriage became actual only after the Italian tour. His relatives and friends were extremely anxious that he make a good marriage, one that would be in keeping with his princely rank and that would bring him at the same time a valuable connection with a reigning house. A number of alliances of this sort existed as distinct possibilities; German princely families, blessed as always with a surplus of marriageable daughters, were the leading contenders. For a time, the Prince considered marrying Wilhelmina Amalia of Brunswick-Lüneburg (she was later to become the wife of Joseph I, the friend of his Viennese youth and the implacable foe of the final period of the Rebellion), but she did not hold his attention for long. After thinking of a princess of the House of Hesse-Darmstadt, he finally decided to marry Princess Charlotte Amalia of Hesse-Rheinfels. The young lady was extremely attractive, and their marriage had all the appearances of a brilliant match.

His bride was pleased to exchange the confining society of a small German court for the life of an immensely wealthy Hungarian magnate and the prestigious position in Viennese society which this involved. Rákóczi had been impressed by the value of the Hessian connection rather than by Charlotte's charm or personality.[19] The

Emperor and his ministers were caught unawares by this marriage, and faced with the fait accompli, they were understandably annoyed. But Leopold revealed the presence of a warm paternal heart in his character by suddenly restoring the family estate to the young couple. The young man of nineteen and his wife were able now to go to Munkács and reestablish there the life he had known as a boy. Since he was the hereditary Lord Lieutenant of the *comitat* of Sárospatak, he had an excellent vantage point from which to bring the family influence to bear in local affairs.

These properties represented the largest single collection of real estate in the hands of a private citizen in Hungary. Composed of the properties of Bethlen, Báthory, and Rákóczi families, it provided the Prince with the material basis necessary to make him the most important figure in Upper Hungary. The largest single property was the Duchy of Makovicza, which had formerly belonged to the Báthory family, a territory that included most of the Ruthenian population dwelling in the Subcarpathian area. But the lands of the Prince extended virtually without interruption from the Tisza line at Tokay as a western limit to the Transylvanian frontier on the east and the Polish border on the northeast. It would not be too much of an exaggeration to say that the young man controlled the whole northeast section of Hungary in virtue of this act of the Emperor. The income from these lands permitted him to live in great style, while in the time of revolutionary crisis it would constitute a major part of the Rebellion's annual budget.

The married life of the young couple gradually deteriorated. Charlotte was a grasping young woman whose personality was completely at variance with that of her husband. She dutifully presented him with sons, and she remained loyal to him in the years of separation that followed his flight to Poland. But Ferenc Rákóczi did not seem to suffer from the disappearance of his wife as a factor in his life. Though his name would be linked now and again with other women, his mode of living was virtually that of the celibate. His rather puzzling lack of interest in women is somewhat analogous to Eugene of Savoy's indifference. Strange that the two most distinguished men of the

Habsburg Monarchy of this period survived quite happily without assistance from the 'second sex'. The solution of this mystery awaits the biographer with a training in depth psychology.

The seven years that he had been away from Hungary had made of him a Hungarian magnate of the type of Prince Esterházy. The heir of 'free princes' had lost sight of his hereditary vocation in the fleshpots of his Viennese captivity, and it was only natural that the centripetal tendency of the baroque court culture should exert a powerful attraction on him. Once he returned to the Rákóczi bailiwick, it became of crucial importance for him to rediscover his Hungarian heritage. The question of language and dress (the Hungarians of the day wore a distinctive costume) was the merest beginning in the process of acclimation, but in speaking Hungarian and wearing Hungarian dress he served notice that he had taken up where he had left off seven years before. His friendship with Count Miklós Bercsényi assisted this process, ·for Bercsényi encouraged him to think of himself as a Hungarian once more.

Bercsényi, a close neighbor of Rákóczi's had the advantage of greater maturity and broader political experience. His career bore certain likenesses, moreover, to that of the young Prince. The Bercsényi family tradition had been one of relentless opposition to the Habsburgs, and the Count's father had been an important supporter of Thököly. But the widespread enthusiasm for the liberation of Hungary from the Turks had brought him to adopt a position of loyalty to the King and Emperor. His courageous showing during the ensuing campaigns had secured him the Imperial favor, but the tragic state of liberated Hungary drove him once more into the opposition to Austrian rule. In the company of this political realist, this fiery devotee of Hungarian liberties, Rákóczi could not fail to reestablish the closest of spiritual ties with his native land.

The last decade of the century had not been kind to Hungary, and all classes of Hungarian society were driven toward a more and more hopeless position. Ferenc Tokay's peasant uprising in the summer of 1697 brought Rákóczi his first adult experience of the revolutionary forces at work in Hungarian society. The uprising had been a purely peasant affair, though the peasants had been pathetically eager for Rákóczi's leadership. Rumors circulated in Vienna that he was actually involved in the affair, and to give the lie to these reports he found it necessary to go to Vienna and there establish proof of his innocence. His manner of accomplishing this gave evidence of a developing political ability. For he sought out the Emperor's confessor, Padre Menegatti, S.J., and requested the Jesuit's assistance in clearing his name. Since his most outspoken enemy at the moment was Count Kinsky, the choice of Menegatti was a brilliant move. Kinsky and Menegatti had a long history of personal antipathy, and it was only natural that a 'victim' of Kinsky's malice would receive a most sympathetic hearing. The confessor's influence eventually secured the restoration of the Emperor's good will. But the suspicions about Rákóczi's loyalty, once they had become current, continued to flourish despite the Emperor's favor, and the coldness with which he was received in Austrian circles became a contributing factor in his decision to assume his rightful position as the leader of the Hungarian revolutionary movement.[20]

Fate provided him with a magnificent opportunity to do just that with the death of Carlos II in November, 1700. The resumption of hostilities between the Emperor and Louis XIV offered Rákóczi the possibility of gaining French support for an insurrection. The Prince in a very foolhardy way was determined to approach the King of France through the medium of a member of his own household, Captain Longueval, whose trips back and forth to his home in Lorraine would not arouse Austrian suspicions. He conferred with Bercsényi about the proposals they were to make to the French, and they decided to remind Louis of France's traditional friendship for the Hungarian people and to ask him to assist the Hungarians in regaining their freedoms. Communications of this kind were clearly treasonable from the Austrian standpoint, though Rákóczi and Bercsényi believed that they had every moral right to intrigue with the French. For reasons that have never been entirely clear, Longueval now informed the Austrians of the real nature of his trips. The leaders were immediately implicated; Bercsényi had time to escape to Poland, but Rákóczi was seized on one of his Hungarian estates and removed to Wiener-Neustadt.[21] History was on the very verge of repeating itself, for his Zrinyi grandfather had been imprisoned and executed for high treason in similar circumstances thirty years before.   The Austrians had every intention of bringing Rákóczi to trial for treason, but with the connivance of the commander of the fortress, Captain Lehmann, and of highly influential people at Court, he managed to escape and make his way to his friends in Poland.[22] In the period of his confinement in the fall of 1701 in the fortress of Wiener-Neustadt, he discovered once again the perennial merit of the ancient laws of the Kingdom of Hungary, particularly those which made it unlawful to try a Hungarian noble in a court of extraordinary character that was convoked beyond the territorial limits of the Kingdom. The laws were magnificent but impotent to save him from the legal machinations of the Austrians; Count Buccelini, the Austrian Court Chancellor, was obviously not impressed by Rákóczi's references to Hungarian laws.   When the prisoner was informed of Longueval's disclosures, he summarily dismissed them. In any case, it was not legal for a man of the captain's humble station in life to testify against a Rákóczi.[23]

The Polish friends of the Hungarian leaders were all key members of the French party in Polish politics that had recently been disappointed by the election of Augustus of Saxony as King of Poland.   Thier solicitude and interest enabled the exiles to establish contact with the French Ambassador at Warsaw, the Marquis du Heron. All the while the Prince and Bercsényi were forced to live in semi-retirement, because Leopold's ambassodor was constantly protesting against the granting of Polish asylum to these would-be traitors.   But powerful support appeared in the person of Helena Sienawska, the wife of the Crown General and Palatine of Belz, Adam Sienawska. "Madame la Palatine" had great talent for intrigue, and once Rákóczi's plight had enlisted her sympathies, she performed minor miracles of political maneuvering in his behalf. In his close contact with the great Polish families, the Hungarian magnate found much that reminded him of Hungary. But the constitutional organization of the Republic of Poland struck him as a system which might well be adopted in Hungary. The Polish aristocrats had a wide measure of autonomy in thier own bailiwicks, and this appealed to a man whose family controlled so much of northeastern Hungary. The Polish practice of institutionalizing minority opinion through Confederation of the dissidents was even more a propos. This form was to be adopted by the Hungarian rebels as the most meaningful expression of their constitutional authority.[24]

The Hungarian leaders had meanwhile become prisoners of the King of France, though they had not received any assurances that aid would be forthcoming in the event of a revolutionary diversion in Hungary. Louis XIV intended for the time being to confine his assurances to large annual grants to the exiled leaders. His royal conscience reportedly had scruples about a French alliance with men who were planning to rebel against their legitimate sovereign. But with the financial assistance from Paris, Rákóczi managed to establish himself on the broad acres of Brzezan in Galicia; this provided him with an excellent observation post from which to follow developments in Hungary.

The candidate for the leadership of a Hungarian rebellion did not have long to wait. The peasants in the neighborhood of Munkács were becoming increasingly restive as a result of the *executions* carried out by the Imperial soldiers. At the same time, all of Hungary was well aware that the number of German troops stationed in Hungary had been drastically reduced; twelve thousand effective soldiers were left in the whole country, and a large portion of this force was tied down to strongholds throughout the country. A delegation of peasants travelled across the Carpathians to find out where thier Prince was staying in Poland. They came eventually to Brzezan, and their simple joy at seeing Rákóczi again was a moving sight indeed. He gave them promises of his assistance in the event that the peasants found it necessary to resort to military action against the Imperial troops. The delegation departed for home with the assurance that their movement would not lack direction the next time they came to blows with the Germans.

The actual uprising in the spring of 1703 caught Rákóczi off guard; the peasants had not waited so that his plans could mature and his appeals to France and Sweden might receive favorable answers. Peasants like Tamás Esze, Mihály Pap, and Albert Kis, and their followers had already taken the initiative of attacking the Austrians when their appeal came for Rákóczi's fulfillment of the pledge to come to the aid of the peasants. It was a moment of great crisis for Rákóczi. There was a good chance that the uprising might be crushed before he could arrive on the scene. The whole affair had an air of improvisation about it that was deeply disquieting to men like Rákóczi and Bercsényi. But the international situation could not be more favorable -- the French and Bavarian armies were in control of southern Germany and the Elector Max Emanuel of Bavaria was moving now into an invasion of the Austrian lands, and on June 7, 1703, the pledge was fulfilled as Rákóczi assumed personal leadership of the Rebellion on Hungarian soil. This was the formal commencement of the fight to regain Hungarian liberties. A year later, Rákóczi was to issue a manifesto explaining the reasons for the Rebellion. The document was his inspiration, though it was largely the product of the pen of Paul Ráday, the director of Rákóczi's Chancellory, and in token of thier enthusiasm for the obscure beginnings of the Rebellion, it was issued under the date of June 7, 1703.[25]

This manifesto, known under the title of *Recrudescunt inclytae gentis Hungarae vulnera* ("The wounds of the renowned Hungarian people have broken out afresh") consisted of a list of *gravamina* that was addressed not simply to the Emperor, as had so often been the case in the recent history of Hungary, but to all the princes and republics of the whole Christian world, indeed, to all the men whatever their condition in life. The manifesto did not spare its readers, for the list of grievances was a long one, and for those who had read such lists before, there was little in the way of surprise or novelty. The articles followed no particular order of importance or logical development, as complaints that referred to conditions of recent vintage mingled comfortably with *gravamina* that went back almost as far as Mohács. The Prince's recent experience of Austrian tyranny contributed to the tone of exasperation in the document; one of the articles specifically referred to the treatment meted out to him and eighty other Hungarian leaders who had been accused of involvement in the conspiracy of 1701.

A place of prominence was given in the manifesto to a full-scale attack on the changes in the Hungarian constitution which had been made at the Diet of Pozsony in 1687. The Hungarian Rebels pointedly refused to accept the establishment of hereditary monarchy in Hungary (they regarded the elective character of that monarchy as a fundamental law that could not be changed) or the abolition of the right of resistance, the *jus resistendi*, an article in the Golden Bull of King Andrew II in 1222, which made it legally possible for the Estates to defend their privileges against royal encroachment. Pozsony had meant that the Hungarian Estates no longer had any protection from the arbitrary practices of Habsburg absolutism. The Rebels made the disavowal of that Diet the cornerstone of their programme; they made it clear that they regarded the decisions at Pozsony as illegal promulgations which had been wrung from the body by Austrian pressures.

Another group of articles was aimed at the Austrian practice of excluding Hungarians from participation in their own affairs -- the Peace of Carlowitz was cited as an instance of the Emperor's failure to consult the wishes of the Hungarians, even when he was engaged in establishing the limits of the Kingdom -- and the repeated pattern of subordinating Hungarian administrative agencies to the Hofkammer and the *Commissio neo-acquistica*. Under the last heading, the fifth article complained that the Austrians had been refusing to restore lands to their rightful owners in the newly-acquired districts. A number of leading families of the Kingdom had been drastically penalized in this way.

The recent Austrian innovations in the matter of tax collecting evidently had left deep scars on the Hungarian psyche. The Imperial government established the amount of the annual *contribution* without consulting Hungarian officials (this was not quite the whole truth, as we have seen), and mention was made of the failure of the government to come to an agreement with the assembly of notables in 1698. The

Hungarian position on that controversy was reiterated: the taxes had been converted from an annual levy to a standard *contribution*, and in such arrangements the wishes of the *comitats* could easily be disregarded. Moreover, the ministry had made proposals which would have abolished the last remnants of Hungarian liberties; the gentry would have been depressed to the level of the "Common People," and the position of the magnates would have been seriously weakened.[26] The manifesto expressed great concern about the way Hungarian ecclesiastical preferments had been bestowed on foreigners who could have little interest in Hungarian affairs, whether spiritual or temporal, and who customarily did not reside in their sees, abbeys, and chapters. To this valid complaint was added censure of the general religious policy of the Imperial government. The illegal methods it had resorted to in strengthening the position of the Catholic Church had only sowed further dissention in the strife-torn kingdom.

The modern reader of the Recrudescunt will find it a disappointing document -- the lengthy list of grievances fails to convey a sense of great revolutionary ardor. But since it was composed in the very early period of the Rebellion, when the significance and goals of the movement were still somewhat obscure, it wisely confined itself to listing the alleged causes of its break with Vienna. Much of the description of the state of Hungary was true enough, and few would deny that it presented a cogent indictment of the crimes and omission and commission of a nascent Austrian absolutism. Exception might be taken to its excursions into the dimension of recent history in the cases of the Diet of Pozsony and the assembly of notables at Vienna, but in so far as it confined itself to the day-to-day *modus operandi* of Austrian officialdom it had a solid basis in fact. The humanistic flourishes of its Latin phrases had caught something of the cynicism of the Austrian ministers in their dealings with 'ancient laws and customs' and of their callousness in disregarding the tender sensibilities of the Hungarians, particularly those who were interested in appointment to office.

What the manifesto could not possibly say was that its somber picture of the tragic aspects of Hungarian life under Austrian rule did not tell the whole story. Certainly a country so recently liberated from the Turks might be expected to possess a sense of gratitude for its release. But the presence of the Germans overrode any unpleasant memories of the Turkish occupation.[27] And the manifesto, since it sought to influence European public opinion, could hardly be expected to present a moderate and balanced report on the intolerable conditions it intended to change. What in essence was the program which Rákóczi and his peasant followers desired to carry into effect? The nature of the Rebellion's goals will emerge with greater clarity once we have completed our reconstruction of its social context. But a preliminary observation can be made at this point. The manifesto falls down seriously in its failure to speak of a new state of affairs in Hungary, of the building, if you will of a 'New Jerusalem' on the Hungarian plain. The program did not even include the deposition of the Habsburg king (this extreme limiting point of Rákóczian political radicalism would be reached only after five years of bloody conflict had reduced the Rebellion to a state of desperation); at best it was an ominous warning to His Apostolic Majesty in Vienna to give his close attention and paternal care to the grievances of hid Hungarian subjects. But beyond the area of domestic conflict between the sovereign and the nation Hungary now laid claim to a position of its own in the European system, and the diplomacy of guarantees which it pursued was a direct consequence of the renewed sense of its own importance.

Now that we have followed the evolution of Rákóczi to the time when he assumed leadership of the Rebellion, we can hope to establish a logical connection between his movement and the society whose anxieties and growing exasperation it expressed so well. Hungary at the beginning of the eighteenth century existed on a bewildering variety of social and temporal planes. Few societies could lay claim to such variations of social status and intensities of ideological commitment. The forms of medieval Hungarian society had survived the period of Turkish occupation by a state of suspended animation only to appear as a hopeless historical curiosity in the rapidly changing world of mercantilism and absolutism. The Catholic clergy and the magnates had an unquestioned position of primacy in the society, and they were followed in turn by the gentry and the citizens of the Royal cities and towns. The peasantry was the broad foundation upon which this pyramid rested, but it did not figure very prominently in the social thinking of the classes above it. This reluctance to display an interest in the underdog was not the consequence of a bad social conscience but simply the result of a myopia common to baroque society as far as peasants were concerned. They bore the oft-repeated title of the *misera plebs contribuens*, and this designation was obviously deemed sufficient description of the peasants' role in society.

The increased pressures brought to bear on this society by the Austrian government had not encountered a solid front of resistance, because of the high degree of stratification and the intense egoism of class on each and every level. Every segment of this society had its limited view of what was necessary for the maintenance of the status quo, and these views understandably enough failed to coincide with one another. The Catholic clergy, for example, had a bad reputation for avarice, and even its most distinguished representatives had evinced an embarrassing interest in preferment and in ecclesiastical properties.[28] In an ideological way, it gave violent support to the extension of Catholic influence and the extirpation of Protestantism, a position which clearly failed to consider the good of the society as a whole. The clergy's spiritual ties with Vienna were exceedingly strong, and only an awareness of its traditional role in the Hungarian constitutional system encouraged it at times to adopt a middle of the road position, a compromise between its fidelity to the Hungarian constitution and its support of the Habsburg connection.

The magnates' position revealed strikingly similar ambiguities. Nominally, they formed the most influential group in Hungarian politics, since they presided over the *comitats* as hereditary lord lieutenants and had a virtual monopoly on the chief offices of the Kingdom: the Palatine, the *Iudex Curiae*, the Protonotary, and the Procurator. But recent developments had brought about a high degree of alienation of the magnates from the rest of Hungarian society. The patriarchal way of life which was so characteristic of this overwhelmingly agrarian society no longer attracted this group. In virtue of its superior economic position it had been enabled to establish itself in Vienna, and even in these days of Leopoldinian, rather that Theresian, Austria, the capital and its suburbs were dotted with palaces and residences of the magnates. The great charm of life in Vienna was its hint of the modernity of the European world, and this compared more than favorably with the static way of life on their estates in Upper Hungary or the Transdanubian region. Education in Jesuit colleges had enabled the magnates to adopt the distinguishing marks of the Austrian and Bohemian aristocracy, and associations made in these schools inevitably led to family and political connections. The Court of Emperor Leopold had acted as a powerful magnet; its wealth of music, ballet, and stately ceremonial (the Hungarians had a predisposition to take particular pleasure in the complexities of the Spanish court ceremonial) made it difficult for the magnates to refuse the unspoken invitation to settle down in Vienna. Once established there, they deemed it unnecessary to undertake many long and fatiguing trips to their distant estates. Vienna had a decided geographical disadvantage, and attendance at Court inevitably meant that the greater part of the life of a magnate was lived far from home.

The return to Catholicism had been almost universal in this class (the Rákóczis were a case in point), and once this step had been taken, the magnates found it possible to ally themselves by marriage with the great families of the Hereditary Lands. That complex pattern of family connections, which served as one of the major transmission lines of power and status in Hungarian society, extended now to include Hungarians, and a melting pot process of aristocratically limited dimensions came into operation. The acquisition of this new social status had unfortunate consequences, for the Hungarians were prone to develop a bad case of an inferiority complex. The Austrians had accepted them with an air of patronizing interest, and it was evident that Austrian society as a whole, much less to act as Vienna's proconsuls in Hungary. Poor Esterházy was a truly pathetic figure in his well-meaning efforts to please the Court and his countrymen. Much of what he did proved to be financially rewarding, but it failed to win the trust of the *Au̧liker* or the confidence of the Hungarians. In the event that the Austrians hurt these magnates deeply enough in their self-esteem, the wounded party might seek revenge *vi et armis*, but this was an uncertain foundation for devoted and selfless support of the Rákóczi movement.[29]

The gentry (the *nobiles*) in contrast to the clergy and magnates wore a straightforward air. Its position was far more consistent, so its reactions could be more easily predicted. The Western observer was doubtless struck by the similarities between the gentry class in Hungary and the English squirearchy. The Hungarian gentry was far more numerous, since nearly ten per cent of the population regarded themselves as *nobiles*, and it covered a wider range of social variations from a class of prosperous independent landowners through the Hungarian equivalent of a 'stout yeoman' to a layer of impoverished nobles (the *bocskorosnemesek*) who were hardly distinguishable from the peasants. But the class loyalty at whatever point in this scale was incredibly strong, and this cohesiveness made it possible for the gentry to dominate the local political and social scene perhaps even more effectively than its English counterpart.

Time had brought few outstanding changes to the life of the Hungarian countryside, and the mentality of the gentry was an almost miraculous survival of the Hungary that had gone down to defeat at Mohács. István Verböczy's *Tripartitum*, the great codification of Hungarian customary law which he had produced on the very eve of Mohács, was its great vade mecum, for it had established as the eternal law of the land the favored position of the gentry in Jagellonian Hungary. Since there were perilously few careers open to talented members of this class within the Habsburg system (the army and the Church offered little chance of rapid promotion), the squires tended to study law and to devote much of their intellectual energies to the immensely complicated legal problems that flourished at the comitat level. Minor elective positions in the local administration and judiciary reverted to their care. The legalistic gentry mind, moved easily by a sense of injustice, became the chief source of the Rebellion's inspiration. Diets, Congresses, and Confederations -- these were the especial delight of this class, though the nation as a whole probably suffered from this overdose of legal education. The gentry was politically alert and strongly anti-Habsburg, but these radical tendencies were curbed by its legal and political conservatism.[30]

Hungarian Protestantism flourished in the gentry class. In the eastern part of the country, the squires belonged to the Calvinist Church, while in Upper Hungary Lutheranism predominated. The devotion to religious freedom was another factor that militated in favor of the gentry's support of the principles of Rákóczi's manifesto.

The relative weakness of the urban centers and of the bourgeois class constituted one of the major obstacles to a full-fledged revolutionary movement in Rákóczi's Hungary. In this situation Hungary did not differ from the rest of Eastern Europe. The pragmatic temper of a merchant class was missing from the Rebellion, and in its absence the movement's ability to maintain its grasp on the political and economic realities of the struggle left much to be desired. In many cases, the inhabitants of the cities were Germans and inclined to retain their loyalty to the Emperor, but the Vienna government could generally count on its support -- however lukewarm it proved on occasion -- of the Hungarian burghers as well. The pitifully small urban class hesitated to place itself in jeopardy by an alliance with the feudal countryside. Moreover, the military expeditions of the rebel armies often bore an unpleasant likeness to the depredations of armed robbers, and not infrequently degenerated into a war between town and countryside. Sound business practice encouraged the citizens of Pozsony, Sopron, and even Debrecen to maintain a markedly guarded attitude to the Rebellion and its goals.[31]

The timeless tragedy of the peasants' lot (it had been getting progressively worse since the end of the fifteenth century) has been noted more than once, and the negotiations carried on between the Deputation and the Hungarian leaders, which we discussed in the preceding chapter, give sufficient evidence of the inhumane conditions

in which the peasants lived. This was a state little better than that of
beasts of burden -- reminiscent of the conditions prevailing in Germany
at the close of the Thirty Years' War. The demands of the landowners
for goods and services had increased at the very time that Imperial tax
collectors and unpaid troops made life ever more troubled and uncertain.
Every rebellion against the Habsburgs had furnished the peasants an
opportunity to take matters into their own hands. The *kuruc* with his
swashbuckling way of life exerted a constant siren lure for a peasantry
that lived without even the appearance of hope. The Rákóczi Rebellion
owed its inception to a desperate attempt by the peasants near Munkács
to escape from the crushing burdens imposed by the Hungarian
landowners, as well as the Imperial taxgatherers.

These peasants were simple Ruthenians for the most part, but
they were shrews enough to realize that they required leadership. In
their search for this quality, they turned almost automatically to the very
class which was responsible for so much of their misery. They sought
out, as we have seen, the greatest landowner of all and entrusted their
cause to his safekeeping. The Prince could bring the full force of his
Christian charity to bear on the peasants' problems, but he had
absolutely no interest in bringing about radical changes on their behalf.
Amelioration perhaps, and concessions as far as services and taxes were
concerned for peasants who served in his army, but his inborn blind spot
where they were concerned led to one of the more tragic flaws of the
Rebellion. The one class which might have brought him substantial
military victory was slowly but surely reduced to a role of passive
participation. The grand seigneur in Rákóczi felt uneasy in the presence
of great masses of peasant followers, and as soon as it was practically
possible to do so, he encouraged the magnates and the gentry to assume
direction of the fighting forces.[33] The sense of inferiority vis-à-vis the
standard European military procedures was increased by the obvious
contempt of his French military advisers for the undisciplined forces
under his command. But with every increase in military efficiency
something of the flaming spirit of rebellion was lost; his army
reproduced the inequalities present in Hungarian society, and the

peasants began to lose their interest in the Rebellion.[34]

The historian's defective hindsight may well lead to the commonplace conclusion that the decline and fall of the Rákóczi Rebellion was implicit in the character of the society that produced it. Divided and fragmented as it was by countless barriers, Hungarian society was not surprised to discover that its centrifugal forces were more powerful than the unifying appeal of freedom. For freedom itself was refracted by class egoism; it could be comprehended only in terms of the pattern of thought proper to each class. Baroque Austria was not wrestling with one cohesive society; it was actually engaged in a dialogue (not simply with the sword) with three time dimensions: the almost pathetic modernity of the milieu of the magnates and the clergy, burdened with all the ambiguities that the baroque is heir to, the largely medieval frame in which the gentry moved, quite unaffected by the long Turkish occupation, and finally the world without time in which the peasantry, reduced by sheer misery to a life not unlike that of the beasts, sought refuge from history.

An untried young man with the best of family antecedents and an endless capacity for feeling alienated from his surroundings had established himself as the focus of the cause of Hungarian freedom. The Rebellion he led ultimately proved to be a blessing in disguise for him, since it required him to think long and hard about himself and the Hungary he had understood so poorly at the beginning of the Rebellion. His way from Muncáks led ultimately to Grosbois and to the knowledge of self he found there, and beyond that to a degree of spiritual eminence that most sovereign princes could envy.

But the Hungarian 'worlds' he left for the life of an exile did not have his transfiguring good fortune. The political compromise that the leaders made with Vienna rested on the assumption that the social spectrum would survive unchallenged -- in arrogance or in misery depending on your point of view. But this society could at least be absolved of one sin; it had not been the primary cause of the Rebellion's defeat. If any force or set of circumstances could be said to have done just that, it was the European power relations at the beginning of the eighteenth century. And it is to this that we will turn our discussion of "Ferenc Rákóczi and the Great Powers".

Notes to Chapter 2

[1]My excursus on the Hungarian 'national character' was developed on the basis of a sampling of travelers' accounts and a good deal of attention to the diplomats' offhand remarks on the Hungarians and their rather special way of life. The materials which I used for my study of "Rákóczi and the *Weiner Zeitung*", an epilogue to Part Three, also helped me to establish the common European notion of the Hungarian at the turn of the eighteenth century. No claim is made, of course, indeed it could not be made, to accuracy in the setting up of this necessary composite picture.

For the early life of Ferenc Rákóczi, I have concentrated heavily on his *Principis Francisci II. Rákóczi et Aspirationes Principis Christiani* (Commissio fontium historiae patriae Academiae Scientiarum Hungariae) (Budapest, 1876) (hereafter *Confessiones*). For interesting comments on the state of Hungarian society in his time, the *Memoires du Prince Francois Rakoczy sur la guerre de Hongrie, depuis l'année 1703 jusqu'a sa fin* -- tome II of the *Histoire des Revolutions de Hongrie* (La Haye, 1739) (Hereafter *Memoires*) -- was especially helpful. The most impressive and certainly most detailed biography of the Prince is Sándor Márki's *II. Rákóczi Ferencz* (Budapest, 1907-1912), in three volumes. Márki prepared this study under the influence of late nineteenth century Hungarian nationalism, and the tone is hagiographical in the extreme. But its careful study of the relevant sources and wealth of illustration make up for its tendentious character. The reproductions of contemporary engravings and the facsimiles of important documents make it particularly valuable in creating the tone and appearance of the society of the time. Márki and all other students of Rákóczi's period are vastly indebted to the lifework of Kálmán Thaly in publishing an innumerable series of sources, many of them devoted specifically to the life and times of Rákóczi. Thaly was, if it be possible, an evebn greater votary of the Rákóczi Myth than Márki, and his publications must be used with great care. Only a complete survey of the existing sources in Hungary would enable us to determine how extensive deletions and outright suppression of evidence were in his work. But his *Archivum Rákóczianum* (Budapest, 1873-1889), 10 vols. is still the major source for the military and somestic career of the Rebellion.

For the modern sociological approach, I have relied on the impressive chapters of Gyula Szekfu, in the fifth and sixth volumes of the *Magyar történét*, which treat the baroque period in Hungary. But even more helpful was the detailed study of Elemér Mályusz, "A Rákózi-kor társadalom", *Rákóczi emlékkonyv kétszázéves fordulójára* (Budapest, 1933?), II, 25-68. This article, which was published in a Rákóczi *Festschrift* is almost impossible to find, and I considered myself extremely lucky to discover it in the British Museum. One difficulty in the work of both Szekfu and Mályusz is that they follow the *Geistesgeschichte* school in laying far too much stress on their categories. The use of the 'baroque' as a concept which explains amost everything runs into certain difficulties when applied to the society of Rákóczi's day. But their studies devote much-needed attention to the class structure in Hungary, and both men are happily bereft of any illusions about the 'good old days' of Hungarian feudalism.

[2]I have not thought it necessary to footnote the following section in detail, though where the sources contain particularly happy indications of this state of mind, I have made reference to them. On Hungarian volatility, Count Wratislaw to the Duke of Marlborough, Vienna, July 19, 1705, quoted in Coxe's translation in William Coxe, *Memoirs of the Duke of Marlborough with his Original Correspondence* (revised edition) (London, 1847), I, 340.

[3]George Stepney to Robert Harley, Vienna, February 24, 1706, contained in Ernö Simonyi, *Angol diplomatiai iratok* (*Archivum Rákóczianum*, II osztály) (Budapest, 1873), II, 398-399. (Hereafter *Simonyi*).

[4]*The Weiner Zeitung*, Nr. 2, August 8-11, 1703, reported that many Hungarians were joining the rebel cause "weilen der Ragotzi inhen alle Freyheit verspricht."

[5]The notion that the Hungarians had been especially prolific in the way of insurrections was one on which Rákóczi in particular frequently enlarged; cf. his remark to Stepney: "...That the cause wherein they are now engaged is the 7th Revolution to which their unhappy country has been exposed in a few years, reckoning from Bathory, Botzkai, Bethlem Gabor, two Rákóczis and Teckely down to the present conjuncture:", Stepney to Sir Charles Hedges, Schemnitz, November 3, 1704, *Simonyi*, I, 533.

[6]A brief but illuminating discussion of the Germanophobia is to be found in Oswald Redlich, *Das Werden einer Grossmacht*: Osterreich, 1700-1740 (Wien-1942), 154-155.

[7]"We recieved with all splendour and courtesy; except that the Prince affected to take the precedency of us in his own house, which point it was impossible to contest with him there, nor would it have been seasonable to discover any uneasiness on that account, since I take for granted we are employed here to compose differences, and not to dispute about Ceremonials.", Stepney to Sir Charles Hedges, Schemnitz, November 3, 1704, *Simonyi*, I, 531; Bruynincx described a meal attended by thirty-four guests which consisted of seventy-two

dishes and "behalven het decert, ende daernae coffee, thee, rossolis en andere liqueurs; maer als hondert Edellyden en nog so vell andere van syne domestiques en bedienen standen ront om de toffel, ende wierden geduyrende de maeltyd oerse heyde musiquen van Trompetten, kettel tromen, houtbois en vercheyde swaeren Spel, gehoort, het welcke alle de twee volgende daegen op de deselve wyse gecontinuieert heeft ....", Bruynincx to the States-General, Schinta, March 22, 1704, *Secrete Brieven, Staten-Generaal* (Rijksarchief, the Hague), fascicle 6160.

[8]Rákóczi, *Memoires*, 71-72.

[9]One of the many examples of Stepney's rough calculation of the number of Protestants in Hungary is to be found in his letter to Harley, Trinau, July 20, 1706, *Simonyi*, III, 159.

[10]"Car la Nation aviot cela de commun avec toutes celles qui ignorent la Science militaire qu'elle étiot prete d'entreprendre tout avec impetuosité; mais elle s'en désitoit aiesement, dès que les idées ne répondoient pas aux espérances, et que les espérances n'etoient pas rem;lies par le succès.", *Memoires,* 55.

[11]"Il (the Memoires) contiendra un récit succinct, et non une exagération, de ce wque j'ai fait. Je cous ai, dans les lives de mes Confessions, exposé devant vous, mes actions extérieures. Ils sauront par les prémières, quel furent les motifs qui me firent agir: ils connoitront par les secondes, ce que j'ai fait. Je ne souhaite rien, sinon que par la connnoissance des prèmières, ils reconnoissent que je suis un pécheur, et que vous etes un Dieu plus rempli de miséricorde que de justice; enfin que vous etes un père tendre, et que j'ai été un enfant profigue.", *ibid.,* 3.

[12]*Confessiones,* 5.

[13]"Absit Domine a me historiam scribere familiae meae at confitens tibi in humilitate recitare seriem Principum Transylvaniae avorum meorum...." is followed by some account of the family background, *ibid.,* 5-6.

[14]"Ducebar te protegente inter medios Turcarum et Tartarorum exercitus, qui propter belligerationem avi mei contra ipsos Domui meae infensi fuerant. Saepa ad deviandum a Religione mea tentabar insidiose....", *ibid.,* 9.

[15]The Countess had declared "nec posse se illorum arcem tradere, quam nemo

justa ab lis petere potest."; this is followed by an exceedingly mournful account of the separation of the family., *ibid.*, 13-20.

[16]Quoted in German translation by F.R. Krones, "Die Literatur sur Geschichte Franz Rákóczi II im letzten Jahrzehnt (1872-1882)", *Historisches Jahrbuch*, IV (1883), 120-121.

[17]"Sufficit enim mihi te nosse, num re vera saepe dictus Imperator in re indifferens fuerit, Cardinalem vero intendisse, ut rebus ut dixit, dispositis, sorore nempe Moniali, me vero Jesuita facto, Domus nostra exstingueretur et successionis in Patres Jesuitas redundaret beneficium.", *Confessiones*, 26.

[18]He was to find even more fualt with a Capuchin confessor in his bachelor days in Vienna: "Confessarius mihi a sorore recommendatus fuit Pater quidam Capucinus suavis et indulgens; recitationem criminum meorum subsequebatur absolutioo nulla intermissa aut correctione aut exhortatione, quamvis omnia propemodum peccata devenere mihi habitualia.", ibid., 32.

[19]But cf. his own comment: "Ducebar vel maxime politicis retionibus, quibus juvenilis ardor, elegantiae formae sponsae incitatus sat praeceps consenserat;", *ibid.*, 43. The marriage took place in September, 1694, when the Prince was eighteen.

[20]"Sed me innocentiae meae condiere non credebam consultum; aula enim Viennensis Hispanicis regebatur maximis, et propterea omnium suspicionum fuit susceptibilissima; Cardinalis Kolonics, cujus in rebus Ungaricis plurimum praepollebat consilium, impalcabilis fuerat mihi; et Comes Kinski, qui primi Ministri tunc fungebatur officio, ex solo politices nefandae principio Imperatorem Domum meam suae semper inimicam in Hungaria exstirpare debere illo quoque fuerat infensior.", *ibid.*, 60. The following two pages describe the winning over of the Emperor by "Pater Manegatti".

[21]Rákóczi knew Villars, the French Ambassador, personally, but he did not feel that it would be safe to contact the King of France through him: "...sed nimia ejus cum Principe Sebaudiae Eugenio et aliis proceribus familiaritas et discursuum levitas ac in pluribus imprudentia avertebat ab eo confidentiam;", *ibid.*, 72. The Longueval incident is fully described in a later section of the *Confessiones* ("sed homo, qui edebat panem meum, supplantavit me."); it and the story of his escape and flight to Poland constitute the most extensive part of the book, cf. *ibid.*, 102-135 passim.

[22]At a meeting of the *Conferenz* "wegen des entwichenen Ragozi" on November 9, 1701, Count Mansfeld delivered himself of the following opinion: "er glaube das er (Rákóczi) hohe protection gehabt habe, habe es JRM (the Emperor) zu Laxenburg gesagt er werde den process verlühren, J. M. die Kayserin, die fürstin von Lokowiz, beede Landtgrafen von Hessen Darmstatt, Pater Miller, undt P. Wolf, hätten sich umb ihme angenomben, undt scheinet das JRM selbsten dise fluct convirt, undt eingewilliget have, mann solle ihme citiren....", *Konferenzprotokolle (Gräflich Harrachsches Archiv*, Vienna), Fasz. 187.

[23]*Confessiones*, 113 ff.

[24]The section dealing with the Prince and Bercsényi's stay in Poland and the prehistory of the Rebellion is based on Márki's two chapters, "Lengyelországban" and "A nép behivja Rákóczit" in his *II. Rákóczi Ferenc*, I, 208-219 and 231-238.

[25]The text of the manifesto is printed in the *Histoire des Révolutions de Hongrie*, 55-108. For a brief discussion over the confusion on the actual date of its issue, cf. Márki, *op. cit.*, 242n.

[26]A detailed study of the convocation of 1698 appears in the preceding chapter.

[27]"Die Unterthanen empfänden solcher Gestalt repectu des vorigen türkischen Jochs keinerlei Ergötzlichkeit....", H. Bidermann, *Geschichte der österreichischen Gesamt-staats-idee*, I, 122, quoting from the *Einrichtungswerk des Konigreichts Ungarn*.

[28]*Confessiones*, 158-162, paricularly "Magnates et potiores erant Catholici, Clerus Hungarus dominandi et cupidus et asuetus; minor nobilitas cum potior militantium manu praenominatos sequebatur errores et auctis a diffidentia in me clamoribus, qui precum loco haberi debebantur, funestae et violentae repraesentabantur sequelae denegationis justitiae.", 159.

[29]Mályusz, *loc. cit.*, 36ff.; Rákóczi draws a rather unsympathetic picture of the magnates: "Ceci étoit cuase qu'ils favorisoient de coeur les Autrichiens, et leurs fortunes; ou bien, faisant peu de cas de la famille, et de la personne du Comte Bersény, ils aboient de la peine á embrasser mon parti, crainte de se mettre dans un rang inférieur au sien; car il est certain qu'aucun d'entre eux n'avoit de mauvais sentiment sur la cause, dont j'avais embrassé la défense.", *Memoires*, 40.

[30]Mályusz, *loc. cit.*, 39-41.

[31]"An old and permanent evil was the absence of a middle class ....", *ibid.*, 33.

[32]Cf. the enlightening discussion of Mályusz on the peasantry, *ibid.*, 27-31; the peasants in the Rákóczi movement devoted much of their attention in the very early days of the Rebellion to raids on the estates, and "...la Noblesse des Comtés ne sachant quel part prendre, craignant également le peuple et les Allemands, se retiroit bien dans les Chateux des Seigneurs; mais peu s'enfermoit dans les lieux gardés par les Allemands.", *Memoires*, 22.

[33]"Enfin étant tous ignorans, et desunis, ils n'etoient pas meme capables de remplir les fonctions de Caporal. Cependant, comme ils étoient estimés par le peuple, on ne pouvoit ni leur oter leur emploi, ni en trouver alors de meilleurs pour mettre á leur place.", *ibid.*, 14; "Comme je ne pouvois pas faire tout á la fois la réforme des Colonels paysans, je commencai dés cette secondé Campagne de faire des Brigadiers, pour donner á la Noblesse un rang supérieur á ses propres Sujets et Vassaux.", *ibid.*, 55.

[34]Cf. Fákóczi's excellent formulation of the law which had appeared to operate in the military aspects of the Rebellion: "Il me semble avoir rapporté que notre guerre, commencée avec beaucoup d'ardeur, sembloit languir depuis la Négóciation (i.e. at Nagyszobat) rompue. La remède meme que nous employames pour la soutenir produisit cet effet. La ferveur dans son commencement causoit les desordres qu'j'ai rapporté; et l'ordre nécessaire, et unique remède du desordre, commencoit á éteindre la ferveur, et introduisoit nécessairement la tiédeur.", *ibid.*, 117.

Part Three

Ferenc II Rákóczi and the Great Powers

"... je confesserai en toute humilité, que j'ai souvent agi inconsidérément, & plus souvent avec imprudence. Combien de productions d'seprit, & de prévoyance humaine, la Posterité ne trouvera-t-elle pas dans mes Négotions au dehours, qu'elle regardera la plupart comme trop vagues & trop étendues, si elle n'examine pas avec attention les circonstances des tems, & le génie des Princes & des Cours avec qui il a fallu traiter."

- Ferenc II Rákóczi

Introduction

In that perplexing period for European statesmen that followed the death of Carlos II of Spain, the power alignments in the approaching conflict were by no means obvious or certain. Into this general atmosphere of confusion -- it was particularly noticeable in England -- stopped Mr. George Stepney, poet, diplomat, and Whig publicist. He had published a most forceful *Essay upon the present interest of England* (London, 1701), and in this pamphlet he argued the case for the restoration of the Grand Alliance. In his view, France once again threatened to upset the "balance of power", and sheer self-interest, rather than any sense of loyalty to her old allies, demanded that England join once more with the Emperor and the Dutch -- this time to dispute the passing of the entire Spanish inheritance into the possession of France. The very freedoms which enlightened England enjoyed and which it felt to be established on a permanent basis since the 'Glorious Revolution' were fatefully involved in this struggle. The establishment of French preponderance on the Continent would inevitably entail the isolation and weakening of France's traditional enemies. And once she had reduced the Dutch and the Empire to the position of secondary powers, it would be England's turn next.

Stepney knew how to make an effective case for English intervention. His prose had always possessed a good deal of verve, and he was at his dialectical best in maintaining in the Essay that the balance of power must be preserved in Europe. Once he had demonstrated that European (and this certainly included England) freedom of movement rested ultimately on a dynamic balance between the two camps, he proceeded to the 'discernment of spirits', a ticking off of the remaining Powers of Europe in terms of the positions they would probably take in the forthcoming struggle between France and the Grand Alliance. A number of the European states would presumably remain neutral:

Switzerland and Venice, for example. Portugal would soon see the wisdom of joining the Allies, since it had much more to lose from Philip's domination of Spain than from that of the Archduke Charles. Savoy would suffer a case of mixed feelings but would eventually take its place in the coalition. The one great mystery was the role that the 'Young Swedish Hero', Charles XII, would play. There was always good reason to suspect a French orientation on the part of the makers of Swedish foreign policy, but the moody and unpredictable Charles might break with that tradition. Stepney and his readers were absolutely certain of one thing: Sweden and Denmark would always be in opposing camps. For whatever Charles XII did, the King of Denmark was sure to do the very opposite. The distant powers of Eastern Europe did not bulk large in Stepney's prognostications, for he conceived the coming war within a Western European frame, and as such only the Powers he had mentioned had to be taken into account.

The picture he painted of Allied prospects was definitely an attractive one: the combination of the naval strength of the Maritime Powers and of the armies of the Emperor and the German Princes would turn the tide in favor of the Archduke Charles and effectively contain France within her present limits. The European system, as Stepney described it, was straightforward enough. Indeed, it bore a suspicious likeness to the mechanical methods of political activity which had come to be the principal stock in trade of European political theorists. Its basic element was the assumption that European freedom required an equal balance between the two constellations of powers. France and the Grand Alliance acted as the foci of these groups, and the others tended to pair off in a rather mechanical way, for if one party to an ancient controversy favored France, the partner would be moved to join the Alliance. The weaknesses of Stepney's analysis were not immediately apparent, but he failed to take the Great Northern War into sufficient account and had completely overlooked the possibility that France would have the good fortune to find diversionary assistance in the very heart of the Emperor's dominions.

Within three years of the publication of his pamphlet, most of what he had predicted had actually occurred. The Grand Alliance had been reconstituted and was already deeply engaged on a wide range of fronts: Italy, Spain, southern Germany, and the Spanish Netherlands. Portugal had come into the war on the side of the Allies, and the ever ambiguous Savoy had finally opted for war with France as well. Neutralism flourished in the expected places, and the 'Young Swedish Hero' while devoting his energies to defeating the combination of the Tsar and Augustus of Saxony and Poland, remained as enigmatic as ever, as far as his intentions in the West were concerned. But in Hungary, unexpected support for France had materialized in the Hungarian insurrection, and in the early months of 1704 the Rebels and the Elector of Bavaria were moving in the direction of Vienna, where a junction of their forces was expected to take place. This was one of the most important variables in the system, and Stepney had failed to take into his calculations; historical accidents were playing hob as usual with the experts.

Before attempting to elucidate the impact of this 'accident' on the European power politics of the period, it will be necessary to provide a brief summary of the history of the Rákóczi Rebellion. Its life story may be roughly divided into four periods: a glorious adolescence, a difficult youth, a despairing middle age, and a tedious and humiliating demise.

Its first months were precarious indeed, but in the course of the summer of 1703, it gained control of most of eastern Hungary. Rebel raids probed deeper and deeper into Upper Hungary and the *Alföld*, and by autumn reached close enough to Vienna to make the capital uncomfortable. The Elector of Bavaria's threat to Vienna was growing in magnitude, and Rákóczi's plan seemed to be working. At the beginning of 1704, the situation was so desperate that Prince Eugene had to turn his attention from the threat in the West to the Hungarian theater of war. He hurried to Pozsony to reorganize Austrian defenses in West Hungary and to lend the aura of strength by his very presence in Hungary. The Emperor Leopold had appointed the aged and irascible Field Marshal Count Siegbert Heister to the command of the Imperial troops in Hungary. This move encountered heavy opposition from Eugene, for Heister was renowned for his ability to wear down his own troops by endless indecisive maneuvers. But his victory at Gyarmat on June 13, 1704, was a hopeful beginning, particularly since it closely coincided with the Allied victory over the Franco-Bavarian army at Höchstädt on August 13. Rákóczi's depression in the wake of these blows partially disappeared with the news that the Estates of Transylvania had elected him Prince. Here was a golden opportunity to restore the line of 'free princes' in Transylvania, and the affairs of that Principality began to monopolize much of his attention. This first period of little more than a year had witnessed an incredible initial spurt of energy, but Höchstädt meant that the Rebellion would have to proceed on a new and less attractive course. A shift from military to diplomatic considerations took place, as the leaders began to realize that the fate of the movement rested with one or more of the Great Powers.

The first attempt at a diplomatic solution involved negotiations with the Emperor through the intermediary services of the Anglo-Dutch Mediation. In talks held at Selmec, the Mediators had their first test of strength. Since both sides failed to give any indication of real interest in a settlement, Rákóczi continued his hopeful overtures to France, Sweden, and Turkey. He had become involved much against his will in the struggle over the Polish crown, and this meant that he would inevitably find himself caught in the crossfire between the Swedes and the Russians. The death of Leopold in the spring of 1705, opened the way to a new set of talks with Vienna. The young Emperor Joseph I was known for his moderate views on Hungary and his personal friendship with Rákóczi, but since the Hungarians did not wish to yield the point of hereditary succession to the Hungarian throne, Joseph's attitude stiffened appreciably. For while talk of peace continued, the advisers of the Emperor secured the replacement of Heister by Count Heberville, who was sent to the relief of Count Rabutin, the hard-pressed Imperial Governor of Transylvania. Numerous attempts were made to halt the passage of this force, but Heberville eventually reached Transylvania after inflicting a stunning defeat on Rákóczi at Zsibó on

November 11, 1705. His relief of Rabutin saved the Principality in great part for the Emperor, but the great stretch of Hungary between the Leitha and Transylvania continued in Hungarian control. That September, the Prince had met with the representatives of the disaffected *comitats* at the Congress of Széczény. The meeting had declared itself in favor of instituting a Confederation on the Polish model. The Prince was elected *dux*, and a Senate was established to advise him on the conduct of the Rebellion's affairs. Leadership remained throughout the revolution in the hands of the *dux* and his close advisers, Bercsényi, Károlyi, and Antal Esterházy. The last two men were representative of that group of magnates who had thrown in their lot with the Rebellion because of injured *amour propre* rather than any deep ideological commitment. They had been anxious at the outset to demonstrate their loyalty to the Emperor -- Károlyi had inflicted one of the first serious defeats on the Rebel forces -- but official Austrian indifference had driven them finally into the arms of the Rebellion. But the movement had finally clothed itself in constitutional finery at a time when the prospects of lasting success were not particularly bright. The battle of Ramillies, which forced the French to evacuate most of the Southern Netherlands, was a sign that the Rákóczi Rebellion had entered upon the depressing period of middle age.

While the victory of Marlborough at Ramillies encouraged Louis XIV to intensify his peace feelers, it only made the Austrians more intractable in their dealings with the Rebel leaders. The failure of new negotiations at Nagyszombat in July, 1706 -- a companion piece to the previous failure at Selmec -- reduced Rákóczi to the alternatives of French or Russian succor. His embarrassment only increased when Peter evinced a tremendous interest in making Rákóczi the King of Poland, now that Augustus of Saxony had been forced to renounce the Polish throne. The Prince's motives in agreeing to the Tsar's suggestion will always be somewhat mysterious, but certainly fear of offending such a powerful and unpredictable friend played a part. The Hungarians and the Russians concluded the Treaty of Warsaw on September 4, 1707, but the agreement was fated to remain a mere 'piece of paper'.

For Charles XII suddenly abandoned his stance of outraged concern about the Protestants in the Emperor's dominions, and resumed his campaign to establish Stanislas Leszczynsky securely on the throne. In the very period that Rákóczi was negotiating with Peter, the Hungarian Confederation met at Ónod. After unusually stormy deliberations (two partisans of moderation were brutally struck down in the Prince's presence by some of his closest associates), the Confederation formally declared its 'abrenunciation' of Joseph I on June 14, 1708. Now that they had renounced the Habsburg, the likeliest candidate was not Rákóczi, but the Wittelsbach Elector of Bavaria, who was currently unemployed. But it was the last dramatic drive for a French alliance that made Ónod what it was, and Rákóczi soon discovered that even the Rebel repudiation of Joseph I would not move Louis to give full aid. A disastrous defeat of Rákóczi's main force at Trentschin late in the summer of 1708, made it quite clear that the 'beginning of the end' was already well advanced.

Yet the death struggle of the Rebellion was to be ever so slow and deliberate. The Prince turned once more from the bitter realities of the home front to the illusions and dreams of his foreign policy, and his diplomatic activity, though never so energetic, lost contact with the politically possible. Only the Tsar held out hope in the years that separated his victory at Pultava and his humiliating defeat on the Pruth. But long before 1711, Count János Pálffy, now the commander of the Imperial forces in Hungary, undertook the mission of weaning the magnates away from Rákóczi, and by a dexterous mixture of amnesty and grants of land he eventually brought Károlyi and Eszterházy back to the Imperial hold. The desertion of leaders of this magnitude insured that the Rebellion's small fry would begin to think seriously about its own future. Joseph's death in 1711 interrupted negotiations for a time, but Charles IV through the agency of the Regent, the Empress Dowager Eleonora, carried on the work of compromise to its conclusion at the Treaty of Szatmár on May 26, 1711. The offer of amnesty to the leaders of the Rebellion did not encourage the Prince, Count Bercsényi, and a large collection of retainers, to return from Poland. In the treaty, the

Emperor gave his solemn oath to the Hungarian nation that the right of hereditary succession would not be used as a weapon to dislodge the traditional liberties of the Kingdom. The compromise had been struck at last, and both parties had yielded something of their claims to undisputed mastery of Hungary's future. And the Hungarians, after their extended moment of glory and prominence on the European scene, with hardly-concealed pleasure entered upon a long and uneventful eighteenth century.

Modern students of this period have considerable less excuse than Stepney had for their tendency to overlook the role of the Rákóczi Rebellion in the interplay of power politics at the time. The Hungarian Rebellion, though initiated as a protest against German misrule by the peasant masses, owed much of its existence as a full-fledged fight for Hungarian freedoms to the War of Spanish Succession. The terrific demands on Vienna imposed by the requirements of the early Italian campaigns had caused a military vacuum in Hungary, thus giving the Rebels a great initial advantage, which permitted them to assume control of the country with the exception of a few fortresses still in Imperial hands. The threat to Vienna and to the Hereditary Provinces forced the Austrians to recall regiments from the Italian and German theaters. The annual cost of the Rebellion hovered in the neighborhood of seven million gulden -- a third of the whole Imperial budget. Louis XIV owed an immeasurable amount to this second front so perilously close to Vienna; he expressed his gratitude by sending what financial and technical support he could, though he never went to the extreme of concluding an actual treaty of alliance with Rákóczi.

The customary reading of this situation reduces the Rebellion to the position of an episode in the history of the War of the Spanish Succession. Accordingly, Rákóczi's movement was a simple continuation of the diversionary work of the Princes of Transylvania and Turkey, who had frequently forced the Emperor to fight on two fronts while he was engaged in a major conflict with France. But such an assessment of the Rebellion does not do it full justice. Its range of contacts with the Great Powers was far wider and more complicated than the partisans of the 'episode' theory would allow.

But since there have been so few attempts to elucidate the more general significance of the Rebellion, this limiting view can be easily forgiven. The Rebellion has suffered a further quirk of historiographical fate in that its diplomatic aftermath has been studied in detail, although the diplomatic history of the Rebellion has failed to attract much interest. Szekfü, who is responsible for this state of affairs, cannot be entirely absolved of the charge that he put the cart before the horse in approaching the problem.

The reasons for this reluctance to undertake a comprehensive treatment of the complex story of Rákóczi and the Great Powers are many. There may well be some surviving disquiet about the fate of the Rákóczi Myth in such a perspective, for a great hero who was quite prepared to deal simultaneously with both sides and was not infrequently caught between angels and demons does not fit any preconceived notions. There are valid practical reasons for this silence. For one thing, these relations constitute one of the most complicated webs of negotiation and intrigue in all of diplomatic history; the territory they cover is immense and the period of time involved is a fairly lengthy one. Further difficulty arises from the question of sources, since the publication of materials relating to the diplomatic activity of the Rebellion has not kept pace with that devoted to its domestic policies and military campaigns. Vast amounts of unpublished sources lie still untouched in half a dozen European archives, and there is little chance that they will see the light of day in the near future. The novice in such matters with an inclination to block out the full range of this particular Hungarian Rebellion's impact discovers to his amazement that the sources do not yet permit him to describe the whole process in detail.

But this almost forgotten chapter in the history of international relations literally cries out for attention. For it is meaningless to study the Rebellion in the isolation of Hungary's internal development, since it was the stepchild from start to finish of the European system. French and Bavarian victories in 1703 encouraged Rákóczi to take the plunge, while the victories of Marlborough and Eugene of Savoy in the next campaigns made his eventual defeat inevitable. No more convincing proof can be found perhaps for the validity of the Rankean principle of the primacy of foreign affairs in the determination of the internal political configuration of the European states. More recent revolutionary movements in Hungary stand as further proof of the same principle.

But does it demean the importance of the Rákóczi Rebellion when one says that whatever successes it achieved on the home front it could not evade the iron laws of European power politics? I think not; it only adds a further dimension of pathos to this movement and to others caught in the same vise. Hungarians have not been masters of their own fate in moments of great awakening such as these, even though they controlled the greater part of the country and took on all the airs of national independence. The unchanging tragedy of Hungarian history gains form and substance from the invocation of the Rankean insight.

The contemporaries failed to see this pattern at work; they did not have sufficient foresight to see that the Rebellion was doomed to failure. Instead, they turned their attention to conjunctures which might have had favorable consequences for the Rebels. Such a 'catastrophic theory' of the Rákóczi Rebellion is the one I will develop in my treatment of its diplomatic history. It may be in apparent contradiction of what has been said so far, but further explanation should obviate any misunderstanding. Its main weakness is its inclination to trespass upon the dangerous territory of the conditional in human history, for in three particular cases I will demonstrate that an extraordinary change in the relationships of the major powers could have worked a miraculous change in the fortunes of the Rebellion. That these three crises so potentially favorable to Rákóczi passed without radically changing matters does not diminish their value as keys to the importance of that Rebellion.

For the outcome might have been vastly different if the Turks had gone to war with the Emperor, and the compromise that was eventually achieved between Vienna and the Hungarians at Szatmár might have been vastly more favorable to the Hungarians if the Anglo-Dutch Mediation had brought sufficient pressure to bear on the Emperor. It will not be necessary to follow the development of Austrian relations, on the one hand, and Hungarian relations, on the other, with Turkey, the Maritime Powers, and Sweden through the entire course of the Rebellion. It will be my interest to present evidence adequate to support the 'catastrophic theory' of the Rebellion's foreign relations.

Rákóczi himself appears to sanction such a procedure. For in his *Memoires,* he underlines the fact that he assumed control of the movement only in the expectation that he could win: by establishing a common front with the Elector Max Emanuel under the walls of Vienna he would force the Emperor to make substantial concessions to his Hungarian subjects. When Höchstädt rendered this fundamental premise nugatory, Rákóczi was forced to take this into account. The possibility remained that the French might reverse the decision of Höchstädt. The Prince believed that even after this fatal reverse there were two moments of destiny for him and his cause. The first was the prospect of establishing a common front with a French army in Croatia. When Vendôme reached the Adriatic in the campaign of 1705, Rákóczi hoped that this would provide a springboard for the landing of a French expeditionary force on the Dalmatian coast and its eventual meeting with larger forces of Hungarian Rebels. A hope without substance, since the French did not have the troops and the supplies necessary for such an undertaking, and Venice had already received France's pledge that it would not disturb the Republic in its control of the northern reaches of the Adriatic.

The second favorable conjuncture was Rákóczi's last minute expectation that the Tsar would join forces with him in Transylvania or eastern Hungary. Peter's relations with the Hungarian leader easily take the prize for diplomatic puzzles. In the period from his victory at Pultava (1709) to his humiliating defeat at the hands of the Turks on the Pruth (1711), Peter was the likeliest candidate for the role of *deus ex machina* in Hungary's tragedy. But all the discussions did not move a single Russian soldier to the rescue, and the moment -- it was always partially Rákóczi's fantasy -- passed by.

The Prince had also entertained the hope that his negotiations with the Austrians at Nagyszombat (1706) would be productive of an agreement that would guarantee the achievements of the Rebellion on the domestic scene. In the second chapter of this final section we will treat those negotiations in detail to determine whether he was in earnest in his optimistic view of the Mediation.

The character of the two crucial periods that we have chosen to examine impose a further shift in the orientation of Part Three. Secure in our belief that the fate of Hungary never for a moment depended on the excursions of the Rebels, we will move into the foreground of our consideration the all-important relations of the Austrians and the Powers from whom help might have come. This enables us to establish an immediate connection between the Rebellion and two of the developments which bulked large in Part One: the Austro-Turkish settlement at Carlowitz and the early successes of the Anglo-Dutch Mediation. For a large part of the diplomatic tentatives of Rákóczi ran directly into these pre-existent situations.

When viewed in the long perspective of the Habsburg Monarchy's history, the Rebellion's showing on the diplomatic front posed one of the most dangerous challenges to Austria's role as a Great Power that modern history has witnessed. Austria's mismanagement of its affairs turns up again in the course of the diplomatic struggle. This was a time of maximum strain on the Austrian system, and curious quirks and flaws that appeared should not surprise us. The exertions of the Austrian ministers may occasionally steal the limelight from Rákóczi and his diplomatic agents, but the record of men like Eugene of Savoy and Wratislaw was a solid and impressive one. Incompetence and official shortsightedness were not the whole story as far as the Austrians were concerned. An Austrian spirit was convincingly displayed in the tenacity of purpose and the deep attachment of the more distinguished ministers to the Monarchy. These men, who managed to introduce their reforming conceptions under the patronage of Joseph l, gave Austria a new lease on life. They fought the Rebellion with all the weapons at their disposal, but they ultimately produced in the settlement of Szatmár a realistic and moderate solution of the Hungarian question.

Chapter 1

Rákóczi and the Sultan

"C'est le sort de la pluspart des grandes affaires, ce que l'on peut au plus est de le prevenir ou le diminuer par les mesures que l'on peut prendre à la Porte."

- Marquis de Pomponne

"We want but one Disturbance more to be as miserable a state as it is possible, I mean a breach with the Ottoman Port, and of that there is too great appearance."

- Mr. George Stepney

"But all things considered, I believe it may be affirmed that these people (the Turks) have carried themselves as fairly as could be expected from them in such a Conjuncture."

- Sir Robert Sutton

In the years that immediately followed the conclusion of the Peace of Carlowitz, Constantinople enjoyed a period of prominence in European power politics and a consequent quickening of diplomatic activity that was to be rarely equalled in the last centuries of the Ottoman Empire. The Turks had only recently established themselves as members of the European system, and now they found to their scarcely-concealed delight that their former enemies were engaged in the precarious business of currying favor with the Turkish government. The Solemn Embassies that formally ratified the various separate treaties came and went, but the interest of the European powers in the direction that Turkey would take did not suffer any appreciable decline. For

Europe was by this time at war again, and Turkey was a factor to be taken into the calculations of statesmen in every major capital.

Pera had witnessed diplomatic flurries in recent years, but they did not even remotely approach the activity of the first decade of the eighteenth century. A set of colorful personalities had gathered in the diplomatic colony which was memorable enough even if their intrigues did not lead to the resumption of war in the Balkans for the time being. The Marquis de Ferriol had succeeded the discredited Châteauneuf. He had experience of affairs in Eastern Europe through his service with the army of Thököly in the post of France's observer, but the Marquis was unquestionably psychotic, and he would end his embassy in the state of insanity. The Turks were not at all surprised by this, for they had seen it coming. Ferriol had figured in an incident known as the Affair of the Sword in which his refusal to remove that offending weapon had led the Turkish officials to deny him admission to the Sultan's presence. In the course of his fairly extended stay, Ferriol never had an audience with the Sultan.[1] But with or without the formal presentation of his credentials, he pursued the same tack as his predecessor, and in this he was ably seconded by the learned and influential Père Benien of the Society of Jesus. The French priest had the reputation of a man of parts. He made good use of a previous stay in Turkey to learn Turkish and Arabic, and his personal charm, his linguistic ability, and a specialized knowledge of mathematics and astrology made him especially popular in the Turkish capital, particularly with the men of the law.[2]

France had lost something of the clear predominance it had once exercised in Pera, but its prestige in Turkish circles was still immense. In these years of great activity, moral support for France appeared in the form of the diplomatic agents of Prince Rákóczi, a shadowy group of men, these 'Hungarian deputies' or ministers of Transylvania. They set up housekeeping at the customary residence of the Transylvanian Ministers to the Porte and immediately fell in with the latest French diplomatic maneuvers. The Principality of Transylvania constituted a real temptation for the Turks, and the Franco-Hungarian coalition frequently dangled this tempting morsel in the view of the Emperor for the losses which Köprülü had been forced to sanction at Carlowitz was an alluring one indeed.

It was at this time, too, that Russia established permanent diplomatic representation in Turkey, and Russia began to occupy more and more of the thinking of Turkish policymakers. The two empires had only recently shown an interest in participating as an ordinary practice in European affairs, and from this contact with European trade and diplomacy innovations had resulted that involved a certain amount of Europeanization. Russia soon made great strides in this direction, but in the first year of the eighteenth century Turkey was about equal in the adoption of European ways. The amazement which the Turks experienced at the Petrine reforms in dress was mirrored in an amused description by Lord Paget of an incident which had occurred in the course of the visit of the Russian Embassy that concluded the Treaty of Constantinople:

> The Muscovite Ambassador and his retinue, have appeared heer so different from what they allways, formerly were, that the Turks can't tell what to make of them, they are all accouter'd in French habit, with abundance of gold and silver lace; long periwigs and (which the Turks most wonder at) without beards; The last Sunday being at Mass in Adrianople the Ambassador and all his company, did not only keep all their hats off during the whole ceremony, but at the Elevation, himself and all of them pull'd off their periwigs, that was much taken notice of and thought to be an unusual act of devotion ...[3]

Lord Paget had returned, as we have seen, to Pera in February, 1699, excited with the stunning success of his 'Method' in Mediation, and anxious to try his hand again at the earliest possible opportunity. And chances for keeping in practice seemed at first abundant. But thoughts of England and of the peace and comfort of Beudesert Hall in his declining years (His Lordship was approaching sixty) became foremost in his mind as the Solemn Embassies completed their business without experiencing appreciable difficulties. To be sure, his old bete noire Marsigli was bringing his 'disordered visions' to play in the meetings of the Boundary Commission and had managed to worry the most complacent and permissive Turkish delegate into a state of resistance to Austrian proposals and ... presents. But this did not seriously muddy the peaceful waters of the Carlowitz settlement, and Paget's ill health made it unlikely that he would be of much assistance in any further revival of the almost dormant Mediation.[4]

William III had appointed George Berkeley, Earl of Berkeley, to succeed Paget in October, 1698, and it was expected that Berkeley would arrive in Turkey in time for the finale of the Peace Congress. But Berkeley had begged to be excused, and the King had not brought pressure to bear on him to accept such a difficult assignment. Even as Berkeley refused the appointment, Paget suggested to Whitehall that the title of Mediator Plenipotentiary be added to Berkeley's title of Ambassador of the King of England in order to point up the continuity in the work of Mediation. This would then establish the ad hoc role of Paget in the preliminaries and the actual negotiations at Carlowitz on a permanent footing, but Berkeley never appeared and the title was allowed to lapse.

Paget's desire to return to England finally led him to suggest that Robert Sutton, the British Minister Resident at the Court of Vienna, should succeed him in the Constantinople embassy. Sutton was known to Paget largely through their long correspondence, and the older man had come to value the discretion and poise of the younger diplomat. And there was no denying that Sutton, alone among the British diplomats in Europe, had a detailed knowledge of Austria and Turkey; the first he knew at first hand, and for his information on the second he was indebted to Lord Paget's letter and to his acquaintance with Ibrahim Pasha, the Turkish Ambassador to Vienna.[5]

One finds it difficult to assess the degree of influence that Paget possessed in Whitehall, but shortly after his suggestion was received there, the government entrusted Sutton with the most important assignment of his career -- the arduous task of representing England in Constantinople. Sutton was assisted through the complicated labyrinth of Turkish court ceremonial on his arrival at Adrianople in March, 1702, by the experienced Paget, and both men were pleasantly surprised by the extraordinary cordial reception accorded the new English Ambassador by the Turks.[6] When Sutton had his first public audience with the Grand Vizir, Sultan Mustafa followed the ceremony with great interest from a jealousy high above the company's heads. On the next day, he gave an even more tangible proof of his friendly feelings by replying to the address of the newly-accredited Ambassador in a 'clear and distinct voice', an act contrary to the custom by which the Sultan did not deign to reply personally or whispered his remarks into the ear of the Grand Vizir.[7] And the burden of his discourse was even more pleasant to the English:

> The English are our good and trusted friends, and we intend to give them proof on every possible occasion that we harbor similar sentiments. We will strive especially to demonstrate to the King our gratitude for his friendly Mediation and the confidence which we have in his friendship.[8]

Mustafa's sentiments were probably sincere, for his whole bearing during the audience had clearly exceeded the limits of a routine expression of good will. And his ministers were similarly committed to a friendship with the Maritime Powers and to a policy of adherence to the provisions of the recent Peace. For the men who ruled Turkey at the time of Sutton's arrival were the very officials who had been responsible for Turkey's role in the peace settlement, and once the treaties had been signed they saw little point in upsetting the delicate balance that had been achieved with so much difficulty. So much had to be done in Turkish internal affairs, and the task of building up the economic resources of the Empire and restoring order where chaos had become the order of the day was a congenial one to men like the Grand Vizir Hussein Köprülü and Rami Pasha, the Reis-Effendi at Carlowitz.

Köprülü was forced by age and infirmity to request permission to retire in September, 1702, and, after a brief interlude, Rami Pasha became Grand Vizir at the beginning of 1703. The Grand Mufti Feishullah moved influentially behind the scenes, and the influence of the men of the Law was apparent in Rami's appointment. The new Vizir had won the respect of the European diplomats at the Peace Congress, and his deep personal culture and administrative ability commended him to the Sultan and the cadis. But the predominance of the jurists had not been achieved without creating eddies of discontent in the ranks of the Janissaries and of the urban proletariat of Constantinople. These groups still smarted under the sense of humiliation that Carlowitz had caused them, and the soldiers, in addition, feared that power slipping from their control into that of the jurists and bureaucrats . The retirement of old Köprülü had caused a minor war scare in Pera circles; Sutton was plainly alarmed by the general talk of war and the common agreement that Hussein Pasha's retirement strengthened the hand of the war party.

It was difficult to predict which one of the newly-acquired friends of the Ottoman Empire would be chosen to bear the brunt of the Turkish attack. In the fall of 1702, Venice led all the other contenders for this doubtful honor. The Turks had been particularly distressed by the loss of the Morea, and Venice was thought to be the weakest of the former members of the Holy League.[8] But once the question of a war of *revanche* raised its head, it did not require an excess of intelligence to see that the Emperor was also a strong contender for Turkey's bellicose attentions, especially since he was at the moment so deeply involved in his war with Louis XIV. Marquis de Ferriol was having a field day in encouraging the Turkish ministers to consider the prospect of war; he did not have to be too specific in making suggestions, since the Turks were well aware that the French were anxious to embroil them in a war with Austria.

But the Turks were adamant on one point: they had no intention of going to war with Russia. Their brushes with Tsar Peter convinced them that his was a force with which they would soon have to reckon, and the diplomats remarked how especially careful the Turks were to keep the Crimean Tatars as quiet as possible, lest Tatars' obstreperousness involve them suddenly in a war with the Russians.[9] Sutton had been quick to discover the profound lack of interest in Turkish circles in such a conflict, for he had thought of deflecting the ominous attention of the Turks from Venice and the Empire to Russia. He had even gone to the extent of requesting permission from Lord Manchester, the Secretary of the Southern Department, to use English influence in this way:

If therefore it be apparent that they are resolved to take advantage of the conjuncture (all Christendom being embroyled in a war) to pick a quarrel with some one of them, I desire to know whether His Majesty will be pleased to allow, that endeavours may be used to show them that it is more their Interest to break with the Muscovites than the Venetians, who are in League with the Emperor and Poland.[10]

But the Turks were plainly not interested, and Lord Manchester provided him with no directives on the policy he would follow.

The European diplomats continued to be anxious as they observed the constant military preparations going on around them. While Sutton had come to the conclusion that the Turkish menace should be directed at Russia, Carlo Ruzzini, now acting as the Venetian Bailo, was doing his best to save the Morea for Venice by encouraging the Turks to think of regaining their position in Hungary. Venice's ambiguous role in Constantinople was conditioned by the Republic's great fear of losing the Morea, and its signal absence of loyalty to its alliance with the Emperor was thus the product of its primary interest in self-preservation with the Emperor. There was a lingering dissatisfaction in Venice at the treatment it had received at the Peace Congress, but even more ground for dispute was to be found in the occupation of neutral Venice's territory by the army of Prince Eugene. While the military situation in Italy remained in doubt, Venice thought it wise to speak fair words in Vienna and to support the intrigues of Ferriol in Turkey.[11] The Austrian ministry was duly informed of Venetian double-dealing, since its resident agent in Pera, Johann Michael Thalmann, dutifully reported on his efforts to counteract these Franco-Venetian intrigues.

Thalmann was a recent arrival in Pera, and his coming naturally strengthened the hand of the English and Dutch Ambassadors in their campaign to keep Turkey out of a war with the Emperor. The Austrian ministers had been incredibly slow in despatching a diplomat to represent the Emperor's interests in Turkey. Lord Paget had been the first to sound the alarm; he was not particularly worried about the course that Turkey might pursue. On his way home to England in the autumn of 1702, he stopped off in Vienna and made use of his great prestige there in pressing home the need "to hasten an Internuntio, or some other Minister". The ministers assured him that a 'fit Person' would be despatched in a week's time, but Paget was not too sanguine about the chances of such a decisive move. The outlook, as far as Austro-Turkish relations were concerned, was even more depressing:

> .... For the Turks are a Proud Humorous People, who when they take a prejudice against, or resent, any Neglect or slight offered them are not easily appeased. The German Carelessness and disposition to delay, and suspend Business, has occasioned many inconveniences, and yet they will not reform their displeasing, vexatious, indamaging temper, as is apparent in this) as well as many other) transactions; which suffer and languish because they are not sustain'd with a little mettle, vigour, and Diligence.[12]

Needless to say, Paget's surmise was quite correct, and Vienna allowed the question to drag on. Sutton, once he had grasped the explosive character of the Turkish situation, took up the cry for the appointment of an Austrian Internuncio. His understanding of the reluctance on the part of the Austrians to send a diplomat differed, however, from Paget's view.

> The Emperor neglects his concerns with the Port as much, as if he were indifferent whether he was to continue in Peace with this Empire or not. As far as I can perceive, the Imperial Ministers suppose it to be more the Concern of the Queen and the States-General than their own to maintain the peace between their Master and Sultan, and so perhaps it may be found in effect.[13]

His last phrase was certainly a rare moment of prophetic insight; he was to spend the next years in proving just how right he had been. The Austrians finally relented at the beginning of 1703, but the appointment of Thalmann only partially satisfied the English requests. For the man was a graduate of the school of Oriental languages in Vienna and had acquired a reputation as a Turkish expert. But something more was needed to fill the gap than an interpreter with the humble rank of Secretary of the Internunciature.[14]

Russia, meanwhile, had been displaying a marked interest in exploiting the current Turkish military buildup to her own advantage. Chancellor Golovin, doubtless on the order of the Tsar who still bore a grudge against the Emperor for the 'desertion' at Carlowitz, ordered Dmitri Tolstoi, the Russian Ambassador in Constantinople, to use his contacts with Turkish officials to encourage them to resume war with the Emperor. Russia was at the moment engaged in a life and death struggle with Charles XII of Sweden, and the threat of a Turkish attack must have assumed nightmare proportions at times for the Russians. Tolstoi did not choose to act on the Chancellor's suggestion (it was originally made in 1703 and repeated in 1706); he reported to his superior that a suggestion of this kind on his part would carry little weight with the Turks and would only augment their suspicions of the Russian policies.[15]

The formal raising of the standard of revolt in Hungary by Prince Ferenc Rákóczi in June, 1703, added further complication to the diplomatic puzzle in Constantinople, and, from the standpoint of the Emperor and his English and Dutch allies, it made the chances of a Turkish attack ever more likely. For almost from the start of the Rebellion it was a painfully evident that the Emperor no longer possessed the military initiative in Hungary and Transylvania, and that this would only whet the appetite for easy conquest. Even in the mind of the most peaceful Vizir there would be a dangerous reawakening of the thought that victory for Turkish arms would improve the Ottoman Empire's position in international affairs.

Months before the Rebellion began, the movements of the Crimean Tatars struck Sutton as being most suspicious, and he reported to London early in 1703, that there was a good reason to believe that a great design had been formed against Transylvania; his proof of this was the "secret intelligence with the Prince of Ragozzi and his party" that had been established by the Turks. At the beginning of April, he again remarked that the Turks might be encouraged by France to help Rákóczi regain Transylvania:

> Whether the French may not at present endeavor to prevail with the Turks to give the Prince of Ragotski any indirect assistance in order to attain that Principality, or to countenance a Rebellion in Hungary in his favour, especially during the confusions in Poland, I am not able to judge ...

And he could only complain about the inadequate character of the information he received on French intrigues and the reactions of the

Turkish officials; it all went back to the notoriously poor quality of his dragomen and the lack of funds with which to give presents to the Turks. Sutton's information in this instance was obviously not correct, but he had had the prescience to see the approaching disaster, which was more than could be said of the bulk of Austrian officials. The ensuing Rebellion became a specialty of Robert Sutton; he followed its development with care and did his best -- with an occasional assist from Jakob Coyler and Johann Thalmann -- to present it in the most unfavorable light possible whenever his conversations with Turkish officials gave him an opening.[16]

It is ironic indeed that the temptation to fight the Austrians reached its apex at the very moment that Turkish domestic affairs made it absolutely certain that Turkey would be unable to go to war. The exact degree of connection between the Rákóczi Rebellion and the Turkish revolution of the summer of 1703 will probably never be elucidated in any completely satisfying way. The historian notes that the Turkish disturbances followed closely on the heels of the events in Hungary, and this may lead to the conclusion that the revolutionary disease was communicable. But apart from the question of contagion, it is likely that the reports of the outbreak in Hungary, which circulated in Constantinople, merely occasioned the sudden decision of the soldiers and the city crowds to rid the country of the peaceful regime of Rami Pasha. The Sultan and his ministers were in residence at Adrianople, and for the first few days did not suspect that anything out of the ordinary was happening. But the disorders grew progressively worse, and officials began to go over to the revolutionary movement. The foreign diplomats were treated to a prolonged spectacle of mob rule in Constantinople, but somehow Sutton was not touched by these events. He reported on these disorders in his letters to England, but his mind was so made up -- chaos was the natural order of Turkish politics -- that manifestations of this kind did not strike him as unusual. The crisis continued through the months of July and August and was resolved only with the deposition of Rami Pasha and his inept master Mustafa and the accession to the throne of the latter's brother as Ahmed III. This revolution had been less drastic in its effects than similar outbreaks of the Janissaries the century before, but the victorious troops were allowed to vent their hatred on the person of the Mufti Feisullah, and his most barbarous demise acted as a reminder that the Turks had not completely mastered the rules of European moderation and decorum.

The new regime was most uncertain in its movements, for it had the thankless task of appeasing the forces which at the same time it made absolutely certain that there would be no repetition of the uprising. Constantinople continued in a state of mild alarm, though the forces of law and order were already exacting a reckoning with the officials who had sided too prematurely with the forces of revolt. Sutton was of the considered opinion that the Turks were still in a position to pursue a vigorous foreign policy; more than one Turkish regime in a situation like this had sought salvation in war.[17]

The great conundrum which still puzzled Sutton and his colleagues was "where the storm may fall". A count was taken once more of the choices open to the Turks, and once again Sutton discounted any chance of war with Russia. The Turks, according to the informants, would secure their common frontier with Russia and "abandon the Czar to the revenge of the Swede". Secure on that flank, they could then devote their full attention to Venice and the Emperor, and Sutton was fearful that aid to the Hungarian Malcontents, albeit of an unofficial variety, would be the first step on the road to a complete break with Vienna. Disaster could be avoided only through a swift and decisive victory of the Imperial army in Hungary. Once the Rebels had been crushed, the temptation for the Turks to intervene would automatically disappear. And so in his letters to London and to George Stepney, Her Majesty's Minister in Vienna, he multiplied his urgent appeals for an immediate decision in Hungary.[19]

But any thought of crushing the Hungarian Rebels with dispatch was sheer fantasy in the closing days of 1703. For the Hungarians, after making a speedy recovery from a series of minor setbacks they had received in the summer, had now pressed deep into the *Alföld* and Upper Hungary, and advance units of their forces occasionally carried out raids that reached the outlying suburbs of Vienna. The capital's defenseless condition produced real panic in official circles, and special levies of troops from Lower Austria were called up to ensure the safety of the Emperor, the Imperial family, and finally the capital itself. Leopold had just begun to suffer from the collection of physical complaints that would finally prove fatal in May, 1705, and his debility at this crucial time was almost as troubling to his advisers as his usual indecisiveness. The Imperial ministers struck Charles Whitworth, the Secretary of the English Legation, as a most dispirited group of men, and he feared that the extremity at which they found themselves might move them to negotiate with France.[20]

Yet the presence of Eugene of Savoy, Count Gundacker von Starhemberg, and Johann Wenzel Wratislaw in key positions gave reason to hope. These were young and capable men committed to a vigorous prosecution of the war, and their sense of purpose was in heart-warming contrast to the inactivity and defeatism of the older ministers.

The Monarchy had lived in the presence of crisis for at least a century, but if one had to choose the most critical period of all, the winter of 1703 would, in my opinion, win hands down. The Bavarian armies were moving relentlessly into the Alpine *Länder*, and the 'Back door', as Whitworth so felicitously described the Hungarian front, was open and unguarded. A combination of Bavarian and Hungarian forces before Vienna might have led to the disappearance of Austria as a Great Power. It was with a real sense of urgency then, that Eugene set out for Pozsony to inspect the defenses in that area and to breathe something approaching confidence into the Hungarian officials still loyal to the Emperor and the Austrian military commanders who had become incapable of any sort of reaction to the Hungarian attacks. Eugene's reports from his headquarters in Hungary were even less encouraging, and since the crisis permitted a certain license in his expression, he bluntly told the Emperor that the Habsburgs faced the greatest moment of trial in their long history. Only a brief period of time remained in which to "save your Imperial Majesty, together with the Most Serene

Dynasty, from the loss of his kingdom". Time was in incredibly short supply, and each passing day witnessed the development of the menace from both east and west with the additional danger that it would also "come to a war with Turkey".

Eugene did not frighten easily; his marvelous sang froid was one of the sure supports of Austrian morale while he lived, but he left no illusions in the minds of the Emperor Leopold and Joseph, the King of the Romans, that this was a threat that made 1683 look like child's play. It was definitely within the range of possibility, as far as he was concerned, to hold off the Bavarians and the Hungarian Rebels; the first inspired more annoyance than fear, while the second were too undisciplined to be victorious in a pitched battle with the professional soldiers of the Emperor. But the entry of Turkey into this situation would be decisive, and we have the expert testimony of Leopold's greatest general to support this conjecture.[21]

Contact had been established in the meantime between the Rebels and the Turks. The first agents of Rákóczi to reach Turkey arrived in the very wake of Ahmed III's accession. Their mission was understood to consist of requesting 'succours' of an undisclosed kind from the Turks, but the English Ambassador's information was not complete. The Hungarians devoted most of their attention to propagandizing for the Rebel cause. The French Ambassador availed himself of every opportunity to bring their first-hand reports of the parlous condition of the Emperor's forces in Hungary to the hearing of prominent Turkish officials. Exchanges of a more substantial kind had already taken place on the frontier of Hungary and the Ottoman Empire, though the fortresses along the border remained in Imperial control. The Pashas of Belgrade and Temesvár followed a far from scrupulously neutral course in dealing with the Rebels, and they frequently exchanged emissaries. The Sipahi Osman, recently restored to his homeland after years of confinement in Austria as a prisoner of war, undertook a mission from Ali Pasha, the Pasha of Belgrade, to Rákóczi. His report on his diplomatic errand would, if it were available in a Western language, cast an interesting light on the conditions of the Rebel camp as viewed by a

Turkish observer, and would allow for a more balanced view of the relations between the Hungarians and the Turks. The obvious pro-Hungarian sympathies of Ali Pasha eventually became so embarrassing to the government in Constantinople that he was demoted with full assurances that his policy had not coincided with that of the government which retained complete loyalty to the Treaty of Carlowitz.[22]

Eugene of Savoy and the Allied diplomats would have been even more concerned if they had realized that the Turks were engaged in a comprehensive discussion of their policy in regard to peace or war at this very time -- January, 1704. There were rumors current to that effect (with the usual hint of French overtures), but it was only three years later that the Austrians realized how close they had been to war with the Turks at the time. The information given to them in 1707 has not been corroborated by official Turkish documents; it consisted simply of the reminiscences of the self-styled chief actor in the drama, but his report is sufficiently in keeping with other testimony to deserve a good degree of credence. The circumstances in which the story was told were typical of the period. On the homeward trip from Adrianople, Christopher Guarient von Rall, a special Imperial Envoy to the Sultan, stopped off in Sofia. And there he had been the guest of the local Pasha, a garrulous fellow apparently, and in the course of their conversation he was treated to a most interesting revelation of the part of hist host, who had been one of the associates of Hassan Pasha in the Vizirate in 1704, had played in preserving the peace.[23]

The Grand Vizir Hassan Pasha had not been slow to realize that the Ottoman Empire, thanks to developments in Hungary, faced one of the most crucial periods in its history. He was constantly plagued by requests for governmental action and by unsolicited bits of advice from the Pashas and their subordinates in the border regions, and at his suggestion the Sultan issued a call to the notables of the Empire to meet in a special session of the Divan and there debate the policy which his government should pursue in relation to Hungary. Ahmed was relatively untried in politics, but his inexperience was not so great that he did not make an effort to influence the deliberations in the direction of a moderate decision. The Pasha (of Guarient's report) was accordingly summoned to his presence the evening before the scheduled meeting and was commanded on the pain of death to express the opinion he had formed of the wisest policy for Turkey to follow in the open meeting.

The meeting of the Divan began with a lengthy commentary by the Grand Vizir on the general situation, and then the question was put to the members: whether the Porte should content itself with observing Hungarian developments or should go into the attack "against Hungary".[24] (Throughout the discussion the Turks talked as though they planned to launch an attack on a hypothetical Hungary; they were obviously trying to avoid referring to the Emperor in this context.) The Vizirs showed great reluctance to express their opinions. This 'conspiracy of silence' rested on their firm belief that there was little point in warmly espousing a position that might later on be held responsible for a political catastrophe. Vizirs who made mistakes of this kind had a way of paying for their miscalculations with their lives. Far too much was at stake at the moment, and it was impossible to foretell whether the Turks would run into streak of good luck or bad.

In the very midst of this embarrassed silence, our Pasha stepped forward, performed his obeisance at the feet of the Sultan, and launched into his prepared statement. The 'midnight oil' had been burned in great quantities in his polishing up of this homework assignment, for he was suspiciously prolific of reasons to support his general thesis that Turkey should not go to war. The original question was restated (without changing its meaning): was it to the advantage of the Ottoman Empire to stamp out the fire of Rebellion that was sweeping Hungary and Transylvania or should it continue to watch the conflagration develop from the security of its neutral position? The first and most cogent reason for electing the second alternative was that the effective power of the German Emperor was still an imposing quantity, and Leopold would probably be able in the case of war with Turkey to patch up an agreement with his enemies in the West -- the allusion to Rijswijk was pointed enough -- and then, reinforced by the German "kings and princes" turn the full force of his military power against Turkey. As far as the Hungarian Rebels were concerned, their pretended power was still too shaky a foundation for an alliance, and the Pasha reminded his hearers that Rákóczi's forbears, and Ferenc I in particular, had been lifelong enemies of the Porte and had more often done harm to it than good.

His next two reasons centered about the preponderant role of France as the support of the Rebellion. The wounded *amour propre* of the Turks came to the surface and with it the often unexpressed fear that France and her client states might soon pose a threat to Turkey. For the Pasha listed as his third reason the fact that Rákóczi was far more devoted to the French tie than he was to Turkey. If he had been in complete good faith in his professions of attachment to the Porte, he would have given it sufficient advance notice of the uprising (instead of relying so completely on the French from the very beginning), he would have pledged his fealty to the Sultan and, in general, displayed subservience to Turkey's wishes. And because this had not been the case, the Pasha concluded that Rákóczi was not sincere in his proffers of loyalty to the Porte. And in addition, the expansive tendencies of the Rebellion which were encouraged by the French might bring about a situation in which the Ottoman Empire would find itself under attack.

The Pasha next turned to a discussion of the juridical and ethical considerations involved in any violation of the Treaty of Carlowitz. That treaty had been formally ratified by the sworn oaths of the contracting parties. And so far, the Emperor had given the Turks no reason to believe that he would fail to honor his oath. The Pasha's devoutly Mohammedan conclusion was to assert that divine justice would surely punish the Turks if they broke their solemn oath without sufficient reason. The members of the Divan had certainly had cause in recent months to deplore the violation of oaths in their own country -- the Pasha was hinting none too subtly that the Hungarian Rebellion and the Turkish revolution of the preceding summer were similar in nature. In summation, he suggested that, while the present conjuncture was favorable, the points which he had advanced made it entirely probable that any Turkish intervention would have a disastrous outcome. "The Porte should place far more weight on the enmity of the Emperor than on the friendship of Rákóczi and twenty others like him."

At this point, the Sultan pressed the Pasha to be more specific about the policy that the government should pursue. The Pasha was well-primed for this question, too, and his answer was a logical development of his reading of the power situation in Eastern Europe. The Sultan must not undertake anything of an unfriendly nature against the Emperor to whom he had pledged his friendship, but should rather seek to demonstrate his peaceful inclinations by sending an impressive embassy to Vienna with an offer of Turkish support in crushing the Hungarian Rebellion. The Pasha and his colleagues were well aware that the Emperor could not accept such a proposal (the Austrian ministers would regard this as a most suspect move), but the avowal of interest would give confirmation to the Turks' assurances of their amicable feeling. Furthermore, since the Rebellion possessed long-range possibilities of danger for the Ottoman Empire, it behooved the Turks to be extremely careful and to require the Pashas on the frontier to be excessively circumspect in their actions.

The Pasha's vigorous espousal of a policy of continued friendly relations with the Emperor and of guarded neutrality on the Hungarian frontier carried the day, and Ibrahim Effendi was duly dispatched to Vienna with the customary notification of the accession of a new Sultan to the throne and with such solemn pledges of Turkish goodwill that the Emperor would conclude that the Turks did not intend to take advantage of his misfortunes by denouncing the Treaty of Carlowitz. The offer of fraternal assistance in crushing the Rákóczi Rebellion was actually made, but as the Turks had expected the Austrians made no move to accept the Sultan's offer. The diplomats had been aware that something was afoot in Turkish official circles, and Sutton in particular had been apprehensive that the mission of Ibrahim Effendi was but a prelude to the resumption of hostilities. His relief was extreme when he learned of the pacific nature of the embassy, and the happy Turkish inspiration of proffering aid struck him as being particularly neat -- "we are not here

so barbarous, but we can make a civil compliment sometimes."[25] What
he could not know was that the moment of greatest danger had been
passed, and for a long time he continued to see the grim specter of war.
Clearly, the Turks had not laid down a permanent policy at the meeting
of the Divan, but since this was the single opportunity they would have
of achieving a cheap victory at the Emperor's expense, the provisional
policy advocated by the Pasha became by necessity a standing order of
Turkish foreign policy. The highwater mark in Austro-Turkish relations
during the Rákóczi Rebellion had been reached at this point, for what
the Turks refused to venture at the nadir of the Austrian crisis, they
could not possibly contemplate in years when the Emperor was
evidently the master of his own house.

The Habsburgs had been saved by the peace party (this included
the Sultan) in Constantinople. The activities of Sutton, Coyler, and
Thalmann had obviously helped to maintain the Turkish sense of respect
for Austrian power, but there was no indication that the Austrians, or
the Hungarians for that matter, had influenced the thinking of the
Turkish ministers. The dark days that had preceded Carlowitz were far
more responsible, for they had left an indelible imprint on the minds of
Turks of that generation. The men who remembered Zenta were in no
mood to renew the dangerous dialogue with the Austrian armies,
however straightened Austria might appear for the moment. The blithe
promises of Rákóczi's friendship made by the Hungarian Deputies had
not blinded the Turks to the obvious fact that his orientation was
western and that he nurtured ambivalent feelings toward them.

Sir Robert Sutton was heard to complain on another occasion that
the Turks were too tied to the dimension of the immediate present to be
really successful in international politics.

> The Turks can scarce be brought to look far into the future, or to examine their
> interests at a distance. That which is nearest to 'em is always the object of their care or fear,
> and they apprehend nothing that is remote.[26]

But surely that meeting of the Divan gives impressive proof that this
nearsightedness was not always the rule. The Turks, if anything, had

been so bemused by the inscrutable character of future events that they had been reduced to inactivity. They had balanced the known quantity of Imperial reverses in Hungary against the unknown of an imminent comeback, and on this basis had concluded that it would be foolhardy to go to war. Indeed, one might profitably invert Sutton's observation and say that the trouble with the Turks at this point was that they had not sufficiently aware of the myriad potentialities of the present. In adopting a long perspective they had failed to capitalize on the amazing opportunity that existed for them to join with France, Bavaria, and the Hungarian Rebels in those first weeks of 1704, and thus to destroy, possibly for all time, the Habsburg hegemony in Central and Eastern Europe.

The period of maximum danger for Austria was fated to be brief enough; the victory of Eugene of Savoy and Marlborough at Höchstädt that summer removed the threat of another great Siege of Vienna and brought to a close the first period in the life of the Hungarian Rebellion. The military successes in southern Germany had immediate repercussions in the Hungarian headquarters and in the palaces along the Golden Horn. Now that Rákóczi could no longer win a decisive military victory he realized that he was forced to transpose his struggle to the area of diplomatic negotiation. Not that he had failed to make steps in this direction already, but the emphasis from now on would rest heavily on the contacts he had with most of the Great Powers of Europe. A most high-minded, and as far as diplomatic practice went, most naive young man, he soon found himself caught up in such a complicated web of negotiations -- they were frequently at cross-purposes -- that the most hardened devotee of *Realpolitik* would be bound to express admiration for the feat. The lamb was playing a game with many foxes, and he soon developed such apparent mastery of the game that it blinded him to the depressing state of the Rebellion's position in Hungary -- the pattern of military defeat and the obviously faltering support of the Hungarian gentry and *misera plebs*. The Turkish officials would, of course, witness a definite increase in Hungarian diplomatic activity in Turkey; Rákóczi's election as Prince of Transylvania gave additional substance to his involvement with that Principality's erstwhile suzerain.

The transition from the military phase to the diplomatic phase of the Rebellion was underlined by the arrival at Durazzo in July, 1704, of Louis XIV's personal envoy to Rákóczi, an elderly general, Pierre Pucho Count de Clinchamp, Marquis des Alleurs (he was generally known by his last title).[27] The Marquis, whose good looks as a youth had won him the favor of influential ladies of the French Court, had had a good deal of experience in diplomatic work in Western Europe, but there was little in his training and in his immensely cultivated way of life that prepared him for service in Hungary as France's envoy, paymaster, and expert consultant on military affairs. He had set out in May somewhat nonchalantly for his distant post. An entourage of twenty-five officers and a sum of money, reported to be as large as seven hundred thousand livres, accompanied him. The trip to Durazzo via Genoa, Naples, and Sicily consumed two months, and the good Marquis would have been horrified if he had known that the remainder of his journey would take nearly eight more months.

His sudden appearance on Turkish soil created a ticklish problem for the Turks. Sutton and his collaborators were almost immediately aware of the presence of the French party in the Albanian port, as they were quick to note the Turks' friendly reception of the Marquis and the constant communications between Ferriol and Des Alleurs.[28] But Turkish embarrassment did not constitute an obstacle to his progress towards Hungary. He and his party travelled with Turkish protection to Belgrade, and there he was received by the Pasha as if he were a representative of a foreign power on his way to take up residence in Constantinople. But the Pasha of Belgrade happened to be the very same man who had dominated the meeting of the Divan six months before. His appointment to a Pashalik on the border was doubtless a consequence of the position he had taken then. He was understandably loath to allow Des Alleurs to proceed on his journey, and before he allowed the French diplomat to leave for Temesvár, he subjected him to a close interrogation.[29] At the very outset of their exchange, the Pasha, not to beat about the bush, raised the pointed question of the purpose of the Frenchman's trip. The reply was candid enough: since the Emperor's forces were causing great hardship to the King of France in Germany and Italy, it was only natural that he seek to reciprocate by making trouble in Hungary. Almost as an afterthought, Des Alleurs declared that Louis was now in the course of responding to urgent appeals from Rákóczi and Hungarian leaders who were anxious to restore the Kingdom of Hungary, which had been made a hereditary monarchy by guile and force, to its rightful state of liberty. The Pasha's practical nature found it difficult to believe that the general and his party could be of much assistance to the Hungarians in achieving this program. If the King of France was really sincere in his desire to lend a helping hand to the Rebels, thousands of men and great sums of money would be required. And this brought the Pasha around to the surmise that Des Alleurs was in fact carrying large sums with him and promises of more. Since the Pasha was of the opinion that the nature of Des Alleurs' mission was a question of grave importance to the Porte, he requested a complete account of its plans before the French party would be allowed to continue its journey.

The next day, Des Alleurs admitted that he had been officially commissioned by his sovereign to serve as minister at Rákóczi's headquarters, and that in the course of his stay in Hungary he did not merely intend to encourage those already in arms against the Austrians but hoped to encourage others to imitate their example. In passing, he noted that he was carrying sums to the Prince, but he maneuvered to distract the Pasha's attention by observing that it would be much better for the Turks if the Emperor -- their ancient enemy -- did not have control of Hungary.

Once again, the Pasha failed to see how the withdrawal of Imperial forces from Hungary would work to the Turks' advantage. Rákóczi had certainly made far-reaching promises to the French to get financial assistance from them. And it was quite natural for a Turkish official to suspect that in the new state of affairs the Prince -- or to be more realistic about it -- the King of France might prove a more dangerous neighbor than the Emperor in the long run. Des Alleurs sought to ally his suspicions by presenting the Pasha with a document containing the terms of a proposed alliance between the Hungarians and the Turks which would rejoice in the guarantee of the King of France. It is difficult to imagine who had been responsible for this remarkable state paper, but whatever its provenience, it fell certainly into the class of French devices to win over the Turks to the Hungarian side.

According to the provisions of the proposed treaty of alliance, all fortresses, cities, and other places that the Prince captured with Turkish help were to be handed over to the Seraskier, the commander-in-chief of the Turkish armies in the field, or to the Pasha in the vicinity. Captured supplies were to be retained by the Hungarians in the amount that was required for the further prosecution of the war; the excess was to go to the Turks. The manpower of the jointly-conquered territories was to provide soldiers for the Rebel army, but the rest of the population was to be subjected to the Sultan and pay him tribute as it had done during the Turkish occupation. The King of France promised to bestow his royal protection on this agreement.

The discussion finally got around to the question of whether or not Rákóczi wanted to become King of Hungary. Des Alleurs expressed the opinion that, since the Prince would hardly undertake anything now or in the future contrary to the wishes of the Most Christian King, he would be satisfied with any title that the Porte might care to bestow upon him and with his possession of the Principality of Transylvania. But since this implied the cynical abandonment by Rákóczi of the cause of Hungarian freedom, Des Alleurs was careful to say that he did not care to commit himself to writing on this point. Neither Louis nor the Prince had authorized him to discuss the matter.[30]

Thought the Sultan was immediately informed of the project of alliance, the Turkish government evinced no further desire to detain the French embassy, and Des Alleurs and his party continued their trip to Hungary by way of Temesvár. In Constantinople, meanwhile, the Turks were publicly salving their conscience by declaring that such a small group of French officers would be of no great help to Rákóczi and arguing quite speciously that the Treaty did not require them to pursue a policy inimical to France.

Des Alleurs, after an extensive and fatiguing journey through the Banat, Transylvania, and eastern Hungary, finally caught up with his quarry at Eger on March 11, 1705. He made a really triumphant entry into the city and was received with great ceremony at Rákóczi's residence in the shadow of the Palace of Eger's bishop, István Telekesy, the most prominent supporter of the Rebellion in the Hungarian episcopate. The princely Court was a stickler in matters of etiquette, but on this occasion, Des Alleurs was surprised by the dispatch with which the Hungarian leader got down to business. Formalities were waived, and a series of long, confidential discussions on the state of the Rebellion followed.

The French envoy presented Louis XIV's letters to Rákóczi and delivered in addition a long memorandum which discussed in awesome detail the general course of the war, the Hungarian military potential, and the state of the Rebel army. Des Alleurs was even more surprised when he received the Prince's comprehensive reply only two hours after the conclusion of the first interview. The Hungarian position on the points raised in the memorandum was developed at length, but Des Alleurs' trained eye was quick to notice the very core of the document: it contained assurances from the Prince that all available means would be employed to forestall the conclusion of a peace with the Emperor. An interesting sidelight on the work of the Anglo-Dutch Mediation, it also calmed the French fears that the Hungarians in the wake of their great disappointment at Höchstädt would be moved to make as favorable a separate treaty with the Emperor as they could.

Once the relations of the Prince and the Marquis had fixed on such a comfortable footing, Des Alleurs felt that he could give the Hungarians some very pointed advice on the future course of their relations with the Turks. The journey through Turkish territory had given him some insight into the workings of the Turkish official mind, and his newly-acquired grasp of the situation in Hungary, gleaned from talks with the Prince and from his own observations, furnished him with material for his *Reflexions sur l'état present des affairs d'hongrie à l'égard de la Porte Ottomane.* This liberal dose of well-meaning advice was presented to the Prince on April 1.[31]

The basis of Des Alleurs' argument in these *Reflexions* was that Rákóczi could no longer permit his relations with the Turks to continue in their present dubious state. A certain lack of decision had been understandable in the Rebellion's early stages, but the movement was now two years old, and it could no longer evade the responsibility of clarifying its position vis-à-vis the Turks. For one thing, Rákóczi could not be sure that the Turks would not take it into their heads to restore their authority in Hungary and Transylvania. Turkish legal grounds for such a step could be based on their view that the cession of these territories to the Emperor had only been a temporary one. The lands had been mortgaged to the Emperor for a period of thirty years, and at the expiration of the Treaty the Turks would no longer be bound to respect the Emperor's frontiers. Sine the signatories of the peace treaty had not foreseen the advent of the Rebellion, the Turks might reassert their claim at any time on the ground that the mortgagee was no longer in actual possession of these holdings. It was high time, then, for Rákóczi to head off such a move by regularizing his relations with the Turks to the extent that a real exchange of views would be possible. Des Alleurs believed that the Prince absolutely required the tacit support of the Porte in continuing his fight. The confusion that reigned in Eger, Constantinople, and even Vienna on the exact nature of the understanding between the Rebels and Constantinople might well threaten the existence of the whole movement. For if the Turks gave even the least indication that they were interested in reviving their occupation of Hungary, Rákóczi's foreign policy and his position as the great spiritual leader of the forces of Hungarian freedom would suffer an irremediable blow. The Transylvanians with whom the French envoy had talked on his trip through the Principality had repeatedly indicated their great fear that Turkey might take advantage of the present confusion by reasserting its former claims. What a magnificent gift this would be to the propagandists for the House of Austria. Any confirmation of the rumors which they circulated to the effect that the

Turks were at the bottom of the Malcontents' conspiracy would be catastrophic, since its effect on the devotees of the Rebellion would not be difficult to gauge. Des Alleurs concluded his considerations with the strong appeal that an emissary be dispatched to Turkey without further delay. This envoy could work in concert with the French Ambassador, and together they might succeed in putting an end to the present uncertainty.

Rákóczi was quick to act on this wise suggestion. And afterwards, he must have commissioned Ferenc Horváth to represent him in Turkey. He presented Horváth with a comprehensive *Instructio* to serve him as a guide in the course of his most delicate negotiations.[32] In its introductory paragraph, Rákóczi felt called upon to give reasons for his desire to initiate more formal relations with the Turks. The astute hand of Des Alleurs was visible in all of this. The Prince remembered that the French Ambassador had been most successful up to now in handling Hungarian interests at the Sublime Porte but this mutually satisfactory arrangement could not continue. For the party at the Turkish Court that favored the Austrians had been making political capital out of the activities of Marquis de Ferriol as a representative of Hungary; this proved that Rákóczi was merely a pawn in France's elaborate and devious Eastern European policy. A show of independent action at the Porte by the Hungarians would serve to dispel any misunderstanding of Ferriol's position which might have excited Turkish suspicions or wounded Turkish *amour propre*.

The Instructio was anxious, however, that Horváth combine his show of independence with the greatest possible care to avoid attention. The chief object of his negotiations was to convince the Grand Dragoman Mavrokordatos that it would be a wise move to establish formal diplomatic relations with Rákóczi. Horváth was enjoined to be especially careful in his conversations with this master of the diplomatic trade. He was on no account to make any damaging admissions until he was certain of a favorable reception. Once he had been received, he might make his opening by asking if Mavrokordatos was interested in the current state of affairs in Hungary. If the answer was a positive one,

Horváth was instructed to report that the Diet of Transylvania had elected Rákóczi as Prince, and that the recent death of Emperor Leopold visibly strengthened the Prince's claim to Transylvania from both a legal and a moral point of view. Mavrokordatos would soon begin to give some indication of the direction in which his sympathies lay, and if it appeared that he was not positively committed to the party that supported strict compliance with the Treaty of Carlowitz, Horváth could then present his credential to Mavrokordatos with the request that the Turkish government inform him in the very near future as to its readiness to receive a permanent mission from Ferenc II Rákóczi, Prince of Transylvania.

This diplomatic offensive could not move on words alone, and the Prince authorized Horváth to make promises of gifts to the Turkish officials so as to weaken the pro-Austrian faction in Constantinople. If ready cash was required, however, he might have recourse to the French Ambassador, who would certainly provide him with the necessary funds. But he was warned not to lean too heavily on the financial resources and the accustomed good nature of the Marquis; it would be most unwise to alienate such an influential and determined friend of the Rebellion.

As if to head off the approaching Hungarian diplomatic offensive, Johann Michael Thalmann had been more than usually active in these early months of 1705. He had reached the conclusion that Ali Pasha, the Pasha of Temesvár, and Prince Brancoveanu, the Hospodar of Wallachia, were the chief intermediaries between the Turks and the Rebels; through these "two canals" flowed French funds and Turkish military supplies, an important part of the Rebellion's war potential. And so he decided that damming up these 'streams' had first priority, but unless extraordinary measures were taken the usual Austrian protests about this flow of supplies would be ineffective. Thalmann reported to his superiors in the *Hofkriegsrat* that the only solution to the difficulty was to win one or two of the Turkish ministers for the 'Austrian interest' and through these means effect a change of personnel in Temesvár and Bucarest. He had his eye on the Kihaja, the deputy of the recently appointed Grand Vizir Mehmed Pasha. Thalmann had already approached him with the innocent comment that the friendship between the two Empires would be wondrously improved if the Banat and Wallachia had more capable rulers. The Kihaja had expressed a mild degree of interest in such a worthy cause, and he intimated to the Austrian that his assistance would, of course, depend on a large outlay of Imperial funds.

The ministry in Vienna did not show any enthusiasm for his plan, since it felt that any change of officials would probably not improve matters, indeed, it might only make the situation a lot worse. At the end of May, Joseph I, who had succeeded his father at the beginning of the month, addressed an Imperial Rescript to Thalmann in which he declared that he was opposed to any policy of financial subsidies as an instrument of Austrian diplomatic pressure at the Porte, and that he wished Thalmann to confine his activities to the collection of useful information on Turkish plans and to formal representations to the Vizir that assistance to Rákóczi, whether public or secret, must be regarded by Austria as constituting a clear violation of the Treaty of Carlowitz. This rescript's tone detailed perfectly with the strong stance in international affairs that Joseph adopted at the beginning of his reign. The note of unshakable decision, so refreshing in light of previous developments, was evident in this communication. But Joseph did not further the solution of the problem of Austria's representation at the Porte; Thalmann continued in his post. The bright Josephinian promise was so often a facade behind which the veterans of his father's administration carried on business as usual.[33]

Joseph did adhere to a well-established custom in Austro-Turkish relations by sending Christopher Ignatious Baron von Guarient to Constantinople with official notification of his accession. Though this mission was necessarily brief, the presence of a more prestigious personality in the Internunciature could not help but strengthen Allied influence in Turkey. The situation that the Baron found in Constantinople did not differ strikingly from that which had been reported by Thalmann. It was clear enough that the Turks were allowing the French to send arms, money, and technicians through Turkish territory, and the Turks were themselves furnishing Rákóczi with an unspecified amount of assistance. The Imperial Envoy Extraordinary made a very poor impression on Robert Sutton, and Sutton's report on the new arrival is certainly one of his better flights:

> But Monsr Guarient is such a stick of Wood, as I believe never was sent into this Country by any Prince, & I cannot conceive how he came to be pitched upon in this conjuncture. Certainly never did any Minister take so little care of his Masters Interests or live so much to his dishonour. Besides his pusillanimity & weaknesse, wch are become a jest to the Turks, his miserable covetousnesse is a Proverb to all the world. He minds nothing but scraping up a little pelf ... What a Special Spark they have sent to menage their affairs here at this Juncture.[34]

Guarient for some inexplicable reason proved attractive to a number of minor Turkish officials, and he was soon in receipt of a good deal of information about the latest French moves as well as the communications between the Grand Vizir and Rákóczi. One Turkish confidant supplied him with copies of a 'project' which had allegedly been submitted to the Grand Vizir by Mihály Pápay, the leading Hungarian Deputy in Constantinople. The project, Guarient was further informed, had actually been drawn up by the French Ambassador with the assistance of the Venetian Bailo, and then the Hungarian envoy had been allowed to convey it to the Grand Vizir Mehmed Pasha. Though Guarient did not descend to details in reporting on the project, one can assume that it involved Turkish recognition of the Prince as rightful sovereign of Transylvania and an increase in more tangible assistance to the Rebels. Guarient had found that Mehmed Pasha had been greatly improved over the summer of 1706, and he was quick to alert the Grand Vizir to the baselessness of such reports.[35]

Perhaps it was the same confidant who passed on a particularly choice bit of information which only served to support Austrian claims that the Rebels were now in desperate straits. At the end of September, 1706, a most imposing embassy arrived from Hungary. It had carried with it, according to Guarient's informant, a letter from the Prince to Ferriol that had been full of gloom about the immediate future of the

Rebellion. For the moment at least, the Hungarians were in reasonably good spirits. The siege of Esztergom was proceeding nicely, and the territory in the immediate vicinity of the primatial city had fallen quickly enough into the control of Rebellion. But extensive preparations by the Austrians boded ill in the long run. Once the Emperor's two armies were ready for the next campaign, the Rebels would be forced to yield large sections of the country to these well-trained regulars. It was the Prince's intention, if Divine Providence continued to look with such favor on Imperial arms, to exchange the role of *dux* for that of guest at the Court of Versailles. The moment he was convinced that further organized resistance was pointless, he and Des Alleurs would proceed incognito to Pera, and continue their journey to France with the aid of Ferriol.[36]

A highly confidential report of a meeting which the Hungarian Embassy had had with the Grand Vizir also reached Guarient. The Hungarians had presented a letter of credence in the name of Prince Rákóczi and the Hungarian magnates, and had assured Mehmed Pasha that the Estates of Hungary and Transylvania were prepared to return to the *status quo* which had prevailed before 1683. This would be a relatively easy matter to arrange if the Porte would provide sufficient auxiliary forces to capture the remaining German strongholds in Hungary. Four hundred thousand dollars was set as the payment for the Turkish troops, and the Deputies promised to leave unimpeachable security for the payment on a specified date. The French Ambassador made an additional offer of two hundred thousand dollars in the event that the Turks would actually declare war on the Emperor. But the Sultan reiterated his wish to maintain peace, while at the same time he encouraged the Grand Vizir and the Mufti to confer privately on these offers. The two Turkish leaders had a long conference on October 21, and it was then decided to wait for the outcome of the next campaign in Hungary before making any decisions to help the Hungarians.[37]

In the absence of Rákóczi's letter and of dependable eyewitness reports of the audience granted to the Hungarian Deputies by the Grand Vizir, it is difficult to say with any hope of certainty just how much truth there was in the reports that reached Guarient. Although they doubtless exaggerated the extent of the Prince's pessimism and the readiness of both the Hungarians and Transylvanians to place themselves under the suzerainty of the Sultan, they tie in with Rákóczi's known preoccupation at the time to find a solution to his problems in Eastern, rather than Western, Europe. This 'eastern orientation' was a logical consequence of the shift in the Rebellion's sphere of interest from Upper Hungary and Transdanubia to the traditionally strong Rákóczi supporters -- the *comitats* along Transylvania's western and northern boundaries. The danger for Austria in this new development was that a desperate Rákóczi might unleash the whirlwind of a Turkish invasion on the Danubian lands. But it was more likely that he would seek safety in flight, for his Christian instincts which naturally rebelled at the thought of another Turkish occupation might outweigh his commitment to the Rebellion.

The long-awaited campaign was largely confined to Transylvania. At long last, the Prince appeared to claim his throne, and his immediate success in winning over large areas of the country had an immediate effect on the Turks. Messengers travelled back and forth, and Rákóczi was now attended by a Turk who acted as a messenger and as an interpreter in his communications with the Porte. The Turks, when they realized that he had supported his claim to the princely throne by the present campaign, were once again in a quandary. The majority of the ministers now favored war, but the Nischandji (the Chancellor of the Empire), Bekir Pasha, who had for some time been in the pay of the Austrians, convinced them to postpone their decision yet another time.[38]

The Nischandji's most effective delaying action is evidence that Thalmann had finally overcome the Emperor's scruples about giving presents to Turkish officials. Indeed, he had created a complicated system of information-gathering and bribery. An excellent indication of its inner workings is to be found in an itemized report that he sent to Vienna at the end of July, 1707, on the manner in which the funds that he had received from Vienna had been spent.[39] He had started the year with a letter of credit for six thousand thallers, and by means of a complicated series of advances from Dutch and English bankers and from Sir Robert Sutton he had been enabled to secure the sum in currency. Since Sutton had been so cooperative in these arrangements, it was only natural that he should have some say in determining the manner in which the funds were allocated.

Thalmann's sources of information were a very mixed bag. He customarily received reports *in secretis* from a servant in the household of the Grand Vizir, from a German servant of a Chihaja, who desired eventually to return to his native land, and from a German woman in the Harem who collected odd bits of political gossip that she could glean from the conversations of the Turkish officials and their women. These sources received a monthly pension of then thallers or more, and though they occasionally furnished him with important tips, the cost of maintaining these contacts was but a small part of his total expenditures.

Larger sums were involved in presenting gifts to pliable Turkish officials. Two agas in the suite of the Grand Vizir served as go-betweens, and they also were expected to testify to the wisdom of keeping the peace when official conversations turned to the possibility of war in Hungary. But Sutton rightly believed that it was essential for the Austrian to secure the permanent services of one of the key ministers, particularly since the early months of 1707 had witnessed a repetition of the war scare of 1704. Acting on Sutton's advice, Thalmann paid a secret visit to the Nischandji, who possessed excellent qualifications for the job -- he had served some years before as the Reis-Effendi and was usually summoned to participate in any high-level discussions of foreign policy. Bekir Pasha had the additional merit in Thalmann's eyes of being reputed to be the most influential advisor of the Grand Vizir. The Nischandji displayed a most heart-warming interest in the preservation of friendly relations between their two countries, and shortly after this meeting his pacific sentiments were rewarded with a present of two bags of gold pieces worth one thousand thallers.

Now that contact had been made, both sides to the implicit agreement were well aware of just how they must proceed. The

Nischandji performed valuable service in setting obstacles in the way of the Hungarian Deputies, and on one occasion he demonstrated such clear talent and interest in this work that he received another gift of two bags of gold. It had appeared for a time that the Grand Vizir might accede to the latest request for official Turkish recognition of Ferenc Rákóczi as Prince of Transylvania. The immediate consequences of such a move on the part of the Turks were difficult to predict, but Sutton and Thalmann obviously felt that the Emperor could not possibly overlook such an outright violation of the Treaty of Carlowitz. In an effort to bolster the Nischandji's position with as much support as possible within the Sultan's entourage, Sutton told Thalmann that it might be feasible to enlist the services of the Reis-Effendi as well. The Austrian Resident immediately acted upon this advice, and in the course of an official conversation with the Reis-Effendi, he let the information slip out that a favorable view of the Austrian position at this critical moment would be well rewarded. Another thousand thallers did in fact go to him for his assistance in warding off the recognition of Rákóczi.

All through the summer of 1707, Thalmann grew increasingly exercised about the prospect of Turkish intervention in Hungary. By autumn he was noting the powerful effect that the reports of the declaration of an interregnum in that Kingdom had had on the Turks. This new development, combined with the evidence of the loyal support for the Prince by the Estates of Transylvania, had encouraged the Grand Vizir to undertake another study of the whole problem. Thalmann was particularly fearful lest this survey lead to the conclusion that the present moment was the best opportunity the Turks had in years to make their power felt in Central Europe. Peace seemed to be suspended by a single thread, and Thalmann renewed his warnings to the *Hofkriegsrat* that it might expect to see the full force of the Turkish army thrown into the Hungarian war at the beginning of 1708. The Grand Vizir reportedly favored such a move, but his mind was still subject to change if large presents were forthcoming from the Austrians.[40]

For once the *Hofkriegsrat* took Thalmann's warnings seriously -- his perennial sense of urgency had at last communicated itself to the generals' deliberations. In the formal report, which they submitted to the Emperor on November 17, 1707, the seriousness of the threat of war was made clear. The report urged that every possible step be taken immediately to crush the Hungarian Rebellion; delay would only increase the chances of Turkish intervention. This view had been repeated with such agonized insistence in the notes of the Anglo-Dutch Mediators and in the reports of the Austrian Resident in Constantinople, and now at last it had found its way into the thinking of the *Hofkriegsrat.* The Emperor replied with his accustomed show of decision: in the event of war with the Turks he would be forced to come to terms immediately with France. In the meantime, additional funds should be dispatched to Thalmann and more reserves committed in the campaign in Hungary. His Imperial Majesty concluded with the pious hope that the Porte would think better of the whole affair, though his directives made it abundantly clear that Joseph was fully alive at last to the danger of war.[41]

It may seem to be a precarious bit of reasoning indeed to conclude from his Imperial Resolution that there had been a pronounced change in direction of Habsburg policy. But the strain of the long war on two fronts and the realization that a mood of compromise was growing in Western Europe may have influenced the Emperor to give priority to problems closer to home. The balance between the *Erzhaus'* involvement in Western and Eastern Europe appeared momentarily to be in favor of the East. Whether he based this conclusion simply on what he felt to be the realities of power politics or on a burgeoning sense of Austrian mission in Eastern Europe, the statement that it would be necessary to make peace with France in order to save his Hungarian and Transylvanian possessions was a memorable one.

Joseph's hope for the continuation of peace was matched by yet another decision of the Sultan to refrain from attacking the Austrians. Thalmann was of the opinion that this latest happy inspiration of Ahmed was the result of a clever ruse that he had played on the Sultan which involved the well-known tendency of the Turks to be superstitious. He had hit on the idea of combining fact and prophetic fiction into a piece of logic that would force the Sultan to conclude that peace was absolutely necessary. Through the medium of one of the Sultan's familiars, he had called the Sultan's attention to the passage in the Koran which prophesied the conquest of Constantinople by the Turks. In the very same passage, there was a statement that one day a monarch with blonde hair (the 'beniasfer') would someday conquer the Turkish dominions and destroy the Ottoman Empire. Joseph I was notoriously blonde, and in case the Sultan was insufficiently aware of this fact, Thalmann had taken the precaution of presenting a portrait of the Emperor to the Sultan. The minor premise of his syllogism was thus proven beyond the shadow of a doubt, and apparently the significance of all this had not escaped Ahmed. For in the meeting which was to settle the question of war or peace, Ahmed spoke in very brotherly terms about Joseph.

> We are -- the two of us -- young Emperors, and it is our greatest wish to continue our present state of friendly relations. You (addressing the Grand Vizir) are a young Vizir, and it is most unlikely that you could carry out any great project (i.e. war) that would redound to my benefit.[42]

There was, of course, a less far-fetched explanation for the success which Thalmann had scored in averting the catastrophe. To the more pragmatic minds of the English and the Dutch the war threat had seemed vastly exaggerated. Coyler was convinced that Thalmann was to blame for creating so much unnecessary stir about the menacing attitude of the Turks, while Sutton with an air of closing the whole incident informed Phillip Meadows, then the British Resident at Vienna, that there was no longer any need to fear that the Turks would engage in hostilities with the Emperor or the Venetian Republic. Both these diplomats regarded the days of the Hungarian Rebellion as numbered, and as long as the process of its decline continued uninterrupted there was no valid cause to speculate on sudden Turkish invasions of Transylvania and Hungary. If any threat of war could be said to exist, it came from quite a different direction. The Turks were now apprehensive that Charles XII and the Tsar would reach a compromise, and this would free Russia's hand for action against Turkey. But apart from this none too likely possibility, the diplomatic horizon was most serene. Sutton and Coyler evidently believed, and in this way they were joined by such a perceptive observer of international politics as Daniele Dolfin, Venice's Ambassador in Vienna, that the period of real stress and strain in Austro-Turkish relations had ended. Thalmann was naturally reluctant to accept such a view, and it was only in the closing days of 1708, that he finally got around to reporting that "the Turks will not undertake anything of a hostile nature against Hungary in the foreseeable future."[43]

This was the long overdue *finis* to the threat of Turkish intervention. For at least four years it had excited extraordinary interest and concern in a number of European capitals and in the migratory headquarters of Prince Rákóczi. We have demonstrated on the basis of the available sources that it was only at the very beginning of this period that there was a serious chance of war breaking out. Few people realized at the time how close the Turks had been to intervention and how fateful this would have proved for the course of the War of Spanish Succession. Opportunities of this kind are infrequent, and the Turks may have rued the day they let themselves be swayed by the eloquence of a certain Pasha.

The remainder of the chapter had consisted largely of unconvincing protestations of good faith and compliance with the Treaty of Carlowitz from the Turkish side and a constant flow of protests about secret aid to the Rebels from the Austrian side. Roughly from 1708 to the end of the Rebellion, relations between the Hungarians and the Turks were more a matter of stage business than anything else. Hungarian Deputies continued to wait upon Grand Vizirs; Rákóczi and his advisers produced improbable projects, and all the substance of political reality had disappeared from such contacts and plans.

Constantinople could lay claim to being the scene of one of the most bitterly contested struggles produced in the diplomatic sphere by the Hungarian Rebellion. Both the Austrians and the Rebels had shown a profound lack of interest in the reactions of the Turks throughout the period of the Rebellion's early successes. Only after Höchstädt did

Austria come to realize that the preservation of Turkish neutrality in its war with the Hungarians was necessary if it was to maintain its territorial integrity. Rákóczi had also tended to underestimate the importance of friendship with the Sultan, and this was as true in the last convulsive moments of the Rebellion as it was in the beginning. It was a difficult, perhaps impossible decision for a man of his delicate fiber to face, since any close collaboration with the Turks might prove an entering wedge for their reappearance in Hungary, and he eventually compromised to the extent of accepting assistance from them in secret. This deep distaste for the Turks was most likely a holdover from his youth; the painful experience of his stepfather, the 'dog of the Padishah', were too vivid in his mind to be overlooked. But this did not prevent him from using the threat of an alliance with the Turks and consequent Turkish intervention as his final trump in the diplomatic game -- Europe had to understand that if it came to the worst, he would be literally forced to unleash the Turkish and Tatar hordes on Christendom.

We now know that he never had the possibility of making good his threat. When the Rebellion entered upon its last and most critical period in 1708, the Turks were in no mood to risk the gains they had made in the years of peace on such a quixotic venture. The time was long past for great political profit on a small military investment; the Hungarian Rebellion was simply not a good risk. Moreover, when Peter the Great's victory at Pultava made him the only available candidate for the role of *deux ex machina* as far as the Rebellion was concerned, the Turks began to lose the little enthusiasm they had once possessed for Rákóczi. The role of the peaceable Ahmed III should not be underestimated. Even at the very height of the crisis, he had managed to oppose any overt action in favor of the Hungarians. For the rest, it suited him to be courted by the leading powers of Europe at the same time that his Empire slowly made its convalescence from the disastrous war with the Holy League. He remembered that he had come to the throne as the result of an insurrection (which he could not fail to reprehend), and it was likely that a painful experience of that kind had made him more than usually sympathetic to the case for law and order that was typified by the young 'beniasfer' in Vienna.

This analysis of the evolution of the diplomatic relations of the Turks and the Emperor, on the one hand, and the Rebels on the other, reduces the importance of the work of Johann Thalmann and his numerous Hungarian counterparts. Their energies were consumed in an atmosphere that could not help be anti-climactic. Thalmann's efforts could not hide the fact that the Emperor was represented in Constantinople by a well-trained interpreter (in this most difficult profession Thalmann must be accounted a great pioneer) and not by a diplomat of the rank and stature of Sir Robert Sutton or Count Coyler. And it was this show of 'German Carelessness' that lent currency to Sutton's suspicion that the Austrians felt that it was more important to the Maritime Powers that there be peace between the two Empires than it was to the Austrians themselves.

Thalmann found it wellnigh impossible to operate as an independent factor in the 'united front' against France and Hungary, and much of the time he was content to follow Sutton's lead. On the few occasions that he struck out on his own path, he found that his superiors had little enthusiasm for his show of independence. The very money he used to maintain his system of spies and bribes usually was borrowed from English and Dutch bankers. But the years he spent in Turkey were not entirely unproductive, for he was able to fashion the foundation of permanent and continuous Austrian diplomatic representation at the Sublime Porte and thus initiate a tradition that would soon free itself of the tutelage of the Maritime Powers. In this way, he was luckier than the Horváths, the Henders, and Pápays. They had had the misfortune to serve their Prince when this demanded complete subservience to the wishes of the psychotic Marquis de Ferriol, and when their services were no longer required by Rákóczi and France, they had disappeared without leaving a trace in the diplomatic colony in Pera.

Notes to Chapter 1

The course of Austro-Turkish relations during the time of the Rákóczi Rebellion has not, to my knowledge, been studied before. Confirmation of this point comes from T. Esze, "A Rákóczi-szabadságharc", *Magyar törtenexa Kongresszus: 1953 Junius 6-13* (Magyar Történelmi Tarsulat: Budapest, 1954), 77, who points out that the whole range of the Rebellion's relations with the Turks has received no attention. Hammer-Purgstall makes reference on occasion to Turkey's relations with the Austirans and the Hungarians, but his attention naturally focuses on Cahrles XII at Bender and the Turco-Russion War of 1711. The present chapter cannot hope to tell the whole story (the role of France which was of tgreat improtance will remain partially obscure until a study is made of the dispatches of de Ferriol), but it may well serve as an introduction to a little-known area of Turkish and European diplomatic contacts and as a continuation in part of the developments treated in Part One.

The chapter is based on three collections of unpublished sources. First of all, the letters of Lord Paget and, when he returned to England, of Sir Robert Sutton, his successor. They are preserved in London's Public Records Office under *State Papers Foreign, Turkey.* There is, unfortunately, a great gap in Sutton's dispatches fron 1705 to 1710. An occasional letter of his to George Stepney and the latter's successors in Vienna -- they are printed in *Simonyi,* III, passim -- gives some indiaction of his view of the diplomatic situation in Turkey for those years. I have quoted liberally from this collection; the letters contain a good deal of information that is presented in a most trenchant and lively style. For a brief and informative discussion of Sutton's career and his views on Turkish affairs, see A. Kurat, *The Despatches of Sir Robert Sutton, Abassador in Constantinople (1710-1714),* Camden Society, Third Series (LXXVIII), 1953, 6-10.

Secondly, I have referred to the *Turcica, Berichte und Weisungen (Haus-, Hof- und Staatsarchiv,* Vienna) for the years 1702-1711. Largely the reports of Johann Michael Thalmann, the Imperial Secretary and later Resident in Constantinople, the dispathches of Baron Christopher Guarient which relate to his special mission to the Porte in 1706, also offer many important sidelights on Austro-Turkish relation. Excerpts fron this collection have been pulished in Hurmuzaki, *Documente,* VI, but to avoid any of the usual discrepancies I have cited only the *Turcica.*

Occasional reference has also been made to the dispatches of Daniele Dolfin III, the Venetian Ambassador to the Emperor. He was a well-informed observer in the best tradition of Venetian diplomacy, and in addition he occasionally reports on commmunications he has received from the Bailo in Pera-- material which I have not been able to consult. Dolfin's dispatches are preserved in copies in the *Haus, Hof- und Staatsarchiv's* collection of *Dispacci degli Ambasciatori Veneti in Germania*, Bände, 186-189.

(In citing the letters of Paget and Sutton, I have used the form S. P. F., as a standard abbreviation. The *Turcica* items are listed simply according to date.)

[1]"Ce que j'ai dit de la manière de s'habiller de M. de Ferriol et des affaires qu'il avait eues, fait voir que son esprit n'étiot pas dans une assiette entièrement tranquille.", Marquis de Bonnac, *Mémoire historique sur l'Ambassade de France á Constantinople*, ed. Charles Schéfer (Paris, 1894), 57. The sdiscussion of Ferriol is baded on the section devoted by Bonnac to the "Abassade de M. de Ferriol", 48-60.

[2]Robert Sutton to the Earl of Nottingham, Per, November 18, 1703, in *Simonyi,* I, 52-53.

[3]Lord Paget to James Vernon, Pera, December 6, 1700 0. S., *S. P. F.*, 97 #21, 51.

[4]Paget to Mr. Blathwayt, Per, July 20 0. S., S. P. F., 97, #21, 54; "The Solemn Embassies are over; the Lymits are so adiusted, as not to want any more the help of out Offices.", Paget to Vernon (?), Pera, August 27, 1699, *S. P. F.*, 97, ä21, 51.

[5]*British Diplomatic Representatives*, 151; Paget to James Vernon, Adrianople, June 3, 1699, *S. P. F.*, 97, #21, 51.

[6]The same letter of August 27, 1699, *S. P. F.*, 97, #21, 64; Paget to James Vernon, Pera, August 27, 1699, *S. P. F.*, 97, #21, 72.

[7]Robert Sutton to Lord Manchester, Pera, March 10, 1701 O. S., *S. P. F.*, 97, #21, 77-80.

[8]Hammer-Purgstall, *op. cit.*, VII, 28. The description of Turkish internal politics is based on Hammer's same volume, especially 71-90.

[9]Sutton to Lord Manchester, Augus 7, 1702 O. S., *S. P. F.*, 97, #21, 87.

[10]Sutton to Manchester, Pera, November 30, 1702 O. S., *S. P. F.*, 97, #21, 96.

[11]"...non farci dubitare dells realtá della politica ambigua praticata in questo temp da Venezia a Constatinopoli, tanto più che vediamo il nostro Dolfin temere che i torbidi di Ungheria possano attirare le mosse dei Turchi e che una volta scoppiata la guerra tr l'Imperatore ed il Sultano potesse esservi a tratta anche la Serenissima, giachè "accesso il fuoco nella casa del vicino bisogna temerlo nella propria"; M. Giudici, *I Dispacci di Germania dell' Ambasciatore Veneto Daniel Dolfin 3^d* (Venezia, 1907), 119.

[12]Lord Paget to the Earl of Nottingham, Vienna, rev'd. Whithall January 4, 1702 O. S., *S. P. F.*, 97, #21, 65.

[13]Robert Sutton to Lord Manchester, 370era, April 23, 1702 O. S., *S. P. F.*, 97, #21, 96.

[14]Dr. Johann Michael von Thalmann arriced in Turkey in 1703 as Secretary. He became Resident on January 30, 1704 and Internucio only on April 15, 1712. These dates can only be regarded as approximations, though they appear in the *Repertorium der diplomatshcen Vertreter aller Länder seit dem Westfälischen Frieden*, I (1648-1715), ed. Bittner u. Gross (Berlin, 1936), 172.

[15]T. K. Krylova, "Russko-turetskie otnosheniya vo vremya sevrnoi voini", *Istoricheskie zapiski*, 10 (1941), 253ff.

[16]"...I have not any body in the Nations service, who is capable to procure me any good intelligence, or qualified to manage any affair for me at the Port in my own absence... as well as the other great defect of mony or present, the afficacy whereof is well known in this Country, where all people are wonderfully affected with them.", Sutton to Nottingham, Pera, April 2, 1703, O.S., *S. P. F.*, 97, #21, 130-131.

[17]Sutton constantly tended to underrate the danger inherent in Turkish popular disturbances; six months before the Revolution he declared that "an Insurrection might be well apprehended, if the Court was not out of their reach.", Sutton to Nottingham, Pera, January 28, 1702 O.S., S. P. F., 97, #21, 121, and he was content to provide his superiors with "a naked relation of hte matter of Fact" when the insurrection acutally occured,; Sutton to Nottingham, Pera, Augus 20, 1703, *S. P. F.*, 97, #21, 135.

[18]"As far as I can understand the genus and maximes of these people *their designe is* to make *good Frontier* against *Muscovy* and then, abandon *the Czar*

the the *revenge of the Swede and being by those means secure from* so *power-full an Enemy make use of thier opportunities elsewhere.* I hope *thier first enterprise is not against the Emperor* but *'tis to be feared they will underhand encourage the Rebells in Hungary* (cipher underlined), Sutton to Nottingham, Pera, August 20, 1703 O. S., *S. P. F.*, 97, #21, 138.

[19]"'Tis very much to be desired that this Rebellion may be wholly suppressed this winter, that the temptation may not be any longer before these people.", Sutton to Nottingham, Pera, October 18, 1703 P. S., *S. P. F.*, 97, #21, 145.

[20]"Their danger is much greater than when the Turks last besieged Vienna, they had then one side open and the whole Empire to their friends; and you may please to remember it was their Neighbours and not their own efforts which saved them from their ruine; and it can be much less expected they should do wonders at present...Another great misery is the dispirited ness of several of these Ministers...", Charles Whitworth to Charles Hedges, Vienna, January 16, 1704, *Simonyi*, I, 108-109.

[21]"...allein ich könnte es bei Gott nicht verantworten, wenn es nicht thäte; denn die Sachen sehe und erkenne ich in einem solche betrüben Stand, als sie vielleicht noch niemals gewesen, solang Dero glorwürdiges Erzhaus regiert.", Eugen of Savoy to the Emperor, *Feldzüge*, I, 6, *Militärische Correspondenz* (Pressburg, January 12, 1704), 18. Cf. also his letter to the King of the Romans of January 14, 1704, *ibid,* 24.

[22]Thalmann reported on the fall of Ali Pasha: "...das gedachter Aly Bassa bey gegewertigen Hungarischen troublen beide reich in eine missverständnuss zu verwickhln gesuecht, welches weill es der auf richtign intension dess grossvesiers zuwider, have er ihn von der gränz avociren und an seiner stadt den erwehnten Hassen Pasha, als welcher vorhero alldorten mit denen Teutschen in gueter verständnuss gelbet nach Belgrad beordern wollen.", Thalmann to the *Hofkriegsrat,* December 2, 1703.

[23]It is impossible to be exact in dating this meeting of the Divan; on the basis of the available evidence, January, 1704 would seem most likely. Guarient submitted a "Konferenzprotokoll" of a meeting he had with the Pasha of Sophia, who also had the title of "Rubbe Veziri", which I take to be rightly *Kubbe veziri*, on January 4, 1707. (The statement of the Pasha begins, "Sihe, alss dem Ragoczy vor 3 jahren...") On the role of the Kubbe vizir, "The viziers with the grand vizier...were called the Kubbe wezirleri "viziers of the dome" because

they sat with the grand vizier, whose name they shared but not his power, under the same dome in the Diwan...When they appeared thogether before the Sultan, only the grand vizier could speak of offical business. The other viziers stood silent beside him with hands crossed.", "Wazir" *Encyclopedia of Islam* (Leyden, 1927), vol. 4, part 2, 1135-1136. This protocol runs from fol 53v. to 54v., *Turcica,* January 24, 1707.

[24]Hassan Pasha's question: "...ob bey diser rebellion und wie es das ansehen hat, ganz Hungarn von dem Teutschen kayser abzufallen und hingegen den Ragozi vor ihren könig zu erklären gednckhet, di portten noch länger zusehen und mit dero macht zurcukhalten oder aber gegen Hungarn anruckhen solte?", *ibid.,* 53v.

[25]Sir Robert Sutton to Vienna Legation, Pera, February 20, 1703 O. S., *Simonyi,* I, 147.

[26]Sutton to Nottingham, Pera, November 2, 1703 O. S., S. P. F., 97, #21, 161.

[27]In discussing the mission of Des Alleurs, I have relied heavily on the article of Sándor Márki, "Desalleurs altábornagy Rékóczinál", *Hadtörtenelmi Közlemények* (1917), 1-12. For the characterization of the man by Rákóczi, see Memoires, 70. A comparable description is to be found in the *Memoires de Saint-Simon* (Paris, 1911), IV, 283-284.

[28]"The Port hath not only granted passage to Monsr Desalleurs and his attendance, but the Passha of Temeswar gave him a convoy of 300 Horse, which conducted him to the Confines of Transylvania, where he was delivered into the hands of an Hung[n] officer, that came to receive him on the part of Pr. Ragoczi, in which they have acted directly contrary to the Vizir Azem's Promises and Oaths. By this insistance Your Honour will observe the Turks begin opely to countenance the Hung[n] Malcontents, to which they are induced by French *Mony,* as well as their own inclination.", Sutton to Sir Charles Hedges, Pera, March 18, 1705, *S. P. F.,* 97, #21, 190.

[29]The Pasha's report on this interrogation is also contained in Baron Guarient's *Konferenzprotokolle* for January 24, 1707, in the *Turcica,* 1707, fol. 55-56.

[30]Des Alleurs' answer, according to Guarient's information, "Was mein könig jezt und in dass khönfftige haven will, deme wird der Ragoczi gewislichen nihmall entgegen sein khönnen und glaube, er wurde sich mit einen ehrentitel (den ihme die portten vergönte) und besizung des fürstenthumbs Sibenbürgan gar wohl befridigen, obschon hernach ganz Hungarn in die Türchkhische

underthänigkheit fallen solte. Welches jedoch allein für mich und nicth auf befelch meines, königs oder würcklichen einwiligung des Ragoczi sage, noch weniger dises leztere schrifftlich von mire geben khan.", *ibid.*, fol. 56.

[31]These *Reflexions* exist in a copy the George Stepney collection (the basis of Ernö Simonyi's publication), S. P. F., 105, #62-81; this particular document is under #78, 102ff.

[32]"Instructio pro Egregio Francisco Horváth , secreto ablegato Nostro ad Fulgidam Portam", no date, Kalman Thaly, *Archivum Rákózianum, I osztály: Had- és Belügy.*, I, 376-377. I have been unable to discover anything further about Horváth's mission, though it is fairly obvious that the Turks did not extend official recognition to Rákóczi, however willing they may have been to treat with him in an unofficial way.

[33]Thalmann had observed, "Zu diesen aber wurde allein ein blosse remonstration keineswegs gnung sein, sondern wurde mit gewisser bey ein und andern minister mit discretion angewendeten geld zum effect gebracht werden.", Thalmann to the *Hofkriegsrat*, Constantinople, January 27, 1705; for the Emperor's statement of policy, *Turcica*, May 21, 1705.

[34]Sir Robert Sutton to George Stepney, Pera, September 26, 1706, *Simonyi*, 252-253.

[35]Relation of Baron Guarient to the Emperor, Constantinople, *Turcica*, September 3, 1706.

[36]"...darbey vertraute mir gedachte person in gleichmässig höchster gehaimb ein originalschrieben, in welchem der Ragoczi untern 1. ten septembris dem Französischen ambassadeur zugeschrieben....", Relation of Baron Guarient to the Emperor, *Turcica*, October 24, 1706.

[37]Thalmann to the *Hofkriegsrat*, Constantinople, *ibid.*, October 25, 1706.

[38]Thalmann to the *Hofkriegsrat*, Constantinople, *ibid.*, May 16, 1707.

[39]"Beylage, worinnen gestzet wirdt, waszgestalten auff guethbefindten des. Engl. Herrn Pottschafters von denen Krafft Creditsbrieff zu anfang diese 1707-ten Jahrs übermachten 6000 Thaller zu Ihro. Kays. Mays. diensten 4000 Thaller angewendet worden.", Thalmann to *Hofkriegsrat*, July 30, 1707, published in

Hurmuzaki, *Documente,* VI, 61-63.

[40]"Die hier anwesende Ragocz. comissarien Henter, Hirod Ferenz und Papai richten alle ihre sollicitation ein auff arth und weise, die ihnen der Französische bottschaffter vorschreibet, welche meistens in ungegründeten vorstellungen der grossen so in Hungarn als Sibenbürgen ihrem vorgeben nach von zein zu zeit erhaltenen vortheillen bestehen, absonderlich haven sie uber die in der rebelliondieta zu Onoth gefaste resolutionen, worinnen die Hungarischen ständte das interregnum declariret und die ihro. kays. may. alss ihrem rachtmässigem könig schuldige obedienz völlig verworffen haben sollen...und davon die ihnen zugeschickte weithleuffige afta dem grossvezier unlengst eingehändiget, wecher sie übersezen lassen und in genaue consideration gezogen hatt.", Thalmann to the *Hofkriegarat,* Constantinople, *Turcica,* October 13, 1707.

[41]The report of the *Hofkriegsrat* and the "Resolutio Caesarea" are in the *Turcica,* November 14 and 19, 1707.

[42]Thalmann reported to the *Hofkriegsrat* on the success of hi "Beniasfer" ruse, and he learned through the Kislar Aga what th eSultan had remarked: "Wir seindt zwey junge kayser, wir wollen die freundschafft noch längermiteinander unterhalten und du bist auch in junger vezier, welcher grosse sachen zu unserem vorheill nit wurdte ausführen khönnen...". *Turcica,* January 19, 1708.

[43]Dolfin included extracts of Sutton's letter to Meadows of January 4, 1708, and of Colyer's letter to Bruynincx, January 19, 1708. The conclusion -- "Doppa la mia ultima letters null é successo, che possi dar ombra d'una guerra contro l'Imperatore o contro la Republica di Venezia.", Daniele Dolfin to the Senate, Vienna, February 11, 1708, *Dispacci di Germania,* 1707-1708, #515.

Thalmann reached the same conclusion in his report to the *Hofkriegsrat, Turcica,* Constantinople December 23, 1708.

Chapter 2

Rákóczi and the Mediators

"Thô this is in some sense a Domestick Affair, yet ye present situation of affairs makes it of Universal concern;"

- Anne R.

"Les victoires de Catalogne sont belles et bonnes, et les Te Deum aussy, si les Portugais etoient seulement meilleurs, si la paix d'Hongrie se pouvoit faires, et si notre bon allié l'Emper^r avec tout son Empire n'etoit pas si foible."

- Hamel Bruynincx

    The War of the Spanish Succession discovered the Anglo-Dutch Mediation busily engaged in closing out its Carlowitz accounts -- the few remaining items of business of the great peace settlement of January 26, 1699. The golden afterglow of the Mediation's success continued in the Pera atmosphere (it found some reflection, of course, in the English and Dutch missions at Vienna), and the resumption of hostilities in the West, while it must have given Paget and Coyler pause, did not for the moment indicate that there would be an immediate call for their mediatory services. The Grand Alliance, for one thing, was notoriously slow in re-establishing itself, and the Turks displayed no immediate intention to intervene in Western Europe's quarrel over the fate of the Spanish Empire. But if the occasion should arise in which they would be needed, the Mediators were sure to respond with all of their accustomed enthusiasm and their blithe disregard of the enormous difficulties involved in halting a conflict once it had reached the stage of open warfare.

The Mediators guild consisted of a small, select group of English and Dutch diplomats. Lord Paget and Count Coyler were its acknowledged leaders, but virtually all of the seasoned diplomats of the Maritime Powers in Eastern Europe had taken part in these negotiations. Jakob Hop and Conraad von Heemskerck had been prominent at one time or another, and Lord Lexington qualified for membership by reason of his brief stint in Vienna. The younger generation of diplomats had won its spurs in the prolonged work of Mediation. George Stepney had shown a most precocious interest in bringing about a peace between the Emperor and the Sultan; Robert Sutton had made his mark by his splendid work as the contact between Whitehall and Lord Paget during the Peace Congress, and Jakob Jan Hamel Bruynincx had spent his diplomatic apprenticeship assisting or substituting for Hop and Van Heemskerck and now that he had been appointed the Resident Minister at Vienna he might on occasion be expected to give evidence of the liberal education he had received in "meddling in the business of other people."

The years of negotiation leading to Carlowitz had been a 'School for Mediators,' and this younger generation had proved to be apt and devoted pupils. The intellectual character of the training they had received could not be described with any hope of accuracy, but they had been subjected to vast amounts of practical training. And they had come in time to regard this part of their diplomatic work as an enormously difficult and thankless task that only infrequently brought rewards of diplomatic prestige and professional advancement. Disposed to complain about the sheer physical strain imposed by the role of the intermediary, they presumably recalled the example of Paget and Coyler in discovering a virtual bonanza at Carlowitz.

Paradoxically enough, it was George Stepney, the man who had had the briefest training in this highly-specialized form of diplomatic practice, who became the Mediator par excellence of the first decade of the eighteenth century. In the English 'line of succession' he was a worthy successor to Paget, and he, in turn, prepared the way for Sir Robert Sutton's solid contributions to peace in Eastern Europe in the following decade. Coyler had the distinction of having lived through the whole course of the Anglo-Dutch Mediation from its primitive beginnings in the anxious period before the Siege of Vienna to the conclusion of its efforts with the signing of the Treaty o Passarowitz in 1718. But mere longevity and patient application were not enough; the English brought more wit and dash to the work, and just as Paget occupied the center of the stage at Carlowitz, so Stepney clearly overshadowed his Dutch colleague Hamel Bruynincx in the course of the negotiations between the Emperor and the Hungarian Malcontents.

George Stepney could lay claim to eminence in a number of fields. Passionately devoted to the craft of poetry in his spare time (he was to find his last resting place in Westminster Abbey's Poets' Corner), he had proved himself to be a first-rate diplomat during the business hours. His years in the English diplomatic service had been largely spent at a varied array of German Courts, and when he was transferred to Vienna in 1701, it was understood that he had reached the pinnacle of his career. His previous experiences had furnished him with the reputation of a sound and well-informed observer of German affairs, and he was already acquainted with the Austrian Court, having served as Secretary there nearly ten years before. As an almost perfect specimen of an English diplomat of the William III model, he possessed an immense capacity for hard work, a talent for realistic appraisal of men and events, and an extreme loyalty to his sovereign. Few English kings or queens would have the good fortune to be represented at the Hofburg by Stepney's equal in intellectual distinction and attractiveness as a personality (Lord Paget was the only serious contender in this period), and the close and fruitful contact he had maintained with Austrian diplomatic enterprise in the German byways inspired hope that he would be well-received by Austrian official circles.

But the very gifts of intelligence and emotion with which he was endowed would constitute unmovable obstacles to the success of his stay in Vienna, and his sojourn there, though it would prove to be the most noteworthy period of his career, could hardly be called happy or successful. He left Vienna in 1706 a sick and embittered man, convinced that he was pursued by the unwearying enmity of the Austrian ministers and the "immortal hatred" of the Society of Jesus. The reasons for his failure derive partially from his independence of mind and his Whig principles, though the breakdown of the Mediation had much to do with this depressing finale as well.

Stepney's amazing facility of expression, combined as it was with a high sense of responsibility, produced an immense collection of official dispatches and private letters in the course of his years in Vienna, and this full-scale running commentary on a wide range of developments has happily survived in great part. Even the most casual reading of a Stepney dispatch produces a quickening of interest that the copybook exercises of his colleagues would fail to do. His was a world far richer in content and far more profound in its bent than they could lay claim to; its colors infinitely sharper and its shadows more extreme, yet he manages to convey the very substance of the life about him, often with an aphoristic compression. Written usually in great haste and not infrequently with great agitation and addressed to superiors who customarily failed to respond as the occasion demanded, these letters form an integral part of George Stepney's literary achievement. Any student of diplomatic history would be most fortunate to have as his guide through the perplexing maze of negotiations someone with half the candor and the commitment of this man.

The anonymous perversity of historical accidents had brought to the Court of Vienna at one of the darkest periods in its existence. And though the Hofburg could not expect to find a more literate observer of its activities, his pronounced anti-Austrian bias -- and it had mammoth proportions -- required that he etch out the literary representation of its mixture of arrogance and impotence that no envoy of Louis XIV could hope to improve. When he discovered weakness and carelessness in his path he castigated them in phrases that have lost none of their incisiveness. Little that he wrote was entirely free of an undercurrent of antipathy, though common sense demanded that he be as circumspect as possible. For he was in the unenviable position of disagreeing violently with the assumptions on which the whole Austrian system was based at the same time that he was required to work in close harmony with some of the more notable exponents of that system. Some of the motive force for this extraordinary sense of alienation from the Vienna scene can be traced to the powerful feeling of *ressentiment* he nurtured towards the Habsburgs. At some point in his career, his tenders of devotion had been rejected, and he had come to the depressing knowledge that for the House of Austria "virtually was its own reward."[1]

And yet the Habsburgs could surprise him by a show of kindness and puzzle him with the numinous quality of their religious devotion.

> I am not so very superstitious as to imagine the pious Emperor has the art of divination, yet I think it worthy of observation that the 13th was the very day (i.e. of the victory of Höchstädt) on which the Bishop of Vienna began the solemn Devotions... and I have been told since the Emperor should have said; In those three days the destiny of his House of Austria might be decided.[2]

In his work as a Mediator, Stepney was further handicapped by his natural tendency to sympathize with the underdog, in this case the Hungarian Rebellion, and to lay a lion's share of the blame for the failure of his efforts to bring about a compromise at the door of the Austrian ministers. The reason for his sympathy -- and he found it difficult to hide -- extended beyond the Englishman's traditional love of fairplay. For one thing, both Stepney and Bruynincx believed that the future of Protestantism in Hungary was at stake in this struggle and that a thorough-going victory by the Austrians would allow those perennial mischief-makers, the Jesuits, to carry out the enforced Catholicization of the country.

But more than religious liberty alone attracted him about this Rebellion. A man so obviously pleases with the settlement that had followed the 'Glorious Revolution' in England would be prone to admit that the Rebels were fighting the extension of the very same 'despotic principle' that had led to James II's downfall. But a feeling of ideological kinship with the Hungarians often ran counter to the demands of his official position and contributed greatly to the weakening of his position in Vienna.[3]

As early as March, 1702, Stepney had had a premonition that there would be trouble in Hungary. The Emperor had been drawing "almost all his force" out of that country, and the King of Poland might avail himself of this opportunity to assist Rákóczi and Bercsényi to carry into execution their original plan of insurrection. Paradoxical though it may seem for a diplomat of a Maritime Power to complain that the Emperor was slighting his interests in Hungary in favor of the Italian campaign, Stepney expressed grave misgivings on this point. Though a closer look reveals that it was perfectly in keeping with the English desire to have the Austrians concentrate the bulk of their attention on Germany; the English, it might be added, had "little or no thought of assisting the Emperor toward the *conquest of Italy* which has ever been esteemed of *infinite consequence in comparison of the other pieces of the Monarchy* (cipher underlined)."[4]

A year later when the Rebellion actually broke out in Hungary, the English Envoy displayed an attitude of proven prescience; he had predicted that the removal of the Imperial troops and the oppressive *contribution* of four million gulden would set off such a movement. Immediately alive to the importance which the nascent Rebellion might have for European power politics and more specifically for the success of the Grand Alliance, he and Hamel Bruynincx promptly announced their readiness to work for a peaceful solution of the problem. Mediation had not as yet been suggested, but the motivation of the subsequent Anglo-Dutch Mediation certainly had:

> Care must be taken to shutt this Back-Door, or the Diversion (joyned with what we already suffer by the Elector of Bavaria) will hinder the Emperor from continuing the Warr, as he ought to do, against France either in Italy or in the Empire.[5]

As an appraisal of the origins of the Rebellion and the degree of danger involved for the Alliance, this report was penetrating enough, but it simply failed to take into account the limiting conditions within which the Austrian Monarchy was forced to operate. The Austrian ministers were probably no slower than he in coming to such conclusions; it was just that they were helpless to move from an intellectual realization of the danger to any vigorous, decisive response to it. Limited concessions to the Hungarians might have had some success; the Palatine could have been pressed into service to assume that office's traditional role of Mediator between the King and the nation. We have the testimony of no less an authority than Prince Rákóczi that if Esterházy and the magnates in Vienna had acted in concert at this stage and won over the Ministry to a policy of prudent concessions the Rebellion would have had a happy conclusion.[6] But this judgment presupposes, of course, that the Austrians would be willing to receive suggestions from the Palatine and his circle and that Rákóczi and his party would have been satisfied even then with solemn promises of Imperial good behavior in the future.

An egregious error soon replaced Stepney's original reactions to the news of the disturbances; he now was of the opinion that the Rebellion had been a mere flash in the pan. He was not alone in this mistaken view, for many diplomatic observers concluded on the basis of early setbacks suffered by the Rebels, particularly that of Dolna, which was administered to them by Károlyi, marked the end of the struggle. But by the middle of August, the Rebellion had upset their all too fragile calculations and had become a force to be reckoned with. Stepney now reported that the continued show of strength on the part of the Rebels had finally forced the government to take concrete action; for one thing, the Emperor had agreed to remit one million of the four million gulden that the Hungarians had been expected to pay for in 1703. But such tardy measures could not now quench the flame of the greatest insurrection that the Hungarians had witnessed up to that time. Prince Eugene had only five or six thousand effective troops in Hungary to hold off a Rebel force at least five times that size, and the future looked even blacker, for Eugene had no available reserves which he could commit in Hungary.[7]

At this critical juncture in November, 1703, George Stepney returned to England for consultations with his superiors, Secretaries of State Robert Harley and Charles Hedges. In his absence, England possessed a worthy substitute in Charles Whitworth, who was later to become one of the finest men in the English diplomatic service. The

Austrian ministers regarded Stepney's trip as a most suspicious development, and they made a clumsy effort to get to the bottom of the mystery. During the time of Stepney's stay in England, Hamel Bruynincx came forward to assume charge of the local diplomatic campaign for compromise in Hungary, and in doing so he earned for himself the unenviable reputation of the person most likely to go on the hundred thankless errands that were involved in subsequent negotiations.

The Austrians had had the poor taste to leave an opening through which the English and Dutch could introduce an offer to mediate: the Emperor repeatedly requested that the Anglo-Dutch army take up its winter quarters in southern Germany -- an arrangement which had the obvious merits of reducing the threat from France in that area, thus affording the Austrians a breathing space.[8] England took immediate advantage of the Emperor's plight; Sir Charles Hedges informed Whitworth that the Queen was aware that the Emperor could not manage an Italian, a German, and a Hungarian campaign simultaneously, and:

> ... the only way to put an end to these disordres will be, to give good terms to those Malcontents that are in Arms, and you are in her Maj[ys] name to press the Emperor on that head, as far as you can without giving him offense, representing to him that it may be more convenient to connive at some things at present and give them favorable conditions rather then not to put an end to a business which gives so much Disturbance to his other affaires. Especially considering the advantage the Turcks may take at this Juncture if they are encouraged....if you find His Imperiall Majesty gives any ear to what you offer upon this subject, you are to desire, he will be pleased to lett you know which way her Ma[ty] may contribute to the putting it in Practice, her Ma[ty] being willing to be Guarand of any Propositions that may be offered, if the Emperor thinks fitt to admitt of such an overture between him and his Subjects, her Majesty wants only to know in what manner the Emperor likes best that she should concern herself in putting an end to these intestine Broiles, whether by interposition, mediation, or any other way that may be most agreable to his Imperiall Majesty.[9]

Naturally the Austrians must realize that Her Majesty's tender solicitude did not extend to the increase of her present heavy subsidies to the Emperor. Money and mediation had a well-recognized relationship from the very beginning, since the English instinctively knew that his perennial short supply of the former would compel the Emperor to be particularly attentive to suggestions that London and The Hague might care to make in regard to the latter. But an excess of gulden in the *Hofkammer* would have as deleterious an effect on any Mediation as a string of Austrian victories in Hungary.

Barely five months had passed since Stepney's first notice of the Rebellion's existence, and England had already made her first offer of Mediation. It had been the brain-child of Sir Charles Hedges, and he managed to carry the day in Whitehall against the opposition of George Stepney "whose perfect knowledge of the State and Constitutions of the Austrian Monarchy" allowed him to entertain no illusions about the reception such a proposal would receive in Vienna.[10] But Hedges and Harley approached the problem not with great knowledge and great prejudice but with the English impatience of complications that foreigners indulge in for their own sake. Viewed from the distance of London, the Austrians' involvement with Rákóczi looked largely factitious in nature. How relatively simple a matter to make some concessions to Malcontents (the Secretaries did not care to be specific) and then top it off with the guarantee of a foreign sovereign that the Emperor would honor his agreement. Nevertheless, even Hedges' usual matter-of-fact style did not conceal the fact that he fully expected that the Austrians would react most unfavorably to the offer.

The Dutch did not fail to take the cue from England, and Anthonie Heinsius, the great *Raadpensionaris,* quickly duplicated England's proposal in the name of the States-General. Count Goess, the Imperial Ambassador at the Hague, expressed his gratitude for the Pensionary's interest, but he was quick to point out that such a proposal would encounter strong resistance in Vienna, since the Austrian government was well aware of the notoriously evil consequences of foreign intervention in internal politics. Goess could be of little assistance in suggesting the name of an Austrian minister who might be approached on a matter of this delicacy.[11] In Vienna, Charles Whitworth was equally conscious of the dangers of heavy-handed diplomacy in winning Austrian agreements to the offer of mediation, and he followed the circuitous route of approaching Prince Salm, the first minister of the King of the Romans, and sounding him out as to the likely reaction from the Court. The Prince showed little enthusiasm for the idea but indicated that the Ministry would probably not flatly reject it.

The Austrians, when faced with the threat of Allied interference, suddenly discovered that they had more ordinary mediatory offices at their disposal. Prince Esterházy and Prince Eugene were at Pozsony (these were the critical days of January, 1704), and they had initiated a number of peace feelers. The content of the offers was vague enough: liberty and security for the Hungarian nation and proper consideration would be shown to the leaders of the Rebellion.[12] Such attempts on the part of the Austrians to by-pass a foreign Mediation should cause no surprise, for among the numerous drawbacks of the Mediation form, the Austrians found nothing more difficult to bear than the publicity which such negotiations gave to their relations with disloyal Hungarian subjects. And because they could not refuse to accept the good offices of the English and Dutch, they kept waiting for the opportunity when they "might be able to shuffle (them) out of the Mediation if they could handsomely."[13]

As eminently practical men, the ministers were convinced that compromise when it came would not be achieved on the basis of an adjudication of legal or constitutional points at dispute but on a hard-headed division of the political spoils. This unalterable conviction led to the development of a home-grown Mediation, a tenuous system of 'cobweb intrigues' that allowed for continuous contacts between Vienna and the Rebellion without foreign participation. The instrument ready at hand for this work was the party of Hungarian moderates whose position was best exemplified by Archbishop Széchényi. That prelate's attachment to the traditional liberties of the Kingdom had been demonstrated at the meeting of the notables in Vienna, and yet he had not thrown his support behind the Rebellion. Most of the support for such a balanced view came from the circle of magnates in Vienna and high Catholic ecclesiastics, but it was bound to evoke sympathy in Rákóczi's camp as well. For the conservative wing of the Rebellion found it literally impossible to think of casting loose from all connections with the Habsburgs; they tended to think of themselves as fighting *for* Hungarian liberties and not *against* the Emperor. The leaders of the Rebellion appreciated the wisdom of making concessions to this group by appearing to favor negotiation.[14] The Archbishop and his two assistants, the 'Hungarian Deputies,' Provost Visa of the Kalocsa chapter and Pál Okolicsányi, a Lutheran leader in Upper Hungary, made this all the easier by their countless trips between Vienna and Rebel headquarters.

The story of this secondary Mediation need not concern us here, though on occasion it cooperated closely with Stepney and Bruynincx. But it should be pointed out that its irenic endeavors encountered tremendous opposition and misunderstanding on both sides. Because the Archbishop was anxious to provide each side with an honest account of the aims of the others, he not surprisingly came under suspicion of being a traitor to his nation or two his King. The Austrian Ministry had very grave reservations about his activity with the result that it failed to make the best use of his well-meaning advice.[15] The Anglo-Dutch Mediation, on the contrary, came to appreciate the value of his contacts and the accuracy of hid reports on the constantly- changing situation. Occasionally, the two Mediations carried out combined operations. The Deputies carried the burden of sustaining the contacts during the interludes between Congresses and of working out the armistices which prevailed during the Congress deliberations. At this point of transition from semi-official Mediation, Stepney and his Dutch colleagues generally took charge of affairs. But no exact rule of procedure controlled the part that any group would play. The Hofburg availed itself of the services of now one and then the other with the self-same lack of conviction that characterized its oscillation between fair words and promises and threats of imminent retribution on the field of battle.

In light of an obvious Austrian reluctance to agree to the proposals of the Queen and the Pensionary, the favorable reaction of Vienna came with breath-taking alacrity. It was hedged about with repeated declarations that a formal Mediation was out of the question.

But the increasingly desperate situation of the House of Austria made it very likely that it would have to yield on that point as well.[16] Count Kaunitz in his capacity as 'minister of foreign affairs' and as a member of the committee on Hungarian affairs of the *Conferenz*, may have been largely responsible for this show of Austrian compliance. Kaunitz had a reputation for being very sensitive where matters of personal finance were concerned, and the thought of his large estates in Moravia being plundered by Hungarian raiders was thought to have influenced him. Now that the Austrians had yielded to their Allies by accepting the proposed good offices, they ran the great danger of being surfeited with Mediators. The Maritime Powers had barely enforced their claim to this office, when the King of Poland and Charles XII of Sweden expressed a like interest in serving the cause of peace. Even the King of Prussia was reported to fancy himself in this role, though he never got around to bringing this to the attention of the Hofburg. The threat of a joint Bavarian-Hungarian attack on Vienna was enough to reduce the Emperor's advisers to a state of profound despair, and their embarrassment in the face of so many offers was only the more extreme.[17]

The English and Dutch felt offended by the growing threat to a monopoly of the Mediation; at this stage it was a more attractive prospect than it would be when the actual *pourparlers* commenced. In the press of competition, they discovered that they had a good prior claim to consideration, and Stepney sensibly advised the Secretary to use the phrase -- "that whereas the Crown of England and States Generall had by their Mediation at Carlovitz procured Peace and Tranquility to the Kingdom of Hungary" -- in drawing up his Full Powers, for in that way, the interest of the Maritime Powers and the precedence it gave them over any rivals would be securely established.[18] The existence of a line of succession, a continuity in Mediation effort in Eastern Europe, had been affirmed, and occasions would not be lacking in the course of the present Mediation when the resemblance to the 'parent' would be striking.

The Austrian ministers soon began to show signs of life in the

Hungarian negotiations, and they invited Bruynincx and Whitworth to participate in a number of conferences at which the forthcoming negotiations with Rákóczi were discussed.[19] The older generation still controlled these meetings: Count Harrach, acting as chairman, Count Mansfeld, Count Buccelini, the ailing Count Kaunitz, and -- a solitary exception to the role -- Eugene of Savoy. At the meeting of February 23, 1704, the diplomats read the text of a letter which they hoped to send to Count Bercsényi as the opening salvo of their diplomatic offensive. It raised the question of whether the Hungarians were willing to accept the 'interposition' (a euphemism for Mediation perhaps) of England and Holland in their quarrel with the Emperor. Recent reports from Hungary led them to believe that the Hungarians would insist on the participation of as many Powers as possible, and Bercsényi's answer would presumably clear up this mystery. The members of the *Conferenz* had assumed their most ingratiating manners for the occasion, and they were quick to praise the good intentions of the Mediators before passing on to a discussion of the wording of their letter. The Austrians were particularly careful about phrasing that might suggest that the quarrel between the Emperor and his Hungarian subjects was a 'lawful War,' or that he was in any way responsible for what had occurred. Eugene in his *votum* betrayed the soldier's professional interest in the terms of the armistice which was to be arranged before the actual peace conference began, particularly those relating to the provisionment of the beleaguered Imperial fortresses in Hungary.

A second meeting was held a week later, and the discussion was largely devoted to the points which the Mediators were expected to raise during the talks with the Hungarians. A major obstacle to an agreement existed in the Hungarian demand for a Guarantee, but the official mind displayed quite as much concern about the title to be used in communicating with Rákóczi. After prolonged deliberation on this point of etiquette, they concluded that the style of 'Prince' could be used without seriously weakening the Imperial position. In the matter of the Guarantee, caution had to be exercised in coming to a decision. The

Hungarians had frequently stated that they would not negotiate without such a Guarantee, and any precipitate action on Vienna's part might remove any possibility of an accommodation from the very start. It finally struck them as a very neat compromise to offer the Rebels the Guarantee of the King of the Romans in addition to that of the Mediating Powers.

Since Hamel Bruynincx had agreed to undertake the trip to Upper Hungary where contact might be more effectively made with the Rebel leaders, he was deluged with instructions on his *modus operandi.* Eugene warned him to be especially circumspect in dealing with the Archbishop and the Deputies "since it was not certain how far they were to be trusted, and that their negotiation seemed to be at an end by his journey...." The cyclical movement of official and semi-official Mediation had obviously just completed another phase. Harrach's conclusion set the tone for this early period of Mediation: the ministers were sending Bruynincx on a voyage of exploration -- he was charged to discover whether the Rebels wanted to negotiate or not. If they displayed a sincere interest in coming to an accord, he might then receive any proposals that they cared to give him. At a later meeting of the committee of the *Conferenz,* Bruynincx was empowered to sound out the Rebel leaders on the question of compensation, since they might care to exchange their commanding position in an insurrection in Hungary for a petty principality in the Empire. If talk of bribes failed to make any impression, he was to make it very clear that the Emperor fully intended to undertake a more vigorous campaign in the spring. One statement in the set of answers which Bruynincx received to his questions on how to conduct himself represented an important change of tactics; the Hungarians would have to be content with the Guarantee of the King of the Romans "against whose person the Hungarians can have no objection."[20]

The bearer of all these instructions could still manage to be optimistic when he reached Pozsony; the traditional 'honeymoon of the Mediation' still dominated his mood. And with the excitement of the prospector about to discover a rich vein of ore, he encouraged Stepney, who had returned to Vienna shortly after Bruynincx' departure, to join him as soon as possible.[21] But Stepney, though he was armed with impressive Full Powers, appeared undecided about his next step, perhaps because he had less appetite for travel into Hungary than Bruynincx possessed. The period of indecision lasted long enough for the word to come from Schinta, the town not far from Pozsony where the Dutch Minister had been conferring with Count Bercsényi, that there was no point in Stepney making the trip.[22] The very first contact with the Hungarians had destroyed most of Bruynincx' illusions; he now realized that the abyss that separated Rákóczi and Vienna was much greater than he had at first imagined. The Hungarians, whose real interest he had so much at heart and whose sympathy he felt he had, showed themselves lukewarm on the question of Mediation -- they were not ready to accept it or reject it. And so confident were they of approaching victory that Bercsényi told him that they expected to be treated "as a people no longer under subjection but a nation entirely at liberty to dispose of themselves as they think fit."[23]

Rákóczi's choice of Miklós Bercsényi as his representative in the talks with Bruynincx had a certain amount of good political reasoning behind it. As the Prince did not think it would be wise for him to be present at these preliminary discussions, being represented there by his oldest associate in the revolutionary movement, his second-in-command, was the next best thing. Bercsényi would keep him well-informed on the progress of the discussions, and he could rely on his alter ego to express his own views with the greatest accuracy. Yet from the standpoint of diplomatic relations, the choice of Bercsényi would have fateful consequences. For outsiders quickly came to the conclusion that the Count had an undisciplined and restless spirit that exhibited itself in arrogance and pretension, and more than one would-be partisan of the Rebellion had been alienated by the presence of this man in an important position. Thus the character of the movement and the nature of its leadership made it virtually certain that he would receive and treat with each delegation that arrived from Vienna, but the very fact that he presided in the absence of the Prince constituted *prima facie* evidence for the view that the Hungarians were not sincere in their avowed desire to end the war with the Emperor.

Stepney, Bruynincx and Count Rechteren d'Almelo, who later joined them in the Mediation, had frequent opportunities in the course of these negotiations to confer privately with Bercsényi and Rákóczi. The atmosphere surrounded each discussion varied according to the general political situation, yet they inevitably took on a stylized air, as though the participants were proceeding according to a preconcerted plan. The conferences began with an exchange of compliments in the course of which the Hungarians assured the Mediation of their gratitude for the continued friendly interest of England and Holland. This provided the Hungarians with an opening in which to state their case, and they enlarged on the many abuses attendant on Imperial rule in Hungary, its illegal procedures, and its violation of the religious liberties of a large portion of the population. If the Rebel leaders took the calculated risk of making peace with the Emperor after all this history of maladministration they could expect to find that he would violate his promises to them the moment circumstances were more favorable to the House of Austria.

The Mediation found it wise at this point to turn the direction of the conversation towards power politics by bluntly suggesting that Rákóczi's understanding with France was at the bottom of this hesitancy to compromise with the Emperor. A dimension of *Realpolitik* had now been added to the exchange of views. The Hungarians candidly admitted that they admitted that they maintained a close tie with France but sought to explain it as a by-product of the basic weakness of the Rebellion. Since they could not expect to achieve victory without foreign aid, they were required to seek friends and allies among the Powers of Europe. The Hungarians obviously expected that the English and Dutch would sympathize with their plight; after all both people had had plenty of experience with revolution and the ambiguous foreign policies which were usually involved. The Mediation in its reply was not unsympathetic, but since it did not believe that these cases were analogous, it terminated the discussion with the solemn warning to the

Hungarians that those who looked to France for support were inevitably disappointed.[24]

The negotiations between the Dutch Minister and Count Bercsényi at Schinta in the first two weeks of March, 1704, followed this pattern and produced little in the way of agreement. Schinta marked the end of the Mediation's 'honeymoon,' since it could no longer expect any easy solutions to the problem of peace or war. The further development of the contacts with the Hungarians might produce real results, but for the moment indecision reigned supreme in Hungary and in Vienna.

This was the situation which faced the meeting of the Conferenz on April 9, 1704. The Emperor Leopold had expressed the wish that the members of the committee on Hungarian affairs continue their discussion of the current peace negotiations with the Hungarians with the hope of producing some concrete policy-decisions, particularly on the line of his government should take with the Mediators. Harrach's summation of the discussion indicated that the meeting had not arrived at any very definite conclusions. Taking its keynote from the observation that "the right time to negotiate is when one had the advantage," the group turned to consider such expedients as existed for people like themselves who clearly did not possess the upper hand. They agreed that the Mediation should be allowed to continue its efforts, but they expected that the English and Dutch would bring more pressure to bear on the Hungarians in the future. The main device that commended itself to them was the summoning of a Hungarian Diet. Though this was not a very imaginative idea, the ministers were prolific in the way of practical points to be taken into consideration in planning for the Diet. For one thing, the leaders of the Rebellion automatically were denied the right to participate. The Emperor, it was expected, would solemnly open and close the sessions of the Diet, and the King of the Romans would remain at the place of meeting for the whole time. Particular attention was to be devoted to ensuring the safety of these royal personages on their way to and from the Diet, and Sopron appeared for that very reason to be the likeliest spot. Two other points were touched on: the Archbishop of Kalocsa's activities continued to disturb the Austrians, but they agreed that the offer of Mediation made by the King of Sweden should be accepted, after it had been discussed with the present Mediators.[25]

Further meetings managed to hammer out the answer to be given to Stepney and Bruynincx on the next step to be taken with the Hungarian negotiation: the Emperor declared his willingness to agree to an armistice in Hungary on the basis of "possideatis uti possidetis" and his readiness to accept the Mediation of Sweden, though he was not prepared to accept Sweden's Guarantee of any eventual agreement. The details of time and place for the Congress could be worked out with the Hungarian leaders. Shortly after this statement, however, the Austrian government reversed itself on the point of the Swedish Mediation. The reasons for the reversal of attitude remain obscure, since there is no indication that Stepney or Bruynincx proposed objections to this move, however much they may have disapproved of it privately. The Emperor politely declined the Swedish proposal on the grounds that a similar offer on the part of Poland made it impossible for him to accept it. It was manifestly impossible for two states at war with one another to act as Mediators in his difficulty with the Hungarians, and he could not, of course, accept one without offending the other.[26]

Minute negotiations in preparation for the Congress consumed the summer months. This Congress at Selmec (the Hungarian name for the town which the Mediation and the Austrians called Schemnitz), located in modern Slovakia at no great distance from Pozsony, was the first real meeting of the Austrians and the Hungarian Malcontents. The contacts between the two parties had been numerous enough -- one only had to think of the all too frequent visits back and forth of the Hungarian Deputies, the expert maneuvers of their superior Archbishop Széchényi, and the intermittent correspondence which Bruynincx had managed to maintain with Bercsényi -- but this was the first time that these enemies in a war of Rebellion would sit down at a conference table with the accompaniment of such international publicity as the Anglo-Dutch Mediation would provide.

The Emperor had not been at all happy in his choice of the chief of the Imperial Delegation. Baron Johann von Seilern was a 'new man' but recently raised to the rank of Privy Councillor, and though his career bore many external likenesses to that of the much lamented Strattman, his excessive convert's zeal and annoying care for legal precision made him an unlikely negotiator of a compromise with the Rebels. Indeed, even before the actual sessions had begun in the middle of October, Seilern had muddied the waters considerably with prolonged disputes over the wording of the passports with which the Austrians and the Mediators would travel. The least concession to the national pride of the Hungarians and Rákóczi's considerable *amour propre* made him conscience-stricken, since in his view the leader of the Malcontents was an outlaw condemned for high treason *in absentia* by the Austrian court. In this scruple he showed his tendency to disagree with the rest of the ministers, who expected that the title of 'Prince' might be used by the commissioners sent to negotiate with Rákóczi. Only more complication developed in the appointment of Archbishop Széchényi to the second place in the Delegation. According to Hungarian custom, the Archbishop of Kalocsa was the third ranking officer in the Kingdom, following immediately after the Primate and the Palatine, and the position he was expected to assume at Selmec only acted as an abrasive to his feeling of outraged status. He felt this to be a studied insult to his dignity, and so for much of the Congress, which desperately needed his talent as a go-between, he kept to his room with the excuse of sickness so that he would be spared the humiliation of appearing in a subordinate role to that of the parvenu Seilern.[27]

Thus it was Seilern's show from the very outset. Charles Whitworth met him the day before the Austrians left for Pozsony and was horrified to discover that Seilern did not intend to budge from the Hungarian capital until Rákóczi had abandoned some of his pretenses to titles appearing on the passports. Violent argument on forms of address and questions of seating at meetings continued to be a forte of the European diplomat, though there were definite signs that the Mediation's conception of the diplomatic craft had advanced beyond this point. But Whitworth felt even more disturbed when Seilern declared that the peace talks were pointless from the start -- only a military decision would solve the Hungarian problem. In the meantime, he went off to the Congress, as Whitworth said, "with a spirit rather to receive Criminals to grace, than to treat with a body of men who still think they have some just claims to freedom and good usage."[28]

After an understandable number of misadventures, Bruynincx (Stepney was conferring at the moment with the Duke of Marlborough at his German headquarters) and Seilern arrived at Selmec, and were soon engaged in a tight struggle over the *Curialibus,* the necessary, if time-consuming, preliminaries to the actual discussions. Here the main point at issue was the proposed armistice of three months, since neither side was ready as yet to move to a discussion of a general peace agreement. In the period immediately before the Congress much thought had been devoted on both sides to the application of the "uti possidetis" clause and to the question of the provisioning of the isolated Imperial fortresses, and a compromise had seemed to be in the offing. But Seilern now started the whole process over again and in so doing made as strong a case for the Imperial side as he could. This marked no striking deviation from standard diplomatic bargaining practice, and the other party would then be expected to submit an equally extreme set of demands which would prepare the scene for bartering back and forth. But Seilern and Bercsényi did not excel in diplomatic maneuvers of this kind; they were, if anything, lawyers with briefs rather than diplomats with compromise on their minds.

Faute de mieux, initiative in the talks now passed to the Mediation. Bruynincx made a last minute effort to win concessions from Seilern, but the Imperial Commission had no intention of yielding an inch or a phrase in its demands. Under the strain of the Mediator's persistence, Seilern made an interesting revelation of the mentality that now prevailed in Austrian official circles. He used the phrase *"rerum facies erat mutata,"* and this was taken to mean that the battles Höchstädt and Gyarmat, which had made the Congress of Selmec possible had developed at time when the Hungarians had a clear advantage, but the summer of 1704 had definitely erased this, and the Austrians now intended to negotiate from this diplomatic *tabula rasa*. Bruynincx somehow managed to infuse the desultory tasks that followed with the appearance of life; something must be left for the wit and energy of Stepney to work on, and in this way he secured an agreement on a further partial suspension of hostilities.

The Congress atmosphere which greeted Stepney on his arrival was most depressing; the Mediation's hopes as far as the Selmec talks were concerned had proved evanescent. As a last resort, Stepney decided on a meeting with Prince Rákóczi, who was taking the cure a Vihnye in the vicinity of Selmec, in the expectation that such a meeting would be productive of some good. The long and generally candid conversations which ensued give particular interest to the last days of the Congress. For the first time in the whole affair, the purveyors of good offices had a chance to size up their most important prospective customer. They were conscious, of course, of the danger they ran that reports of their 'partiality' in dealing with the Rebels would get back to Vienna, but they did not allow considerations of this kind to stand in their way.

At the very outset, the Prince made it perfectly clear that the Rebels could not accept the 'conditions' which had been handed to them by Seilern. In addition, they still refused to believe that the Emperor was sincere in his promises of freedom and security. By this point, the usual pattern of the talks between the Mediation and the Hungarians asserted itself. Rákóczi was oppressed with the notion that the present Rebellion was the last that Hungary would be able to manage for a long time to come, and the consequences would be doubly disastrous for Hungary if the leaders allowed themselves to be deceived by the empty promises of the Emperor and his minister. Self-preservation alone compelled them to take every possible step that might assure the success of the Rebellion, and it was in this dimension that the recourse which they might be forced to have to the help of the Sublime Porte must be understood. Stepney followed this bit of Rebel bluff with a reminder of the fate of the Elector of Bavaria and his brother, the Elector of

Cologne, who had depended on the French for support and who were now recipients of the King of France's hospitality. Rhetoric alone was all the Hungarian could muster as an answer: an honorable death on the field of battle would be preferred to an "ignominious life in bondage." The Mediators had accomplished one thing at least: they had driven Rákóczi to the point of admitting just how problematical his hope of salvation from the outside happened to be.[30]

This conversation had also helped to clarify the Mediation's thinking on its relations with the Malcontents. In the Rebellion's first year, Stepney and Bruynincx had adopted an ambivalent attitude: the countries they represented were officially allied to the Emperor and desperately anxious to have as large an Imperial force as possible available for the Western Front. On the other hand, the insurrection of the Hungarians exerted a large claim on English and Dutch sympathies. A sense of kinship to which the Hungarians frequently made reference existed not too far beneath the surface. The Hungarians reciprocated this feeling and were grateful for the almost impartial interest of the Mediation, but they had been forced, as they were never tired of repeating, to ally themselves in a loose way with the traditional enemy of the Habsburgs and the more recent foe of the Grand Alliances. In this way France had made of the Rebellion a counter in the customary French policy of diversion in the East. And so the Mediators approached a more balanced view in the realization that what ideology united, power politics could easily break asunder. The Hungarians were right in thinking that England and Holland were too far removed geographically and spiritually from the Central European scent to ever be greatly involved in the dramatic developments in Hungary.

The Congress of Selmec and the Mediation's 'most impertinent Embassy' ended in a stalemate, and Stepney's pessimistic summary of the Congress' work distributed the blame for its failure with a good deal of objectivity:

> I impute the cause of our miscarriage equally to both sides: If the Emperor had really been resolved to treat, his Commission might have been otherwise composed, and their demands less exorbitant. For I hope one may say without profaneness that his will and Power (like that of Providence) might have been but one and the same act if he had been so

pleased; on the other hand the malcontents are extremely to blame for not making a better use of this mediation among them, and ought not to have grown obstinate and untractable because the first proposal was not to their liking.[31]

The failure to accomplish anything at Selmec did not lead, however, to a relaxation of the Mediation's efforts. London and the Hague now began to toy with the idea that special emissaries should be sent to Vienna to add greater force to the work of Stepney and Bruynincx, and in this case the envoys should be of sufficient social rank and prestige to influence the rank-conscious Austrians. This was the genesis of the Noble Embassy -- two men of aristocratic stamp, armed with a new set of Full Powers, would assume direction of the Mediation's work in Vienna. The Dutch could lay claim to having originated the idea, though it meshed easily with the usual patterns of thought in Whitehall. Harley expressed England's willingness to cooperate and turned to a consideration of likely candidates. His first thought was of Lord Paget.[32] Paget's amazing success at Carlowitz argued in his favor, as did the enthusiasm which the Emperor had lavished on him on his return to England by way of Vienna. Perhaps Paget would succeed in moving the Emperor and his ministers to a desire to compromise where Stepney's approach had failed. The Resident Minister quickly sensed the implicit condemnation of his effectiveness as a Mediator contained in this latest move, and he soon began to show evident signs of hurt feelings. The Secretary of State consoled him as best he could: the Queen most certainly appreciated what Stepney had done; it was simply that she and the States-General believed that two Envoys Extraordinary would lend éclat and additional conviction to further efforts on the part of the Mediation.[33] But the younger generation of Mediators saw no reason for the sudden intrusion of the old guard. Sutton in a letter to Stepney commiserated with him and repeated the general rule that "all men are best able to finish their own work, besides that 'tis unreasonable that one man should reap what another man hath sown."[34]

Paget delayed making his decisions known. For a man of his years, the journey to Vienna and all too familiar discomforts of a

Mediator's life acted as deterrents; it was only his manifest satisfaction in "playing the mediator" that led him to entertain the thought at all. He decided to consult with an old comrade in arms of the Carlowitz days, Count Schlick, and the Austrian apparently advised him that he would be wrong to accept Harley's offer.[35] Mediation between the Emperor and the Turks was one thing, but in mediating between the Emperor and the Rebels he would be involving himself in a totally different situation. While Paget hesitated, the Austrian Ambassadors in London and The Hague sought to convince the men in charge of foreign affairs that sending a new set of envoys would prove a grave mistake. The Hungarians showed concern only in the case of Paget, for Stepney received a letter from Prince Rákóczi in which he expressed grave displeasure at the report of Stepney's recall to London (this had not been envisioned by the plan of the Noble Embassy) and puzzlement at Paget's disappointment. Hungarians generally had developed an antipathy to Paget, because they believed, without any particular good reasons for their view, that Paget had had a hand in the treatment which had been meted out to Count Thököly by the Peace of Carlowitz.[36] Paget politely declined the appointment at the end of April, 1705, thus removing any objections which the Rebels might have had to the endeavors of the Noble Embassy.

Harley's next inspiration was to approach Charles Spencer, the young Earl of Sunderland, whose fame consisted of his profession of republican principles as a youth and his marriage to the daughter of the Duke of Marlborough. Sunderland's acceptance raised no great expectations in either Vienna, where he was unknown, or The Hague, where Heinsius had difficulty explaining his appointment to Count Goess. The Dutch had had better fortune in picking Count Adolf Hendrik Rechteren d'Almelo, a member of one of Holland's most aristocratic families, who had served many years as a Dutch diplomat in Germany.[37] London and The Hague experienced a sense of renewed hope at the prospect of the imminent change in the composition of the Mediation. The hope was based on the illusion that the Austrians would concede points to Sunderland and Rechteren that they had refused to grant Stepney and Bruynincx.

But be sheer accident the preparations for the departure of the Noble Embassy coincided with the death of the Emperor Leopold on May 5, 1705. The Allies paused for a moment out of respect for the memory of the deceased Emperor, for though they had never really understood him they had come in time to respect him as a human being with many attractive qualities.[38] His successor Joseph I gave real promise of putting the tangled affairs of his father's declining years into some orderly pattern. The new Emperor was one of the most prepossessing members of the House of Austria to come to the Imperial throne. Young, handsome, intelligent, even tolerant (he had not been influenced by the Jesuits), he had the additional virtue of picking advisers of real distinction. His Court as the King of the Romans had already been noteworthy for the presence of men of the younger generation: Prince Salm, Count Wratislaw, Count Zinzendorf, and Prince Eugene. There was a tremendous wave of optimism about the failure of the House of Austria throughout Allied Europe; never perhaps had a Habsburg been received with so much enthusiasm in Protestant circles in Western Europe.[39] While his title to the Crown of St. Stephen (he was the first to claim it on the virtue of his hereditary succession alone) was not entirely clear, his interest in bringing about a compromise agreement with Rákóczi could not be questioned. He was an old friend of the Prince, and the Mediation had hopes that Rákóczi's and Bercsényi's obvious respect for Joseph would dispose them to conciliation as well.[40]

But the Mediation was not so sanguine as to overlook the existence of very real obstacles to the adoption of a policy of peaceful compromise in the Hofburg itself. Joseph's accession meant that the long-overdue change of the guard inn the *Conferenz* and in key positions of the administrative apparatus would bring to the fore men who were practically speaking members of a *Kriegspartei,* an orientation that demanded a vigorous prosecution of the war on all fronts, including Hungary. Mr. Stepney had had occasional intimations of the tougher policy which this new 'Cabal' would follow. The recently-acquired holdings of its members in Hungary (Prince Salm and Prince Eugene were cases in point) would encourage them to sabotage any settlement with the Hungarians that would involve a loss of these properties. And thus the land grant practices of Leopold in rewarding his generals and the tutor of his heir with vast acreages in Hungary effectively hamstrung the pacific intentions of his successor.   In addition, the new generation leaned further in the direction of centralism than the men of '83, and Stepney was horrified to report on a conversation with Prince Eugene in which that darling of English public opinion expressed regret that only two hundred Transylvanian villages had been destroyed in a recent Imperial campaign of retaliation "and not two thousand." But these clouds on the horizon did not substantially darken the atmosphere of refreshing enterprise and re-examination of old problems, and in the case of Hungary, Count Wratislaw, taking his cue perhaps from the Emperor's opinion, declared that "we on our part will not fail to present (the Malcontents) with completely sensible conditions."[41]

The long-awaited arrival of Sunderland and Rechteren in August, 1705, presented the new regime in Vienna with a chance to demonstrate the sincerity of its intentions. Sunderland was known to Wratislaw from the latter's years as Imperial Envoy in London, and the report of his eccentric republican views had had a chance to circulate. Wratislaw assured Marlborough that his son-in-law would be well received, though he feared his "inclinations to establish a species of republic in Hungary." The Hofburg realized that it would have to be on its best behavior during the stay of this influential young Lord, but there was a limit to Viennese courtesy even in his case -- the point at which it became clear that he was using the Mediation as a cover behind which to advance his republican principles in Hungary. However tolerant the English might care to be of such vagaries of spirit, the Imperial Court was not yet "Whig to that degree."[42]

Just how the Austrians reacted to Sunderland's presence remains a mystery, but the object apprehensions revealed a most paradoxical lack of sympathy for the Hungarian Rebels. He usually blamed any delays in the negotiations on the Hungarians and was particularly exercised that they obstinately persisted in their demand for the revocation of the law of the hereditary succession. In Sunderland's easy view of the matter, a concession on that point by the Rebels would deprive the Austrians of any grounds for refusing to come to a compromise! Perhaps this growing ennui with the Vienna milieu was responsible for his pique, or was it possible that the 'despotik airs' of the capital had had a momentary unbalancing effect on this erstwhile republican. His stay in Vienna came to a close with the brief visit of Marlborough in November. Sunderland went happily off with the Duke, leaving Stepney, Bruynincx, and Count Rechteren as a Mediation trio.[43]

Joseph and his councillors had been giving much thought in the meantime to the choice of the delegation that was to undertake further negotiations at a forthcoming Peace Congress at Nagyszombat (Trnava). Their final list showed a dexterous blending of pomp and circumstance, proven diplomatic ability, and prolonged contact with the thread of these negotiations. The presiding member of the Delegation was a relative newcomer to the field of peace talks with the Malcontents. This was Charles, Prince of Lorraine, Bishop of Osnabrück and of Olomouc, who was currently campaigning for election to the See of Paderborn as well. This accomplished young pluralist had a family connection with the Emperor, and his princely rank would add importance to the Delegation, at the same time that his profound ignorance of the issues at dispute would give him the appearance of impartiality. In the course of the talks, he would be guided, as he monotonously declared, by the wisdom and experience of the second in rank, Count Wratislaw. Reduced on this occasion to third place was Archbishop Széchényi, who had maintained his valuable contacts with the Rebel leaders. The Archbishop did not feel quite as put out in the present company as he had with Baron Seilern in charge. Count Franz Sigismund Lamberg, who had earned some slight distinction for his success in dealing with the Malcontents in the very earliest days, had the fourth place in the group.

On paper at least, this Delegation appeared to be the most

impressive collection of negotiators that the Habsburgs had yet entered into the lists, but it had serious weaknesses if judged on the likelihood that it would further a peace settlement. The appointment of Charles of Lorraine followed a pattern of sorts in commissioning individuals whose involvement in the Hungarian question could not help but be small to treat with a movement which had made this state of affairs one of its major complaints. The amazing insensitivity of the Ministry (it was to be repeated in the role assigned to Christian Augustus Cardinal of Sachsen-Zeitz at the abortive Diet of 1708) was recognizable in the decision to send Wratislaw. For he was a notoriously bad choice if the Emperor was in earnest about achieving peace at Nagyszombat, for he inclined more and more to a belief that the solution would come only on the field of battle. His long-standing personal enmity to Stepney was an additional drawback, though it played only a minor role in the story of the Congress.[44]

And yet it was no accident that the last and critical period in the life of the Anglo-Dutch Mediation in the Rákóczi Rebellion was dominated by the personal touch of the corpulent and gouty Count Johann Wenzel Wratislaw, the Bohemian Chancellor. At the beginning of the War of the Spanish Succession he had been Leopold's representative in London, and his skillful handling of the negotiations which led to the re-establishment of the Grand Alliance had won him great prominence. His next important assignment brought him into close contact with Marlborough, acting as he did as intermediary between the Allied commander and the Hofburg, and the Duke had learned to prize Wratislaw's keenness of mind, his most informative correspondence, and the proven help he could be in securing a favorable hearing for Marlborough's requests. In the subsequent victory of the younger generation with the accession of Joseph, Wratislaw had assumed a leading role in the formation of Austrian policy. Working in close alliance with Eugene of Savoy and Count Gundacker von Starhemberg, he succeeded Count Kaunitz, who had died in 1705, as the 'minister of foreign affairs.' While Eugene had clear title to the honor of being the "Atlas of the Austrian Monarchy" and Prince Salm, in virtue of the close personal tie with his former pupil, had greater day-to-day influence, Wratislaw operated with great ability on special missions, and in the Congress of Nagyszombat he proved to be a powerful antagonist for Mediator and Hungarian alike. His key position in the Delegation proves conclusively that the Ministry had finally decided to entrust a difficult assignment of this sort to one of its best people. He knew the inner workings of English and Dutch politics and had many important friends in those countries, and the Ministry expected that he would have more success in handling the difficult situations that grew out of the Mediation's role at the Congress than in winning over the Hungarians.[45]

Wratislaw's political views adhered closely to the 'Austrian party' of Count Kinsky. His "radically Habsburg position" differed little from that of Leopold's associate and bore a regional likeness perhaps to the 'Bohemian' orientation of Count Kaunitz. Bohemia had had great success in producing convinced exponents of centralization and a more properly Central and Eastern European tendency in foreign affairs. Wratislaw, personally the most striking of this group, threw all of his tremendous energy and commitment into the service of the Habsburg cause without falling into the sins of pedantry and legalism of a Seilern. It was only natural then that he came to develop a deep antipathy to a man like Stepney who affected the luxury of an impartial view of Habsburg role and policies. And since he was more forthright than was customary in Austrian officials, he did not disguise his feelings. His never ending struggle to have Stepney recalled added immeasurably to the strain under which Stepney labored in his last years in Vienna. Marlborough had the delicate role of peacemaker; he valued Stepney and approved of his work but he admired Wratislaw and needed his support. Only after a series of difficult moments did Marlborough finally and with a typical grace sacrifice Stepney to the Austrian's demands for his recall.[46] The thoughtful solution of transferring Stepney to The Hague had been known to Wratislaw before the Congress of Nagyszombat began. That this only further weakened the position of the Mediation at the Congress is undeniable. But an even greater misfortune appeared in the form of Marlborough's stunning victory over the French at Ramillies on May 23, 1706.[47] By adding this turning point to the expected role of Wratislaw at the Congress even the most confirmed optimist would arrive at zero in prognosticating the chances of a peace treaty with the Hungarians.

At this point it may be possible to sift some of the conflicting evidence on the sincerity of both parties in preparing for the talks. The Hungarians announced that their Delegation had been formed at the direction of the Senate of the Hungarian Confederation. Bercsényi would preside once more, and his appointment, no less than that of Wratislaw on the Austrian side, did not suggest that the Hungarians believed that the Congress would have a successful conclusion. Attention focused more on Rákóczi, who had no intention of leaving such an important mission to the mercy of his close collaborator. The Prince established himself at Vihnye close enough to Nagyszombat so that the Mediation and other interested parties would be able to visit him there quite informally.

In later years Rákóczi gave expression to the view the Hungarians had had at the time of the significance of the approaching talks, and the simplicity of his account gives added weight to its testimony. The battle of Höchstädt had convinced him that he could no longer hope for foreign military intervention, and he had come around to the belief that the only solution was peace, but a peace in keeping with the best interests of the nation. And such a peace, he continues, could only come about if the English and the Dutch exerted sufficient pressure to bear on the Emperor, and there was no doubt in his mind that they could manage this if they went about it in a serious way. Indeed, it had been his expectation of their assistance (a threat to end the Alliance with the Emperor may have been one of the means that Rákóczi envisaged) that had led him to consent to renewed talks. This passage creates the impression that Nagyszombat was the Rebellion's last hope and that the Hungarians, at least, were sincere in their desire for a settlement. But the very next section gives a totally different slant to Hungarian cooperation:

> I informed the Marquis Des Alleurs of what I had done and requested him to inform his Court of this. If the King desired the Estates (i.e. of Hungary) to continue the war, it was absolutely necessary that he conclude an alliance immediately with them and with me in my character of Prince of Transylvania.[48]

One can suspect that the Prince was using the menace of ending his diversion in Hungary as a means of securing favorable French action on his proposal of alliance. Other evidence supports that conclusion.

The defeat at Höchstädt had destroyed the original assumption on which the Rebellion had operated, but it had not prevented the leaders from hoping for assistance in other forms. Rákóczi's *empressement* in the matte of the alliance with France and his subsequent negotiations with Sweden and Russia prove that he was a man who was not disappointed easily. His version of the preparations for Nagyszombat indicate a subtle shift in emphasis from negotiations that focused almost exclusively on Hungary to talks in which Transylvania (and his claim to the princely throne) would play an integral part. By combining the two problems he hoped to insure his possession of the Principality in any peace settlement. This leads us to suspect that Rákóczi, even if he thought of the Congress primarily in terms of winning English and Dutch support for the Hungarian cause and of prying Louis XIV loose from reluctance to conclude a formal alliance, did not absolutely exclude an agreement. If terms had been offered him that he could have accepted, the Congress would have had a very different conclusion.

Wratislaw gives support to this contention by his well-organized drive to reach a secret understanding with the Prince. The intermediary role of the English and Dutch only reduced his chances of a statesmanlike bargain, and he intended to move the Prince by bringing family pressures to bear and offering substantial compensation to the leaders. Such a program derived from Wratislaw's realistic appraisal of the function of the Rebellion's leadership, and all the reports of deliberative councils and the Congresses of the Confederation did not shake him in his belief that the Prince and a small group of magnates formed the very core of the movement. If Rákóczi and Bercsényi could be bought off Vienna would have no further problems as far as armed Rebellion was concerned. Even the dissention and suspicion that such offers would create would seriously weaken the Rebellion.[49] And thus three individuals were drafted into special service: the Princess Rákóczi who was now permitted to visit her husband at his residence at Ersékújvár (in German, Neuhäusel), Countess Julia Aspremont, who paid a similar call on her brother, and Count Lászlo Kéry who was encouraged to bring a son-in-law's influence to bear on the pious Count Bercsényi. All very cozy, this calculating manipulation of family ties, but Count Wratislaw was not a man to shrink from such expedients on grounds of delicacy. In any case, he planned to visit with the Prince himself just to make certain that the Prince had a clear picture of the present state of the conflict between the Emperor and the Hungarians.[50]

Princess Charlotte Amalia displayed reluctance to accept Wratislaw's suggestion when it was first made to her. But it felt good once more to bask in the light and warmth of Imperial favor, and she finally set out on the trip -- it had all the marks of a triumphal procession -- to rejoin her husband. She carried out her part of the understanding with Wratislaw by urging the Prince to come to terms with the Emperor -- she showed some insistence in advising him to exchange Transylvania for a principality in the Empire. At this stage in her troubled career, the security of the Duchy of Leuchtenberg, for example, must have seemed an easy improvement on her husband's situation and her own as well. But once it was clear that she had little hope of convincing the Prince that he should put his family interests first in his plans for the future, she pestered Wratislaw with requests for a passport that would allow her for reasons of health to travel to the spa at Carlsbad. Both the Emperor and Wratislaw informed her that she would have to continue her stay in Hungary: the interest of the common good took precedence over the lady's health.[51] Once the meeting between the Prince and Wratislaw had taken place in her apartments, she received her passport and withdrew permanently from her husband's society and protection. The visits of Countess Aspremont and Count Kéry allowed for brief interludes of family reunion, but they had no traceable political consequences.

The long-awaited encounter of the Prince and Wratislaw took place on June 3, 1706. They met quite casually in the apartment of Princess Charlotte; it was as if the gouty Bohemian Chancellor had merely dropped in for a call on an old acquaintance and discovered to his surprise that the *dux* of the Hungarian Confederation also happened to be present. Since direct seizure of the initiative played an important role in Wratislaw's diplomatic technique, we can imagine that he turned almost immediately to the Emperor's offer of compensation in the Empire. That the Count had seriously misjudged his opponent, Rákóczi's dignified reply made very clear. The Prince candidly admitted that the thought of the Duchy at Leuchtenberg was an attractive one from the point of view of the Rákóczi family interests, but it had not been his intention to improve his family fortunes when he had come to the defense of his country's liberties. Moreover, the tie which bound him so closely to Hungary had gained in meaning in the course of the Rebellion through the many displays of affection and confidence which he had received from the whole nation. At this point, he deserted the dimension of the politician and even statesman to display the ultimate in selflessness. He declared that he would be content to see Transylvania restored to the autonomy which it had enjoyed under the terms of the treaty between Emperor Leopold and Prince Michael I Apaffy. If his person constituted an obstacle to the restoration of Transylvanian liberties, he would willingly surrender the diploma of his election to the Estates, so that they would be able to elect an individual upon whom both sides could agree -- "even if it was the least of my valets."

Wratislaw must have paused in wonder at the spectacle of such monstrous disinterestedness and then reverted, as the Mediators had done so often before him, to the theme of French treachery. "You pride yourself on the promises of France, that hospital of princes whom it has rendered unhappy by its inability to honor its promises and solemn agreements. You will be one of that number, and you will die there." In the years of exile, Rákóczi had frequent occasion to recall the prophetic words of Wratislaw.[52]

While these unofficial meetings took place at Rákóczi's residence, the official deliberations of the Congress consumed all of June and the first two weeks of July. An obstacle in the way of smooth sailing for the Congress had been removed at the outset when the Hungarians abandoned their demand for a specific guarantee from the Emperor that Hungary would receive more favorable treatment than that customarily accorded to the Hereditary Provinces.[53] Though there remained the constant annoyance involved in the frequent renewals of the suspension of hostilities, the Congress settled down hopefully to a consideration of the Hungarian postulata, twenty-three points which differed only slightly from those in the manifesto *Recrudescunt*. Stepney divided these points into three different classes:

> 1st What the Emperor is obliged to grant in conscience, as founded on reason, justice, and law; 2[dly] What he may further allow out of fatherly affection, as well as his own convenience and that of His Allies, without doing any violence or injury to his regal Authority, and 3[dly] What he cannot but reject as insolent and impertinent;

The height of impertinence had been reached, according to Stepney, in the demand that the two chiefs be well rewarded for having caused the Emperor so much trouble![54]

But before the Congress had had a chance to discuss these articles in any detail, the Imperial Delegation challenged the credentials of the Transylvanian Deputies who were present at the Congress. The Austrians possessed authorization by the Emperor to treat with the Hungarians and the Transylvanians, yet Wratislaw now contended that it was impossible to negotiate with the latter if they pretended to represent all the Estates of Transylvania. This would be tantamount to a formal recognition of Transylvanian independence and Rákóczi's formal election as Prince. The Mediation quickly sensed that the Congress had entered upon its critical stage with the introduction of such a difficulty, and it sought desperately to find a formula which would prove satisfactory to both sides. The Austrian had no objection to the form '*Deputati Confoederationis Transylvanicae*,' but the Mediation, knowing full well that something more impressive was required, hit upon the formula '*Deputati Statuum Confederatorum Transylvaniae*' as a compromise. Almost instantaneously Charles of Lorraine and Wratislaw expressed their horror and surprise that the Mediation would make such a dangerous concession on its own responsibility. But Stepney, Bruynincx, and Rechteren reminded the Austrians that the accent here was on the '*Confoederatorum*.' The Austrians failed to see the significance of this variation, and a controversy developed which left the status of the Transylvanians very much in doubt. The Hungarians now assumed a strong line with the flat statement that they could not negotiate without the Transylvanian Deputies, since the law of their Confederation made it mandatory for the two states to reach a common agreement with the Emperor.[55]

The tragicomic logomachy had the effect of uncovering an immovable force in Vienna. The Emperor had reiterated his willingness to make some concessions to the Hungarians and to lavish compensation on their chiefs, but he refused to admit of any change in the status of the Principality of Transylvania. Here was the *fondement solide* of Joseph's policy in this area -- "*conserver la Transilvanie en vertu de la Paix de Carlowitz, dans le meme etat ou Elle a été alors: Et de faire desister les Hongrois de toutes Pretentions à cette Province....*" The battle had been squarely joined: the Malcontents refused to proceed without an Austrian recognition of the independence of Transylvania and the legal character of Rákóczi's claim, while the Austrians were absolutely adamant that, whatever concessions might be made in the case of the Hungarian Confederation, Transylvania must return to a state of strict dependence on Vienna.

Since there could be no resolution of such a dispute, the Congress dragged on to the day one of the parties had the courage to break off the talks. Last minute trips to Vienna by the Mediation and appeals to the Prince proved unavailing, and finally on July 18, Charles of Lorraine and Count Wratislaw informed the Mediation that they were of the opinion that no further purpose would be served by the Congress. The delegations dispersed with haste, for with the imminent end of the armistice both sides could barely wait to come to a solution on the battlefield.[56]   A woefully fatigued and depressed set of Mediators returned to Vienna with the accurate impression that Nagyszombat marked the end of the Mediation's career.[57] The villain of the last act did not escape identification: "Everybody concern'd in it own plainly that Wrat: is the maine cause of our Rupture by his impertinent treatment of Rákóczi at Neuhausel, and by his violent Councills since."[58] Stepney waited impatiently for the moment of his release from the importunities of the Court and the animus of so many of the ministers. Broken in health by the rigors of the long Mediation, he left for The Hague in October, and within a year he was dead at the age of forty-four.[59]   Count Rechteren did not stop to consider whether or not the States-General had an interest in further 'amusements' of this kind; he had reached Holland by the time his superiors discovered that they required his services once more in Vienna.   Needless to say, the surviving member of the once resplendent Noble Embassy absolutely refused to have anything to do with 'one last attempt' at Mediation. Solid and imperturbable Hamel Bruynincx continued on at his difficult post, bound without realizing it to a lifetime of dealings with the Austrian ministries.[60]

The rapid disintegration of the Mediation did not write an absolute finis to the relations of Prince Rákóczi and the Maritime Powers. Towards the end of 1706, when the opinion was current that a general peace congress would be held in the near future, Rákóczi appealed to the Queen and the States-General for their assurances that the case of Hungary would be included in such a Congress' deliberations. The replies of the Queen and the Dutch dripped courtesy and sympathy, but they contained an expression of regret that England and Holland would be so occupied in any general peace settlement with their own affairs that it would be impossible to introduce an extraneous consideration like the Hungarian question.[61] The last links between Rákóczi and the Emperor's Allies were cut on a note of enlightened self-interest.

While the evidence remains too spotty and conflicting to allow for any final conclusions on the role of the Mediation vis-à-vis the

Rebellion, some provisional judgments do emerge. England and Holland had forced the Emperor to accept Mediation in the hope that a compromise in Hungary would free his hand for greater military effort in Western Europe. The Austrians did not fail to regard this intervention as an insult to their rights as a sovereign state and to sabotage the efforts of the Mediators. What was particularly annoying to them was the implication that Austria should put the interests of the Alliance above considerations of self-preservation and territorial integrity. A viable peace with the Rebellion certainly involved the cession of Transylvania to Rákóczi, but this dismemberment went beyond the scope of any alliance loyalty. For the Hungarians the Mediation represented an occasional temptation to secure by negotiation what they were unable to achieve by force of arms.

But in order to be an effective means of helping the Hungarians to achieve this objective, the Mediation required an alignment of the Powers similar to that which had existed between the Treaty of Rijswijk and the Treaty of Carlowitz. At that time, the Emperor was faced with the prospect of carrying on a war on two fronts without the assurance of support from England and Holland. Necessity then dictated a peace with the Turks so that all the Habsburgs' attention could be concentrated on the fate of the Spanish Empire. But in the present instance, Leopold and then Joseph continued to have the security of the Grand Alliance and never felt the imperative need of coming to terms with the less dangerous enemy -- the Hungarians. Only if the Allies had gone to the extreme of *compelle intrare* backed by the threat to renounce the Alliance could a compromise have been reached. But this was a step which the English and Dutch for a variety of good reasons were unwilling to take in the years 1704-1707.[62]

When set against the sweeping continuities of European cultural development, the Anglo-Dutch Mediation in the Rákóczi Rebellion became microscopic in size and importance, and yet in its time it served as one of the indisputable signs of the rising parochialism of several European national cultures, and, in particular, as proof of the growing alienation of Western and Central Europe. For present as one of the causes of the failure of the Mediation efforts was the significant breakdown in communication between these diverging 'worlds.' The tragic and relentless enmity between two distinguished representatives of these diverging patterns of life -- George Stepney and Johann Wenzel Wratislaw -- symbolized the alienation implicit in this process.

Notes to Chapter 2

While this chapter goes over some of the ground covered by Freiherr con Hengelmühller in his unfinished *Franz Rákóczi und sein Kampf um Ungarns Freiheint* (Leipzig, 1913), it is conceived as the sketch for the second section of Triptych on the Anglo-Dutch Mediation: Carlowitz -- Nagyszobat -- Passarowitz. In its inistence on the continuity of Mediation aims, personnel, and methods it marks something of a departure from the more narrowly localized treatments of the Rebellion or Austrian foreign policy in this period.

The main source used in this chapter was Ernö Simnoyi's publication of those Stepney Papers in the Public Record Office which relate to the Rákóczi Rebellion and the Anglo-Dutch Mediation, Anglo diplomatiai iratok (*Archivum Rákóczianum, II. osatály*) (Budapest, 1871) 3 vol. (Hereafter *Simonyi)* The enormous amount of material contained in this work has not received the attention it deserves, and in using it one feels that this really has the status of unpulished sources. I have used, in addition, material derived from Stepney's reports from Vienna in the period 1701-1703, *State Papers Foreign*, 80, #18.

In carrying out my declared intention of making use of the diplomatic collections of the old *Reichshofkanzlei*, preserved in the *Haus-, Hof- und Staatsarchiv*, Vienna, I have consulted the *Anglica* and the *Hollandica*, both for *Berichte* and the *Weisungen*. The reports especially of Count Goess, the Imperial Ambassador at The Hague, help to provide some balance to Stepney's account.

No student of this and related problems in this period can ever quite give up the search for those precious indacations of Austrian ministerial opinion to be found in the protocols of the *Conferenz*. The collection of Vorträge is, unfortunately, almost silent on Austrian dealings with the Rebellion. The next step was to determine whether some of the missing protocols had found thier way into the private archives of important political figures of the time. Through the great kindness of Gräfin Harrach, I was able to obtain copies of the protocols of meetings which had taken place under the presidency of Count Ferdinand Bonaventure Harrach (*Gräflich Harrachsches Archiv*, Vienna; *Konferenzprotokolle*, Fasz. 188)

[1]This discussion of Stepney is based ont he useful article on him in the *Dictionary of National Biography* and on his letters in the George Stepney collection, *S.P.F.*, 105, #62-81.

[2]Stepney to Harley, Vienna, August 20, 1704, *Simonyi*, I, 386.

[3]"...and any man who has had th e happiness of living under a free Government cannot but be a little concerned to see a poor people (whereof 5 parts of 6 are of the Reform'd Churches) depriv'd of their Liberties at on Blow, and given up to the servitude and future persecutions notwithstanding a Powerfull Mediation, of the same Profession with themselves, has been pleased to appear in their behalf.", Stpney to Harley, Tirnay, July 20, 1706, *ibid.*, III, 159.

[4]Stepney to the Earl of Albermarle, Vienna, Marhc 15, 1702, S. P.F., 80, #18, no pagination; Stepney to Vernon, Vienna, April 26, 1702, *S.P.F.*, 80, #18.

[5]Steppeny to Hedges, Vienna, June 2, 1703, *Simonyi*, I, 16-18.

[6]"... mais il (Esterházy) ne remplissoit pas les devoirs de la charge de Palatin, puisque si dès le commencemetn de la guerre, ce Seigneur en se conciliant l'autorité eeut rempli selon sa dignité son caract?re de Médiateur, de concert avec les Grands atachés a l'Empereur, á radsonner les lumières de la prudence humaine, la guerre de Hongrie eut enfin eu un heureux succès.", *Memoires,* 40.

[7]Stepeny to Hedges, Vienna, July 7, 1703, *Simonyi,* I, 24; "...the Rebellion that is broke out in Hungary is likely to prove of more consequence then was first expected, and gives prince Eugene more trouble then any other affaires, as he confessed to me himself last night....", Stepney to Hedges, Vienna, August 22, 1703, *ibid.,* I, 30-31.

[8]Charles Whitworth to Hedges, Vienna, November 21, 1703, *ibid.,* I, 57-58.

[9]Letter from Mr. Secretary Hedges to mr. Whitworth, Whitehall, December 10, 1703, *ibid.,* I, 72-73.

[10]"The truth is, We ought not have concern'd ourselves in this Mediation (and so I represented in my Letter to Mr. Secretary Hedges near 3 years ago when it was at first prpos'd) But since Her Majesty by the advice of her Councill was engaged in it and by the humble address of th Parliamanent was mov'd to ure it with more efficacy...", Stepney to Mr. Cardonnel, Bienna, July 26, 1706, *ibid.,* III, 172.

[11]"...der rathpensionarius fragte mich, ob mann sich alliireten seithen darein legen dörffte? Ich bedanckete ihme vor solche offertum, sintemahlen aber er von selbst wohl begreiffen könte, dass eine frembde mediation zwischen herrn und unterthanen bissweiln von übelen gefolge seyn und darzu ich nicht wuste,

an weme mann sich addressiren muste;", Count Goess to the Emperor, The Hague, *Hollandica,* December 28, 1703.

[12]Whitworth to Hedges, Vienna, January 5, 1704, *Simonyi,* I, 88-89.

[13]Stepney to Marlborough, Vienna, May 27, 1705, *ibid.,* II, 104.

[14]"...les vieillards parmi la Noblesse, les aisés, et les politiques, raisonnoient favorablement jusqu'á la Négociation de Tirnau, puisqu'il voyoient que nonobstant des batailles perdues, les Médiateurs, les Emissaires de l'"Empereur, alloient et venoient; et ils étoient en espérance au moins de qulques soulagemens par la paix. Mais tout traité et pouyparle étant cessé, ils ne voyoient plus rien devant eux.", Ferenc Rákóczi, *Memoires,* 118.

[15]The Referendarius of the *Hofkriegsrat,* Johann Tiel, discussed the role of the Archbishop in a letter to Count Wratislaw, "Mit Herrn Erzbischoff von Colozza have gbestern etliche stunden in familiari discursu zugevracht, de Intentione non iudicat Preator. So vill aber kann ich verstehen, quod inter Hungaros non interim ipsi parem in Doctrina et prudentia, Er kan ein haubt gutt- und nützliches Instrument sein, wen man sich seiner honeste et utiliter zu gebrauchen weiss...So glaube ich Er würde mehr alss keiner im Haubswerk die gemüther ad optatum finem zu lenken vermögen....", Pressburg, *Hungarica,* Faxsz. 190 A. May 10, 1706.

[16]Whitworth to Hedges, Vienna, January 16, 1704, *Simonyi,* I, 103.

[17]Letter from Mr. Sec'y Hedges to Stepney, Whithall, February 8, 1703/4, *ibid.,* I, 130-131.

[18]Stepney to Hedges, The Hague, February 5, 1704, *ibid.,* I, 123.

[19]Charles Whitworth's account of these meetings is to be found in his letters to Hedges of February 27, 1704 and March 5, 1704, *ibid.,* I, 148-163 passim.; the protocols esist in the *Konferenzprotokolle,* 188. In the meeting of the *Conferenz* of February 20, 1704 "uber das snerbieten der Engel- undt Holländischen ministren sich mit denen rebellen hungarn zu interponiren", one of the conclusions had been "das besser ware diese ministri durch ein oder anderen Kaiserlichen ministro instruirt wurden als in conferenz zu beruefen, damit es mehrer verschwigen bleibe, undt nit scheine das JRM (i.e. the Emperor) es verlange.", *Konferenzprotokolle,* Mediators attend the next sessions of the

Conferenz in Hungaricis.

[20]"Questions proposed by Mr. Bruyninx to the Imperial Ministers before he set out for Hungary with the Emperor's answers by way of Instruction thereupon", *Simonyi,* I, 179.

[21]"Tâchez de disposer Mr. de Stepney de me venir joindre, *car il y a de l;'honneur á acquerir...*(italics my own)", Bruynincx to Whitworth, Pressburg, March 6, 1704, *ibid.,* I, 163.

[22]Bruynincx to Whitworth, Schinta, March 10, 1704, *ibid.,* I, 171.

[23]Stepney to Hedges, Vienna, March 19, 1704, *ibid.,* I., 185.

[24]Cf. for example, the decription of the talks of Berscányi and Brunincx in the "Relation secrete de l'Etat des affaires en Hongrie", Bruynincx's report on his negotiations, *ibid.,* I, 192ff.

[25]"Conferenz uber die fridenshandlung mit denen Hungarischen rebellen"; "die recht Zeit zu tractiren ist wann mann die oberhandt hat...was mann von den Erzbischof von Colozca have, weiss mann nit...wann die Engelländischen undt Hollandtischen Ministrij hin-unter gehen solten, müste, es sein das sie insitirten die sachen zu componiren.", *Konferenzprotokolle,* 188, April 9, 1704.

[26]Stepney to Hedges, Vienna, April 23, 1704, *Simonyi,* I, 245-246; Stepney to Hedges, Vienna, April 26, 1704, *ibid.,* I, 252-253.

[27]A complete account of the Mediation's 'impertinent Embassy' to Selmec is contained in Stepney's letter to Robert Harley, Schemnitz, November 3, 1704, *ibid.,* I, 520-539.

[28]Whitworth to Harley, Vienna, October 4, 1704, *ibid.,* I, 467.

[29]Stepney to Bruynicx, Vienna, January 29, 1706, *ibid.,* II, 381.

[30]The account of the conversation with Prince Rákóczi is to be found in Stepney's letter to Harley, Schemnitz, November 2, 1704, *ibid.,* I, 529-535.

[31]*Ibid.,* 538.

[32]Robert Harley to Stepney, Whitehall, February 6/17, 1704/5, *ibid.,* II, 15-16.

[33]"That Her Magesty designs to send another minister hither, si far from giving me any uneasiness; For I am certain to have a witness more of my Zeal and intergrity , and that I ahve reported matters no otherwise then as I found them; who ever he be, He shall have the faires informations I can give him, and my best wishes for success, when my back is turned; For Peace is certainly a good design whoever shall have the honour of making it....", Stepney to Marlborough, Vienna, February 7, 1705, *ibid.*, II, 18; Harley to Stepney, Whitehall, March 20/31, 1704/5, *ibid.*, II, 55-56.

[34]Sutton to Stepney, Pera, April 9, 1705, *ibid.*, II, 61.

[35]Stepney to Lord Halifax, Vienna, May 30, 1705, *ibid.*, II, 105-106.

[36]"En sorte qu'il pretendoient qu'il (Paget) est prevenu contre la Nation.", Ferenc Rákóczi to Stepney, *ibid.*, II, 69.

[37]"...dass der Mylord Sunderland, so ein aidam von dem mylord Marlborough ist...von dessen persohn ich, auss mangel dass die geleganheit nciht gehabt ihn zu kennen, ekine eingentliche beschreibung machen kan, und solcherhalben mich auf den graffen von Wratislaw remittiren muss;", Johann Philipp Hoffman to the Emperor, London, *Anglica,* June 23, 1705.

[38]"It is not to be expressed what general concern and affection they showed towards their Prince during his extremity...."; Stepney was moved by the genuine sorrow of the Viennese, Letter to Harley, Vienna, April 29, 1705, *Simonyi,* II, 70.

[39]Stepney to Harley, Vienna, May 5, 1705, *ibid.*, II, 73-74.

[40]Heinsius was most hopeful about ht eimpact of Joseph's accession on the Hungarians: "...vermeinte und gab seine unrsachen, warumb anjezo ein accomodement mit denen Hungaren liechter geschehen könte; weiln nehmlich die rebellen sich wieder euer kays. may. nicht zu beklagen hetten und dieselbe hingegen ohen verletzung dero höchsten reputation mit ihnen mehrern clemenz und moderation gebrauchen könten.", Count Goess to Joseph I, The Hague, *Hollandica,* May 26, 1705.

[41]Stepney had noted this in the case of the younger ministers as early as the spring of 1704; Letter to Hedges, Vienna, April 23, 1704, *Simonyi,* I, 245; "...undt wir unser seiths werden nicht ermangelen ihnen alle raisonalbe

conditiones zu beben, umb einmahl auss dieser sache zu kommen, undt unss in standt zu setzen anderwertig mit grösern nachdruck zu operiren.", Count Wratislaw to the Archduke Cahrles, Vienna, July 4, 1705, A. Arneth, "Eigenhändige Obersten Kanzler des König- reiches Böhemn, Grafen Johann Wenzel Wratislaw," *Archiv für Kande österreicheische Geschichts-Quellen* (XVI), 1856, 19.

[42]Count Wratislaw to the Duke of Marlborough, Vienna, July 19, 1705, in William Coxe, *Memoirs of the Duke of Marlborough* (London, 1847), I, 340-341.

[43]Sunderland to Harley, Vienna, Septmeber 12/23, 1705, *Simonyi*, II, 210; Stepney to Harley, Vienna, November 21, 1705, *ibid.*, II, 240.

[44]The Emperor's *Instructio* of November 22, 1705, *Ungarn*, Fasz. 188 (1705); Charles of Lorraine to Count Wratislaw, no place or date, *ibid.*, 188, (1705), 205.

[45]The discussion of Count Wratislaw is based in part on the unpublished Vienna dissertation of Margarethe Geyer, *Die Gesandtschaft des Graften Wratislaw in London Bis zu Abschluss der Grossen Allianz vom 7. September 1701* (Vienna, 1748).

[46]Coxe, *op. cit.*, I, 359.

[47]"...I believe the glorious Victory obtained at Ramelly and th estupendious imprvement my Lord Marlvorough hath made of it in so few days will not be without its influence upon that negociation.", Robert Harley to Stepney, Whitehall, May 24, 1706 O. S., *Simonyi*, III, 62.

[48]"Depuis la perte de al bataille d'Hochstet, et par conséquent de l'espérance du secours des Troupes étrangères, j'etois fort porté á la Paix; mais á une Paix convenable au bien de la Nation, que je n'avois lieu d'esperer que par la concurrence des Anglais et des Hollandois, qui auroirent pu, s'ils l'eussent voulu sérieusement, contraindre l'Empereur á nous l'accorder. Je voulois donc convainere les Médiateurs de la justice de notre Cause. C'est ce qui me détermina á venir á une Negociation formelle.", Ference Rákóczi, *Memoires*, 99; he then goes on to mentionhis appeal to Des Alleurs.

[49]A meeting of the *Conferenz in Hungaricis* of May 25, 1706, sheds some light

on the thinking of Wratislaw. "1.) Was dem Ragocy undt dem Berseny zu offeriren? An sit tempus? An cum Regno sit Spes tractandi? An recompensandi rebelles? Quid sit dandum? Leichtenberg." The *conclusum* is interesting: "Non est de tempore proponendi, sed deliberandi quia facilus est retringere mutatis circum stantiis rebus. Ratione Transylvanico nihil, et nullo modo est proponendum...Vel alius locus in Imperio Bersenii satisfactio consilium in arena sumendum?"; *Ungarn*, Fasz. 190 (A), 205.

[50]Stepney to Harley, Vienna, July 28, 1706, *Simonyi*, III, 173.

[51]Letter o fthe Princess Rákóczi to Count Wratislaw, Neuhausel, May 23, 1706, *Ungarn*, Fasz. 190 (1706), 200.; Count Wratislaw to Count Rechteren, Vienna, May 22, 1706, *Simonyi*, III, 41.

[52]Rákóczi's account is containe din the *Memoires*, 100ff. The Prince's allusion to the 'election' of his valet had a curious history, for Stepney in a letter reported, "By some letters I have seen form Prince Rákóczy, He seems extreamly dissatisfyed with the Conversation he lately had with Count Wratislau, who instead of encouragin him by Gratious assurances of the Emperour (sic/) Protection, and by some favorable experdient in the point of Transilvania, flattly declared to his face, that in Case H. I. M. should find himself obliged to leave the Trasilvanians to a free Choice, He might depend upon it, that H. I. M. would admitt the meanest Subject of Hungary or Transilvainia to that Dignity rath then allow of him. After disobliging expression the Court ought not to be much surprised if the Prince is changed of a suddain from the good disposition he discovered of late by promoting everything that might be justdged proper towards facilitating the Treaty, and seems for the future very indifferent whether the Negociation be continued in its ordinary Course, or interrupted by new Hostilities."; Stepney to Harly, Vienna, July 13, 1706, *Simonyi*, III, 140.

[53]Stepney to Harley, Vienna, March 3, 1706, *ibid.*, II, 559-560.

[54]Stepney to Harley, Pressburg, June 15, 1706, *ibid.*, III, 83-84.

[55]"We have at last received some directions by Count Wratislau how we are to behave ourselves in relation to the Trasilvanians; Wherein you see the Cour allows us very little latitude of admitting them to any share in the treaty, thô the Emperor's Powers positively authorize his Commissioners to treat with the Transilvanians as well as the Hungarians; And I heartily with the Austrians with their haught and confident stile may not find themselves mistaken as to the

dispositions of the that people, when the Imperial Army shall be obliged to march ou of that country.", Stepney to Harley, Pressburg, June 15, 1706, *ibid.,* III, 84; "Car au lieu qu'il se devroient nommer *Transilvaniae Confoederationis Deputati*; surquoi les Hongroi aussi bien que les Transilvains insistent si fort, que nous craignons que lExpedient ne reussira pas sants cela."; Mediators to Zenó, Tyrnau, July 2, 1706, *ibid.,* III, 113; Stepney to Harley , Tyrnau, July 6, 1706, *ibid.,* 125-129.

[56]Prince Cahrles of Lorraine and Count Wratislaw to the mediators, Vienna, July 18, 1706, *ibid.,* III, 150-151.

[57]Stepney to Cardonnel, Vienna, July 31, 1706, *ibid.,* III, 179.

[58]Stepney to Cardonnel, Vienna, July 23, 1706, *ibid.,* III, 166.

[59]The Queen's Letter of Revocation for Stepney, *ibid.,* III, 210-212.

[60]Robert Harley to Stepney, Whithall, September 17/28, 1706, *ibid.,* III, 240-241.

[61]Count Goess discussing the response of the Queen and the States-General: "Sonsten ist der inhal sehr civil, der ingrets 'mon tres cher cousin', die courtoisie 'vostre tres affectionée cousine' und der context durchgehends eine freude, dass er Ragozzi an ein accomodement gedencke, dass ihme darzu rathe und man die vorige officia darzu continuiren will, zumahlen man bey dem geralfriedenschluss so viel mit eygenen sachen wird zu thun haben, dass man an frembde schwerlich wird gencken können; wessen der staat sich resolvirt wird, soclhes berichte ich vielleicht mit nechster post gehorsambst;", Goess to the Emperor, The Hague, *Hollandica*, February 25, 1707.

[62]This was Count Rechteren d'Almelo's considered judgment in his final report to the States-General: "...dat de Croon Engelant ende den Staet op het fondament van derselver voor aengetogen resolutie sen de een kant, als by wege van een stercke inductie en als een compelle intrare, het Keyserl. Hof Komen aen te setten tot het Accorderen van aequitable en billiche condititien aen de Ungersche natie....", Report to the Griffier, "Gailsdorff", September 2, 1706, *Weensche Gezantschapsberrichten van 1670 tot 1720*, II, 354-355.

Conclusion

With the collapse of the Anglo-Dutch Mediation's efforts to bring about a compromise between the Emperor and the Hungarian Rebels we came to the appointed term of our investigation. On more than one occasion along the way we have paused to state and to restate the major and minor themes of the work to indicate their projected development in the subsequent chapters, but its finale requires of us a special effort in the way of a retrospective glance that will take into account the thesis' objectives, its underlying assumptions, and its possible contributions to an understanding of the period it treats.

In taking such an inventory I have made use of the device which the Russians call the 'creative history of a work,' that is the analysis of the finished product, not in a mechanistic way by reducing it simply to its component parts, but by treating it as a living organism evolving through different stages in the course of time. In this way the wide range of formative factors of crucial importance in establishing the character of this study will be seen in dynamic relation with each other. Far too frequently the student of history seeks to keep the interval logic of his treatment of an historical problem a deep secret, as if its formulation constituted a betrayal of his responsibility to tell us the truth. But I am convinced that by means of such self-analysis of a historical study, the proper weight can be assigned to the impact of the source materials, the kind of preconceptions about the historical process which are involved, and the presence of the *Zeitgeist* in a generation's historical writing. Marc Bloch believed that the historian has the positive obligation to provide his reader with a detailed explanation of just how he reached his conclusions, and though footnotes and the whole scholarly apparatus fulfill part of the requirement, a more developed presentation of the "why?" of this thesis (for this is clearly what Bloch had in mind) should be of real service in the way of a conclusion.

The whole project had its point of departure in an interest in the diplomatic history of the Rákóczi Rebellion. A novice finds it difficult to resist the temptation of clearing up one of the flagrant lacunae in the historical literature devoted to the period of his special interest, and the absence of any overall treatment of the relations of the Hungarian Malcontents with the European Powers convinced me that I might well make a contribution by making such a study. On closer inspection, I found it necessary to limit the range of my research, for the subject as it stood proved too broad for a thesis topic. I was guided in the direction of limitation by the accidents of the availability of archive collections and of my background and linguistic preparation for a study of the national historical literatures. The fact that I pursued most of my research in the sources in London's Public Record Office and Vienna's *Staatsarchiv* automatically redirected the focus of my attention to Austrian relations with the Maritime Powers and Turkey immediately before and during the Rákóczi Rebellion. Since these relations had not been explored in any detail previous to this time, I once again experienced the bracing feeling of working in virgin soil. I retained my initial interest in the Rebellion's diplomatic relations but I saw them now as an integral part of the rise of Austria as a Great Power, as a threat which Rákóczi had clearly posed to the establishment of the Habsburgs' position in Central Europe.

Once I got down to a detailed investigation of the relevant sources, the discovery of unused or little known materials of particular interest made their special contribution to setting the course which I would follow. The extraordinary degree of interest which Lord Paget's dispatches, the secret correspondence of Count Kinsky and Count Schlick during the Peace Congress at Carlowitz, the protocols of the Deputation (easily the most exciting single find), and finally the detailed reports of Johann Michael Thalmann to the *Hofkriegsrat* so clearly possessed inevitably meant that much of my account of this period would rest on thier testimony.

But the raw materials of themselves could not be completely

decisive; I required a conceptual scheme that would unify a large mass of extremely varied phenomena. The whole problem could not be explained by simply alluding to the iron laws of *Realpolitik,* though these were present without any question, but I preferred to adopt the hypothesis that much of its significance might be elucidated in terms of the developing cultural estrangement of Austria and Hungary, and between these nations and the peoples of England and Holland. This hypothesis rested in turn on the assumption that each national culture at this stage in European history had achieved sufficient self-consciousness to produce characteristic political ideals and institutions. This notion had little that was novel about it, but I intended to derive certain further axioms from it. The kind of diplomatic activity in which a country engaged, I now argued, also bore the indelible mark of its culture, and international politics derived much of its grounds for conflict from this state of affairs. At this juncture the contemporary diplomatic observers appeared to bear me out. For when Paget argued with Kinsky, he was clearly aware that the dispute grew out of differing views of the Alliance's practical objectives and, in addition, from the variant general theories of political activity. What Paget described as the *lenteurs* of the Court of Vienna, the modern student, I felt, would regard as a particularly Austrian approach to the business of making political decisions, indeed, an Austrian view of the degree to which the Emperor should actively intervene in the flow of political events. And the contrasts between English, Dutch, and Austrian diplomatic practices had an analogy in the difficulties experienced by all three Powers in dealing with the Turks. As a necessary corollary to my initial assumption -- it found support, as I have noted, in the striking amount of cultural description in the contemporary diplomatic dispatches -- I had committed myself to a notion of diplomatic and institutional history (in the case of the Deputation) which placed particular stress on the importance of cultural and ideological factors in determining the course of events in Central and Eastern Europe in the years from 1683 to 1711. And I now discovered that I could establish a close causal connection between the preliminaries and the final conclusion of the Treaty of

Carlowitz, the failure of the Deputation to solve Austria's financial problems with the consequence that the solution of the Hungarian 'question' had to be abandoned as well, and the outbreak of the Rákóczi Rebellion and the enormous threat it posed to the continuation of Habsburg power in Europe. Thus three apparently separate developments now fitted easily into one continuing process.

For Austria's prolonged struggle with the Turks which followed on the Siege of Vienna brought most of Hungary and all of Transylvania into the possession of the Emperor. Hungary, as a 'question' for the Imperial administration, became really actual only with the Treaty of Carlowitz. And the form which a settlement for reconquered Hungary would take was left to the political, and cultural history, which once provided such a sense of ordered security are now regarded as frustrating limitations to a broader view of the historian's task. Along with this reaction to compartmentalization has come a need to relate our historical investigation to the deeply problematical character of our present experience. This cannot mean that we conceive history as merely propagandistic or as a transposition of our own partisan loyalties into past time, but rather that we refuse to divorce ourselves from the common effort to work towards a solution of present-day problems, and this in the only way open to us -- as devoted and responsible historians. This view leads automatically to an abandonment of any claim or wish for complete neutrality (an impossibility in any case); in its place we would seek to involve ourselves in the full complexity of the life of human beings at some distance from us in time. On the basis of such intellectual and emotional participation in past events we may hope to clarify the originss of contemporary situations and indicate such analogies as may suggest possible lines of action. In our very involvement in the past we seek to mingle large doses of understanding with occasional careful judgments on the positions and personalities involved. The infuriatingly patronizing judgments of the historians of the Enlightenment have as little attraction for us as does the wan hope of scientific objectivity that was cherished by the positivistic school at the end of the nineteenth century.

The present study's devotion to the ideal of the broad view of history figures in the assumptions about the interactions of cultural and political life which forms its base. In the case of the connection between past events and our present problems, recent history has provided us with a Hungarian uprising that automatically raised serious questions about the meaning of the Hungarian revolutionary tradition and that country's fateful situation in the vortex of European power politics. In addition, the contemporary interest in the problem of communication has clear applicability here. The misunderstandings of a Paget or a Kinsky strike an all too familiar note, for there are those among us who would argue that the Western world and the Soviet bloc encounter similar obstructions in achieveing a peaceful settlement of their differences. It would be a dangerous and unwarranted exaggeration of this view to declare that all conflict between powers can be reduced to a breakdown in communication -- this would be as erroneous for an understanding of events at the beginning of the eighteenth century as it would be in our own day. Conflict between powers takes its start from very tangible, and even in some cases finally irreconcilable, conflicts of interest. But the failure to understand what is at stake only means that further complication has been added to the dispute.

The growth of a European sectionalism thus had an incalculable effect on the sharpening of international tensions. With the addition of Russia and Turkey to the European family at the end of the seventeeth century, the European community experienced a reduction in the degree to which it could be said to possess a common culture. But even without these additions, Europe had begun to divide itself into areas in which a late medieval, a baroque, and an Enlightened spirit was in control. This growing fragmentation may well be but the initial phase of the deepening division of Europe into East and West today. In pointing to the time of Rákóczi as a beginning, I have also tried to keep in mind that it possesses many fruitful grounds for comparison with the October Revolution of 1956. No clear directives for action emerge from this study, but I would argue that it does add to an understanding of the interests which are presently at cross-purposes.

In the much-debated question of assigning ethical values to past action I have thought it wise to pursue a moderate line. Now and then I have found it difficult to withhold praise or blame, and on such occasions I have not scrupled to assume the role of the judge. The cynicism and carelessness of the Austrian ministers, the cant that ran as an undercurrent in the reactions of both the English and Dutch envoys, and the extreme class selfishness of the Hungarian magnates and gentry call forth a moral reaction. In each case I have taken pains to trace out the sociological and spiritual bases for these defects, but to preserve a discreet silence on the ethical dimensions of these defects would be to abandon something of the responsibility to present the whole truth about the period under study. At the heart of this and indeed all historical studies we discover man in a variety of attitudes -- both good and bad. And while we came to moral certainties about the men of this period, we did not forget that the race of man in the time of Leopold I and Ferenc Rákóczi did not alter in its possibilities for good and evil from that of our own day.

Appendix 1

A Facsimile of the *Deputationsprotokoll*

The Transcription of the Facsimile

Deliberatur wegen der Contribuition

Nova Postulata Suppono non esse formanda. Man hatt an die Osterreicher genueg begehret, grosse anlay auff die hauser und auffgeld.

Und wäre die erhlärung au treiben. (Semper nach postulata)

Das quantum wirt sich da verlässlich nicht determiniren lassen. Ess dependirt von der bewilligung, welche (die steckht sich dahir und wirt sich steckhen) wegen des affschlag-- sonderlich von der haus notturft-- sich steckthen derfft (?), der fluechen und vermaledeyen verursachet.

Conclusum: Mitttel auechen und finden, dass regiment webringen zu können. Wan auch Inneröstereich das senign zahle, würden sie gleichwohl liggen bleiben. Die Cammer solle die assignationes geben. Dominus Gundagger: Wan die bewilligung stabiliret, wolle er geld aufbringen. Steyrmarckh mögte die 36.000 fl. aufbringen auff die heyrige bewilligung.

Dominus Kaunitz: putat, man mögte bey den fertigen bleiben. In Siebenbürgen der anfang gemacht mit dem nachlass; mit 200.000 fl. also bestehen bey denen läandern auff die 10 millionen 800.000 fl. Wäare ein landt so reniten mogte man es per impositionem extraordinariam aufflegen.

Die gleichheit betreffend wisse er nicht, wo eine unglechheit seye, esset altioris indaginis.

H. hoffcanzler iustum, das man Ihr May: resolutiones secundire Jedoch alss viehl die möglichkeit zulasse. Wer anders rathe, non daret sanum consilium. Ab utraque parte pax et nulla consolatio.

Man müesse die media nach der arth des landes nemmen: Dahier missrath in trayd und wein gewesen.

Excerpted from the Session of the Deputation on May 18, 1699, Vortäge, Fasz. 37, *Deputationsprotokoll 1699*, fol. 27 v. Crossed out sections have been put in parentheses.

Appendix 2

PROTOKOLL EINER SITZUNG DER GEHEIMEN KONFERENZ üBER DIE
FORDERUNG DER UNGARN, EINEN RECHSTAG ABZUHALTEN,
SIEBENBüRGEN MIT UNGARN ZU BEREINIGEN, DIE ZAHL DER IN
UNGARN STATIONIERTEN TRUPPEN ZU VERRINGERN UND DIE
STEUERN ZU SENKEN.

Appendix 2

Conferenz wegen eines ladtags in hungarn die vereinigung dises Königreichs mit dem fürstenthumb Sibenburgen betreffend. 31 Martii 1699.

Bey Ewer Kay: Mt. batt der fürstliche palantinus und die übrige, so anitzo apud brevia brevium in Ungarn zu Pressburg sitzen, wegen eines landtags im königreich, wegen coniugirung des landes Siebenbürgen mit dem königreich Ungarn und selbiger cantzley mit der Königlichen Ungarischen Geheimen Canzley, wegen ausslogirung eines theils der in winterquartieren subsistirenden militz und wegen litirung des oneris der vier millionen nachvolgendts allerunterthänigist angebracht.

Legatur.

Worüber ewer K: Mt: zu berathachlagen allergändigist anbefohlen, wass zu andtworten seye, welches den 31, Martii be dero obristen cammerern in desselben hoffretirade sub praesidio dess obristen hoffmeisters grafens von Harrach in gegenwarth dess herrn cardinals, graffens Kaunitz, greffens von Stahrenberg und graffens Bucelleni gehorsambst vollzogen und quoad primum wegen dess landtags in consideration gezogen werden de tempore noch loco gewesen, von einen landtag zu deliberiren, der ewer Kay: Mt: und denenUngarn selbst kostbar und beschwerlich fallen mueste, auch wie sonsten ein und anders mahl geschehen.

Ratione incorporationis dicunt, quod diploma vncat.

Vindendum diploma. Sed tamen obstandum.

Transylvani debernt audiri.[a]

4 milliones vix dabunt. Nec aliae provinciae dabunt, aut dare poterunt. So aber der zietn nit[b] so sehr in quaestione. Respondendo in generalibus.

Dominus ob(rister) camm(erer).

Quoad primum wegen des landtags res periculosa. Sie wurden andere puncta nacher bringen.

Si Mtas sua inclinaret, primo dahier alle punct anbringen lassen und sehen, ob man ess dergestalten[c] dahier deattiren und sicherstellen könte, quod non excedant in propositione. Könten ihr Mt. ad audiendam propositionem hinunter, sodan das ausmachen gewissen ministris überlassen. Itaque desiderandum, ut mittant deputatos, qui dicant, was sie proponiren wollen. NB.: ratione fidei.

Ad secundum: Dubitaret, ob ihr Mt. die einverleibung verwilleigen werden. Siebenburgen hettte sien diploma. Quoad contributionem endtlichen.

Je enger ihr Mt. Siebenbürgen hielten, so melius pro Caesare. Pertineret ad Ungariam[d]; non intellexisset, cur Kinsky boluerit separare. Ponenda itaque confinia und regiren lassen wie Ungarn.

Die canzleyen wurden ihr Mt. Hart ändern lassen.

Aussziehung der militz de tempore. Jedoch eine ordtnung.

Kaunitz: Brevis brevium keine versamblung eines landtags

sondern ein udicium.

Dergleichen iudicia wären seapius[e] origo rebellionis.

Respondendum, ess seye nicht huius fori, wo die brevia brevium zu tractiren, non essent similia delberanda.

Ihr May: werden nicht zugegen sein, einen landtag qu verwilligen suo tempore.

Interea hic proponendum, was si auff dem landtag verzubringen vermeinen.

Forte leges in ordinem redigendae.

2. Ratione militiae so vihl ihr Mt. dinst und des landts sicherheit[f] zulasse, vellent reducere. Theils wären schon wurckliche entlassen und giegen hinweg, ut sint sublevanti.

3. Die 4 millionen hetten ihr Mt. ante annum nicht bekhommen, und weillen anderen läander nicht so[g] vihl geben können.

Siebenbürgen zahle 100.000 fl. weniger, iuxta propositionem Hugariae nachzulassen: 400.000 fl.

4. Ratione incorporationis hette Sibenbürgen vor zeiten nach Ungarn gehört, sed obstaret[h] diploma; etiam odia inter has nationes. Tamen putat resituendum Jedoch könne es noch wohl in suspenso gelassen werden.

Starhemberg will auch keinen landtag. Sein vorschlag wegen der logirung wurde practabile sein; casarmen und berackhen machen.

Quad sublevationem: Werden noch mehr ins Reich gehen; heretgegen aus Siebenburgen etwas von der cavagleria herein kommen; selbe könne in Transylvania nicht stehen.

De quatuor millionibus nihil remittendum, multa enim adhuc deessent sine fundo.

Quad incoroporationem: Promissum, das man sie nicht incorporiren wolle; dörffte zum auffstand kommen.

Hungari essent sub palatino. Transylvani wurden sich sehr opponiren. Croaten habe er auch 400.000 fl. auffgetragen.

Herr Hoffcantzler: Ad primum: Dilatorie. Ihr May: wären von selbst bedacht, wie dass königreich widerumben in florirenden standt zu setzen. Die confinien[i] mit Thörckhey[j] erst zu adiustiren. Etiam putat necessarium, ut priums proponantur hic puncta in diaest discutienda.[k]

Eductio[l] militiae iam coepta.

Ratione Transylvaniae res adhuc altioris indaginis.

Ratione cancellariae similiter.

Pari modo, quoad reductionem militiae et 4 millionem: dflatorie.

Herr Cardinal: Quod non sit dies, nec annus; bene dictum a domino Kaunitz, quod non sit illorum officium agere von einem landtag.

Esset primas regni; substitutus personalis etiam non habet[m] mandatum a se cardinali.

Semper intium rebellionis.

Es gebühre ihnen nicht einen landtag zu proponiren. Veniam havere debent ad brevia brevium.

Hetten 21 tag, tantum parerent confusiones. Ihr May. musten zahlen. Scribendum palatino, er solle sich solcher sachen nit unterfangen; ihr Mt. hetten schol lengst darauff gedacht und wurden alle vorsehunt thuen. Vor 200 jahren einer die schwein in des anderen wald getrieben. Modo hac de re iudicatum. Fuissent ducentae sessiones et mandatum, wer etwas fordern wolle, solle sich anmelden; qui non compareret, solte abgewiesen sein.

Mit Siebenbüregen eine accordirte sach, die sich durch einen brieff nicht übern hauffen werfen lasse.

Ostenderent magnam fidelitatem, dicendum.

Ihr Mt. wurden zu seiner zeit schon declariren, (wass nach Ungarn) gehöorig sein soll oder nicht.

Mit der canzley könne es nicht sein. Haberent secretarium arianum, calvinistum, catholicum -- tales non possent poni ad Hungaricam.[n] Sua Mtas non solveret, sed illi ipsi Transylvani. Wären bey gutem willen zu erhalten.

Dicendum:

Partes Regni btreffend°; Wass bekhandtliche partes Ungariae, contribuire nach Ungarn. N.B. Unter Zathmar theils örther, die nach Siebenbügen gehöorig.

Quoad remissionem quatuor millionum, könne niemand von uns sagen, vass thuenlich seye.

Venisset deorsum; petisset a perceptore videre, quis solvisset, - recasasset dare, donec minatus arrestum.

Hetten die grösste khlagen wegen der auxiliaren gehabt, qui omnes dimissi.

Wilderummen einen teutschen mann loco Hoffman ad Cancellariam Ungaricam zu setzen.

Quoad contribuitiones: Fecissent, ut non sciremus, wass eingehe und zahlt werde.

1. Landtag.

2. Incorporatio Transylva (niae).

3. et cancell (ariae).

4. Reductio milit (iae).

5. 4 milliones[p] 12 per zodiacum distrib (uendae).

Conclusum:

Die frag, was zu antworthen: Bey der iezigen zusambenkunft hetten sie darmen nicht zu reden. Ihr May: wäaren schon bedacht, alles dem königreich zu besten einrichten und zu seiner zeit mit ihnen von dem landtag handlen[q] zu lassen, sodan wegen des landtags das gehörige mit ihen qu beranstalten.

Modo Caesari, aulae it ipsis Ungaris molestum et sumpuosum.

Semper propo.......

Ratione Transylvaniae obstaret diploma. Ihr Mt. wurden ihr h. worth nicth brechen wollen. Dicendum, Ihr May: wäaren ietz in anderen beschaftigt.

Ratione militiae et 4 millionum könten ihr May: derzeit nichts statuiren, weillen noch vorhero eins und anders zu adiustirenen.[r] Wegen der militz schon zum abmarch die auxiliaren beordert.

Demissionem quod attinet, videre vellet Caesar[s], was man entbehren könne et inclinaret Caesar sodann, si aliumde haberi possit, zu gratificiren.

Vor einrichtung der gränitzen lasse sich von keiner reduction reden.

Notes to Appendix 2

The origininal is to be found in the *Vorträge*, Fasz. 37, older II (January-November, 1699), fol. 21-26. I am especially grateful to Dr. Walter Leitsch for his assistance in the prepartation of this transcription.

[a]Corrected from "Audiatur Transylvani iam accipient".

[b]Followed by an illegible word that was possible crossed out.

[c]The secretary began to write "dergl(eichen) and then corrected it to "dergestalten".

[d]Originally "Ungariarn".

[e]"Saepius" was added later above the line.

[f]Originally "obstiaret".

[g]"so" corrected from "zu".

[h]Originally "obstiaret".

[i]Originall "confir".

[j]Corrected from "Thurckhen".

[k]"Etiam putat....discutienda" was added later in the margin.

[l]Corrected from "reductio".

[m]Originally "havent".

[n]"tales non possent poni ad Hungaricam" was added later in the margin.

[o]Following this was "Zathmnar wäre" which was crossed out.

[p]After "milliones" there was a word or number which was changed to "12" and then crossed out.

[q]"und zu seiner zeith....handlen" added in the margin.

[r]"weillen noch..." "adiustiren" added later in the margin.

[5]A "wie" following this was crossed out.

Bibliography

I. *Unpulished Sources*

The Hague
Algemeen Rijsarchief
Archief de Staten-Generaal:
Facicle 6160.

London
Public Record Office
State Papers Foreign, Germany, 80: #17, 18, 19

State Papers Foreign, Turkey, 97: #20, 21.

State Papers Foreign, (The Stepney Papers), 105: #78.

British Museum
Additional Manuscripts:
#8880; #28899 (*Ellis Papers*)

Vienna
Gräflich Harrachsches Archiv
Konferenzprotokolle:
Fasz. 187, 188.

Haus-, Hof- und Staataarchiv
Anglica:
Berichte und Weisungen, 1705.
Dispacci di Germania:
May, 1703-1711.

Hollandica:
Berichte und Weisungen, 1700-1711.

Grosse Korrespondenz:
Fasz. 63 II (Kaiser Leopold-Kinsky).

Russica:
Berichte, 1703-1710.

Suecica:
Berichte und Weisungen, 1703-1707.

Turcica:
Berichte und Weisungen, 1695-1711.
Fasz. V: Joseph Hammer-Purgstall, *Die Gesichte der diplomatischen Verhältnisse Osterreichs mit der hohen Pforte vom Beginn des XVI. bis zum Ende des XVIII. Jahrhuderts* (in manuscript).

Ungarn:
1695-1711.

Vorträge (Konferezvota):
1695-1711.

Hokammerarchiv
Gedenkbücher, Ungariche Reihe:
1697-1704.

Hoffinanz, Ungarn:
1697-1703.

Kriegsarchiv
Karten:
B IX C, #99-1. 743, 829, 830, 832.

Staadtbibliothek
Wiener Zeitung:
1703-1711.

II. *Published Sources*

1. *Aktenstücke zur Geschite Franz Rakoczys und seiner Verbindungen mit dem Auslande 1706, 1709 und 1710*, hgg. v. Josef Fiedler, *Archiv für österreichische Gesichte*, Bd. 44, (1871), 399-511; and for the period 1705-1711 in the *Fontes rerum austriacarum*, II. Abt. Bd. 9 (1855) and Bd. 17 (1858).

2. *Archivum Rákóczianum. II. Rákóczi leveltara, bel-es küföldi irratarabol böovitve.* --Kiadja a Magyar Tudomanyos Akademia Törtenelmi Bizottsaga. Elsö osztaly: Had-es belügy. Szerkeszti Thaly Kalman. 10 vols. Budapest, 1873-1889.

3. ------------------. II. osztaly: Diplomatica (Angol diplomatia; iratok. Szerkeszti Simonyi Erno. 3 vols. Budapest, 1871, 1873, 1877.

4. *Bonnac, J. L . d'Usson de, Memoire historique sur l'ambassade de France a Constantinople*, ed. Charles Schefer. Paris, 1904.

5. *Correspondentie van Willem III en van Hans Willem Bentinck, eersten Graaf van Portland*, ed. N. Japikse. 2 vols. 's Gravenhage, 1927, 1928.

6. *Dispacci di Germania dell 'ambasciatore veneto Dan. Dolfin, 22 febbr. 1702-7. luglio 1708, I*, ed. Marcello Giudici. 2 part. Venezia, 1908-1910.

7. *Eigenhändige Korrespondenz des Königs Kar III. von Spanien (nachmals Kaiser Karls VI.) mit dem Obersten Kanzler des*

Konigreichs Böhmen, Grafen Johann Wenzel Wratislaw, Archiv für
österr. Geschichtsquellen, Bd. 16 (1856), 3-224.

8. *Het archief van den Raadpensionaris Antonie Heinsius*
(1689-1720). 3 vols. 's Gravenhage, 1867.

9. *Historical Manuscripts Commission: Report on Manuscripts of*
the Marquess of Bath. 3 vols. Historical Manuscripts Commission,
1904-1908.

10. ----------------------: *Report on the Manuscripts of the Marquess*
of Downshire. Vol. 1. Historical Manuscripts Commission, 1924.

11. *Hurmuzaki, Eudoxiu de, Documente privitore la Istoria*
Romanilor. Vols. V and VI. Bucuresti, 1885-1888.

12. *Lexington Papers, The, or some accout of courts of London and*
Vienna, ed. John Henry Thomas Manners-Sutton. London, 1851.

13. *österreichische Staatsverträge:* England; hgg. v. A. F. Pribram.
(Veröffentlichungen der Kommission für neuere Geschite
Osterreichs, 3). I. Bd. (1526-1748). Innsbruck, 1907.

14. --------------------: *Niederlande,* hgg. v. Heinrich Ritter von
Srbik. (Veröffentlichungen der Kommission für neuere Geschichte
Osterreichs, 10). Wien, 1912.

15. *Rákóczi, Ferenc II, Confessiones et Aspirationes Principis*
Christiani, Principis Franciscus II. Rákóczi (Commissio fontium
historiae patriae Academiae Scientiarm Hungariae). Budapest, 1876.

16. ----------------, *Memoires du Prince Francois Rakoczy sur la*
guerre de Hongrie (Histoire des Revolutions de Hongrie, tome II).
La Haye, 1739.

17. *Relationen der Botschafter Vendigs über (Deutschland und österreich im 17. jarhundert, Die*, hgg. v. Josef Fiedler) (Fontes rerum austriacarum, Bd. 27). Wien, 1867.

18. *Relazioni di ambasciatori Sebaudi, Genovesi e Veneti 1693-1713 durante il periodo della Grande Alleanza e della Successione di Spagna.* ed. Carlo Morandi. Bolgna, 1935.

19. *Saint-Simon, Louis de Rouvroi, Duc de: Memoires complets et authentiques du duc de Saint-Simon sur le siecle de Louis XIV et de la regence.* Collationnes sur le manuscrit original par M. Cheruel et precedes d'une notice par M. Saint-Beuve de l'academie francaise. 21 vols. Paris, 1879-1909.

20. *Sutton, The Despatches of Sir Robert Sutton, Ambassador in Constantinople* (1710-1714), ed. A. Kurat, Camden Society, Third Series (LXXVIII), London, 1953.

21. *Weensche Gezantschapsberichten van 1670 tot 1720*, ed. G. van Antal; J. C. H. de Pater (Riks Geschiedkundige Publicatiën, 67, 69). 2 vols. 's Gravenhage, 1929, 1934.

III. *Secondary Works*
a. Books

1. Angyal, David, *Kesmarki Thöököly Imre 1657-1705* (Magyar törteneti eletrajzok). 2 reszt. Budapest, 1889.

2. Bidermann, Hermann Ignaz, *Geschichte der österreichischen Gesammt-Staats-Idee* 1526-1804. I Abt. (1526-1705). Innsbruck, 1867.

3. Bosscha, P., *De Geschiedenis van oostelijk en noordelijk Europa van 1687-1716.* Zalt-Bommel, 1860.

4. Churchill, Winston, *Marlborough, his life and times.* Vol. 4. London, 1938.

5. Coxe, William, *Memoirs of John Duke of Marlborough with his original correspondence, collected from family records at Blenheim and other authentic sources.* Vol. 2. London, 1847.

6. *Feldzüge des Prinzen Eugen von Savoyen,* herausgegeben vonder Abteilung für Kriegageschichte des k.k. Kriegsarchiva Wien., 20 Bde. u. 1 Registerband. Wien, 1876-1893.

7. Fellner, Thomas, *Die österreichische Zentral-verwaltung.* 1 Abt.: von Maimilian I. bis zur Vereinigung der österreichischen und böhmischen Hofkazlei 1749. Bd. 1: Geschichtliche öbersichte. Bd. 2 und 3: Aktenstücke. Wien, 1907.

8. Gaedeke, Arnold, *Die Politik Oesterreichs in der Spanischen Erbfolgerfrage.* Mit Benutzung des k. k. Haus-, Hof- und Staatsarchivs und des grafl. Harrach'schen Familienarchivs. Nebst Akten und Urkunden. 2 Bde. Leipzig, 1877.

9. Gross, Lothar, *Die Geschite der deutschen Reichskanzlei von 1559-1806.* (Inventare des Wiener Haus-, Hof und Staatsarchivs, Bd. 1) Wien, 1933.

10. Hammer-Purgstall, Josef Freiherr von, *Geschichte des osmanischen Reichs; grössentheils aus bisher unbenutzten Handschriften und Archiven.* 10 Bde. Pesth, 1827-1834.

11. Hantsch, Hugo, *Reichvizekanzler Friedrich Karl Graf von Schonborn (1674-1746). Einige Kapitel zur politischen Geschichte* Kaiser Josefs I. und Karls VI (Salzburger Abhandlungen und Texte aus Wissenschaft und Kunst, 2). Ausburg, 1929.

12. Hengelmüller, Ladislaus Freiherr von, *Franz Rákóczi und sein Kampf für Ungarns Freiheit* 1703-1711. 1 Bd. Stuttgart, 1913.

13. Hora Siccama, J. H., *De vrede van Carlowitz en wat daaran voorafging* (Bijdragen van vaderlandsche 's-Gravenhage, 1910.

14. Horn, D. B., *British diplomatic representatives*, (Camden Society, Third Series, Vol. XLVI). London, 1932.

15. Klopp, Onno, *Der Fall des Hauses Stuart und die Sukzession des Hauses Hannover in Grossbritannien und Irland im Zusammenhange der europäischen Angelegenheiten von 1660-1714.* 14 Bde. Wien, 1875-1888.

16. ------------------, *Das Jahr 1683 und der folgende grosse Türkenkrieg bis zum Frieden von Carlowitz 1699.* Graz, 1882.

17. Kuczunski, Brigitte, *Theodor Heinrich Altet Stratmann.* Berlin diss., 1934.

18. Marki, Sandor, *Rákóczi Ferenvz.* 3 vols. Budapest 1907.

19. Maurer, Joseph, *Cardinal Leopold Graf Kollonitsch, Primas von Ungarn: sein Leben und sein Wirken.* Innsbruck, 1887.

20. Mayer, Theodor, *Verwaltungsreform in Ungarn nach der Türkenzeit.* (Herausgegeben von der Gesellschaft für Neuere Geschichte österreichs). Wien, 1911.

21. Nikiforov, L. A., *Russko-angliiske otnoshenia pri Petre I.* Moskva, 1950.

22. Noorden, Carl von, *Europäische Geschichte im. 18. Jahrhundert.* 1 Abt.: Der Spanische Erbfolgekrieg. 2 Bde.

Dusseldorf-Leipzig, 1870, 1873, 1882.

23. Pastor, Ludwig Freiherr von, *The history of the popes from the close of the middle ages.* Drawn from the secret archives of the Vatican and other original sources, trans. Dom Ernest Graf O. S. B. Vol. XXIV. London, 1940.

24. Pribram, Alfred Francis, *Austria-Hungary and Great Britain 1908-1914.* London, 1951.

25. ------------------------, *Franz Paul Freiherr von Lisola* (1613-74) *und die Politik seine Zeit.* Leipzig, 1894.

26. Redlich, Oswald, *österreichs Grossmachtbildung in der Zeit Kaiser Leopolds I* (Geschichte österreichs, 6). Gotha, 1921.

27. ----------------------, *Das Werden einer Grossmacht: österreich 1700-1740.* (Geschichte österreichs, 7). Wien, 1942.

28. Romein, Jan, *Die Biographie: Einführung in ihrer Geshichte und Problematik.* Bern, 1948.

29. Schwarz, Henry F., *The Imperial Privy Council in the seventeenth century* (Harvard Historical studies, LIII). Cambridge, Mass., 1943.

30. Srbik, Heinrich Ritter von, *Geist und Geschichte vom deutschen Humanimus bis zur Gegenwart.* II. Bd. Müchen, 1951.

31. -------------------------------, *Wien und Versailles 1692-1697. Zur Geschichts von Strassburg, Elsass und Lothringen.* München, 1944.

32. Summer, B. H., P*eter the Great and the Ottoman Empire.*

Oxford, 1949.

33. Stourdza, Alexandre A. C., *L'Europe orientale et le role historique des Maurocordato: 1660-1830* (avec un appendice contenant des actes et documents historiques et diplomatiques inedits). Paris, 1913.

34. Szefü, Gyula, Magyar történet (volume 6 of Homan-Szefu). Budapest, 1932.

35. --------------------, A *szamuzött Rákóczi*. Budapest, 1913.

36. Thompson, Mark A., *The Secretaries of State: 1681-1782*. Oxford, 1932.

37. Zuijlen de Nijevelt, R., *De vrede van Carlowitz*. Utrecht, 1883.

b. Articles

1. Acsady, Ignac, "A Karloviczi beke", *Ertekezesek a törteneti tudomanyok köreböl* (XVIII), 1899, kötet 4.

2. Brunner, Otto, "eine osmanische Quelle zur Geschichte der Belagerung Wiens durch di Türken im Jahre 1683", *Mitteilunen des Vereins für Geschichte der Stadt Wien*, V (1925), 37ff.

3. ------------------, "Österreich und die Walachei während der türkenkriege von 1683-1699", *Mitteilungen des österreichischen Institute für Geschichtsforschung*, (44), 1929, 265-323.

4. Braubach, Max, "Prinz Eugen im Kampf um die Machte, 1701-1705", *Historisches Jahrbuck* (LXIV), 1955.

5. Brinkman, C., "The relations between England and Germany,

1660-88", *English Historical Review* (XXIV), 1909, 247-277, 448-469.

6. Firth, Sir Charles, "England and Austria", *Transactions of the Royal Historical Society,* Third Series (XI), 1917, 1-34.

7. Krones, Franz von, "Die Literatur zur Geschichte Fr. Rákóczi im letzten Jahrzehnt", *Historisches Jahrbuch* (III), 1882, 631-647; (IV), 1883, 96-124. 159-160.

8. Krylova, T.K., "Russko-turetskie otnoshenia vo vremya severnoi voini", *Istoricheskie zapiski* (X), 1941, 250-279.

9. Lane, Margery, "Diplomatic service under William III", *Transactions of the Royal Historical Society,* 4 series (X), 1927, 87-109.

10. Malyusz, Elemer, "A Rákóczi-kor tarsadalom Magyarorszagon", *Rákóczi emlekkönyv ketszazeves fordulojara.* Vol. 2, 25-66. Budapest, 1933.

11. Marki, Sandor, "Desalleurs altabornagy Rákóczinal", *Hadtörtenelmi Közlemenyek* (1917), 1-12.